2009 01 21

Messiahs
and
Machiavellians

Messiahs and Machiavellians

DEPICTING EVIL IN THE MODERN THEATRE

PAUL COREY

University of Notre Dame Press

Notre Dame, Indiana

Designed by Wendy McMillen
Set in 10.3/13.6 Visage Book by Four Star Books
Printed on 55# Nature's Recycle by Versa Press

Library of Congress Cataloging-in-Publication Data

Corey, Paul, 1968–
Messiahs and machiavellians : depicting evil in the modern theatre / Paul Corey.
p.   cm.
Includes bibliographical references and index.
ISBN-13: 978-0-268-02295-2 (pbk. : alk. paper)
ISBN-10: 0-268-02295-x (pbk. : alk. paper)
1. European drama—History and criticism.   2. Evil in literature.   I. Title.
PN1650.E95C67   2008
809.2'9353—dc22

2008010455

FOR AVA COREY AND ELIAS COREY

CONTENTS

ACKNOWLEDGMENTS

The majority of this text was completed during my time in the Department of Religious Studies at McMaster University. The department provided a stimulating environment for intellectual inquiry. At McMaster, I had the good fortune to meet Zdravko Planinc, who originally suggested I examine the history of theatre as a response to evil and then supervised my dissertation. Over the years, he not only showed me how to be a scholar but also taught me what it means to live a philosophic life. This book would not have been written without his teaching. In particular, I must acknowledge his influence on my reading of Shakespeare. In a series of lectures at McMaster, he revealed to me the central problems of *Measure for Measure*. My chapter on this play is certainly the result of his influence. Any errors of interpretation are, of course, my own.

Edward Andrew of the University of Toronto read my dissertation and provided helpful criticisms. I thank him for reading my work with such care. Samuel Ajzenstat, Graeme MacQueen, Louis Greenspan, and Lee Brooks also read drafts, and their criticisms helped improve the text. I am also grateful to the two anonymous referees who reviewed my manuscript for the University of Notre Dame Press. Their reviews proved tremendously insightful and contributed to a more polished text.

There are a number of people at the University of Notre Dame Press who I want to thank: Lowell Francis, my acquisitions editor, for expressing interest in my work and moving the entire project to fruition; Rebecca DeBoer, for overseeing the entire editing process and keeping things on a tight schedule; Susan Roberts, for her work in marketing and promotions; Margaret Gloster, for her work designing the book cover; and Sheila Berg, for her exceptional copyediting of the manuscript.

Preliminary drafts of my research on Machiavelli's *Mandragola* and Shakespeare's *Measure for Measure* were presented at the Canadian

Political Science Association meetings in Ottawa, 1998, and Sherbrooke, 1999. I presented an early version of my chapter on Camus's *Caligula* for the Religion, Holocaust and Genocide Group at the annual meeting of the American Academy of Religion in Boston, 1999. I also presented an edited version of my chapter on Beckett's *Waiting for Godot* to the Eric Voegelin Society at the American Political Science Association's annual meeting in Philadelphia, 2003. I especially thank Ellis Sandoz and the Voegelin Society for being receptive to my work over the years and providing a forum for discussing the highest matters. Finally, sections of the main introduction and conclusion appeared in altered form in my article "Canadian Theatre and the Tragic Experience of Evil" in the journal *Theatre Research in Canada* 27, no. 2 (2006): 282–305.

A number of people contributed indirectly to this project through lectures, academic papers, or informal discussions that influenced my thinking on certain key issues. I thank Jerry Day, Oona Eisenstat, Travis Kroeker, Craig Perfect, Ron Srigley, Susan Srigley, Jeff Tessier, and Stephen Westerholm. Thanks to Rob Virdis for indexing. I also express my appreciation to Elizabeth Daignault, who, more than anyone, experienced the daily challenges of the creative process. My thanks to Liz, for being a midwife for this writing; I know it was a complicated delivery.

There are other people who have supported me in other ways and without whose encouragement this project would not have been completed. I thank Kent Emerson for his love and no-nonsense advice; David Hunt and Fiona Burke, who proved that you do indeed find out who your true friends are when times get tough; the extended Corey family, especially Rachel and Frank Hruska, who were there for me when I needed them most; and Kate Henry, whose counsel has provided both comfort and insight and who has helped me live in accord with the Delphic injunction: "Know Yourself."

I thank Andrea Buchholz, who became my partner during the publishing phase of this project. As always, she arrived right on time. Her intelligence, humor, and encouragement have meant everything to me. Somehow she has managed the difficult task of combining towering ambition with genuine hospitality. Rock 'n' Roll Cleveland!

Finally, and most important, I want to thank my parents, Gerard and Nola Corey. Their unconditional love has been the foundation of my life, and I cannot repay the debt. This book is the fruit of their labors as well.

KEY TO ABBREVIATIONS AND TEXTUAL NOTES

CG   Augustine, *City of God.* Trans. Henry Bettenson. London: Penguin Books, 1972.

D   Machiavelli, Niccolò. *Discourses on Livy.* Trans. Harvey C. Mansfield Jr. and Nathan Tarcov. Chicago: University of Chicago Press, 1996.

MS   Camus, Albert. *Myth of Sisyphus and Other Essays.* Trans. Justin O' Brien. New York: Vintage Books, 1955.

NE   Aristotle. *Nicomachean Ethics.* Trans. Martin Ostwald. New York: Macmillan, 1962.

P   Machiavelli, Niccolò. *The Prince.* Trans. Harvey C. Mansfield Jr. Chicago: University of Chicago Press, 1985.

R   Camus, Albert. *The Rebel.* Trans. Anthony Bower. New York: Vintage International, 1956.

ST   Aquinas, Thomas. *Summa Theologica.* Trans. Fathers of the English Dominican Province. 3 vols. New York: Benzinger Bros., 1948.

Any alterations to these translations are indicated in the notes.

I have used the Loeb Classical Library (Cambridge, Mass.: Harvard University Press) for Greek and Latin texts, unless otherwise indicated. All biblical quotations are from the New Revised Standard Version. All references to Shakespeare are from *The Complete Works of Shakespeare,* ed. David Bevington, rev. 4th ed. (New York: Longman, 1997).

Revaluating Modernity

September 11, the "Death Event," and the Word *Evil*

Evil is a dirty word in most Western liberal democracies. To brand some-one, something, or some event as "evil" suggests that you are speaking of an absolute struggle between the forces of good (us) and the forces of evil (them) in which there can be no compromise. To speak seriously of evil might signify to others that you are a religious or ideological extrem-ist, that you lack a critical intellect, and that you have not considered the various economic, social, historical, and political factors motivating the people and events so designated. Reality is complicated, some will say, and it is crude to divide it into the black-and-white categories "evil" and "good." The best approach is not to speak of evil at all.

In recent years, however, the word has become part of our popular vocabulary once again—at least to some extent. More than anything else, the terrorist attacks by Al-Qaeda against the United States on Septem-ber 11, 2001, gave evil a newfound currency. As we experienced the im-mediate trauma of hijacked planes crashing into the World Trade Center and the Pentagon and killing nearly three thousand people, the word evil seemed suitable. A deluge of articles and new publications appeared dealing with the subject of evil. But as politicians started using the word with greater frequency, most notably U.S. President George W. Bush, the revival of the concept was met by voices of dissent. President Bush was imprecisely, yet pointedly, accused of Manichaeism—of espousing a re-ligious dualism that divides the world into good and evil.[1] Some critics argued that the president's worldview, deeply influenced by evangelical

Christianity, is analogous to that of Al-Qaeda: just as the terrorists brand the secular West as "Satanic" and seek to destroy us, so the Bush administration brands terrorists and anyone associated with them as "evildoers." For these critics, Bush's ultimatum to the world—"Either you are with us or with the terrorists"—simplifies a complicated global dynamic.[2] Furthermore, some argue the president's articulated desire to "rid the world of evil"[3] has encouraged excessive American violence rather than a measured response to the terrorist threat.[4]

Speaking of evil is not something that comes easily in the democratic West, even after an event as catastrophic as 9/11. Given the highly charged nature of the word, and its potential to inspire violence, our reticence to use it is perhaps a sign of health. And yet what word is more appropriate—not just to describe 9/11 and those responsible for it, but the many unprecedented atrocities that have been committed over the past century? It would appear that understanding the experience of evil should be one of our central tasks. This endeavor might help us resist the temptations of fanaticism. But we have been reluctant to broach the subject. Susan Neiman points out in *Evil in Modern Thought* that few major philosophical works published since the end of World War II have dealt exclusively with evil. Hannah Arendt's prediction that evil would be the central issue of postwar intellectual life did not turn out to be true.[5] Given the violent history of the twentieth century and our current geopolitical situation, it is perhaps more imperative than ever for us to reflect on what symbols of "evil" have signified historically and how the experience of evil can best be symbolized today. The hope of such a project is to cultivate an understanding of evil that is more nuanced than most of our current religious and political discourse on the subject.

It is revealing that we still feel the need to speak of evil in reaction to certain events, and it is significant that many people think there is something unique about the violence and destruction unleashed in the modern world. Joan Copjec, editor of a compilation dealing with the question of evil, writes of "our intuitive sense" to "speak of *modern* evil or to claim that an unprecedented wickedness has been introduced into the world."[6] This intuition arises out of the horrible atrocities committed in the twentieth century, evoked by the names "Auschwitz," "Gulag Archipelago," "Hiroshima," "Cambodia," and "Rwanda." Whatever differences may exist between the events signified by these names, they have all come to represent the same thing: the systematic annihilation of human beings that emerged after 1914. Edith Wyschogrod writes, "During World War I a new process burst upon the historical horizon, a multifaceted state of affairs which later included such features as nuclear, biological, and chemical warfare and death camps." Wyschogrod refers to this "social, political, and cultural complex" as "the *death event*"—an event whose roots lie deep in the Western tradition but which was not fully realized until the twentieth century.[7]

The death event compels us to reconsider the traditional problem of evil in its modern context. It calls the entire modern project into question, and possibly heralds a new postmodern epoch. At the very least, we have now entered what the sociologist Zygmunt Bauman calls the "age of revaluation." By "revaluation," he means a critical reassessment of the inclinations and hidden potentials of the past few centuries, and of the modernity that was ultimately conceived in the twentieth century.[8] This is not to say that modernity *is* evil, or that everything the modern world has produced must be abandoned. However, certain impulses were unleashed in modernity that had a violent effect, and these must be reconsidered. Furthermore, we cannot be sure that the death event has passed. As the events of 9/11 portend, it may take new and more destructive forms in the twenty-first century. The constant threat of terrorism, the fear of weapons of mass destruction, the violence unleashed in response to the terrorist threat, and the inability of the United States and Western democracies to bring a definitive end to terror force us to continue re-evaluating what modernity has brought to pass.

———

It is in the spirit of this revaluation that the present work is undertaken. My purpose is twofold: on the one hand, I discuss traditional understandings of evil and consider the modalities of evil in the modern world; on the other, I examine theatre as a site that has symbolized the experience of evil at key moments in Western history. This work discusses Renaissance and twentieth-century drama in the context of the late modern death event. I use the term "late modern" to signify the historical moment when the death event occurred in the twentieth century and the term "early modern" to designate the period when the first glimmerings of modern consciousness arose in western Europe in the late fifteenth and early sixteenth century, during what we now call the Renaissance. Theatre has generally been a marginal art form in the West, but it was a vibrant and popular aesthetic during both of these historical periods, reflecting the impulses that initiated the modern project as well as the sufferings that led to its revaluation. Some dramatic works were symptomatic of the energies unleashed at these times and participated fully in their dynamism; others offered cogent criticisms of modernity. My contribution is to link these two periods of dramatic art in a discussion of evil, to explore the cultural and political tensions that were conducive to the creation of theatre at these times, and to consider theatre both as a symptom and as a critique of the impulses behind "modern evil." It also raises a number of questions about aesthetics, politics, and ethics that are relevant for us today as we struggle with our post-9/11 understanding of evil.

Introduction

Theatre and Evil in the Shadow of the "Death Event"

Evil as a Phenomenon

It is essential to begin by considering the term "evil" itself—what it means, what it has meant, and how I will be using it. In this section I draw on sources from the fields of anthropology, theology, philosophy, and psychology. I begin, however, in the world of mythology.

At the start of Homer's *Odyssey,* Zeus makes a pronouncement before the council of the gods:

> Oh for shame, how the mortals put the blame upon us
> gods, for they say evils (*kakos*) come from us, but it is they, rather,
> who by their own recklessness win sorrow beyond what is given.[1]

In this famous passage Zeus distinguishes between given evils and surplus evils. Humans cannot eliminate or overcome given evils; they are fated to experience some degree of suffering and grief by the very fact that they are alive. They also cause sufferings beyond those given through what Zeus calls "recklessness." The root cause of surplus evil is bad human judgment, through which mortals aggravate their own sufferings and then blame the gods.[2] Zeus claims that this accusation against the pantheon is unjustified. He does not deny that the gods might be responsible for a certain degree of given evil; however, mortals make it worse for themselves through their own foolishness. Despite the emphasis on human responsibility in this passage, the Homeric use of the word *kakon* (evil or bad) is not synonymous with "sin." The former term has a more encompassing signification than the latter. As Zeus's statement makes clear, evil is the harm humans cause *and* the sufferings they experience. In the Homeric sense it is better to speak of "evils" rather than "Evil," for evil is not reducible to a single quality, force, or disposition, either in us or in the world. Evil is rather an experience with many dimensions—a multitude of afflictions, dispositions, and actions that we affect and by which we are affected, by nature and in our social and political relations.

This is not how the term is commonly used today. By and large, we use "evil" to refer to excessive moral wickedness—to actions that cause extraordinary harm and the people responsible. It is rarely, if ever, used to denote illnesses, accidents, natural disasters, or venial crimes. As the anthropologist Martin Southwold writes in *The Anthropology of Evil,* "If we order wrongdoings on a scale of gravity or heinousness, the range of application of 'evil' tends towards the graver end. It is unacceptable to use it of a peccadillo, and uncomfortable to use it of a venial offense."[3] Southwold understands evil as "a special quality of badness" that "is like 'bad' only more so." In this sense, evil is not a given quality; it is determined quantitatively, by the degree of human wickedness, though Southwold does not spell out exactly what quantitative measure we should use to determine if a person or action is merely bad or really evil. Like most of his contemporaries, Southwold chooses to use the word *evil* exclusively in its "strong moral sense" to designate only the worst types of malice, exemplified by the Holocaust or by sadistic crimes. Evil is distinct from immoralities in the "weak moral sense," which he refers to as "bad" or "morally wrong."[4] Furthermore, evil is categorically distinct from what he calls "afflictions" such as accidents or diseases. We should, he claims, reserve our use of the word *evil* for the worst human actions, and not use it to refer to sufferings caused by nature, misfortunes, or minor offenses.[5]

As we observed with Homer, evil once had a broader meaning. Even as late as the eighteenth century evil denoted something more than just extreme human wickedness. During the Enlightenment, the event that prompted the most discussion about evil was not a political or moral atrocity but rather a natural catastrophe: the Lisbon earthquake of 1755, which destroyed the city of Lisbon and killed thousands. However, throughout the eighteenth century, there was an attempt by poets and philosophers, such as Leibniz, Pope, and Rousseau, to deny that there is such a thing as "natural evil."[6] Rousseau, for example, argued that the problem of evil is not a problem with the natural world or God but rather with human beings and the societies they have constructed. For Rousseau, there is nothing wrong with the world as it has been given to us. He writes in the first line of *Emile,* "Everything is good as it leaves the hands of the Author of things; everything degenerates in the hands of man."[7] Nature, for Rousseau, is good; humans suffer because they continually deviate from nature's dictates and from the moral laws that they know by nature. Rousseau believed that human immorality and foolishness are the ultimate causes of suffering, not nature, and that our sufferings are the natural consequence of our wrongdoing. In his 1756 letter to Voltaire, Rousseau goes so far as to claim that humans are to blame for the death and destruction of the Lisbon earthquake because they built tall houses in an environment unsuitable for them. If humans were attentive to nature, argues Rousseau, they would not build fragile cities near fault lines. Rousseau concludes, "most of our physical evils are also of our own making."[8] Perhaps Rousseau is similar to Zeus insofar as he suggests that humans have given themselves sufferings beyond those already given; however, for him, the ultimate responsibility for evil shifts decidedly in the direction of humanity.

According to Neiman, our current tendency to refer to evil as something exclusively moral, and not as anything natural, is something that developed over the course of modern philosophical debate.[9] As a consequence, we no longer speak of earthquakes as "evil." It should be said, however, that the modern effort to make a categorical distinction between natural and moral evils, and then to deny that natural calamities are "evil" at all, is rooted deep in the Christian tradition. We can see the shift toward an exclusively moral conception of evil as early as Saint Augustine. In the *Confessions,* Augustine writes of the "hell of error" that "suppose[s] . . . evil is something that you suffer rather than an act by humanity."[10] For Augustine, such suppositions are erroneous because they assume that evils originate elsewhere than from the human will; indeed, they go so far as to suggest that God is responsible for the existence of evil. Augustine maintains, on the contrary, that there is only one true

God, and this God (unlike any imaginary Greek god) is all-beneficent, incorruptible, and untainted by evil. Furthermore, evil is not a substance within nature, nor is the cosmos itself evil; the world is the creation of the sole beneficent God, and is therefore good (*CG* 11.21–22). This understanding of God and nature gives rise to the theological "problem of evil," or what has come to be known as the *theodicy* question: if God is all-good, all-powerful, and all-knowing, why is there wickedness and suffering in the world? Augustine's answer is categorical: first, genuine "evil" is not found in God or in nature but only in unruly angelic and human wills that freely choose to disobey divine ordinances;[11] second, our sufferings are not truly "evil" but are our just desserts.[12]

For Augustine, the sufferings we experience are not signs of given evils in the natural universe; they are, rather, instances of God's just punishment for our disobedience. As Augustine says in confession to God, "free choice of the will is the reason why we do wrong and suffer your just judgement."[13] It was human sin that introduced sickness, sorrow, and death into the human condition. Human sufferings are understood by Augustine as the "wages of sin"—as the consequence of freely revolting against God—and not as natural "givens."[14] These wages were earned when Adam and his wife freely disobeyed God by eating from the Tree of Knowledge of Good and Evil.[15] As Adam's descendants, humans inherit an inclination toward sin; we are guilty by association and by inheritance. As punishment, God has plagued us with bodies that suffer pain and death. We—as a species—can only blame ourselves for our sufferings and mortality, not God or his creation. Augustine writes in *City of God,* "The corruption of the body, which weighs down the soul, is not the cause of the first sin, *but its punishment.* And it was not the corruptible flesh that made the soul sinful; it was the sinful soul that made the flesh corruptible" (*CG* 14.3; my emphasis). For Augustine, the sufferings and misfortunes that afflict us in the form of illness, corruption, and death are not—strictly speaking—"evil." All our afflictions are just punishments for our desire to exalt ourselves over God. Without God's grace, we can only do evil and suffer its consequences.[16]

In the eighteenth century, Immanuel Kant reformulated this understanding in his account of the "*radical* innate *evil* in human nature."[17] Kant, like Augustine and Rousseau, claims that the only "genuine" evil is "moral evil."[18] He argues that humans have an innate awareness of universal moral laws (such as "Do not kill" or "Do not steal"). We can distinguish these laws from our base impulses through what he calls the "categorical imperative," which he formulates thus: "Act only according to that maxim by which you can at the same time will that it should become a universal law."[19] Kant claims that we have a duty to obey these moral laws, even if they appear to go against our immediate self-interest; however, humans, in order to pursue their selfish desires, have a "natural propensity" to deviate from moral imperatives. Kant writes, "The *corruption* of the human heart is the propensity of the will to maxims which neglect the incentives springing from the moral law in favour of others that are not moral."[20] And like Augustine and Rousseau, Kant claims that this corrupt propensity was "*brought* by man *upon himself*."[21] Humanity is now trapped within this corruption. For Kant, "radical evil" does not designate an immoral act of excessive magnitude; rather, it signifies the general tendency of the human will to pursue its own selfish desires at the expense of universal law. In this way, Kant understands radical evil as something qualitative, not quantitative. Nevertheless, the harmful consequences of this quality in human nature are quantitatively extensive, for it has given us conflict, war, and suffering.

Kant's understanding of evil is not, ultimately, a categorical departure from what we find in Augustine, Rousseau, or Southwold. For whatever differences exist between Southwold (a late modern anthropologist), Augustine (a late classical theologian), and Rousseau and Kant (modern philosophers), there is an element that all have in common. Regardless of whether evil is defined as a quantitatively strong immorality, or as a sinful inclination to rebel against God, or as a qualitative tendency to disobey moral laws that we know by nature, it remains in each case an exclusive moral category. All speak of "evil" only in a strong moral sense. What is lost in such an approach is the broader Homeric understanding of evil as the given harms that we suffer, intend, and commit. Evil, in the Homeric sense, is not the sole consequence of human activity. It encompasses all things "bad," from the most insignificant to the most momentous, regardless of whether they spring from nature or human volition. For Homer, the key distinction is not between what is "merely bad" and "really evil," or between "nature" and "morality," but between the given evils that we will suffer and commit and the surplus evils that we unnecessarily perpetrate. By speaking of evils in this broader way, the approach to the subject takes on the spirit that Nietzsche articulates in the *Genealogy of Morals*: we move "beyond good and evil," insofar as we do not treat "Evil" exclusively as a category denoting sin or extreme wickedness. This does *not* mean, however, that we move "beyond good and bad."[22]

Other contemporary scholars have adopted this broader conception of evil. For example, the anthropologist David Parkin extends the notion of evil beyond "extreme wickedness," based on his cross-cultural analysis of different terms denoting privation, defilement, chaos, maliciousness, and harm.[23] Parkin delineates "three senses" in which we can speak of evil in a cross-cultural context:

> [1] the moral, referring to human culpability; [2] the physical, by which is understood destructive elemental forces of nature, for example earthquakes, storms or the plague; and [3] the metaphysical, by which disorder in the cosmos or in relations with divinity results from a conflict of principles or wills.[24]

In all three senses, evil is whatever antagonizes, corrupts, and destroys, be it human, natural, or divine. Understood in this way, evil denotes any privation, decay, or disorder that detracts from the proper excellence of something. Put differently, "evil" is a name for the privation of the good.[25] For example, the word *ra* in the Hebrew Bible originally denoted anything bad, unclean, harmful, or corruptive; it signified suffering at the natural level, as well as wickedness at the social level.[26] Paul Ricoeur points out that the ancient Israelites make no distinction between the "ethical order of *doing* ill" and the "cosmo-biological order of *faring* ill."[27] *Ra*, in all its human and natural manifestations, is just a fact of existence, a basic constituent of our condition. It is in light of the Hebrew conception of *ra* that the psychoanalyst C. Fred Alford encourages us to consider this lack of distinction between natural and moral evils as "a hard-won insight, not a developmental lag."[28] The attempt to speak of evil more broadly can also be found in the work of the French theorist Jean Baudrillard. Baudrillard writes, "I don't define [evil] in a moral sense, nor, for that matter in an immoral sense. Before being an immorality, evil is first an antagonistic principle. We can, however, retain from the religious vision of evil the idea of negation, illusion, destruction."[29] Baudrillard refers to "extreme phenomena" such as viruses, computer malfunctions, and system breakdowns as "evil"—phenomena that, in common parlance, tend to be designated as "misfortunes" because they are not necessarily the intended results of malevolent human agency.[30] For Baudrillard, evil is something that afflicts us and, to a large extent, transcends us.

With this approach we move closer to an understanding that evil is not just something that we do but also something that we suffer. Alford attempts to recapture this understanding in his own study of evil, but he admits it is "not a view that is dominant in the West today."[31] He asks us to consider "whether there is a category of experience which might help to render commensurable (not identical, but comparable) such radically diverse experiences as suffering, illness, 'falling on evil days,' the malevolence of the human heart, the Lisbon earthquake, the Holocaust, murder, going down into a dark basement, and losing oneself to one's boyfriend."[32] These experiences, according to Alford, are linked in ways we might not understand if we treat evil solely as a moral category. What renders all these various phenomena commensurable is the experience of "dread." Alford writes, "Evil is an experience of dread." He defines dread as the "uncanny experience of discomfort" we have of "being human, vulnerable, alone in the universe, and doomed to die."[33] In dread, we are terrified by the reality of violation, pollution, infection, confusion, and destruction; we fear that the limits that secure our physical well-being, mental health, and societal order will be crossed, afflicting us with suffering and chaos. This fear is aggravated by the ever-present reality of death, which reminds us that ultimately we cannot escape being victims, no matter how secure we are in our daily lives.

The passive experience of dread is directly related to the evils we commit. As Alford explains, "*Doing* evil is an attempt to evacuate this experience by inflicting it on others, making them feel dreadful by hurting them. Doing evil is an attempt to transform the terrible passivity and helplessness of suffering into activity."[34] Or, put differently: "Evil is the attempt to inflict one's doom on others, becoming doom, rather than living subject to it."[35] We fool ourselves into thinking that by causing dread we can escape dread. Through either sheer sadistic maliciousness or an inappropriate pursuit of the good, we lash out at our doom and cause harm. Either way, evil is marked by a loss of judgment regarding the nature of good and bad. It corrupts the evildoer, since the experience of dread quickly becomes a justification for cruelty and destruction. Evil, in this sense, is a principle of reversal and illusion, distorting our judgment and leading us into confusion and immorality.

Baudrillard agrees that the effort to eliminate the experience of dread—to strike all elements deemed threatening or impure in the natural and social realms—can exacerbate violence and wickedness. He suggests it is not in our best interest to aggravate our ignorance of evil through recklessness and, thereby, perpetuate greater evils beyond those already given. We must, he argues, accept the reality of evil and learn to live with it. He writes, "If indeed we were chased from the Garden for the sin of knowledge, we may as well draw the maximum benefit from it."[36] To refuse this knowledge of good and evil—however limited and partial it may be—is to perpetuate catastrophe unwittingly.

Theatre and Theory

The pursuit of knowledge of good and evil in the West has traditionally been associated with philosophy and theology. Here, however, I use works of theatre to discuss the experience of evil and consider how it has been symbolized in modernity. This raises a methodological question: Why choose to discuss evil through dramatic works and not through theory alone? It might be said that theatre, even at its best, lacks theoretical precision. Therefore, one could argue that it is best to concentrate on theory, not theatre, to discern the reality of given and surplus evils. Such an argument revives the ancient tension between "philosophers" and "poets" and insinuates that the theorist and the dramatist are either uneasy allies or outright antagonists. At the very least, it suggests that any serious theoretical discussion regarding evil should not base itself on works of literature.

Certainly, theatrical and theoretical pursuits have distinct characteristics. The playwright struggles to create vivid portrayals of action that are aesthetically compelling in a live performance, bringing an audience closer to the experience of the action itself. The author of a treatise or essay, on the other hand, tries to gain a certain distance from the experience in order to reflect on it. These two approaches are not necessarily antagonistic; on the contrary, they can complement one another. We can see the close relation between theatre and theory by considering the Greek etymologies of the words, which ultimately denote observance or watching. *Theatron* (theatre) literally means "watching place" or "place of seeing" and is derived from the verb *theosthai* (to watch, to look at); *theōria* (theory) primarily means "looking" or "contemplation" and is derived from the noun *theōros* (spectator). *Theōros* originally denoted a Greek public emissary who was sent by a city to observe foreign religious festivals. He was the contemplative outsider at a public event in a strange city. Later, the term was used to designate the spectator in the Athenian theatre. The *theōroi* (spectators) watching the actors onstage, like the observers of ceremonies in alien lands, do not participate in the action; rather, they contemplate the play, just as the theorist contemplates the activities of the cosmos and human beings with a certain degree of detachment.

Though theory is a form of activity, the theorist removes himself as much as possible from everyday activities to create a space in which to reflect. In his day-to-day work, he is immersed in life; life does not play *to* him, as it were, since he is an actor, but it also does not play to him even while he contemplates it. The theatergoer, on the other hand, watches a play that was intended for his contemplation. Whereas the theoretical life is mostly a detached life of solitude, theatre is public and interactive. Theatergoers distance themselves from their everyday lives by entering into a relationship with each other and with the actors onstage. In the theatre contemplation is a reflective dialogue that takes place between spectators and those responsible for creating the drama. The actors present themselves before an audience, which not only triggers emotional responses in the spectators but also challenges them to interpret and assess what they observe. Spectators judge both the aesthetic quality of the performance (Was the play emotionally engaging, well written, well acted, entertaining, pleasurable, effective?) and the content of what is performed (Was the play meaningful, insightful, illuminating?). Actors, directors, and playwrights can respond to the audience's assessment, modifying their aesthetic and moral sensibilities in the future depending on the critical reaction. In this manner, theatre is a peculiar form of public dialogue and contemplation. The issues raised within the theatre are, subsequently, relevant for life outside the theatre. They have a potential impact on how we understand the world and how we live.

The Enlightenment thinkers of the eighteenth century, such as Voltaire, Diderot, and Lessing, understood theatre as a vanguard of moral progress.[37] For them, theatre contributes to the formation of moral character. The audience is encouraged to judge whether the characters in a drama should be praised or condemned for their actions, and the hope is that this will influence how people act when they leave the theatre and return to their lives. Unfortunately, the Enlightenment emphasis on the educative aspects of theatre led to the creation of inferior "didactic plays," in which the representation of engaging dramatic action was often subordinate to the presentation of clear moral lessons.[38] A play, however, need not be didactic or moralistic to inspire moral reflection.

The affinity between theatre and ethical theory is best exemplified by the tragic theatre of ancient Athens. It was a civic requirement for Athenian citizens to attend performances once a year and judge the plays presented. Awards were given to the best actor and the best tragic playwright, chosen by ten judges representing the people. By being required to set aside everyday political tasks and assess the quality of the dramas presented onstage, Athenians were encouraged to theorize about their lives through theatre. J. Peter Euben writes:

> In at least one respect, tragedy was a political institution unlike any other. . . . [T]ragedy's distance from the urgency of daily decisions—which drove the [Athenian] council, assembly, and juries—allowed it to develop a uniquely "theoretical" perspective. This can be seen by the inclusiveness of its understanding, its preoccupation with the status of knowledge, its interrogation of otherwise unquestioned categories and demarcations, and its self-reflectiveness. . . . Freed from the urgencies of making immediate decisions, as in other institutional settings, tragedy encouraged its citizen-audience to think more inclusively about the general pattern implicit in their actions. In this way it was a theoretical as well as political institution.
>
> Drama was also a theoretical act and institution in the sense that the theatre was an occasion, place, and way for theoretical considerations to become relevant to practical affairs.[39]

Euben suggests that the primary purpose of this festival was not simply to give the Athenians diversionary entertainment; it was, on the contrary, an engaging aesthetic institution that was at once political and theoretical. Theatre was a way in which the Athenians as a community did political philosophy. Athenian playwrights used the reflective distance that theatre creates to inculcate practical wisdom in the audience. One of the primary purposes of tragedy was to educate the judgment of the community—a community embarking on a new democratic experiment that, as far as we know, had never been attempted before in history. The heavy burden of political responsibility had fallen on the citizens of Athens. The people, in the days before public education, needed an institution in which they could explore the scope and limitations of action in a hostile world. For this they turned to tragedy, which is different from didactic theatre. Athenian tragedy did not moralize; it portrayed maliciousness and suffering in stark terms, without any character or viewpoint emerging as absolutely good. Such depictions, for the Athenians, were essential for sharpening moral and political awareness—a form of political education distinct from propaganda. Eric Voegelin, in *New Science of Politics,* emphasizes the connection between the struggle for justice in politics and the representative suffering on the tragic stage:

> The tragedy in its great period is a liturgy which re-enacts the great decision for Dike [Justice]. Even if the audience is not an assembly of heroes, the spectators must at least be disposed to regard tragic action as paradigmatic; the heroic soul-searching and suffering of consequences must be experienced as holding a valid appeal; the fate of the hero must arouse the shudder of his own fate in the soul of the spectator. The meaning of tragedy as a state cult consists in representative suffering.[40]

Similarly, Christian Meier points out that tragedy "served to refresh, regenerate, and further develop the ethical basis of politics. . . . This would mean seeing tragedy as a buttress, a precondition for rational politics."[41] After seeing a good tragedy, citizens could return to the immediacy of their daily lives with a better understanding that—in Homer's terms— should not cause more evils beyond those given.

And it was evil—understood as any harm caused, intended, or suffered—that was central to Athenian theatre. As I noted earlier, evil, before being a theoretical category or a theological problem, is an experience of dread. Due to the nature of live performance, theatre can bring the experience of dread vividly to life, for what we see onstage are living human beings creating the illusion of suffering and malice. When mounting or watching a live performance, it is not the experience of dread itself we endure; it is, rather, a representation of it. Such representations of suffering and wickedness can stir emotional responses in an audience, much like the experiences themselves. In this way, we "shudder" at the fate of the tragic hero and empathize with his agony. Aristotle speaks of the great purging (*katharsis*) of "pity and fear" that occurs during tragic performances, a purging that brings the audience back to a balanced state after its pent-up feelings of dread are released.[42] But this stirring and purging of emotions is not the only purpose of theatre. Theatrical symbolizations of dread do not need to overwhelm our critical faculties as the experience itself does. On the contrary, the symbolization of dread onstage provides reflective distance even as it engages our emotions. As such, it offers a unique and potentially fruitful way of theorizing about the given and surplus evils of the human condition.

The present study is a work of political philosophy in the tragic sense. Certainly it is theoretical in form, and refers to various theorists for guidance. However, it concentrates on works of dramatic art in order to reflect on the modern experience of evil. Such an engagement might, in the spirit of tragedy, make possible a clearer understanding of the good life.

Theatre and Evil

Theatre has been a marginal tradition in the West. This fact is often forgotten by those familiar with the respect bestowed on theatre in literary history and the proliferation of commercial theatre in the twentieth century. Albert Camus makes this argument in a 1955 address titled "On the Future of Tragedy."[43] He claims that periods of great theatre are extremely rare. When they do occur, they emerge out of a "tragic age" that gives birth to tragic theatre. He notes that "in the thirty centuries of Western history, from the Dorians to the atomic bomb, there have been only two periods of tragic art, both of them narrowly confined in both time and space."[44] The first of these occurred in ancient Athens and is represented in the tragedies of Aeschylus, Sophocles, and Euripides. The second originated in Italy and reached fruition in England, Spain, and France during the sixteenth and seventeenth centuries; it is represented in the works of Christopher Marlowe, William Shakespeare, Lope de Vega, Pierre Corneille, and Jean Racine. In addition to these two periods, Camus speculates that a third era of tragic art might be taking place in his own time, although he is somewhat skeptical about this prospect; tragedy, for Camus, is a "rare flower," and he thinks the chances are slim that it would bloom in his own day.[45] Later in the twentieth century, and with more hindsight, the theatre scholar John Orr would claim that a third great period of theatrical art occurred in late modernity. He writes:

> There are three major events in the history of world drama. These are the emergence of classical tragedy in ancient Greece, the renaissance of tragic form in sixteenth-century England and seventeenth-century France, and finally the more diffuse tragic drama of modern civilization, written and performed in the period of industrial capitalism . . . between 1880 and 1966.[46]

The third period identified by Orr is represented by the works of Henrik Ibsen, Anton Chekhov, August Strindberg, Eugene O'Neill, Tennesse Williams, Arthur Miller, and Camus himself.

The three major periods of tragic art were also exceptional times for theatre in general, for they generated myriad theatrical forms and genres. In Athens, the great comedies of Aristophanes were being performed alongside the tragedies; and some of the works written by Euripides—such as *Ion, Helen,* and *Iphigenia in Tauris*—are best described as tragicomic. During the Renaissance and shortly thereafter, a multitude of comedies by Niccolò Machiavelli, Shakespeare, Ben Jonson, Pedro Calderón, and Jean-Baptiste Molière were being performed along with tragedies and historical dramas. Finally, the twentieth century witnessed numerous theatrical forms, most notably the innovative dramas of Luigi Pirandello, the "epic theatre" of Bertolt Brecht, and the absurdist works of Eugène Ionesco, Harold Pinter, and Samuel Beckett.

It is widely acknowledged that these periods were the most vital for theatre, the times when the greatest plays—tragic, comic, or otherwise—were being written and performed. Between these periods great dramatic works are difficult to find. The Romans mounted plays derived from Greek comedy and tragedy. Some were popular and had social impact,

especially the comedies, but theatre was not as central to Roman political life as it was for the Greeks of the fifth century B.C.E. For the most
part, Roman plays pale in comparison to Athenian drama.[47] A further decline in and even an eclipsing of the theatre occurred in medieval Christendom. The Western Church was always wary of theatre, often restrict-
ing its subject matter to biblical themes and frequently putting a stop
to staged performances altogether. For nearly a thousand years, from
the decline of the Roman Empire to the Renaissance, theatre was almost
nonexistent. Several liturgical and religious dramas survive from the
high Middle Ages, including the cycle pageants and morality plays, but
these are mostly of "historic interest" only today.[48] These works were
eventually rendered archaic by the power of Renaissance theatre. But
after this brief flowering in the sixteenth and seventeenth centuries, theatre once again declined in Europe. During the English Restoration, the
Enlightenment, and the Romantic period, many comedies, melodramas,
and didactic plays were written and performed; however, throughout
these times, philosophy, science, literature, symphonic music, and opera
overshadowed theatre.[49] Though Shakespeare's plays became canonical
as "literature" and were respected throughout Europe, they were largely
neglected as works of "theatre" between the late seventeenth and late
nineteenth century. For almost two hundred years, during a period of
increasing optimism in science, reason, and historical progress, Shakespeare's plays were infrequently performed. When they were staged, they
were almost always rewritten and modified to make their tragic themes
more palatable. It was not until the late nineteenth century that theatre once again became a vital aesthetic, thriving until at least the 1960s.
This coincides with a renewed interest in Shakespeare. But as the twentieth century concluded, theatre was once again pushed to the margins,
this time under the pressure of mass media. Despite the proliferation
of commercial theatre in city centers such as New York and London, public attention has been focused elsewhere. Television, cinema, videos, and
computers have gradually become the dominant media of information
relay and "entertainment."

   None of this is to suggest that there are no good works of theatre
outside of ancient Athens, the Renaissance, or Western late modernity;
nor does it mean that every play written during these historical epochs
is equally significant. It is to say that theatre has been at its best during

what Camus calls "tragic times." A "tragic age," according to Camus, is one that is marked by crisis, violence, and transition, and yet also contains enough social stability for the tragic arts to flourish. It was during such historical epochs—when the experience of evil was extremely acute and yet there was space to reflect about it—that theatre arose as a dominant aesthetic. Camus writes:

> Great periods of tragic art occur, in history, during centuries of crucial change, at moments when the lives of whole peoples are heavy both with glory and with menace, when the future is uncertain and the present dramatic. Aeschylus, after all, fought in two wars, and Shakespeare was alive during quite a remarkable succession of horrors. Both, moreover, stand at a kind of dangerous turning point in the history of their civilizations.[50]

Not every age of tumult and change necessarily gives rise to tragic art. Nevertheless, each of the three great flowerings of Western tragedy developed under such circumstances.[51] In Athens, the City Dionysia reached its creative climax in the fifth century B.C.E., between the Persian and Peloponnesian Wars.[52] This tumultuous period would see the rise and fall of Athens as the major political power in Greece and the advent of philosophy as a predominant mode of reflection. The political shape of the Greek world was also on the verge of a major transformation, as the small, loosely affiliated leagues of cities would be absorbed into the single totality of Alexander's empire within a generation. Twenty centuries later, tragic theatre was revived during the tumultuous disintegration of Western Christendom in national and religious wars and the widespread questioning of Christian doctrine and practice. Finally, the theatre that developed during the late nineteenth and twentieth century was concurrent with the growth of industry, the advancement of technology, the rise of modern bureaucratic states, the horror of two world wars, the realization of death camps, and the threat of nuclear war. The magnitude of these events suggested that modernity had reached a crisis point.

Given the tumult and change characterizing the three periods of tragic art, it is not surprising that questions concerning the nature of evil should arise. These concerns are clearly present at the birth of theatre in ancient Athens. Alford claims that tragedy was conceived out of the

Greek anxiety of being unable to distinguish good and evil.[53] He uses the term "Dionysian crisis" to describe this anxiety. As the chorus in Sophocles' *Antigone* states, "Evil seems good to one whose mind the god leads to ruin."[54] This, according to Alford, "is the real meaning, and the real terror, behind the proverb that those whom the gods would destroy they first make crazy—that is, unable to distinguish good and bad. Tragedy's strength lies in its ability to tell this truth."[55] In Athens, theatre took place at the City Dionysia, a five-day festival in honor of the god Dionysus. The Athenian *theatron* was the "watching place" where citizens were required by civic ordinance to observe depictions of evil—to gaze upon those things that disrupt civilized life and contaminate good with evil. As Mera Flaumenhaft points out, "The tragedies reveal rape, parricide, incest, cannibalism, and defiled corpses. . . . In the theatre, spectators must face what is mixed and mingled, mangled and impure."[56] Dionysus, god of wine and ecstasy, was the appropriate divinity to honor with these spectacles. In Greek mythology he is the god who, in Euben's words, "liberates men . . . from the monotony of ordinary life and familiar social categories."[57] He emancipates human beings by abolishing the classifications, divisions, and boundaries that normally apply. Dionysus is part god and part beast, part male and part female, part gentle and part violent.[58] His celebrants "recognize none of the usual boundaries" between "city and wild, sanity and madness, . . . purity and transgression."[59] This is not to say that Dionysus is entirely evil; on the contrary, he brings some of the greatest goods to humankind. We are told repeatedly in Euripides' *Bacchae* that Dionysus's gift of wine helps alleviate our miseries.[60] Dionysian intoxication, however, is a mixed good; humans become drunk and possibly lose their better judgment. Alford observes that appearance and reality are "confounded" under the impact of Dionysus, and "good and bad [are] so mixed up that they cannot be sorted out."[61] This, according to Alford, is the real reason that Greek tragedy is related to the cult of Dionysus.

Anxiety over the confusion of good and evil would emerge again in Renaissance and twentieth-century theatre. In each case, however, the nature of the anxiety is slightly different. In sixteenth century England, a new character type—the Machiavel—arose as a personification of evil in the postmedieval world. The Machiavel was a theatrical response to the political writings of Machiavelli, writings that appeared to challenge both classical and Christian accounts of morality. Explicit in this English response was a concern that traditional moral categories were losing their power, that good and evil were becoming radically indeterminate. Machiavelli, like Dionysus, tried to liberate humanity by abolishing traditional moral limits. But instead of encouraging drunken religious ecstasy, Machiavelli advised his audience to remain sober. Machiavelli demolished ethics not with wild abandon but with a vigilant political science characterized by calculation, premeditation, and efficacy. In the process, he attempted to erase all lines demarcating substantial moral distinctions between good and evil. This new understanding had a profound impact on theatre. It manifested itself first in the plays written by Machiavelli himself and then in the Elizabethan and Jacobean dramas of Renaissance England.

In twentieth-century theatre, anxieties about the nature of good and evil manifest themselves most significantly in absurdist plays. The "absurd" was initially a topic of European philosophy and French existentialist theatre between World War I and II; it later evolved into a theatrical genre of its own, the "theatre of the absurd," which vividly depicted the ridiculousness and suffering of the human condition in late modernity.[62] Portrayals of a world out of harmony, and of human beings unable to distinguish between true and false, appearance and reality, good and evil, dominate much of the theatre of the mid-twentieth century. Patrice Pavis points out that the fixation with the absurd arose out of "a disillusioned picture of a world devastated by conflict and ideology."[63] Many ideologies had promised to liberate humanity from age-old sufferings and confusions, but absurdist theatre revealed that a different reality had emerged in the twentieth-century. The absurdist playwright Ionesco notes, "If anything needs demystifying it is our ideologies, which offer ready-made solutions (which history quickly overtakes and refutes) and a language that congeals *as soon as it is formulated*."[64] These ideologies, according to Ionesco, have produced wars and catastrophes, as well as a "crisis of language" that has distorted human judgment as never before:

This crisis is most often artificially and deliberately produced. Propaganda has consciously obscured the meaning of words in order to throw our minds into confusion. It is a modern method of warfare. When it is maintained that white is black and black is white, it is indeed very difficult to find one's way about.[65]

Ionesco understood his own form of absurd theatre as a reflection of and a critical response to this confusion: the modern inability to distinguish black from white, false from true, and evil from good.

Distinctive Features of the Death Event

Ionesco addresses the new reality of the death event through theatre in order to get his audience to reflect immediately on what modernity has brought to pass. Before embarking on the discussion of Renaissance and twentieth century theatre, it might be best to consider some historical and theoretical details about mass murder in the twentieth century. The death event is the focal point of this study, and it is important to gain an understanding of its distinctive features. I consider the analysis of modern mass murder provided by Camus, Edith Wyschogrod, and particularly Zygmunt Baumann in his book *Modernity and the Holocaust.*

The various genocides and atrocities of the twentieth century suggest that unique and unprecedented evils have taken root in our world. It is not enough, however, to say that modern evil is distinct because of the predominance of man-made mass death. Mass murder is not unique to modernity, nor did moderns invent it. Nevertheless, Bauman contends that twentieth-century mass murder is unique: "Modern cases of genocide stand out for their sheer scale. On no other occasion but during Hitler's and Stalin's rule were so many people murdered in such a short time."[66] This quantitative distinction between late modern genocide and all previous forms of mass murder suggests there are qualitative features that distinguish the death event.

According to Wyschogrod, the "scope" of the death event is distinguished by three characteristic expressions:

[1] recent wars which deploy weapons in the interest of maximum destruction of persons; [2] annihilation of persons, through techniques designed for this purpose (for example famine, scorched earth, deportation), *after* the aims of war have been achieved or without reference to war; and [3] the creation of death worlds [e.g., concentration camps], a new and unique form of social existence in which vast populations are subjected to conditions of life simulating imag-

ined conditions of death, conferring upon their inhabitants the status of the living dead.[67]

For Wyschogrod, what is unique about these phenomena is not so much the unparalleled quantity of murder they have caused but rather that "the *means* of annihilation are the result of systematic rational calculation, and scale is reckoned in terms of the compression of time in which destruction is delivered."[68] The death event, for Wyschogrod, is distinguished by its cold-blooded rationality and routine efficiency. Her argument echoes a point articulated by Camus at the beginning of *The Rebel,* where he makes a distinction between "crimes of passion" and "crimes of logic" (*R* 3).[69] According to Camus, passionate crime arises from sudden, irrational impulses characterized by intense rage or perverse enjoyment; logical crime, on the other hand, is premeditated and methodical, characterized by industrious application and ideological justification. On the basis of this distinction, Camus claims that mass murders committed before modernity tended to result from passionate exuberance. The extensive slaughters that occurred in the midst of ancient wars and conquests—on or beyond the field of battle—were usually committed in the heat of the moment and sometimes had an element of celebration. Camus writes, "There have been periods of history in which the passion for life was so strong that it burst forth in criminal excesses. But these excesses were like the searing flame of terrible delight" (*R* 6–7). Camus provides ancient examples of such hot-blooded excess: tyrants razing cities for their glory, the conquerors dragging conquered slaves behind their chariots, and assembled people watching enemies thrown to wild beasts (*R* 3–4). Truly modern evil, in comparison, is not characterized by such frenzied, celebratory crime. Modern genocidal regimes are distinguished by what Camus calls a "monotonous order of things" (*R* 7).

Like Hannah Arendt, who spoke of the modern "banality of evil,"[70] Camus observed that modern societies in the mid-twentieth century did not produce barbaric monsters; rather, they produced thoughtless bureaucrats and laborers who participated in mass murder through specific administerial and technical tasks. This banal form of evil is more dangerous than barbaric passionate crime because it is more thorough and more efficient, and can sustain itself for longer periods. Whereas crimes of passion tend to be random and spontaneous, flaring up suddenly in an outburst of rage and fury but dying out quickly, crimes of logic manifest themselves in all-embracing systems in which murder is rationally premeditated, systematically organized, and ideologically legitimized over an indefinite period.[71] Such murder is dreary work, not barbaric play. Bauman writes:

> Rage and fury are pitiably primitive and inefficient as tools of mass annihilation. They normally peter out before the job is done. One cannot build grand designs on them. Certainly not such designs as reach beyond momentary effects like a wave of terror, the breakdown of an old order, clearing the ground for a new rule. Genghis Khan and Peter the Hermit did not need modern technology and modern, scientific methods of management and co-ordination. Stalin or Hitler did. . . . It is the practitioners of cool, thorough and systematic genocide like Stalin and Hitler for whom the modern, rational society paved the way. . . . Contemporary mass murder is distinguished by a virtual absence of all spontaneity on the one hand, and the prominence of rational, carefully calculated design on the other.[72]

This means that the phenomenon of man-made mass death in modernity is not a resurgence of barbaric passions, nor is it something that is antithetical to the general spirit of modernity. On the contrary, logical crime is a conspicuous form in which the modern orientation has expressed itself:

> The Holocaust was as much a product, as it was a failure, of modern civilization. Like everything else done in the modern—rational, planned, scientifically informed, expert, efficiently managed, co-ordinated—way, the Holocaust left behind and put to shame all its alleged pre-modern equivalents, exposing them as primitive, wasteful and ineffective by comparison.[73]

Bauman characterizes the modern spirit as a drive towards total rationality, absolute efficiency, and omniscient management. This spirit presents itself as the greatest manifestation of "civilization," but it is not a sufficient barrier to mass murder. On the contrary, it can precipitate genocide if the right conditions present themselves.

None of this is to suggest that there was no premeditated, rational crime before modernity; nor is it meant to imply that none of the perpetrators of modern genocide relished their crimes. The point is that the inclination toward rational, prearranged, organized slaughter has been taken to unprecedented extremes in the modern world. Logical mass murder is best realized not through furious lynch mobs but through systematic bureaucracies in which there is a "meticulous functional division of labour," a division that does not depend on unruly emotions for its proper functioning.[74]

When labor is divided within a bureaucracy, each laborer is employed to perform a specific job that in its own small way contributes to a grander end. All bureaucracies are divided into a series of highly specialized tasks—sorting files, computing figures, compiling statistics, drawing blueprints, ordering supplies, delivering supplies, laying bricks, balancing the books—that collectively work toward achieving a larger goal. However, as Bauman points out, "all division of labour . . . creates a distance between most of the contributors to the final outcome of collective activity, and the outcome itself."[75] When an employee in a bureaucracy is hired to perform the same task each day, he is not necessarily encountering the ultimate end that the bureaucracy is realizing, nor is he expected to think about this end in the actual performance of his specific job. Instead, he is expected to perform his task with the optimum degree of efficiency and effectiveness. It is this for which he is paid, and for which he might possibly be promoted to a better position within the bureaucratic hierarchy. Such material incentives ensure a maximum degree of obedience and efficiency. Furthermore, since most employees do not directly experience the end result of the bureaucratic operation, they are divorced from the human costs of their actions. Because of the apparent innocuousness of the tasks they perform each day at the office or work site, employees do not suffer any ethical qualms regarding their jobs. They are more likely to be concerned with the immediate material incentives offered to them for a job well done rather than the distant harms they do not see firsthand. In such an environment, "morality boils down to the commandment to be a good, efficient and diligent expert and worker."[76] And if a bureaucracy is directed toward a murderous end, it will likely proceed with little resistance from the people working within the system because very few of them are witnesses to the actual killing. In this way, ordinary citizens become complicit in the most horrendous crimes.

Bureaucracy is one of the most salient features of Nazi and Stalinist terror. In both cases, a system of indifferent laborers and "experts" was set up to oversee the expulsion and extermination of whole populations. Most employees within the Nazi and Stalinist bureaucracies did not experience the horrors of the death camps or the Gulag firsthand. Instead, they experienced the daily grind of the office or the workplace. They were not necessarily unaware of the harms they were causing, but they were separated from them.[77] Most kept to their jobs, either in the hope of securing personal benefits or in the fear that they would be punished if they failed. The organization and efficiency of these systems allowed totalitarian movements to realize a level of mass murder that could not have been achieved through mob violence alone. Bureaucracies are what made the Holocaust and other twentieth-century genocides possible. Baumann argues that "bureaucracy made the Holocaust" because bureaucracy is "intrinsically *capable* of genocidal action."[78]

The proliferation of bureaucracies in modernity reveals an inherent shift in the conception of human responsibility. Bauman claims that "moral responsibility," the acute awareness of being responsible for the harms one causes, has been largely replaced in the modern world by "technical responsibility," which is concerned with performing specific tasks with an optimum degree of efficiency and effectiveness regardless of the harmful consequences.[79] Technical responsibility predominates when an action is "judged only by its intrinsic criteria of propriety and success."[80] When activity is measured entirely by these criteria, it is "dissociated from moral evaluation of the ends." It is within this ethos that violence becomes most efficient and cost-effective.[81] The more humans are encouraged to measure their actions by effectiveness, the more likely they lack the moral character to resist the commands of malevolent regimes.[82]

It was not only the shift toward technical responsibility that perpetrated the death event and distinguished it from all previous types of mass murder. The modern predominance of technique originated in utopian visions of the future that justified the use of mass murder to realize perfection. Bauman points out that the motives for mass murder have been varied throughout human history, ranging "from pure, cold-blooded calculation of competitive gain, to equally pure, disinterested hatred or heterophobia."[83] The intentions behind "truly modern genocide" are different:

> *Modern genocide is genocide with a purpose.* Getting rid of the adversary is not an end in itself. It is a means to an end: a necessity that stems from the ultimate objective, a step that one has to take if one wants ever to reach the end of the road. *The end itself is a grand vision of a better, and radically different, society.* Modern genocide is an element of social engineering, meant to bring about a social order conforming to the design of the perfect society.[84]

In other words, modern genocide is a product of the revolutionary utopianism promulgated by totalitarian regimes. In these regimes, entire populations were exterminated—populations that, on the basis of race, nationality, ethnicity, class, religion, or ideological allegiance, were deemed unfit to live in the perfect society.

Utopian activism is what distinguishes the ultimate motives of modern genocide from premodern killing. Though there have been premodern forms of utopianism that have encouraged excess and murder, there was not the bureaucratic and technological means available to pursue utopian dreams. Utopian political projects could not sustain themselves in the past to promote systematic, long-term mass murder. As a result, slaughters tended to be motivated by more worldly inclinations, such as sheer hatred, the desire for more territory, or momentary passion. Bauman claims that truly modern genocide, on the other hand, is "engaged" by a grand messianic visionary—a Lenin, a Hitler, a Mao—with a "bold design" for a "more reasonable and rational social order—say a racially uniform or a classless society." At the same time, this visionary has "the capacity of drawing such designs and determination to make them efficacious."[85] The visionary establishes a system dedicated exclusively to finding the most effective and efficient ways of annihilating undesirable populations in the shortest time. In other words, he initiates a movement that establishes a bureaucracy with a vision. The result is legitimized mass murder, where absolute ends are evoked to justify absolute means. In this way, even if a laborer within a totalitarian bureaucracy is aware that his actions are contributing to grave atrocities, he can continue in his job with a good conscience. These atrocities are made to seem like goods since they are presented as effective remedies for the defects in the world and human nature. Even those who live outside a totalitarian society may sympathize with its utopian intent. According to Camus, this is the reason moderns are unable to condemn modern evil in swift and unequivocal terms. As he wrote in 1950:

> One might think that a period which, in a space of fifty years, uproots, enslaves, or kills seventy million human beings should be condemned out of hand. But its culpability must still be understood. In more ingenuous times, when the tyrant razed cities to his own greater glory, when the slave chained to the conqueror's chariot was dragged through the rejoicing streets, when enemies were thrown to the wild beasts in front of the assembled people, the [conscience remained firm before such unabashed crimes, and judgement remained clear]. But slave camps under the flag of freedom, massacres justified by [the love of man] or by a taste for the superhuman, in one sense cripple judgement. (R 3–4)[86]

For Camus, modern utopianism, with its promises of absolute freedom and superhumanity, encouraged the inclination to legitimize genocide and distorted human abilities to perceive obvious evils. In such circumstances, a revaluation of modern ambitions is imperative. In Camus's words, the "refusal to legitimize murder forces us to reconsider our whole idea of utopia."[87]

Eschatology and Expediency: The Structure of This Work

We can conclude that the modern death event is historically unique for three main reasons: (1) the sheer scale of the catastrophe; (2) the eclipse of moral responsibility by technical responsibility; and (3) the utopian aspirations of the initiating political movements. When we turn to works of Renaissance and twentieth-century theatre, we find significant symbolizations of these characteristics of the death event.

In this book, I begin in the twentieth century, because it is closer to us and because it places us in the context of the death event itself. The desire for utopia was given numerous expressions in late modern drama.[88] The disaster of modern utopianism is best reflected in the absurdist themes of twentieth-century theatre. In Part I, I discuss Camus's *Caligula* and Beckett's *Waiting for Godot*. In these two works we see a reconsideration of the utopianism animating late modernity—a utopianism that, as it turns out, has premodern roots. Both plays concentrate on the traditional figure of the "messiah" who is expected to transform reality and actualize utopia. The plays reveal that twentieth-century utopianism is rooted in ancient and medieval eschatological faith, in the belief that there will be a definitive end of history in which good will triumph over evil once and for all. This belief is found in Judaism, Christianity, and Islam, as well as in the various heretical and Gnostic sects of the Middle Ages. Camus and Beckett uncover what I call the *eschatological impulse* of modern evil. They reveal how the eschatological dream of exterminating evil has culminated in the most atrocious crimes, the most horrendous sufferings, and the most dreadful loss of sound judgment. *Caligula* shows the eschatological "logic" behind modern evil—how the hope for a world without evil can easily become criminal utopianism. *Waiting for Godot* shows how our civilization is having difficulty escaping from its eschatological assumptions. Beckett reveals that late modernity is mired in a multitude of harmful utopian aspirations that humans cling to out of blind traditional habit, desperate nostalgic revival, or sheer cultural inertia. For Beckett, our condition after Auschwitz is not a genuine break from the Western eschatological tradition but a weary and destructive reenactment of old eschatological forms. These forms continue to consume us today and are a central element of our current geopolitical situation. Fervent eschatological expectation is found not only in contemporary Jewish, Christian, and Islamic "fundamentalism" but also in the Western-based fetish for "globalization." The events of 9/11 symbolize the clash between the Western and Islamist eschatological visions and suggest that eschatological violence will be a central aspect of the twenty-first century. Thus *Caligula* and *Waiting for Godot* not only illuminate their own times but also anticipate ours.

My critical exegesis of these two plays in Part I is introduced by a brief discussion of the development of the absurd within European theatre and by a more detailed outline of the main features of eschatology. Following my discussions of *Caligula* and *Godot*, I conclude Part I by arguing that the absurdist vision is both a *critical response to* and a *consequence of* the eschatological excesses of Western civilization. Ultimately, each work is symptomatic of the very disease it condemns.

The late modern emphasis on technique, instrumentality, and effectiveness receives its most acute dramatic rendering in the "Machiavellian" dramas of early modernity. In Part II, I turn to the Renaissance and discuss Machiavelli's *Mandragola* and Shakespeare's *Measure for Measure.* These two plays reveal how the late modern emphasis on "technical responsibility" is in fact rooted in early modern Machiavellianism, for we see characters and societies transformed through the principle of sheer efficacy. As a result, *Mandragola* and *Measure for Measure* uncover what I call the *expedient impulse* of modern evil.

It is significant that Machiavelli, a man widely regarded as one of the founders of modern political thought and modern consciousness in general, has a name that, over time, has become synonymous with evil, or, at the very least, unscrupulous cunning. Machiavelli's reputation as a teacher of evil is largely based on *The Prince* and the *Discourses on Livy,* his two major works of political theory. In these texts, Machiavelli both describes and recommends the effective use of cruelty, conspiracy, torture, execution, theft, deceit, and murder. In *Mandragola,* his comic play, Machiavelli similarly advocates the clever use of adultery to gain control over household affairs. Machiavelli's advocacy of actions traditionally designated as vices led Leo Strauss to remark: "If it is true that only an evil man will stoop to teach such maxims of public and private gangsterism, we are forced to say that Machiavelli was an evil man." Strauss professes himself inclined toward the "old fashioned and simple opinion" that "Machiavelli was a teacher of evil."[89] He is also inclined toward the opinion that Machiavelli initiated the "first wave of modernity." The writings of Machiavelli, according to Strauss, embody the drive toward rationality, efficiency, management, and self-preservation that is often associated with the modern spirit.[90] This suggests that *Mandragola* is not just symptomatic of the modern tendency toward sheer effectiveness; it is, rather, helping to lay the foundation on which this ethos stands.

It is no secret that Machiavelli's account of expediency had a profound impact on the generations that followed. This is especially evident in *Measure for Measure.* Shakespeare was acutely aware that Machiavelli's writings were contributing to the creation of a new ethos of expediency. And Shakespeare also knew that this was affecting both our understanding of politics and our perception of human excellence. *Measure for Measure* tests our critical faculties in the new Machiavellian climate of opinion. Quite simply, the play challenges us to distinguish good from evil in the shadow of purely expedient political and ethical relations. And while Shakespeare could not foresee the catastrophic directions such expediency would take in the late modern world, his play reveals the social and psychological distortions that occur when "calculation[s] of efficiency" are granted "supreme authority in deciding political purposes."[91]

My discussion of Machiavelli and Shakespeare is introduced by an examination of the general response to Machiavelli in English theatre. Following my critical exegeses of *Mandragola* and *Measure for Measure,* I conclude Part II with some general reflections about Machiavelli's innovations. I also argue that *Mandragola* and *Measure for Measure* reveal that the eschatological and expedient impulses of modern evil are not as different as they first seem.

I conclude this work with a general examination of theatre as an aesthetic.[92] In accord with Camus and others, I argue that the greatest theatre—regardless of genre—is intimately connected to the tragic vision articulated in Athenian drama. I show how this vision is distinct from the various eschatological and expedient impulses that have dominated Western society for the past two millennia and that have eclipsed our ancient Greek theatrical heritage.

PART ONE

Evil in
Twentieth-Century Theatre

CHAPTER ONE

Eschatology and the Absurd

The Absurd in Theory

In *The Myth of Sisyphus,* Camus speaks of "an absurd sensitivity that can be found widespread in the age" (*MS* 2). The word *absurd* is popularly used as a synonym for "ridiculous," but it is more precise to say that it signifies "discord," "disharmony," or "incongruity."[1] For Camus, the "absurd" refers to an irreparable antagonism—an unbridgeable rupture— that a person experiences between himself and the world. This experience, according to Camus, has become especially pronounced in late modernity. Humans do not feel at home in the world, especially in a political environment marked by confusion, global war, and mass murder. Indeed, Camus claims that his absurdist meditation in *Sisyphus* was written "in 1940, amid the French and European disaster" (*MS* v).

Camus is aware that the experience of discord is not necessarily a constant factor in human life. For the most part, humans live each day according to natural and social patterns that are familiar and routine.[2] Every individual adapts to these patterns and justifies his or her daily existence with reasons that appear comprehensive and true. Insofar as the daily routine continues without disruption, humans experience a relative degree of congruity with the larger natural and social totalities. However, extraordinary events occur from time to time that disrupt the daily routine and challenge prevailing assumptions. For example, the death of a loved one can "undermine" a person (*MS* 4). In the wake of such an event, a world that once seemed familiar, friendly, and reasonable now appears foreign, hostile, and irrational to a grieving individual. Camus writes, "In a universe suddenly divested of illusions and lights, man feels an alien, a stranger" (*MS* 5). This feeling of alienation may lead a person to consider whether life is worth living and whether suicide is the best option. If this consideration can emerge from the loss of a single loved one, then situations of war and mass murder can only raise more intense doubts about the value of one's life.

Thoughts about suicide are not only generated by extreme experiences. Camus writes, "At any street corner the feeling of absurdity can strike any man in the face" (*MS* 9). One may, in the midst of an everyday routine, suddenly become aware of one's impending and inescapable death; or one may, without any obvious provocation, become lucidly conscious that all human efforts are laid to waste with the passage of time. Daily tasks suddenly appear futile, and the feeling of harmony with the world is replaced by rupture. Everywhere a person looks he encounters "walls" that alienate him from nature, society, and even himself (*MS* 8–16). Camus writes that this "divorce between man and his life, the actor and his setting, is properly speaking the feeling of absurdity" (*MS* 5). And it is consciousness of this divorce that can cause a person to commit suicide.

To speak of the absurd is to speak of evil. Like many of the oldest symbols of evil, the absurd denotes antagonism, disharmony, breakdown, confusion, and chaos. Camus writes, "The world itself, whose single meaning I do not understand, is but a vast irrational" (*MS* 20). We are ultimately left with two certainties: on the one hand, there is humanity's "appetite for the absolute and for unity," and on the other, there is the "impossibility of reducing this world to a rational principle" (*MS* 38). Absurd man realizes that he cannot reconcile these two certainties and that he is in conflict with the world: "Man feels within him his longing for happiness and for reason. The absurd is born of this confrontation between the human need and the unreasonable silence of the world" (*MS* 21). Properly speaking, "the absurd is not in man . . . nor in the world, but in their presence together" (*MS* 23).

Like Camus, Samuel Beckett speaks of an overwhelming experience of incongruity in late modernity. In an early essay on Irish poetry, Beckett speaks of a new type of poet who portrays "the space that intervenes between himself and the world of objects."[3] Such an artist perceives a "rupture of the lines of communication" between the individual and the world.[4] Beckett finds depictions of this rupture not only in contemporary poetry but also in modern art, for example, the paintings of Paul Cézanne. In a series of letters to a friend, Beckett argues that Cézanne's natural landscapes depict a world utterly foreign to humanity.[5] Cézanne's universe, according to Beckett, is an "unintelligible arrangement of atoms" that is "unapproachably alien" and "incommensurable with all human expressions whatsoever." This incommensurability is not just between humanity and the natural world. Cézanne "had the sense of his incommensurability not only with life of such a different order as landscape, but even with life of his own order, even with the life . . . operative in himself." In other words, Cézanne depicts the human subject as alienated from his own thoughts, desires, and social orders.[6]

The absurd experience of alienation, suffering, and confusion, according to Beckett, must be the central concern of all serious contemporary artists, whether they are poets, novelists, painters, or playwrights, for it is precisely this experience that characterizes modern times. "The confusion," Beckett once said, "is not my invention. We cannot listen to a conversation for five minutes without being acutely aware of confusion . . . One can only speak of what is in front of one and that now is simply a mess."[7] Any aesthetic strategy that refuses to represent "the mess" is, for Beckett, deluded, manipulative, or quaint.

The Absurd in Theatre

Theatrical sensitivity to the absurd in the twentieth century is marked by two distinct periods. The first occurred in France between the first world war and the end of the second. During this time, a particular style of drama arose that was subsequently described as "existentialist."[8] Camus's *Caligula,* written during World War II and first performed in Paris in 1945, is frequently cited as a preeminent example of this style of theatre. The second period of theatrical interest in the absurd started in France shortly after World War II and spread throughout Europe and the world. This period gave birth to a new stage genre, marked by radical changes in dramaturgy and theatrical presentation. It would later be referred to as the "theatre of the absurd." Beckett's *Waiting for Godot,* written in 1949 and first performed in Paris in 1953, stands as a paradigm of this type of drama.

Let us first consider the existentialist theatre of interwar France. This includes the plays of Jean-Paul Sartre, André Gide, Jean Cocteau, Jean Giraudoux, Jean Anouilh, Armand Salacrou, and Camus. Salacrou's *The Unknown Woman of Arras* (1935), Cocteau's *Intimate Relations* (1938), and Sartre's *No Exit* (1944) are representative works from this period. The use of the title "existentialist" to describe this generation of playwrights is most likely due to Sartre's popularity, given his advocacy of the term "existentialism" to describe his own thought. Camus, however, did not use the term "existentialist" to describe his own work, and he vehemently disagreed with Sartre's "existentialism." He claimed that his own understanding of the absurd was "directed against the so-called existentialist philosophers."[9] It is important, then, that we do not identify all the dramatists of this period as disciples of Sartre's philosophy. But regardless of which name is used to denote this generation of French playwrights, it is possible to identify several common features in their work.

First, these playwrights were united in their concern with the disorder, suffering, and sense of meaninglessness overtaking Europe at that time.[10] Second, they made concerted efforts to revive classical mythology for the modern world and reconstitute it in a manner that might allow them to explore the moral and political crisis of contemporary Europe. It is noteworthy that almost all interwar French playwrights chose to rewrite at least one Greek tragedy. E. Freeman writes:

> The modern French dramatist . . . made use of a framework of [Greek] archetypal situations and relationships involving death, exile, violence, madness, and love in which to set the crisis of the Western moral conscience in the modern age, especially during its time of sharpest focus: the Second World War and the events immediately leading up to it.

Freeman points out that between 1920 and 1950, "over a dozen leading French authors each wrote an average of almost two 'neo-Greek' plays."[11] Gide's *Oedipus*, Anouilh's *Antigone*, Giraudoux's *Electra*, Cocteau's *Orpheus*, and Sartre's *The Flies* (an adaptation of the Electra myth) are just some examples of this renaissance of tragedy in French theatre. Camus's *Caligula* was part of this restorative movement. Like other plays of the period, *Caligula* uses an ancient subject to illuminate the modern experience of absurdity; however, Camus turned to Roman history instead of Greek mythology to write his tragedy. He chose Suetonius's account of an ancient Roman tyrant over any of the plays of Aeschylus, Sophocles, or Euripides. This makes Camus's play unique in ways that, as we shall see, are significant.

The existentialist and neoclassical dramas of interwar France are not instances of what is now called the theatre of the absurd. Although these plays deal with absurdist themes, the designation "theatre of the absurd" tends to be reserved exclusively for those plays written by the dramatists who emerged after World War II with a radically new style. These dramatists include Ionesco, Arthur Adamov, Jean Genet, Edward Albee, Harold Pinter, and Beckett. With the emergence of this generation in the early 1950s, the "existential" neoclassicist renaissance of interwar French theatre came to a close.

Martin Esslin argues that the main difference between existentialist drama and the theatre of the absurd is stylistic. Existential dramatists "present their sense of the irrationality of the human condition in the form of highly lucid and logically constructed reasoning."[12] Characters in existential dramas often sound like theorists. Camus himself acknowledged this stylistic feature of *Caligula.* Though he was reluctant to characterize *Caligula* as a "philosophical play," he nevertheless calls it a "tragedy of the intelligence," given that its characters meditate on the absurd through discursive dialogue.[13] Esslin claims that Camus and his contemporaries "express the new content in the old convention"—the new content being the omnipresence of absurdity in modern experience and the old convention being the use of theoretical discourse to describe it.[14]

This tendency notwithstanding, the theatre of the absurd largely abandons discursive dialogue. Esslin writes:

> The Theatre of the Absurd has renounced arguing *about* the absurdity of the human condition; it merely *presents* it in being—that is, in terms of concrete stage images. . . . It is this striving for an integration between the subject-matter and the form in which it is expressed that separates the Theatre of the Absurd from the Existentialist theatre.[15]

This means that a number of stylistic elements stand out in the theatre of the absurd that distinguish it from its existentialist predecessor: the dialogue is frequently senseless, the situation is usually ridiculous, the setting is often located in no discernible place or time, and dramatic conventions such as character development and plot are forgone.

Beckett adopted this stylistic approach in his own dramas since he thought it could depict the late modern "mess" with the utmost precision of form:

> [The confusion] is all around us and our only chance is to let it in. The only chance of renovation is to open our eyes and see the mess. It is not a mess you can make sense of. . . . What I am saying does not mean that there will henceforth be no form in art. It only means that there will be new form, and that this form will be of such a type that it admits the chaos and does not try to say that the chaos is really something else. . . . To find a form that accommodates the mess, that is the task of the artist now.[16]

It is helpful to consider this statement in the context of another remark that Beckett made about the work of James Joyce. Beckett writes that for Joyce "form *is* content, content *is* form. . . . His writing is not *about* something; *it is that something itself.*"[17] Beckett would adopt this approach when composing his own works. He did not want his dramas simply to theorize the mess that confronts the absurd man; rather, he wanted to create a form of theatrical expression that accurately embodies the mess in a manner that is stylized and illuminating.

Beckett's concern with "the mess" placed him outside of the modernist aesthetic exemplified by writers like Joyce. The mess, according to Beckett, is characterized by an unprecedented deterioration in human thought and action. This has, in Beckett's words, altered the purpose of art in the late modern world:

> The kind of work I do is one in which I'm not master of my material. The more Joyce knew, the more he could. He's tending toward omniscience and omnipotence as an artist. I'm working with impotence, ignorance. . . . My little exploration is that whole zone of being that has always been set aside by artists as something unusable—as some-

thing by definition incompatible with art. I think anyone nowadays, who pays the slightest attention to his experience, finds it the experience of a non-knower, a non-can-er.[18]

This concentration on ignorance and impotence—on the "non-knower" and the "non-can-er"—is embodied in the very structure of *Waiting for Godot*. As such, it is an archetype of the nondiscursive style of the theatre of the absurd. This is not to say *Godot* is meaningless or that its purpose is to encourage more ignorance and confusion. On the contrary, the play is filled with concrete images and acute observations that illuminate crucial features of the late modern situation. Beckett simply shuns the theoretical discourse that had dominated the existentialist and neoclassical plays in the earlier part of the century. His dramaturgy, however, drew mixed reactions when *Godot* premiered on January 5, 1953, at the Théâtre de Babylone in Paris. Though *Godot* is now widely recognized as a classic, it remains one of the most controversial works of the twentieth century.

Eschatology: Apocalypse and Gnosis

Caligula and *Waiting for Godot* are two noteworthy moments in the development of the absurd in twentieth-century theatre, but they share more than a historical importance. Taken together, they uncover the ancient religious roots that underlie the contemporary experience of absurdity. Specifically, they reveal how the absurd sensibility in the late modern world has been shaped by a multitude of apocalyptic and Gnostic movements within Western civilization. These movements, for all their variety and differences, share an eschatological vision of reality. Walter Schmithals writes, "The understanding of existence that is common to gnosis and apocalyptic[ism] . . . is expressed . . . in eschatology which is dominant in both movements."[19] That is, these movements expect that the world, as it is presently constituted, will come to an end and be replaced by a condition in which evil is purged. "Apocalypticism" and "Gnosticism" are the two predominant schools in which this expectation has been expressed in the Judeo-Christian world. Both *Caligula* and *Waiting for Godot* reveal that these ancient religious movements have contributed to the late modern catastrophe. Furthermore, they suggest that the ostensibly "secular" ethos underlying the modern world and the death event is not a genuine break from these older religious forms but a disastrous continuation. This is not an idiosyncratic claim made in two eccentric plays; it is an argument that has received support from numerous scholars of religion and political theory. As Wyschogrod writes, "The "religious roots of the death event . . . can be traced to Jewish apocalypticism of the intertestamental period and to later Christian apocalypticism"; it can also be traced to the "related speculations of Jewish and Christian gnosis."[20]

Before examining *Caligula* and *Godot* in detail, it is essential to define *eschatology* and differentiate the apocalyptic and Gnostic tendencies within the eschatological worldview. Only in light of such a discussion can we fully appreciate the eschatological nuances of the two plays and how they express the modern experience of the absurd.

The word *eschatology* comes from the Greek *eschatos,* which means "farthest" or "last."[21] *Eschaton,* in its most general sense, refers to any termination, completion, or ending. It is also a morally neutral term that can refer to any goal that we aspire to. If the goal is good, then this aspiration can be understood as an effort to realize excellence or virtue. In this sense, the meaning of *eschatos* overlaps with the Greek *telos,* which also means "end" or "conclusion" but which signifies that something has actualized its best potential.[22]

Eschatology is a modern coinage.[23] It denotes any teaching about "endings" or "last things." It is most often associated with a particular type of religious symbolism that foretells the end of the world and the complete triumph of good over evil. The editors of *The Encyclopedia of Apocalypticism* point out that the word *eschatology* is related to *apocalypticism* ("the belief that God has revealed the imminent end of the ongoing struggle between good and evil in history"), *millennialism* ("belief in a coming better age on earth, such as that described in the thousand year reign of Christ at the end of the book of Revelation"), and *messianism* ("hope for a heaven-sent savior who will usher in the better age").[24] Indeed, "eschatology" is frequently understood to be synonymous with these other terms. Given the various associations of "eschatology," I use it in a specific sense: it is the expectation that the world, as it is presently constituted, will come to an end and be replaced by a new realm cleansed of all evil, a realm that some, but not necessarily all, will inhabit. I use the word *eschaton* similarly, not in its general Greek sense, but in the specific sense of an end state in which evil is purged once and for all.

The eschatological myth has had a major impact on Western consciousness. Norman Cohn writes:

> [The expectation that] there will shortly be a marvelous consummation, when good will be finally victorious over evil and for ever reduce it to nullity; that the human agents of evil will be either physically annihilated or otherwise disposed of; that the elect will thereafter live as a collectivity, unanimous and without conflict, on a transformed and purified earth—this expectation has had a long history in our civilization. In overtly Christian guise it has exercised a powerful fascination for centuries, and continues to do so; and in secularized guise it has been easily recognizable in certain politico-social ideologies.[25]

Not all cultures have lived in expectation of such a "marvelous consummation." Cohn argues that there were many civilizations, some lasting for millennia, which did not know of any such expectation: "Until around 1500 BC peoples as diverse as Egyptians, Sumerians, Babylonians, Indo-Iranians, and their Indian and Iranian descendants . . . were all agreed that in the beginning the world had been organised, set in order, by a god or by several gods, and that in essentials it was immutable." This immutable cosmos was always threatened by evil forces that perpetrated natural disasters and political upheavals, but order was usually maintained through human cooperation with the divine. A wide variety of ancient combat myths portray a perpetual conflict between the forces of universal order and the forces that threatened it. In these myths, it is typical for a young hero god or divine warrior to be "charged by the gods with the task of keeping the forces of chaos at bay." Significantly, the forces of evil are *only* kept at bay: evil can never be entirely contained, assimilated, or exterminated in these myths because there is no single divine or human hero who is all-powerful. The present world—perceived as a divinely established cosmos constantly threatened by chaos—is understood in these myths to be unchangeable in its fundamental characteristics.[26]

Cohn recognizes that societies that knew nothing of eschatological expectation nevertheless had afterlife myths, and that some even had accounts of everlasting heavens and hells where human beings were thought to go after death. These myths are not properly "eschatological" because they only describe the fate of individuals after death, with no implication that human nature or human society might be transformed in *this* world. For instance, Egyptian mythology described an afterlife of eternal rewards and punishments;[27] Mesopotamian, ancient Israelite, and Greek mythologies spoke of dark underworlds where all the dead are disposed.[28] In each case, the afterlife myth was applicable only to the fate of individuals; it did not apply to the state of the present world, which, in all these various mythologies, remained a combination of good and evil ad infinitum. Absent was the idea that the *world itself* would be transformed or annihilated, once and for all, to pave the way for a realm of absolute perfection.[29]

According to Cohn, it was Zoroaster, the founder of Zoroastrianism, who truly initiated the eschatological revolution in ancient mythology.[30] Cohn claims that sometime between 1500 and 1200 B.C.E. Zoroaster broke out of the "static yet anxious world view" of noneschatological mythology by radically reinterpreting the ancient Iranian combat myth:

> In Zoroaster's view, the world was not static, nor would it always be troubled. Even now the world was moving, through incessant conflict, towards a conflictless state. The time would come when, in a prodigious final battle, the supreme god [Ahura Mazda] and his supernatural allies would defeat the forces of chaos and their human allies and eliminate them once and for all. From then on the divinely appointed order would obtain absolutely: physical distress and want would be unknown, no enemy would threaten, within the community of the saved there would be absolute unanimity; in a word, the world would be for ever untroubled, totally secure.[31]

Zoroastrian eschatology flourished in ancient Iran and in the Persian Empire. According to Cohn, it would have a major influence on the ancient Israelites, who were likely exposed to it in their dealings with the Persians during the Babylonian exile (587–538 B.C.E.).[32] As a consequence, eschatological expectation—in the form of a decisive cosmic transformation—spread to the Jewish world, appearing in various apocalyptic texts during the Second Temple period[33] and in movements such as the Essenes and the "Jesus sect."[34] With the rise of Christianity, eschatology became a major feature of both Western and Byzantine culture, predominant within the mainstream churches and the various heretical sects of the Middle Ages. It would also become a central component of Islam, which emerged in the seventh century.

One of the primary features of eschatological religion is what Eric Voegelin calls "de-divinization," "the historical process in which the culture of polytheism died from experiential atrophy, and human existence in society became reordered through the experience of man's destination, by the grace of the world-transcendent God, toward eternal life in beatific vision."[35] The culture of polytheism had a divinized worldview insofar as it symbolized the various powers of this world as divine. The universe was understood as something alive and filled with "intracosmic gods" or indestructible powers—what contemporary scholars sometimes call an "animistic" worldview.[36] In some polytheistic mythologies, a particular divinity or power may have been described as either entirely good or entirely evil. This was, for instance, the case in Egyptian mythology, where the supreme god of order, Ra, was continually at war with Apophis, the evil god of disorder.[37] In other polytheistic cultures, such as that of the Greeks, each god was understood to possess both good and evil qualities simultaneously and was depicted symbolically as distributing both blessings and curses. Regardless of which type of polytheism is considered, the qualities of good and evil are symbolized as divine and indestructible. Egyptian mythology, for example, presented Apophis and his demonic cohorts as immortal; they had always been and would always be in the world.[38] Consequently, evil can never be entirely exterminated or contained; it can, at best, only be held at bay.

In Zoroastrian, Jewish, Christian, Islamic, and heretical revelatory myths, we find a repudiation of evil's indestructibility. Even the demonic symbols of evil, such as Satan, the demons, and the fallen angels, are not "divine" in the polytheistic sense because these agents of malice are either exterminated or completely contained when the *eschaton* arrives. This means that the only genuine divinity is a single, world-transcendent God who has the power to defeat evil once and for all. In this sense, all the powers of this world—in and of themselves—are stripped of their divine status; human experiences of sheer worldly powers, both good and evil, are no longer symbolized as encounters with divinity. Instead, they are at most understood as intimations of the *eschaton.*

Eschatological de-divinization can manifest itself in a variety of ways, but, according to Walter Schmithals, it has taken the two general forms of apocalypticism and Gnosticism. These are not two distinct and homogeneous categories. There is an immense variety of both apocalyptic and Gnostic understandings, and distinguishing between them is often difficult when one considers particular eschatological writings. Nevertheless, it is possible to identify certain general characteristics that distinguish these two tendencies. The decisive difference is how each understands the source of evil in this world.[39] Apocalypticism claims that the world was originally created good by God but was subsequently corrupted by the actions of disobedient angels and humans. Gnosticism holds that the entirety of the creation is evil and has been evil from the moment of its conception; the world is in no way the work of the true God.

In Jewish, Christian, and Islamic apocalypticism, the world is understood to be the handiwork of God—as something originally created "very good" (Gen. 1:31).[40] In this sense, the world was originally "divinized," insofar as all creation was initially a manifestation of divine goodness. The world was degraded when humans and angels chose to disobey God. As a result, the relation between God and his creation was compromised. The present world is the result of this angelic and human disobedience; it is no longer the unblemished expression of God's divine goodness.[41] God is ensuring, however, that things do not remain in this state forever. He will send (or, in the case of Christianity, has already sent but will send again) a messianic savior who will usher in a new age and deliver a select group of humans from the evils that presently plague them. In this way, apocalyptic eschatology is eminently historical—a history that includes a fall (for everyone) and a redemption (for some).[42] Apocalyptic prophecies such as those found in the Books of Daniel and Revelation,[43] or in the Qur'an, speak of a future bodily resurrection of the dead, after which humans will either be eternally rewarded or eternally punished. The world, as it presently exists, must be transformed or annihilated to make way for the resurrection. Only such a cataclysmic event can establish an atemporal paradise in which the saved will live forever and an everlasting hell into which the wicked will be disposed.

In Gnostic symbolism, the world is not depicted as the creation of
a benevolent God; it is symbolized, rather, as the creation of malicious
demons and demiurges who dare to challenge the true God. God exists,
according to Gnostic theology, but he did not intend for this world to be
created. The cosmos is, and has always been, inherently de-divinized; it is
the mundane antithesis of the absolutely transcendent God. As a result,
Gnostic teachings display a radical dualism, expressed through a variety
of antithetical terms and symbols.[44] In general, Gnostic mythologies —
such as those of Marcion, Valentinus, and Mani — pit the "spiritual" God
of "light," "truth," "knowledge," "salvation," "freedom," and "life" against
the "material" universe of "darkness," "falsehood," "ignorance," "misery,"
"slavery," and "death."[45] Hans Jonas writes:

> The deity is absolutely transmundane, its nature alien to that of the
> universe, which it neither created nor governs and to which it is the
> complete antithesis: to the divine realm of light, self-contained and
> remote, the cosmos is opposed as the realm of darkness. The world
> is the work of lowly powers which though they may mediately be
> descended from Him do not know the true God and obstruct the
> knowledge of Him in the cosmos over which they rule.[46]

These "lowly powers," or "Archons," need to use some of the divine spirit,
or *pneuma*, to create the world, for nothing can live without possessing
something of God. When they created the universe, the Archons surrep-
titiously took a part of the divine *pneuma*, and, in Jonas's words, "created man for the express purpose of keeping [the spirit] captive there."[47]
The stolen *pneuma* is thus refracted into particular human beings. Insofar
as *pneuma* is trapped within certain individuals, the corrupt universe can
perpetuate itself in parasitic fashion by feeding off this life-giving spirit.
The humans who possess the divine substance are called "pneumatics,"
and when they die their *pneuma* is reincarnated in new human forms.
Not all humans have *pneuma:* most are mundane combinations of body
and soul, elements that in and of themselves are solely the creation of cosmic powers and therefore absent of divine substance. There is, thus, an
absolute distinction between the pneumatics and all other human beings.
Only the pneumatics can be saved, since only they possess anything truly
divine or transcendent. The division between pneumatics and all other

living creatures is static: no divine act or historic process can bestow *pneuma* on entirely mundane human beings.[48]

It is for the sake of the pneumatics that the transcendental God is forced to become involved in the mundane world. He must gather up the parts of himself that have been scattered and make himself whole once again. Otherwise, pneumatics will continue to be reincarnated in countless human generations. To begin the process, God sends a messenger to this world—a savior who covertly outwits the Archons keeping guard of the cosmos—in order to deliver the saving knowledge (gnosis) that will rescue the pneumatics from their earthly enslavement.[49] Equipped with gnosis, the pneumatic can undertake certain practices to help liberate the *pneuma* and be "reunited with the divine substance" after death.[50] This process will continue until all *pneuma* has been returned to its true home. Jonas writes:

> On the scale of the total divine drama, this process is part of the restoration of the deity's own wholeness, which in pre-cosmic times has become impaired by the loss of portions of the divine substance. . . . With the completion of this process of gathering in . . . the cosmos, deprived of its elements of light, will come to an end.[51]

This is how the Gnostic *eschaton* arrives. The world, including all irredeemable human beings, is obliterated once all pneumatics are liberated.[52] After the extermination of the cosmos, the transcendental God forever reigns triumphant.

We can see, then, the differences between apocalyptic and Gnostic eschatologies. In Schmithal's words, Gnosticism tends to think in "vertical terms," in that each pneumatic saves himself in the present through knowledge and ascends immediately to the divine after death; in contrast, apocalypticism tends to think in "horizontal terms," insofar as the emphasis is on the salvation that occurs for the righteous at the end of history. However, both think in "linear terms" and not of an eternal recurrence of cosmic cycles. There will not be an eternal process of creation, destruction, and re-creation. History culminates in a single decisive change that is permanent and everlasting; the process of fall and redemption happens only once.[53] Nevertheless, the two eschatologies understand this linear historical movement somewhat differently. Bernard McGinn writes, "What sets apocalyptic eschatology apart from its biblical predecessors, as well as from the strong dualisms [of the Gnostic or Manichaean sort], is its conviction of God's absolute and predetermined control over the whole of history, a mystery hidden for all ages but now revealed to the apocalyptic seer."[54] In apocalyptic eschatologies, everything that occurs in this world, even the fall of humanity and the angels, is interpreted as playing a part in a divine process moving toward the ultimate good. Augustine writes:

> It follows that the actions of sinners, whether angels or men, cannot obstruct the "great works of God, carefully designed to fulfil all his decisions," since in his providence and omnipotence he assigns to each his own gifts and knows how to turn to good account the good and the evil alike. (CG 14.27)[55]

For the apocalyptic believer, the world is embroiled in sin, but God is still in control of everything that occurs within it. The forces of evil in the cosmos are no match for an all-powerful God. Even sinners are fulfilling God's agenda, though they might think they are working against it. God's providence governs their actions as well. Such an understanding is quite distinct from the Gnostic account, in which God does not preordain the creation of the universe or control everything that happens within it. Nevertheless, Gnostic symbolism expresses confidence that God will ultimately prevail over the forces of darkness.

The Middle Ages are characterized, in part, by the struggle between apocalyptic and Gnostic forms of eschatology in the Christian West. The Roman Church deemed the various schools of gnosis heretical and worked to suppress them. As a result, the apocalyptic vision of Christian doctrine became the predominant form of religious symbolism during the medieval period. These differences between apocalypticism and Gnosticism notwithstanding, their fundamental similarity is most important for my argument: the *eschaton* is understood by both movements as a final solution to the problem of evil. This is what really unites apocalypticism and Gnosticism as worldviews, despite any historical conflicts that have occurred between them.

Gnostic and apocalyptic eschatologies did not disappear in modernity; on the contrary, they transmogrified into new forms. They were initially revamped as totalizing secular ideologies, which, like their ancient and medieval predecessors, provide a complete interpretation of reality and divide humanity into radically opposed categories. In totalitarian ideologies, however, there is no transcendent God at work in the world; cosmic and historical processes are understood to occur without any assistance from such a deity. Voegelin writes, "Meaning in history become[s] a completely intramundane phenomen[on], without transcendental irruptions." For Voegelin, this "world-immanent" understanding is what constitutes "secularization";[56] and secularization is, according to Voegelin, a *re*divinization of the world—not in the sense of a return to the polytheism, but rather in the form of a new understanding in which "world-immanent" phenomena (humanity, society, history itself) are thought to possess the same powers that belonged exclusively to the transmundane God of eschatological religion. In such an understanding, history is thought to be gradually progressing toward a decisive culmination without the help of a transcendent God. The workings of such an immanent providence might be bloody, but history, it is claimed, will culminate in the establishment of a peaceful worldly utopia. Wyshogrod writes, "In the absence of a transcendental dimension, the new creation is not remanded to an atemporal future. . . . Instead, purity is to be achieved in the here-and-now as the result of a wholly temporal cleansing process."[57] In order for the new utopia to be realized, society, the human species and nature, must be decisively transformed. When utopia is attained, the new world order will be "posthistorical," in that the immanent dynamics of history will have come to an end.

In modern totalitarian ideologies—Fascist, Nazi, and Communist—the events of the past are understood as necessary steps on the path to the realization of the immanent *eschaton*. Radical ideologues do not wait for God to bring about the end of days. This modern impatience, according to Robert Jay Lifton, is what truly distinguishes modern eschatology from most premodern apocalyptic expressions. In the past, the apocalyptic believer understood that God was in control of history and that only God could bring about the end of history. Humans were to live in expectation of the end, but they could not cause it to happen. This, in Lifton's words, tended to "tame" premodern apocalypticism, and it is the reason that "historically the apocalyptic imagination has usually been nonviolent in nature." Modern ideological eschatology, on the other hand, is intent on "forcing the end."[58] The final consummation, it is believed, will be carried out by a revolutionary elite who take it upon themselves to seize power and cleanse the world of impurities. These messianic revolutionaries seek to undermine transcendent theological sovereignty and replace it with an immanent human authority that is complete. The desire is for a radical new order, in which the biological, sociopolitical, and cultural aspects of the human condition have been radically transformed through total control of the state, economy, and science. The process of reordering the given order of being is driven by a radical sorting myth, one that allows the elite to weed out or exterminate all those human beings infected with impurities. In secular sorting myths, particularly those of totalitarian regimes, the distinction between the saved and the damned is established on the basis of ethnicity, race, class, or ideological allegiance. These categories, like those of Gnostic sorting myths, are absolutely static; those deemed impure cannot be made pure. The belief that it is impossible to transform the reprobate is, according to Bauman, a central component of Nazi and Communist utopianism: "People tainted with the ineradicable blight of their past or origin could not be fitted into such [an] unblemished, healthy and shining world. Like weeds, their nature could not be changed. They had to be eliminated for reasons of genetic or ideational heredity—of a natural mechanism, resilient and immune to cultural processing."[59]

Voegelin interprets these modern weeding endeavors as the triumph of the Gnostic understanding, insofar as totalitarian agents do not wait on God to save them but rather endeavor to transform everything themselves through their absolute knowledge. Totalitarianism, in his view, is the "rule of Gnostic activists," and he argues that we should see the "essence of modernity as the growth of gnosticism."[60] Wyschogrod agrees with Voegelin that totalitarian movements are rooted in extreme forms of eschatology, but she does not agree with his identification of them as solely Gnostic. According to Wyschogrod, modern secular sorting myths integrate components of both Gnostic and apocalyptic eschatologies:

> Contemporary sorting myths governing the death event mingle elements from gnostic and apocalyptic myths just as these elements are frequently run together in the sources themselves. . . . Contemporary sorting myths retain the sense of historical urgency found in apocalyptic thought, the experienced separation of past time and present hour, while the division into the saved and the reprobate is interpreted along [static] gnostic lines.[61]

For Wyschogrod, modernity's death event is fueled by an apocalyptic emphasis on historical providence and a Gnostic stress on the irredeemability of certain human beings. The guiding orientation of modern genocidal movements is the beatific vision of a purified world at the end of a cataclysmic struggle; and even when the end is not realized after countless murders, the *eschaton* remains, in Wychogrod's words, a "regulative ideal approached asymptotically but never reached."[62] Consequently, secular societies enraptured by eschatological visions are obliged to continue dividing humanity, separating the reprobate from the pure, in a perpetual process that approaches the *eschaton* but never arrives. This gives birth to the idea of "permanent revolution," which is the inevitable consequence of secular sorting myths.[63] Utopia never comes, but revolutionaries must continue acting as if it is on the horizon.

The Eschatological Features of *Caligula* and *Waiting for Godot*

Caligula and *Waiting for Godot,* taken together, present us with a variety of utopian aspirations, providential orientations, cataclysmic solutions, messianic figures, and selection myths. They show us what it means to accept the general features of Gnostic and apocalyptic eschatologies and their modern secular manifestations. *Caligula* symbolizes the Gnosticism of the modern world; the accent in *Godot,* on the other hand, falls on the modern world's apocalypticism. Together, the plays reflect the state of a civilization that continues to be enraptured by eschatological myths, even when those myths are no longer thought to be persuasive. Camus and Beckett, in their different ways, show how the absurd sensibility is fostered when human beings feel that their true home is not in this de-divinized world but rather in a beatific *eschaton*. Hope for the *eschaton,* without experiencing its immediate presence, aggravates the absurd experience of antagonism between humanity and the world, with catastrophic effects for human thought and action.

CHAPTER TWO

The Gnostic Caesar

Radical Eschatology in Albert Camus's *Caligula*

Caligula and the Passion for the Impossible

Caligula is often spoken of as a theatrical companion piece to Camus's *Myth of Sisyphus*.[1] The central issue for Camus in *Sisyphus* is the "relationship between the absurd and suicide, [and] the exact degree to which suicide is a solution to the absurd" (*MS* 5). Camus claims that the experience of absurdity—an individual's feeling of rupture with the world—does not justify suicide. The truly absurd man will not kill himself out of resignation. Instead, he will continue to live and keep the absurd alive by rebelling against a world that threatens to destroy him. Camus writes: "Negating one of the terms of the opposition [between man and the world] on which he lives amounts to escaping it. To abolish conscious revolt is to elude the problem. . . . Living is keeping the absurd alive. . . . It challenges the world anew every second." For the absurdist rebel, "revolt gives life its value." But it is a revolt that is "devoid of hope," because the absurd man is conscious that existence is unreasonable and that, in the end, he will be killed by "crushing fate" (*MS* 40). The absurd man, then, is caught in a tension. On the one hand, he knows that existence has no discernible meaning and that nothing can be done to free humanity from suffering and death. On the other hand, he is passionate about unifying the world in a coherent understanding and delivering humanity from affliction.[2] The absurd man must live with both assumptions; to deny either the *knowledge* of the world's ultimate meaninglessness or the *passion* for absolute meaningfulness would be to transgress the limits of the absurd.[3]

49

To illustrate this tension, Camus provides a portrait in *Sisyphus* of an absurd type he calls the "conqueror," a man who no longer finds greatness in "conquered territories" but rather in sheer "protest and the blind-alley sacrifice" against "man," the "earth," and "the gods." He is also a man who nonetheless knows that the aims of his revolt are impossible. Camus has the conqueror reflect on his circumstances: "Conquerors know that action is in itself useless. There is but one useful action, that of re-making man and the earth. I shall never remake men. But one must do 'as if'" (*MS* 64–65). How far the conqueror should go in his efforts to remake the world is not clearly spelled out by Camus. This opens the danger that the conqueror's desire to transfigure the universe might overpower his knowledge that this transfiguration is impossible. In *Sisyphus*, Camus refers to the passion to remake the world as "metaphysical revolt" (*MS* 40).[4] He provides a more extensive definition of metaphysical revolt in his later theoretical text, *The Rebel*:

> Metaphysical rebellion is the movement by which man protests against his condition and against the whole of creation. It is metaphysical because it contests the ends of man and of creation. . . . [T]he metaphysical rebel declares that he is frustrated by the universe. . . . [He] opposes the principle of justice which he finds in himself to the principle of injustice which he sees applied in the world. Thus, all he wants, originally, is to resolve this contradiction and establish a unitarian reign of justice. . . . Metaphysical rebellion is a claim motivated by the concept of a complete unity, against the suffering of life and death and a protest against the human condition both for its incompleteness, thanks to death, and its wastefulness, thanks to evil. . . . At the same time that he rejects his mortality, the rebel refuses to recognize the power that compels him to live in this condition. (*R* 23–24)

Caligula is Camus's attempt to represent such a metaphysical revolution on the stage. In the play, the Roman emperor Caligula can no longer accept the given evils of the world; the "scheme of things" becomes "intolerable" for him (8). This realization spurs him on a mission to transform the universe, human nature, and the gods. In place of the imperfect cosmos and its incessant suffering, Caligula desires "the impossible"—a realm where "men will die no more and at last be happy" (17). In his move toward the impossible, the emperor systematically perverts all accepted values through mass murder, torture, and uninhibited sexuality. He is a fanatical incarnation of Camus's conqueror, acting "as if" the impossible can be made possible.

The passion to remake the world through metaphysical revolt is an extreme reaction to the absurd. In *Caligula*, this passion is presented as an eschatological yearning with strong Gnostic attributes. Caligula, like a gnostic, perceives creation as evil and attempts to bring about its destruction. In an early essay, *Christian Metaphysics and NeoPlatonism*, Camus refers to Gnosticism as a "monstrous Christianity" ("monstrueux Christianisme"),[5] as a type of eschatology that is "obsessed" with evil and that takes its desire for purity to the furthest possible extremes.[6] The "Gnostic solution,"[7] as Camus puts it, desires the "complete destruction of creation" ("la destruction complète d'une création").[8] In *Caligula*, the emperor desires exactly the same thing and thinks he can satisfy this desire through his own revolutionary efforts. Paul Archambault was the first to see this, arguing that the play is "an experimentation with the 'Gnostic solution'" because "Caligula's vision, like the Gnostic vision, is fundamentally acosmic, alien to the world of the possible."[9]

Camus himself claimed that his intention in *Caligula* was to illustrate the "frenzy," "havoc," and "failure" of the "passion for the impossible."[10] The play, undoubtedly, depicts the excesses that result when the passion for a transformed world overwhelms the intellectual awareness that such a transformation is impossible. Camus, however, was not entirely unsympathetic to all such passions. While the play criticizes the excesses of metaphysical revolution, it simultaneously celebrates the Gnostic perception of the world and the Gnostic passion for utopia. Camus's lingering sympathy for such eschatological desires often leads to theoretical confusions within the play, making it difficult to interpret consistently.

Camus as Playwright

Camus is mostly celebrated for his novels (*The Stranger, The Plague, The Fall*), his theoretical treatises (*The Myth of Sisyphus* and *The Rebel*), and his short essays. He was also active in theatre up to the time of his death in 1960; for most of his adult life, he participated in theatre as actor, director, or playwright. He wrote four original plays—*Caligula,*

The Misunderstanding, State of Siege, and *The Just Assassins*—as well as several adaptations for the stage, including Dostoevsky's *The Possessed* and Faulkner's *Requiem for a Nun.* Despite such extensive involvement, his dramatic works never had the same impact as his novels and essays. They received mixed reviews at their debuts and are rarely performed today. Albert Sonnenfeld writes, "The technical flaws in Camus' works for the stage are apparent to every reader or spectator."[11] *Caligula,* while perhaps Camus's best dramatic work, is no exception. Though it has several moments of greatness, it is an uneven piece of drama.

Critics often point out that *Caligula* reads and plays like an extended theoretical discussion rather than a lively drama with distinct characters and believable dialogue. Characters such as Caligula, the poet Scipio, and the colonel Cherea, seem like "philosophical spokesmen" for Camus, not flesh-and-blood human beings brought to life on the stage.[12] In a review of the first performance of *Caligula* for *Le Monde,* the theatre critic Robert Kemp bemoaned, "When I listen to *Caligula,* I can't stop thinking about Albert Camus. . . . I never wonder: What is Caligula going to do? What are Cherea and Scipio thinking of?—but: what does M. Camus want to say?"[13] At the same time, much of the dialogue in the play has a lyrical quality that is not well suited for the stage. Consider this exchange between Scipio and Caligula describing the sensual pleasures of the natural world:

> SCIPIO: Yes, yes! And that fantastic moment when the sky all flushed with red and gold wings round and shows its other side, spangled with stars.
> CALIGULA: And the faint smell of smoke and trees and streams that mingles with the rising mist.
> SCIPIO [*in a sort of ecstasy*]: Yes, and the chirr of crickets, the coolness veining the warm air, the rumble of carts and the farmer's shouts, dogs barking . . .
> CALIGULA: And the roads drowned in shadow winding through the olive groves. (36)

Consider also the words of Caligula's mistress, Caesonia, in this passage:

> Oh, don't you realize what it can be to live and love quite simply, naturally, in . . . in purity of heart. (68)

Lines such as these are scattered throughout the play, and they are difficult, if not impossible, for an actor to speak convincingly. Sonnenfeld writes, "In a novel, this lyricism can effectively convey a vision of beauty. When spoken aloud in the theatre, especially after the highly theoretical language which dominates so much of the dialogue, the tone seems rhetorical, almost oppressive."[14]

We accept the caveat: *Caligula* is a flawed work. And yet it is worthy of serious consideration, for it has insight into the utopian pathology driving the modern death event. Even its failures are illuminating, both of the nature of theatre and of the modern confusions about the experience of evil.

Roman Tyrants and Modern Totalities

Many of the circumstances and events in *Caligula* are taken from Suetonius's historical biography of Gaius Caesar (37–41 C.E.), third emperor of Rome.[15] Suetonius tells us that Gaius was fond of wearing a miniature military uniform when he was a child. This earned him the ridicule of Roman soldiers who called him "Caligula," which means "little boot."[16] When Gaius became emperor, he endeavored to abolish any link between himself and something as lowly as a bootikin. He was perhaps the first Roman emperor to insist unabashedly on being worshiped as a god while still alive.[17] Suetonius reports that Caligula proclaimed his divinity by taking revered statues of Greek deities and having their heads replaced with his own.[18] Caligula's divine status was used to justify a remarkable series of evils. Suetonius reports that Caligula raped his sisters, murdered his friends, ordered countless executions, demanded grisly tortures, created his own famines, took part in gladiatorial contests, and killed innocent bystanders with his own hands. For these reasons, Suetonius refers to Caligula as "the Monster,"[19] and he links Caligula's monstrosity with a desire to do the impossible:

> [Caligula] built villas and country houses with utter disregard of expense, *caring for nothing so much as to do what men said was impossible.* So he built moles out into the deep and stormy sea, tunnelled rocks of hardest flint, built up plains to the height of mountains,

and razed mountains to the level of the plain; all with incredible dis-
patch, since the penalty for delay was death.[20]

Camus was obviously struck by Suetonius's account of an emperor attempting to change the very structure of creation.

Camus's use of a classical source to create a modern tragedy is not
unusual, given that so many of his fellow French playwrights were doing
the same thing at that time. But whereas most neoclassical dramas of
this period were based on ancient Greek tragedies, *Caligula* was developed from a work of Roman history. This is a curious choice, given the
influence of the Greeks on Camus's thought,[21] and also given his claim
that imperial Rome was a denigration—indeed, the very antithesis—
of tragic Athens. In a 1937 address titled "The New Mediterranean Culture," Camus insists that the Roman Empire is not to be confused with
Greece. The former was a monolithic totality with a single debased culture obsessed with domination; the latter was a loose association of
diverse peoples with a rich cultural center in Athens. Camus claims an
error "lies in the confusion between Mediterranean and Latin, and in attributing to Rome what began in Athens."[22] It was Rome, according to
Camus, that propagated this very confusion. He argues that the Greeks
are "the very denial of Roman and Latin genius."[23] The only "genius" that
the Romans had over the Greeks was in conducting war to facilitate
political expansion:

> These imitative and unimaginative people [the Romans] had never-
> theless the imagination to substitute for the artistic genius and feel-
> ing for life they lacked a genius for war. And this order whose praises
> we so often hear sung was one imposed by force and not one created
> by the mind. Even when they copied, the Romans lost the savour of
> the original. And it was not even the essential genius of Greece they
> imitated, but rather the fruits of its decadence and its mistakes. Not
> the strong, vigorous Greece of the great tragic and comic writers,
> but the prettiness and affected grace of the last centuries. . . . [I]t
> is easy to acknowledge Mussolini as the worthy descendant of the
> Caesars and Augustus of Imperial Rome, if we mean by this that
> he, like them, sacrifices truth and greatness to a violence that has
> no soul.[24]

In this passage, Camus makes a direct link between imperial Rome and twentieth-century totalitarianism. Modern totalitarian movements such as Mussolinian fascism have a Caesarian desire for total domination. This is key to why Camus chooses a Roman emperor as the subject of his first play: imperial Rome prefigures the modern desire for totality through violence.[25] Camus writes in his later essay, "Helen's Exile," that it is "indecent to proclaim today that we are sons of Greece."[26] Instead, he claims, we are the spiritual descendants of Caesarian Rome:

> We [moderns] have preferred the power that apes greatness— Alexander first of all, and then the Roman conquerors, whom our school history books, in an incomparable vulgarity of soul, teach us to admire. We have conquered in our turn, have set aside the bounds, mastered heaven and earth. Our reason has swept everything away. Alone at last, we build our empire upon a desert. How then could we conceive [like the Greeks] that higher balance in which nature balanced history, beauty, and goodness, and which brought the music of numbers even into the tragedy of the blood. We turn our backs on nature, we are ashamed of beauty. Our miserable tragedies have the smell of an office, and their blood is the colour of dirty ink.[27]

Camus frequently speaks of the modern enterprise as "Caesarian."[28] In *Caligula,* Camus uses a Caesar to critique the modern Caesarian passion for totality and to show, in the style of Greek tragedy, the disaster to which such hubris leads. But Camus gives his Roman emperor Gnostic aspirations: Caligula does not desire to expand the empire into new political territories; rather, he wants to establish an impossible empire by conquering human nature and the cosmos. In this sense, Camus uses Suetonius's "monster" to present a "monstrous Christianity," independent of any consideration for the "historical Caligula."

It might be objected that Caligula is too flamboyant, too erratic, and too "Roman" to represent acosmic Gnosticism adequately, or, for that matter, modern totalitarianism in all its bureaucratic and banal aspects. Undoubtedly, the tragedy of Caligula does not "smell like an office."[29] However, Caligula manifests the same nihilistic disenchantment with life that Camus associates with Gnosticism and modernity. According to Camus, nihilism is not, as is often thought, a rejection of all "beliefs";

it is a rejection of life as it is imperfectly constituted. Camus writes, "A nihilist is not one who believes in nothing, but one who does not believe in
what exists" (*R* 69).[30] And further, characterizing modernity as he saw it
in 1951, Camus observes, "The men of Europe . . . no longer believe in the
things that exist in the world and in living man; the secret of Europe is
that it no longer loves life" (*R* 305). Caligula, like a modern European,
does not commit evils out of a perverse ecstasy for this life but out of an
intense dissatisfaction with the world and its impurities. His methods are
less efficient than the systematic operations of modern totalitarianism,
but they stem from the same nihilistic impulse to annihilate the world.

Caligula: The Monstrous Christian

*Perceiving the World as Nothing: The Absurd, the Impossible,
and the Law of Radical Equivalence*

Caligula begins with a group of Roman patricians discussing the sudden
disappearance of the emperor. We learn that Caligula has not been seen
since the death of his young sister, Drusilla (3). Inquiries concerning the
whereabouts of the emperor, and questions regarding what should be
done in the meantime, are met with responses of "Nothing" (3, 6) and
"Still nothing" (4, 5). The very first word attributed to the emperor is
nothing:

> THE OLD PATRICIAN: When I saw [Caligula] leaving the palace, I no-
> ticed a queer look in his eyes.
> FIRST PATRICIAN: Yes, so did I. In fact I asked him what was amiss.
> SECOND PATRICIAN: Did he answer?
> FIRST PATRICIAN: One word: "Nothing." (3)

The word *nothing* (*rien*) occurs throughout *Caligula,* and it begins to
take on significant nihilistic implications as the play progresses. Caligula
continually emphasizes that he perceives "nothing": he says that there is
"Nothing, nobody left" (18), that there is "Nothing, nothing yet" (73), that
love is "nothing" (17), and that there is "nothing in this world, or in the
other" (73). By the end of the play, Caligula says he has chosen "a path

that leads to nothing" (73). He starts to experience the world as "nothing" after Drusilla's death, but we are told that he once held the world to be something. Scipio reports:

> [Caligula] told me life isn't easy, but it has consolations: religion, art, and love one inspires in others. He often told me that the only mistake one makes in life is to cause others suffering. He tried to be a just man. (10)

Other characters confirm this portrait of Caligula as a man striving for goodness in a harsh world. The patricians attest to a young, naive, yet likable emperor, who is a little "too fond of literature" (5).

Caligula's youthful love of books, however, is not the most obvious indication that something is wrong with him. As we hear from the First Patrician, Caligula's fondness for Drusilla "was something more than brotherly." "Shocking enough, I grant you," he says (5). But however shocking this might be, the patricians make little of Caligula's appetite for incest. It seems they are willing to ignore this indiscretion for the sake of preserving the status quo. But Cherea's description of Caligula as "perfection's self" is certainly an exaggeration, given the emperor's incestuous relation with his sister (4). Something within Caligula is predisposed to breaking fundamental taboos.

Drusilla's untimely demise shocks Caligula to such a degree that he leaves the imperial palace and spends three days in the rain and wilderness, apparently in mourning. But when he returns to the palace, disheveled and covered with filth, he tells his servant Helicon that Drusilla was not the specific object of his grief (8). Instead, he claims to have spent the past three days trying to get "the moon." When Helicon asks why he would want this, the emperor responds, "Well . . . it's one of the things I haven't got" (7). Like a true Caesar, Caligula desires new acquisitions, but what he wants lies far outside the realm of politics in first-century Rome. Caligula's desire for a dead satellite suggests that his aspirations are antithetical to the conditions of life on this planet, even though he explicitly denies that his sudden desire for the moon is a sign of madness. On the contrary, he claims to have a "reasonable" (*raisonnable*) understanding of both the world and his own aspirations.[31] Caligula explains to Helicon:

> What happened to me is quite simple; I suddenly felt a desire for the impossible. That's all. Things as they are, in my opinion, are far from satisfactory. (8)

When Helicon points out that many people share this opinion, Caligula responds:

> That is so. But in the past I didn't realize it. Now I know. Really, this world of ours, the scheme of things as they call it, is quite intolerable. That's why I want the moon, or happiness, or [immortality]— something, in fact, that may sound crazy, but which isn't of this world. (8)[32]

Caligula claims that Drusilla's death is "not the point" of his newfound aspiration for the impossible; rather, her passing is merely "the symbol of a truth that makes the moon essential." The "truth" is: "Men die; and they are not happy" (8). In place of this world and its unacceptable truth, the emperor wants to found a "kingdom where the impossible is king" and where "men will die no more and at last be happy" (16–17). Caligula's desire for the moon symbolizes his extraterrestrial aspiration to make the "impossible possible" (13)—to realize immortality and eternal beatitude, even if it means destroying life in its present constitution. As he says later in the play, "Suppose the moon were brought here, everything [would change]. . . . Then the impossible would become possible, [and at the same time, in a flash, all things would be transfigured]" (49).[33]

Caligula, then, is no ordinary Roman tyrant seeking to expand the empire. His yearnings for the "impossible," for a "transfiguration," for "immortality," for something "not of this world," for a "kingdom" where "men will die no more," are all unmistakably eschatological—and eschatological in a revolutionary sense. Caligula does not wait, faithfully and resignedly, for God to bring about the final apotheosis; on the contrary, he decides to conquer and transform creation himself. He says:

> What's the use to me of a firm hand, what use is the amazing power that's mine, if I can't have the sun set in the east, if I can't reduce the sum of suffering and make an end of death? . . . [I]t's all one whether I sleep or keep awake, if I've no power to tamper with the scheme of things. (16)

Caligula's sudden consciousness of the impossible makes him extremely sensitive to any type of decay. He now knows that nothing lasts, and he plans to use this knowledge to encourage the destruction of the universe (71). For Caligula, genuine knowledge of mortality renders the entire terrestrial world unsubstantial. Even human emotions are empty because they too pass away.

This extreme sensitivity to corruption and mortality causes Caligula to accept a doctrine of radical "equivalence." Death, for Caligula, renders everything equal—which is to say, equally worthless. Camus informs us in *Sisyphus* that this perception of radical equivalence is a central feature of absurd experience (*MS* 34). It is Caligula's awareness of the absurd that leads him to pronounce, "Everything's on an equal footing: the grandeur of Rome, and your attacks of arthritis" (11). In Act 1, he decides to follow through with this doctrine of equivalence; he plans to be "logical right through, at all costs" (8), or, as Cherea says, he "pushes the absurd (*l'absurde*) to its logical conclusion"[34] by "converting his philosophy into corpses" (51, 21). To claim that everything is equivalent means there is no such thing as crime, since crime presupposes a value that has been violated, a worldly measure of good and evil. To be logically consistent means that everything is permitted and that crime can range freely without troubling the conscience. Caesonia points out to Caligula that this absurdist doctrine is wrong. She argues that there are clear distinctions within the world between "good and bad, high and low, justice and injustice," and that "these will never change." Caligula, however, responds that he is "resolved to change them" by leveling everything out and renewing the world (17). For Caligula, Caesonia's hierarchical and ethical distinctions are simply terrestrial illusions that cause pain so long as humans accept them. Insofar as humans abide by the illusory rules of this world, nothing changes; men and women will continue to live, suffer, and die. Caligula expects that by terrorizing people into seeing that all worldly distinctions are unsubstantial, he will precipitate a catastrophe that will force humans to seek the impossible and generate a cosmic transfiguration.

Caligula first practices his doctrine of radical equivalence on the Intendant. He gets him to agree that matters concerning the Treasury are of "prime importance," and then announces that the economic system of Rome will be changed in two "drastic and abrupt" steps: first, all patricians will be ordered to disinherit their children and leave their property to the Roman state; second, these patricians will be randomly executed as the need for money arises. The Intendant, of course, objects to Caligula's economic proposals, but Caligula reminds him of their earlier agreement that the Treasury is of absolute significance:

> If the Treasury has paramount importance, human life has none. That should be obvious to you. People who think like you are bound to admit the logic of my edict, and since money is the only thing that counts, [you] should set no value on their lives or anyone else's. I have resolved to be logical, and I have the power to enforce my will. Presently you'll see what logic's going to cost you. I shall eliminate contradictions and contradicters. If necessary, I'll begin with you. (12–13)

With such tactics, Caligula admits that he is "singleminded for evil (*mal*)" (36).[35] He is only "evil," however, according to the illusory standards of this world. Caligula thinks he knows a superior ordering of good and evil—an ordering whereby "good" is absolutely transcendent and thoroughly acosmic. As Caesonia says, "Caligula is creating a new order of merit" (30). He will remain logically true to this "new order" by systematically transgressing every commonly held perception of good and evil until "the consummation" (50).

Caligula's attempt to commit every possible outrage for the purpose of salvation is one possible moral consequence of what Hans Jonas calls "Gnostic acosmism." On the one hand, a Gnostic pneumatic can adopt an extreme form of asceticism or self-annihilation, in which he avoids all contact with the world as much as possible; on the other, he can embrace an extreme form of libertinism, in which he indulges every bodily desire and flouts every moral law.[36] This latter option seems contradictory to the goal of acosmic transcendence, but it is "logical." In the mind of the pneumatic libertine all natural and moral laws are simply the product of the evil "demiurge" and his demonic "Archons" who create the cosmos and establish universal rules of order.[37] These rules, in the mind of the pneumatic, are equivalent—that is to say, they are all equally worthless—yet if they are obeyed they are extremely oppressive. Jonas writes, "The law of 'Thou shalt' and 'Thou shalt not' promulgated by the [demonic] Creator is just one more form of the 'cosmic' tyranny."[38] The pneumatic thinks he is under no obligation to obey any natural or moral laws; on the contrary, through "intentional violation" of cosmic norms "the pneumatic thwarts the design of the Archons and paradoxically contributes to the work of salvation. This antinomian libertinism exhibits . . . the nihilistic element contained in gnostic acosmism."[39] Caligula shares the ethos of the Gnostic libertines. He understands the command "Thou shalt not kill" as an evil ordinance and wants to teach others how they too can perceive this and rise above it.

Caligula's mission is both pedagogical and messianic. His acute awareness of "the truth"—that men die and are not happy—as well as his consciousness of the impossible makes him a potential educator and savior. His position as emperor also gives him an unprecedented opportunity to enforce his teaching. Caligula speaks of himself as a teacher with a special understanding, a *connaisance,* which is clearly not of this world. People, according to Caligula, are "without understanding (*connaisance*)" (9).[40] Above the common worldly opinions regarding good and evil there is a superior understanding that is not illusory. It is this *connaissance*— this gnosis—that Caligula wants to give humanity. Humans need to be made fully aware of the impermanence and equivalence of all things, and thereby break their attachments to the world.

To become a savior, Caligula must become as inhuman as possible. At the end of Act 1, he symbolically erases the remnants of his humanity by gazing into a mirror and effacing his reflection with a mallet. If he must continue to live for a while longer within his mortal body, it is because his body is the vessel of the *connaissance,* the transcendental "idea," that will save others. This "idea," for Caligula, is the only essential thing in a world that is nothing. As Caligula effaces his image in the mirror, he says, "All gone. . . . Nothing, nobody left. Nobody? No, that's not true," and he forces Caesonia to declare the one thing left: "Caligula" (18). Since he is all that remains, Caligula attempts to create a new world ex nihilo.

Universal Guilt and Homicide

Act 2 begins three years after Act 1 (19). It opens with the patricians complaining about the injustices they have suffered at the hands of Caligula. We hear stories of murder, confiscated properties, and wives forced to become prostitutes. Scipio is also present at this discussion, complaining that his father was tortured and murdered by Caligula without justification. Unsurprisingly, the emperor has made many enemies. The only characters who remain loyal to him are Helicon and Caesonia. At the start of Act 2, the patricians decide to overthrow the emperor immediately, but Cherea enters and stops the revolt. He offers to lead a conspiracy to kill the emperor, but he argues against assassinating him at the present moment. His reasons, as we shall see, are hard to comprehend; nevertheless, the patricians agree to wait with Cherea for the appropriate moment, effectively giving Caligula more time to act on his fantasies (19–23).

For the most part, what occurs from Act 2 to Act 4 is not a story, but a series of crimes and grotesque spectacles, interspersed by theoretical discussion. In Act 2, we see Caligula commit a number of outrages: he taunts a man named Lepidus, whose son he has killed (24–25); he takes Mucius's wife and rapes her within earshot of her husband (26–28); he closes the public granaries to create a famine throughout the empire (28); he rewards citizens who most frequently patronize the "National Brothel" (30); and he kills the elderly Mereia with his own hands, simply because the old man swallows a remedy for asthma (31–33). In Act 3, Caligula dresses as the goddess Venus and forces the Romans to worship him in a grotesque religious ceremony (40–42). In Act 4, he dances a horrible ballet, wearing a ballerina's outfit and garlanded with flowers (59). He then has Caesonia announce to the patricians that he has died, only to reappear immediately and berate everyone for their false grief (62). Near the end of the play he also stages a poetry contest, forcing a group of Roman poets to write verses on the theme of death. They are given one minute to compose their poems and are cut off by a whistle if Caligula deems their work inadequate (63–66).

Throughout these three acts there is the constant threat that Caligula will strike at any moment in a completely arbitrary manner, like an epidemic. At one point Caligula laments that there has been no "world-wide plague" during his reign. To compensate, he announces that he will personally "replace the epidemics we've missed" (62). In Caligula's mind, all humans deserve to be killed because they are all guilty—guilty insofar as they have agreed to abide by the false moral rules of the universe and insofar as they have accepted suffering and death as given evils. In these ways, humans have facilitated the continuance of the world. Caligula codifies and justifies arbitrary execution with a proclamation stating that "all men are guilty" and that execution "relieves and liberates" (29). This edict reveals that Caligula is not directing his eschatological fury against a specific group of people but rather against the entire human race. At present, only Caligula is elect, but through universal condemnation and terror, other human beings can be saved.

The first group that Caligula terrorizes is the patricians. Caligula is appalled by their concern for wealth, power, and reputation, as well as by their willingness to lie, cheat, and forgo honor for the sake of worldly success. In his eyes, they are vermin who can be disposed of without any loss: "All these executions have an equal importance—from which it follows that none has any" (12). But Caligula's doctrine of universal guilt is also directed at "literary men" like Cherea and Scipio, who are not petty or hypocritical like the majority of patricians but who are guilty of far more serious crimes. Caligula says to Cherea:

> Lies are never guiltless. And yours attribute importance to people and to things. That's wh[y] I cannot forgive you. . . . This world has no importance; once a man realizes that, he wins his freedom. And that is why I hate you, you and your kind; because you are not free. You see in me the one free man in the whole Roman Empire. You should be glad to have at last among you an emperor who points the way to freedom. (14)

For Caligula, attributing value to people and things is the original sin. Intellectuals like Cherea and Scipio are most deserving of execution because they actually think the world has value.

Caligula, however, does not execute Cherea or Scipio. When killing and ordering executions, he exercises arbitrary grace and punishment. He tortures Scipio's father to death, kills Lepidus's youngest son and murders the elderly Mereia, though none of these men is guilty of any obvious wrongdoing. While Caligula is busy killing the innocent, he lets the ostensibly guilty and dishonorable live. For example, in Act 3 the Old Patrician betrays his comrades by informing Caligula of the conspiracy against his life. Caligula does not thank the Old Patrician for his information. On the contrary, he threatens to kill him for disloyalty to his fellow conspirators. And then, just as arbitrarily, Caligula does not follow through with his threat, even though the Old Patrician embodies the very hypocrisy and pettiness that he cannot tolerate (47–49). Caligula also lets Cherea live after being given a tablet proving the latter's involvement in the conspiracy. This tablet is legal "evidence" of Cherea's guilt, by which Caligula can have him executed (53–54). Caligula chooses instead to burn the document and absolve Cherea. He says to Cherea, "Admire my power. Even the gods cannot restore innocence without first punishing the culprit. But your emperor needs only a torch flame to absolve you" (54). Caligula wants to render the old gods obsolete by bestowing unwarranted mercy.

Deicide: Caligula's De-divinized Pedagogy

Caligula's attempt to overcome the old divinities is central to the play. When Caesonia first hears of his desire to "tamper with the scheme of things," she accuses him of wanting to be "a god on earth." Caligula assures her that "it's something higher, far above the gods," that he wants (16). But as an emissary of the impossible, he deems it necessary to play the part of an intracosmic god to teach the Romans a lesson about true and false divinity

At the beginning of Act 3, Caligula reveals to Rome the "secrets of the gods" by having himself grotesquely attired as the goddess Venus. The patricians, in the presence of a transvestite emperor sitting on a pedestal, are forced to recite "the litany of Venus called Caligula":

> Our Lady of pangs and pleasures,
> Born of the waves, bitter and bright with seafoam,
> O Queen, whose gifts are laughter and regrets,
> Rancors and raptures,
> Teach us the indifference that kindles love anew.
> Make known to us the truth about this world—which is that it
>   has none.
> And grant us the strength to live up to this verity of verities.
> Bestow your gifts upon us, and shed on our faces the light of your
>   impartial cruelty, your wanton hatred; unfold above our eyes
>   your arms laden with flowers and murders.

Welcome your wandering children home, to the bleak sanctuary
of your heartless, thankless love. Give us your passions without
object, your griefs devoid of reason, your raptures that lead
nowhere.

O Queen, so empty yet so ardent, inhuman yet so earthly, make us
drunk with the wine of your equivalence, and surfeit us forever
in the brackish darkness of your heart.

(40–41)

There is an ironic purpose to the entire ceremony. Caligula is not trying
to revive religious fervor in Rome for the "imaginary gods" (43); on the
contrary, his intention is deicidal. He wants to kill the old pagan deities
by making them appear disgusting to the Romans. First, he mocks the
female goddess of love by dressing in drag, the effect of which is simultaneously grotesque and comic. He then has the Romans recite the litany,
the content of which emphasizes the cruel indifference of Venus. She
oversees a world filled with "flowers and murders," "impartial cruelty,"
and "raptures that lead nowhere." Caligula wants to demonstrate that
the cosmic gods are unworthy of human devotion because they cannot
satisfy our deepest longings for happiness and immortality. They are like
the Archons in Gnostic mythology—the debased deities who rule over a
thoroughly evil world.

Caligula claims that "any man, without previous training," can "get
even with the gods. All that's needed is to be as cruel as they" (43). But
the point, for Caligula, is not simply to become a god on earth. He refers
to his incarnation as Venus as merely a "small advance . . . upon the path
of freedom" (43). Caligula has a much bigger agenda in mind: he wants
to use his power to "compensate" for "the hatred and stupidity of the
gods" (43). Such compensation can only be had by revealing the impossible, which shows the ancient pagan gods to be disgusting and illusory.
Love of the impossible de-divinizes the present world. True divinity, whatever that might be, is absolutely transcendent.

The pedagogical purpose of Caligula's incarnation as Venus is to reveal that the gods cannot offer liberation from evil; they can only give
human beings a life of cruelty and waste, alleviated by brief moments of
happiness and ecstasy. But by taking on their role—by "play[ing] their
[ridiculous] parts to perfection"[41]—Caligula wants to blaspheme the old

deities by following their cruel and indifferent example (43). His intent is to incite the Romans to revolt, not only against his leadership, but also against the world and its false divinities.

Indifference and Solitude

Human beings can attempt the impossible only if they become completely indifferent to the things of this world. In the Venus liturgy, the Romans recite, "Teach us the indifference that kindles love anew" (40). Expressions of "love" that cling to the things of this world prevent humans from attaining perfect indifference. Love must be made "anew" by cutting all relations with earthly realities. Caligula says the "truth about love" is that "it's nothing." To "really live"—that is, to have eternal beatitude—one must realize that "living . . . is the opposite of loving" (17). Loving attributes importance to people and things. In place of terrestrial love, Caligula seeks complete isolation and detachment. He discovers that such solitude is hard to find. As he says to Scipio:

> You prate of loneliness, but you don't know that one is never alone. Always we are attended by the same load of the future and the past. Those who we have killed are always with us. But they are no great trouble. It's those we have loved, those who loved us and whom we did not love; regrets, desires, bitterness, and sweetness, whores and gods, the celestial gang! Always, always with us! (37)

The reality of others, along with the love or hatred they inspire, continues to intrude on Caligula. And yet, despite the difficulties of achieving "real solitude," he knows that it is the solution he craves (37). Total indifference to the world will allow him to achieve the "godlike enlightenment of the solitary" (72).

In his struggle to realize this solution, Caligula divorces himself from civic relations, nature, and romantic attachments. With regard to civic relations, Caligula wants nothing to do with the "common human solidarity" represented by men like Cherea.[42] For Cherea, humans must care for each other in a socially responsible way if there is to be "security" and "happiness." The possibility of a decent community means curbing the desire for the superhuman, since such a passion only wreaks revolutionary havoc on society. But for Caligula, these desires are not enough to defeat evil once and for all. Instead of Cherea's earthly happiness, Caligula points to a "splendid, sterile happiness" that lies "beyond the frontier of pain" (71).

Along with his rejection of fraternity, Caligula isolates himself from the natural world. Many references are made throughout the play to the replenishing and beneficial aspects of nature. In the first scene, the Old Patrician proclaims that "Nature's a great healer" because it allows humans to overcome their grief with the passing of time (4). For Caligula, the fact that nature erodes a sincere emotion like grief is just another example of the world's maliciousness (71). The subject of nature's beneficence is raised again in Act 2, when Scipio alludes to a poem he has written on "nature":

> CALIGULA: And what has nature done for you?
> SCIPIO: It consoles me for not being Caesar.
> CALIGULA: Really? And do you think that nature could console me for being Caesar?
> SCIPIO: Why not? Nature has healed worse wounds than that. (35)

In this passage Scipio confesses to feelings of inadequacy because he is not the most powerful man on earth. However, the omnipresent cosmos and the beauties of the natural world remind him that Caesars, by comparison, are not as glorious. Caligula sympathizes with Scipio's vision of nature, but he condemns it as "anaemic" because it lacks the vitality of the impossible. Since the consolations of nature do not outweigh its cruelties and since it cannot offer eternal life, nature must be transfigured. As Caligula says, "My appetite for life's too keen; nature can never sate it" (36).

Finally, Caligula isolates himself from erotic attachment. It is Caesonia who symbolizes the possibility of this type of love. She claims the only god she has ever worshiped is her body, which she will use to bring the emperor back (10). By using her sexuality, Caesonia tries to revive Caligula's natural senses and immerse him in the physical realm of the possible. But for Caligula, humans are not free insofar as they love anything mortal. This makes sexual love a sin of the worst sort in Caligula's new order of merit. Nevertheless, he does not practice celibacy, nor does he demand abstinence from his subjects. Instead, he founds an empire of vice in which citizens are ordered to immerse themselves in constant sexual activity. He awards a monthly badge of "civic merit" to citizens who patronize the national brothel "most assiduously"; any citizen who does not get the badge within a year is either exiled or executed (30). The ostensible purpose of this law is to raise profits for the state, but it actually promulgates a sexuality of indifference. Sexual relations will occur not because of love, or even lust, but rather terror.

Caligula frequently engages in violent sex, but even this threatens the very solitude he so desperately desires. He says to Scipio:

> When I am with the women I make mine and darkness falls on us and I think "now my body's had its fill" that I can feel myself my own at last, poised between death and life—ah, then my solitude is fouled by the stale smell of pleasure from the woman sprawling at my side. (38–39)

Sexual activity immerses Caligula in the reality and imperfection of life, bringing him back into the physical world. Caesonia tries to encourage Caligula in this direction, asking him to "live and love quite simply, naturally" (68). Caligula confesses that he still feels a "shameful tenderness" for Caesonia, making her the "last witness" of his human nature. But he cannot tolerate this, and he attempts to strangle Caesonia in the final moments of the play so that he may "perfect at last the utter loneliness that is my heart's desire" (72).

Superior Suicide: The Sacrifice of the Messiah

There is one final witness to Caligula's humanity: Caligula himself. He eventually comes to realize that his nihilist logic demands his death. At one point, Scipio says to Caligula, "You've done everything that was needed to rouse up against you a legion of human gods, ruthless as yourself, who will drown in blood your godhead of a day" (45). Caligula replies that this is exactly his intention, which he proves by refusing to act against his assassins. He does nothing during the course of the play to stop the conspiracy against his life, though he is completely cognizant of it. Once again Caligula is "logical" to the end: if he must be indifferent to everything, then that must include his own existence. This is presented symbolically in the final scene when he shatters the mirror showing his reflection. At this very moment, the armed assassins enter and stab him to death.

In the American preface to the play, Camus addresses Caligula's refusal to resist assassination:

> One cannot destroy everything without destroying oneself. This is why Caligula depopulates the world around him and, faithful to his logic, does what is necessary to arm against him those who will eventually kill him. *Caligula* is the story of a *superior suicide*. . . . Unfaithful to mankind through fidelity to himself, Caligula accepts death because he has understood that no one can save himself all alone and that one cannot be free at the expense of others.[43]

In *Sisyphus,* Camus speaks of "superior suicide" in relation to the character Kirilov in Dostoevsky's *The Possessed.* Although the point of *Sisyphus* is to prove that truly absurd men do not commit suicide, Camus claims that Kirilov is nevertheless "an absurd character." In other words, the absurd condition does not completely disallow every type of suicide; there is a particular type of self-murder that it permits. Camus refers to Kirilov's death in *The Possessed* as a "superior suicide" because it is done for "an idea, a thought" (*MS* 78). Unlike a suicide committed in resigned despair over the world's indifference to humanity, Kirilov's suicide is a vehement act of revolt against the world. Like Caligula, Kirilov aspires to a "painful independence" that, according to Camus, makes him a fully transcendent "God" (*MS* 80). Camus has Kirilov declare, "The attribute of my divinity is independence" (*MS* 79). Kirilov refuses to be subject to anything that transcends him, including death. He will choose the moment of his death independently and of his own accord. He realizes, however, that others are not free insofar as they "entertain blind hopes" of deliverance through imaginary divinities. To make them realize that "everything depends on us," not on an imaginary God, Kirilov thinks it is necessary to kill himself. Kirilov's suicide, according to Camus, is a "death without future, imbued with evangelical melancholy" (*MS* 80). That is to say, his death cannot promise personal immortality, even though, as a suicide, it shows hope for a decisive transformation of humanity. It is the first shot in an eschatological revolution:

> [Men] need to be shown the way and cannot do without preaching. Consequently, Kirilov must kill himself out of love for humanity. He must show his brothers a royal and difficult path on which he will

be the first. It is a pedagogical suicide. . . . But once he is dead and men are at last enlightened, this earth will be peopled with tsars and lighted up with human glory. Kirilov's pistol shot will be the signal for the *last revolution.* Thus, it is not despair that urges him to death, but love of his neighbour for his own sake. (*MS* 80; my emphasis)

Like Kirilov, Caligula does not commit suicide in despair; rather, he lets himself be killed in order to teach humans the "difficult path" of freedom. His sacrifice is, likewise, "pedagogical," and could potentially transform humans into immortal Caesars if they would only accept the lesson he is teaching. Caligula thinks that his own assassination could bring about the last revolution—or, in Caesonia's words, "the one [final] revolution in this world of ours if people would only take it in" (33).[44]

The notion that a single suicide can transform the world is not as peculiar as it might first seem. The "logic" of superior suicide is at the foundation of Christian civilization, and is present in both Gnostic and apocalyptic readings of Christ's passion.[45] In *Sisyphus,* Camus speaks of Kirilov's superior suicide as an "annexing" of Christ's crucifixion. Christ, it is believed, allowed himself to be killed in order to save humanity; he submitted himself to the evils of this world as a revelatory and redemptive sacrifice. Jesus' life, according to Camus, is the "most absurd" because his notion of the "Kingdom of God" could not be reconciled with the world as presently constituted (*MS* 79). This led to his superior suicide through the crucifixion, which revealed the absurd rupture between him and the world. Likewise, Caligula willingly submits to his own execution. In a manner similar to Jesus, he does not employ worldly prudence because his kingdom of the impossible is entirely transcendent; instead, he imprudently allows himself to be assassinated.

The final scene of *Caligula* echoes Christ's passion. Christ, just before his arrest, prayed in Gethsemane to be relieved of his mission.[46] So too Caligula, with the conspirators circling around the palace, has a moment of weakness that resembles Jesus. For an instant, Caligula—like Christ looking at his sleeping disciples in Gethsemane—wishes he was not the savior but among the saved:

How bitter it is to know all, and to have to go through to the consummation! Listen! That was a sound of weapons. . . . Why am I not in their place, among them? And I'm afraid. That's cruellest of all, after despising others, to find oneself as cowardly as they. Still, no matter. Fear, too, has an end. Soon I shall attain that emptiness beyond all understanding, in which the heart has rest. (72–73)

Even in this passage Caligula still seems somewhat determined to finish his mission. However, he expresses doubts about his entire enterprise in the moments before his death. He feels that somehow he has been forsaken by the impossible, since Helicon was unable to get him the moon (9). His last-minute plea to Helicon resonates with Christ's desperation on the cross. Caligula's anguished cry, "[Helicon! Helicon!] Nothing, nothing yet," recalls Jesus' cry in the Gospels, "My God, my God, why have you forsaken me" (73).[47] Even if the reference is not explicit, the point of Caligula's cry is similar. The moon never arrives, and Helicon, like Jesus' God, does not respond.

Without the possibility of the impossible, Caligula claims that humans "shall be forever guilty" (73). If Caligula is forsaken, then humanity is not saved. With this recognition, Caligula condemns his own messianism. He says to himself, "I have chosen a wrong path, a path that leads to nothing. My freedom isn't the right one" (73). This leads him to the conclusion that "killing is not the solution" (72). Perhaps this is a moment of tragic realization: he had tried to put an end to the absurd condition, but he only succeeded in reinstating it intact.[48] His life still exemplifies the hopeless rupture between humanity and the world from which he had tried to escape. But the possibility that Caligula now rejects his murderous project is uncertain because he remains defiant to the end. He says, in his last moments, "There's nothing in this world, or in the other, made to my stature" (73). And as the assassin's knives hack him down, Caligula screams, "I'm still alive!" (74).[49] These last words reveal that his messianic purpose has been successful, at least in part. Caligula's nihilistic spirit does not die at the end; it lives on in the nihilism of the modern world.

Metaphysical Revolt, True Rebellion, and Greek Tragedy

Archambault provides a summary of what has been discussed thus far:

> Caligula's dissatisfaction with a physical universe that he considers
> evil; his dualistic obsession with the concepts of purity and impurity;

72 | Evil in Twentieth-Century Theatre

his faith in a superior knowledge, of which he is the purveyor, as the sole means of escaping from the realm of the possible; his contemptuous asceticism in matters of love and friendship, or anything that implies an admission of value; his radical conviction that all men are guilty; his sense of history, that is, his vision of life as a drama, as an inescapable engagement in a process toward catastrophe—these ideas bear a close resemblance to those which Camus in *Christian Metaphysics* had called "the fundamental Gnostic themes."[50]

Both the gnostic and the absurd man perceive everything in the world as "equivalent," a perception closely related to the desire for a different world. Camus shows how such perceptions and desires contribute to a revolutionary ethos, one that does not preclude murder or certain types of suicide. Even if the absurdist rebel is aware that the impossible can never be made possible, the insubstantial nature of the world provides no apparent decree against killing. He can rebel "as if" it were possible to transform nature and humanity through murder. The tendency of the absurd sensibility to slip into murder is discussed by Camus in *The Rebel*:

> Awareness of the absurd, when we first claim to deduce a rule of behaviour from it, makes murder seem a matter of indifference, to say the least, and hence possible. If we believe in nothing, if nothing has any meaning and if we can affirm no values whatsoever, then everything is possible and nothing has any importance. There is no pro or con: the murderer is neither right nor wrong. We are free to stoke the crematory fires or to devote ourselves to the care of lepers. Evil and virtue are mere chance or caprice. . . . Hence, if we claim to adopt the absurdist attitude, we must prepare ourselves to commit murder, thus admitting that logic is more important than scruples that we consider illusory. (*R* 5–6)

In *The Rebel*, written after *Sisyphus* and *Caligula*, Camus tries to modify his understanding of "revolt." It is here that Camus formulates an understanding of what he calls "true rebellion"—a type of rebellion that avoids the murderous excesses of metaphysical revolt and unequivocally condemns legitimized mass murder. In *Caligula*, we see Camus taking his first steps to depict this type of rebellion with the character Cherea.[51]

However, exactly what "true rebellion" is, and how it differs from Caligula's metaphysical rebellion, is a matter of confusion in both *The Rebel* and *Caligula.*

Let us first consider *The Rebel,* for its theoretical account provides a framework within which to consider the types of rebellion presented in *Caligula.* In *The Rebel,* Camus gives an account of rebellion at its phenomenological "origins." Camus variously refers to this as "true," "original," or "slave" revolt. According to Camus, the initial impulse to rebel is not nihilistic in the Caligulian sense:

> [Rebellion] is not, originally, the total negation of all existence. Quite the contrary, it says yes and no simultaneously. It is the rejection of one part of existence in the name of another part, which it exalts. . . . Then, when rebellion, in rage or intoxication, adopts the attitude of "all or nothing" and the negation of all existence and all human nature, it is at this point that it denies itself. Only total negation justifies the concept of a totality that must be conquered. (*R* 251)

Camus claims that when humans feel the need to rebel against suffering, murder, and injustice, they are not simply saying "no" to everything; rather, they are also saying "yes" to some things that have intrinsic value. A person is not initially at odds with the whole of creation when he feels the need to rebel; rather, he is motivated to revolt against something specific because it has violated something else. By rebelling, the rebel affirms the value of a particular thing against whatever harms or threatens it. Camus writes, "Every act of rebellion tacitly invokes a value" (*R* 14). Any revolt that forgets this original "yes," and subsequently attempts to realize a total transformation of humans and nature, is untrue to its origins. Although such revolutionary efforts are reactions to murder and injustice, they ultimately perpetrate the same evils. In this way, genocidal revolutionaries contradict their original purposes.

Camus postulates a type of rebellion that is different from the one expressed in *The Myth of Sisyphus.* In *Sisyphus,* Camus describes the absurd man's rebellion as a metaphysical revolution that pits the individual against the entirety of creation and that can only say "yes" to human revolt. In *The Rebel,* Camus criticizes this understanding by examining how it potentially legitimates madmen like Caligula. He tries to arrive at an alternative understanding of revolt that says "yes" to the good in humans and nature. It is not the case, as Camus states in *Sisyphus,* that "revolt gives life its value" (*MS* 40); rather, revolt is undertaken in the name of those things *within life* that are valuable. Camus, in this new understanding, calls into question the absurdist presumption that "everything is equivalent" and instead proposes a type of rebellion that takes place in a world containing high and low, justice and injustice, goods and evils. This rebellion is characterized by what Camus calls "a strange form of love"—a love not inspired by what things might become in a perfect world but by what they are in an imperfect one (*R* 304). In this sense, the true rebel's response to evil is noneschatological.

Camus argues that this type of rebellion is embodied in the tragic mythology of the ancient Greeks, particularly in the myth of Prometheus, who fights on behalf of humankind. Camus writes:

> The Greeks are never vindictive. In their most audacious flights they always remain faithful to the concept of moderation, a concept they deified. Their rebel [Prometheus] does not range himself against all of creation, but against Zeus, who is never anything more than one god among many. . . . It is a question of settling a particular account, of a dispute about what is good, and not of a universal struggle between good and evil. (*R* 27)

The Promethean rebel is not engaged in an eschatological battle between absolute good and evil but in a fight on behalf of the relative goods of this world. He does not think that all of creation is rendered worthless by the fact of evil. Instead, he acts to affirm specific goods whenever these are threatened. The Promethean, in Camus's words, takes the "measure of life" as his guide, a measure that will moderate both the ends and the means of rebellion (*R* 298). Indeed, Camus writes, "rebellion in itself is moderation" (*R* 301). The true rebel realizes that there are limits to what any revolt can accomplish and that disaster will occur if these limits are crossed.[52] This, according to Camus, is one of the central lessons of Greek tragedy: "The Greeks never said that the limit could not be crossed. They said it existed and that the man who dared ignore it was mercilessly struck down."[53] This is why "the chorus in classical tragedies generally advises prudence. . . . The constant theme of classical tragedy . . . is the limit that must not be transgressed."[54] The true rebel must understand that his revolt, whether against political injustice or natural afflictions, is limited even with regard to his specific issue. His "no" to specific evils must be accompanied by a lucid awareness that he cannot realistically negate all evils. It is a matter of recognizing which evils are given and which are surplus. If the Promethean is prudent, he can reduce surplus evils to some extent, but he must accept that evil in general is ineradicable. Camus writes:

> Rebellion indefatigably confronts evil, from which it can only derive a new impetus. Man can master in himself everything that should be mastered. He should rectify in creation everything that can be rectified. And after he has done so, children will still die unjustly even in a perfect society. Even by his greatest effort man can only propose to diminish arithmetically the sufferings of the world. But the injustice and the suffering of the world will remain and, no matter how limited they are, they will not cease to be an outrage. (*R* 303)

The Promethean, when responding to evil, must distinguish possible alleviations from impossible solutions. Even if a specific alleviation is possible, he must consider whether it is desirable. Upon this deliberation he acts, even if it means putting his own life at risk. This continual dynamic and constant tension—between his love of the world, his need to revolt, and his awareness of limits—characterizes the psyche of the true rebel and makes him proceed with prudence.

This account of Promethean revolt suggests that Camus is trying to move beyond all permutations of the eschatological myth and not just the secular and Gnostic radicalizations of it. Camus often argues that Christian apocalypticism is not a sufficient remedy for Caligulian nihilism. He writes: "If, in order to go beyond nihilism, we have to go back to Christianity, we might very well carry on the movement and go beyond Christianity into Hellenism."[55] Camus suggests that two thousand years of resigned Christian apocalypticism bred an immoderate hope for another world and that this unintentionally encouraged more radical forms of eschatology to flourish in modernity: "Origins of modern lunacy. It was Christianity that turned man away from the *world*. It reduced him to himself and to his history. Communism is the logical consequence of

Christianity. [It is a history of Christians]."[56] Camus also speaks of the "Christian origins of all types of historic Messianism, even revolutionary Messianism[s]" such as fascism and communism (R 193). In this sense, the source of modern nihilism is not found within Gnosticism alone but within eschatology in general. Modern ideological movements, with their advanced technology and revolutionary politics, radicalize the eschatological impulse. For Camus, the desire to transform nature, society, and the human species through technology and violence is not a definitive departure from Christianity but a radical continuation of its denigration of nature:

> When the Church dissipated its Mediterranean heritage, it placed the emphasis on history to the detriment of nature. . . . When nature ceases to be an object of contemplation and admiration, it can then be nothing more than material for an action that aims at transforming it. (R 299)

This nihilistic ethos, according to Camus, is antithetical to the ancient Greek understanding of the world and human action.

Beyond Nihilism: Cherea and True Revolt

In *Caligula,* Camus offers an alternative to Caligula's nihilism through the character Cherea, who in many ways anticipates his later formulations of true rebellion in *The Rebel.* Camus, however, is unsuccessful at bringing true rebellion to the stage. Many of the weakest moments in the play are those dealing with Cherea's resistance to Caligula. The conspiracy against the emperor is initiated when the patricians voice their intent to overthrow Caligula at the start of Act 2. Cherea stops them from acting immediately. He argues that "a frontal attack's quite useless when one is fighting an imperial madman in the full flush of his power" (21–22). He claims that Caligula's malice is "disinterested" and that this should stop them from taking "arms" at the present time (22). He advises them instead to be patient and to use "cunning." The cunning Cherea recommends to "actively encourage [Caligula] to carry out his wildest plans" so that he is isolated from all his subjects (22–23).

Cherea's argument is puzzling. Presumably, Cherea wants to bolster Caligula's monstrosity in order to sway popular opinion against him. There is an underlying sense that Caligula is still loved by many of his subjects. The First Patrician claims that the masses would oppose Caligula's assassination at this point (22). Cherea does not articulate this consideration directly, however, and nothing more is said about popular opinion for the rest of the play. The conspirators allow Caligula's madness to continue without resistance for the next three acts. It is not until Act 4 that Cherea decides the time is right to assassinate Caligula. It is not clear why this time is more opportune than the earlier moment in Act 2. We are not told that popular sentiment has turned against the emperor or that he has made himself more vulnerable to attack. In fact, we are not offered any coherent explanation as to how the delay has benefited the conspirators.

The plot against the emperor has the potential to be dramatically engaging, but this possibility is squandered by the ineptitude of the conspirators. The conspiracy is transparent, easily spotted by Helicon, Caesonia, and Caligula himself. In Act 3, Helicon gives Caligula a tablet written by the conspirators, containing all their names and citing Cherea as the ringleader. Why such an incriminating document exists in the first place and why Helicon easily discovers it, is never addressed. Cherea, we should recall, wanted his fellow conspirators to use extreme cunning. Instead, he and his colleagues are so incompetent that it borders on comedy. There is, however, a serious idea that Camus is trying to illustrate, even if he has trouble presenting it. Through Cherea, Camus is struggling to symbolize true Promethean rebellion and distinguish it from Caligula's Caesaro-Gnostic revolution. Cherea fights to affirm the goods of this world by continually reminding the Romans of the worldly things they "venerate" and "hold most deeply,"[57] and he encourages the conspirators to oppose Caligula for the sake of these things.

The distinction between Cherea and Caligula is presented clearly in Act 1. Caligula condemns Cherea for "attributing importance to people and to things" (14), but Cherea retorts that "it is necessary to plead for this world, if we want to live in it."[58] This statement reveals that Cherea is not rebelling to annihilate the universe, or to revenge his own humiliations, but to "combat a big idea . . . whose triumph would mean the end of [the world]" (21).[59] What most "appals" Cherea is that Caligula uses "unlimited power . . . [to the point of denying mankind and the world]" (21).[60] He tries to affirm humanity and the world by reminding the Romans that the universe does not correspond to Caligula's perception of it.

Cherea's revolt is not against the totality of life but against Caligula alone. He does not hate the world but rather the empire of madness that Caligula has created. His rebellion against evil is more modest than Caligula's, both in its methods and in its aims. He wants a relatively "secure" world where people can "live and be happy," as opposed to Caligula, who wants a "renewed" world where "men will die no more and at last be happy" (51, 17). Cherea knows that his rebellion against Caligula can make life better but not perfect. These modest aspirations make Cherea contemptible in the eyes of the emperor. Caligula accuses him of being "an ordinary man, sound in mind and body," with "no desire for the extraordinary" (53), but Cherea's distaste for the superhuman keeps him from becoming a methodical killer.

Nevertheless, Cherea must murder the emperor. That Cherea both organizes and actively participates in Caligula's assassination is significant because it reveals that his love of life does not preclude certain types of murder. The true rebel, according to Camus, must be willing to use violence in extreme circumstances but must never rest easy with it:

> If rebellion exists, it is because falsehood, injustice, and violence are part of the rebel's condition. He cannot, therefore, absolutely claim not to kill or lie, without renouncing his rebellion and accepting, once and for all, evil and murder. But no more can he agree to kill and lie, since the inverse reasoning, which would justify murder and violence, would also destroy the reasons for his insurrection. Thus, the rebel can never find peace. He knows what is good and, despite himself, does evil. . . . In any case, if he is not always able not to kill, either directly or indirectly, he can put his conviction and passion to work at diminishing the chances of murder around him. His only virtue will lie in never yielding to the impulse to allow himself to be engulfed in the shadows that surround him and in obstinately dragging the chains of evil, with which he is bound, toward the light of good. (R 285–86)

Though Camus acknowledges it is occasionally necessary for the Promethean to commit evil, he does not say murder is good.[61] He demands that the true rebel acknowledge that murder is evil, regardless of how "justified" it may be, for otherwise revolt becomes embroiled in logical crime. The Promethean must choose the "lesser evil," but this choice must be recognized as an evil nonetheless. The refusal to turn good into evil, mixed with a modest expectation of what can be accomplished, limits the violence that a rebel like Cherea will commit. He murders, but he does not, like Caligula, "codify" or "legitimize" murder, nor does he think that murder can put an end to all killing. In this sense, Cherea echoes Camus's understanding of political resistance in "Neither Victims nor Executioners":

> People like myself want not a world where murder no longer exists (we are not so crazy as that!) but one where murder is no longer legitimized . . . for we live in a world where murder is legitimized, and if we do not like that we must change it. But it seems we cannot change it without running the risk of murder.[62]

The demand for a thoroughly nonviolent rebel, according to Camus, is as utopian as legitimizing mass murder in the name of a perfect world. Extreme circumstances force a Promethean to consider using political insurrection or war, for these might be the only means at his disposal when confronting a greater evil. Cherea's circumstances ostensibly present us with a situation where violence is the best option.

Cherea could, of course, refuse to kill the emperor. The alternative is Scipio's peaceful acquiescence. Scipio, much to Cherea's displeasure, decides to leave the conspiracy at the last moment, claiming that he can "never again take anybody's side" (56).[63] But the refusal to take any side simply affirms all sides, and this ultimately means consenting to those, such as Caligula, who codify murder. Though Scipio's nonviolent approach has the appearance of purity, it is, for Cherea, the wrong reaction in this instance. Scipio is hardly, as Caligula says, "singleminded for good" (36). On the contrary, Scipio's passivity facilitates Caligula's nihilism.

Return to Nihilism: The Essential Goodness of Metaphysical Revolt

It appears, on the basis of what has been said, that Camus is proposing a politically astute form of rebellion free of any eschatological expectations.

Camus claims he is trying "to define the conditions necessary for a political position that is modest—which is to say, free from both messianism and nostalgia for an earthly paradise."[64] But if the point of *Caligula* is to show "the folly of attempting the impossible" (*R* 301), this is mitigated by Camus's obvious sympathy for the protagonist. There is another less dominant but nonetheless quite obvious tendency in the play that compromises Camus's critique of Caligula. Camus continually tries to salvage something good—even essential—from Caligula's eschatology by presenting him as a misguided hero who is essentially right but goes too far. In this sense, it is not Caligula's passion that is wrong but the direction it takes. This suggests that Camus does not want to depart from the eschatological myth entirely but simply mitigate its excesses.[65]

Surprisingly, Camus had originally intended *Caligula* to be a straightforward celebration of metaphysical revolt, even in its most murderous manifestations. I. H. Walker points out that Camus initially had "a sympathetic view of Caligula, stressing his idealism, his flamboyance and his lonely suffering."[66] Camus's admiration for the emperor is evident in a January 1937 *Notebook* entry titled "Caligula or the meaning of death"— the first written indication of Camus's interest in Caligula. He gives a tentative outline of the play that is very different from the one he eventually published. The most noteworthy difference is that Caligula is not assassinated at the end but instead emerges triumphantly from behind the closing curtain to tell the audience, "No, Caligula is not dead. He is there, and there. He is in each one of you. If you were given the power, if you had the courage, if you loved life, you would see this monster or this angel that you carry within yourselves break loose."[67] Camus presents the emperor as both a "monster" and an "angel"—a significant departure from Suetonius, who unequivocally declares that Caligula is a monster. But this epilogue of a resurrected Caligula encouraging the audience to discover the Caligula within themselves was eventually scrapped by Camus, as was the entire 1937 outline. Over the course of World War II, Camus gradually reconstructed both the form and the content of the play. Manuscript versions of these efforts exist that reveal not only Camus's structural deviations from the original plan but also a gradual change in his attitude toward Caligula.[68] The play that Camus eventually published in 1944, and subsequently revised in 1947 and 1958, contains a much stronger critique of the emperor's monstrosity. Perhaps Camus's experience of the war and his involvement in the French Resistance made him reconsider his previous desire to encourage new Caligulas. However, Camus does not entirely relinquish his impression of Caligula as a noble hero, even in the final revised version of the play. The 1958 text continues to suggest that there is something extraordinarily good—even angelic— in Caligula's desire to murder.

The goodness at the core of Caligula's revolt is signified by the other characters. Helicon, Caesonia, Scipio, and even Cherea claim that Caligula's nihilism has a benevolent origin. Caligula's purity of heart persuades other characters to acquiesce to his nihilism for reasons that are not always obvious. Camus's own understanding cannot necessarily be identified with the opinions of these characters, but it is clear that he wants us to empathize with Caligula to a certain extent. It could be argued that this aspect of the play is the residue of Camus's youthful enthusiasm for Caligula—something he tried to mitigate in the later editions of *Caligula*. But few of Camus's revisions dissuade us from the impression that Caligula is essentially good. As late as 1958 Camus added a passage in which Helicon identifies Caligula's basic goodness:

> Gaius is an idealist, as we all know. In other words, he hasn't yet understood. I do, and that's why I take charge of nothing. But if Gaius begins to understand, then he—on the contrary—is capable, with his good little heart, of taking charge of everything. And God knows what that would cost us.[69]

This passage is difficult to interpret, but its general point is discernible. Helicon claims to understand that the world is nothing, but he will do nothing about it. Instead of "taking charge," Helicon will acquiesce to Caligula's wildest plans because he has "no reason not to" (9). He acknowledges, however, that Caligula's nihilism expresses itself differently from his own passive indifference. Unlike Helicon, Caligula has the power, the ambition, and the idealism to "take charge of everything," and he claims that this ambition comes from Caligula's "good little heart."

The moral ambiguity surrounding Caligula's passion is also apparent in Caesonia. She, as opposed to Helicon, privately disagrees with Caligula's nihilism but publicly supports him. Caesonia agrees—albeit reluctantly and under Caligula's coercion—to be "cruel," "cold" and "ruthless" (18). Consequently, we see her participate in all Caligula's schemes throughout the play. She also tries to justify Caligula to the Romans.

She criticizes all "dolts" who claim that he has a "disease," arguing instead that, far from having a corruptive illness, the emperor has "too much soul" (63). Once again there is a sense that Caligula is too much of a good thing. This is what Caesonia wants Scipio to understand in Act 2. Scipio hates Caligula for torturing his father to death, but Caesonia tries to "speak to what is best" in Scipio so that he will "understand" Caligula. She gets him to recollect the graphic torture of his father—the tongue being torn out of his mouth—along with the image of Caligula, who ordered the torture (34). For Caesonia, grasping the meaning of these two images would bring about the "final revolution" if humans could only accept it (33). Though Caesonia's reasoning is unclear, her intention is not: she wants Scipio to comprehend the purity of Caligula's intent, a purity that demands grisly torture and arbitrary homicide.

Caesonia is successful in changing Scipio's mind, and by the end of the play Scipio says to Caligula, "I've come to understand you" (67). Scipio now sees what is "best" in himself as a poet: his poems should not celebrate the beauty in nature but rather illuminate the revolt against the whole of creation. He now understands the "murderous powers of poetry" advocated by Caligula in his book *Cold Steel* (28). The degree to which Scipio comes to understand Caligula is revealed in his poem about "death" in the poetry contest of Act 4. In the heat of the moment, Scipio writes:

> Pursuit of happiness that purifies the heart
> Skies rippling with light,
> O wild, sweet, festal joys, frenzy without hope.
>
> (66)

Touched by this enigmatic meditation, Caligula declares Scipio the winner of the competition. Scipio, as if thanking Caligula, says he learned about death from the murder of his father (66). The poem suggests that Scipio has reevaluated, and to some extent accepted, Caligula's enterprise. Even if the "pursuit of happiness" is a "frenzy without hope," it nevertheless "purifies the heart" to rebel as if the impossible could be made possible. The "frenzy" in Scipio's poem might refer to murder—perhaps even the murder of his father. But Scipio does not become a murderer himself. He chooses to leave Rome to "discover the meaning of it all" (67). But his unwillingness to resist Caligula, along with the compliant nihilism of his poetry, reveals he has become more like the emperor. In the last act he says, "Something inside me is akin to [Caligula]. The same fire burns in both our hearts" (56).

It could be argued that Camus is implicitly criticizing Helicon, Caesonia, and Scipio for their acquiescent nihilism. But when Cherea, the character who mounts the strongest resistance to Caligula, suggests that Caligula's revolt is honorable, the play becomes more difficult to interpret. Cherea defends Caligula for his seriousness and sincerity, and he claims that this stems from Caligula's ability to act in the service of an "idea" without considering his own interests (20–22). For Cherea, "disinterest" is the mark of a superior man, and he argues that Caligula's assassination will be honorable if the men who commit it are equally "disinterested" (55). He does not understand the conflict between himself and Caligula as a fight for power, or as a struggle of vanities, but as a disinterested clash over ideas. For this reason, Cherea considers Caligula more of a comrade than most of his fellow conspirators, who are merely out to avenge their "petty humiliations" (21). Cherea also has respect for Caligula's homicidal pedagogy, since it jolts the patricians out of their pettiness. Cherea says, "There's no denying it's remarkable, the effect this man has on all with whom he comes in contact. He forces one to think. There's nothing like insecurity for stimulating the brain" (58). This comment suggests that Cherea, like Caligula, has a taste for catastrophe. The desire for "insecurity" might be the real reason he delays Caligula's assassination in Act 2 and advises the patricians to help Caligula pursue the impossible. Cherea thinks the patricians need to be taught a lesson in disinterestedness through terror.

Despite Cherea's admiration for the emperor, he still agrees to carry out the assassination. In contrast to Scipio, Cherea claims to have "silenced in [his] heart all that might be akin to Caligula" (56). But Cherea also admits he struggles with nihilistic impulses within himself that resemble Caligula's. Indeed, he claims to dislike Caligula precisely because "one cannot like an aspect of oneself which one always tries to keep concealed" (50–51). He says to Caligula:

> True, there are moments when, to feel free of them, I desire the death of those I love, or hanker after women from whom the ties of family or friendship debar me. *Were logic everything, I'd kill or fornicate on such occasions.* But I consider that these passing fancies have no

great importance. If everyone set to gratifying them, the world would be impossible to live in, and happiness, too, would go by the board. (52; my emphasis)

Cherea has high regard for the emperor's "logic," which leads to murder and rape. In another passage, Cherea claims that Caligula's "philosophy" is "irrefutable" ("une philosophie sans objections") (21),[70] but this is true only if one assumes that all worldly actions are equivalent. Cherea's response to Caligula's doctrine of equivalence is somewhat ambivalent:

> CALIGULA: So, I take it, you believe in some higher principle?
> CHEREA: Certainly I believe that some actions are—shall I say?—
> more praiseworthy than others.
> CALIGULA: And I believe that all are on an equal footing.
> CHEREA: I know it, Gaius, and that's why I don't hate you. *I understand,
> and, to a point, agree with you.* But you're pernicious, and you've got
> to go. (52; my emphasis)

In the 1947 edition of *Caligula*, Camus expunged Cherea's admission that he understands and agrees with Caligula.[71] This suggests that Camus became uncomfortable overemphasizing the similarities between Cherea and the emperor. However, even in the final revised version of the play that Camus prepared in 1958, Cherea still says he does not "hate" Caligula precisely because he holds all actions on an "equal footing."[72] Cherea is of two minds: on the one hand, he fundamentally disagrees with Caligula's radical equivalence and thinks that some actions are more praiseworthy than others; on the other, he thinks that Caligula is right and therefore accepts that no single action is better than any other. If Cherea accepts that Caligula's philosophy is "irrefutable," then, like Caligula, he would perceive the world as having no intrinsic value. He would then be distinct from Caligula only insofar as he clings to an illogical moderation instead of pushing the absurd to its "logical" conclusion. This moderation would not stem from a Promethean perception of goodness in the world but from a fear of unmitigated murder.

Cherea's position is not clear. We are left asking: Does Cherea silence the Caligulian elements of his soul because they are fundamentally wrong, or does he moderate them because they are right but dangerous?

If the latter is Cherea's position, then Caligula is perhaps justified in criticizing Cherea for lacking the courage to follow through on the truth.

These ambiguities in *Caligula* not only reflect Camus's youthful sympathies for the gnostic Caesar but also anticipate his later theoretical confusions in *The Rebel* regarding true revolt. Ronald D. Srigley has clarified the nature of these confusions in a chapter on *The Rebel* in his manuscript "Albert Camus's Political Philosophy."[73] My central argument regarding similar confusions in *Caligula* is based on Srigley's analysis. As we have seen, Camus states in *The Rebel* that true rebellion "is not, originally, the total negation of all existence" (*R* 251). This makes true rebellion categorically distinct from metaphysical revolt, which protests "against the whole of creation" (*R* 23). However, as Srigley points out, there are other moments in *The Rebel* where Camus speaks of the "true" rebel having eschatological yearnings like the metaphysical rebel. Camus blurs the distinction between "metaphysical revolt" and "true rebellion" by occasionally suggesting that every form of revolt, at its origins, desires the impossible. For example, Camus writes, "In *every rebellion* is to be found the metaphysical demand for unity, the impossibility of capturing it, and the construction of a substitute universe. Rebellion, from this point of view, is a fabricator of universes" (*R* 255; my emphasis). In this passage and others like it, as Srigley argues, the metaphysical rebel's desire for a substitute universe is not a nihilistic deformation of original rebellion but the essence of "every" type of insurrection—including true revolt. Camus also says that the true rebel will "conquer existence" and that his rebellion "embraces the entire universe" (*R* 291, 293). Such aspirations for totality seem contrary to the modest aims of true revolt as Camus describes them elsewhere.[74]

Srigley argues that though Camus often condemns metaphysical revolution as a nihilistic deformation of true rebellion, he also suggests there is something indispensable about metaphysical rebellion that all rebels must embrace. Camus writes, "Metaphysical insurrection, in its first stages, offers us the same positive content as the slave's [i.e., true] rebellion" (*R* 25). Later, Camus says that the "consequences of nihilism" must be studied "without losing sight of the truth innate in its origins" (*R* 102). He seems to praise the eschatological passion driving metaphysical revolt while condemning the extremes to which this passion often leads.[75] His attempt to retain the eschatological passion of metaphysical rebellion confuses his account of true revolt, and, as Srigley points out, leads to some disturbing formulations in *The Rebel.* Camus writes, "In every word and in every act, even though it be criminal, lies the promise of a value that we must seek out and bring to light" (*R* 248). Srigley argues that Camus's effort to find "value" in criminal atrocities

> allows Camus both to condemn metaphysical rebellion because of its violent excesses and its destruction of human life, and to excuse—if not justify—these same excesses because they somehow attest to a profound and serious desire to overcome suffering and death and to achieve a kind of immortality. [As Camus writes,] "The destruction of man once more affirms man. Terror and concentration camps are the drastic means used by man to escape solitude. The thirst for unity must be assuaged, even in the common grave. If men kill one another, it is because they reject mortality and desire immortality for all men" (*R* 247). The simple meaning of this rather unfortunate remark is that political mass murderers too are somehow concerned with the salvation of all human beings. The only problem is that their methods are wrong.[76]

We should recall that at the start of *The Rebel,* Camus condemns his contemporaries for not denouncing mass murder "out of hand" (*R* 3). However, he mitigates his own denouncement in the same book.

Let it be said immediately that Camus is one of the sincerest and most eloquent critics of totalitarianism. But Camus, like many of his contemporaries, insists on finding good at the heart of the most obvious evils, and in the process partially justifies the camps.

Beyond Eschatology?

Camus claims that *Caligula* is intended to be an unequivocal condemnation of the passion for the impossible: "For the dramatist, the passion for the impossible is just as valid a subject for study as avarice or adultery. Showing it in all its frenzy, illustrating the havoc it wreaks, bringing out its failures—such was my intention [with *Caligula*]. And the work must be judged thereon."[77] Upon careful consideration of the play, however, it is by no means clear how Camus wants us to respond to the passion for the impossible. Although Camus claims to condemn the desire for utopia, he also celebrates it to a certain degree. He suggests that humans should retain their eschatological passions but that they should never try to realize these passions politically. Thus he presents Caligula as a noble man with the right ideals but a bad ruler who tries to actualize his ideals "as if" they were possible.

Camus's reluctance to denounce Caligula unequivocally is related to his fear of dehumanizing all enemies. Camus does not want the fight between Cherea and Caligula—between the true Promethean rebel and the metaphysical Caesarian revolutionary—to descend into a melodramatic conflict between absolute good and absolute evil.[78] He writes in *The Rebel*, "The enemy remains the fraternal enemy. Even when [the nihilist] has been denounced for his errors, he can be neither despised nor hated" (*R* 248). In this spirit, Camus tries to avoid formulating a new eschatological selection myth that brands all enemies as worthless and disposable. As Srigley writes, "No doubt one of [Camus's] aims in arguing this way is to resist precisely those modern ideologies that divide human beings into two clearly discernable camps—the camps of good and evil."[79] Camus aspires instead to replace melodramatic simplicity with tragic subtlety. But when Camus attempts to show the good intent in Caligula's murderous actions—that is, in the murdering itself and not in other characteristics of the emperor—he perpetuates the same modern confusions that, in other respects, he has already seen through and warned us against. These confusions are inextricably tied to the status Camus bestows on the eschatological passion after the "death event." After reading *Caligula*, we are left in some confusion as to whether Camus is pointing us beyond the eschatological myth altogether or advocating a moderate form of eschatology. Does he think that the source of nihilistic disorder is in the eschatological passion itself or in the radical means that are sometimes used to satisfy it?

CHAPTER THREE

Messianism and the Age of Senility

Perpetual Expectation in Beckett's *Waiting for Godot*

Augustine, Derrida, and Beckett—Waiting

Waiting for Godot presents characters who wait passively for an *eschaton* that never arrives. The eschatology of patient, deferred expectation is frequently advocated as a remedy for the impatient, radical, and murderous eschatology symbolized by Caligula. Those who expect that an "end" will be brought to them by a transcendent power at an indeterminate point in the future are less likely to try to realize the impossible for themselves through an immanent revolutionary program. In other words, living in constant expectation of a future *eschaton* that can only be actualized by a superhuman force minimizes our inclination toward personal and political excess in the present. It is in light of two such arguments that I want to consider the situation in *Waiting for Godot.* The first is by Saint Augustine; the second is by Jacques Derrida.

   Saint Augustine advocates a life of constantly deferred eschatological expectation on the basis of his reading of history. In *Two Books on Genesis against the Manichees,* Augustine charts the progressive spiritual development of humanity since the fall of Adam.[1] He divides biblical history into six distinct epochs and compares these epochs to the six days of God's creation in Genesis 1, as well as to the six stages that constitute a full human life. The division runs as follows: Adam to Noah (infancy), Noah to Abraham (childhood), Abraham to David (adolescence), David to the Babylonian exile (youth), the exile to Christ (maturity), and Christ to the Second Coming (old age).[2] Christ's Second Coming initiates a series of eschatological events that bring the sixth age to a close. For Augustine, the sixth age will be followed by a heavenly "seventh age," an age that corresponds to the "seventh day" when God rested after his creation of the world.[3] With the arrival of the seventh age, the saved will rest with God in his Kingdom on a "day" that "has no evening."[4] And the damned will be tormented in a hell without end.

At present, humans live in the epoch initiated by Christ's first coming. This epoch is the *saeculum senescens*—the "old age of the world"— which is the sixth and last age before the *eschaton*.[5] Augustine writes:

> *The Sixth Age.* Morning came with the preaching of the gospel of our Lord, Jesus Christ, and the fifth day ended. There begins the sixth, in which the old age (*senectus*) of the old man (*veteris hominis*) appears. . . . In this age . . . like the old age of the old man, a new man is born and now lives spiritually.[6]

According to Augustine, the historical event of Jesus is an absolute event that changes human beings and their relation with God; it gives birth to a new "spiritual man" in the old age of history. For the spiritual man, the old age of the world is not a time of monotony and decay but of excitement and vitality. The spiritual man, according to Augustine, finds there is "an abundance of ideas and words which, like the grains, serve partly as an improvement of his conduct in human society, which is like the fruit-bearing trees, and partly to strengthen faith, hope, and charity for eternal life, which is like the green plants."[7] Nevertheless, the appearance of the spiritual man marks the end of spiritual progress. With Jesus, God has revealed everything that he is going to reveal to humans until the Second Coming. This means there will be no further spiritual progress in history as a whole. There will be spiritual development for particular individuals between now and the end, but everything necessary for salvation has been definitively revealed. History now wanes toward the apocalypse in its old age.

One of the central features of Augustine's *saeculum senescens* is its indeterminate length. Earlier generations of Christians before Augustine had expected the Second Coming to occur within their lifetimes, but their predictions had proven false. Augustine proposes that Christians adopt a different approach—an approach that would eventually be accepted by the Roman Church. He claims that the moment of the Second Coming is a divine mystery that no human can apprehend:

> The period of old age is defined by no fixed number of years. Rather, after those five ages, however long one may live, it is counted as old age. In that age of the world we find no generations, and thus the last day is also concealed since the Lord has declared that it should be hidden for our good.[8]

This effectively places the *eschaton* at an indefinite point in the future, a point that is known by God alone and that can only occur through divine initiative. By making the arrival of the eschaton radically indeterminate while emphasizing that only God can bring the eschaton to us, Augustine moderates eschatological hope in the present. First, the Augustinian position corrects all fervent apocalyptic Christians who claim that the arrival of the *eschaton* is imminent. Such heightened expectations are problematic, not only because they have all proven incorrect, but also because they have the potential to disorder those who fervently believe in them.[9] Second, Augustine claims that salvation can only occur through God's initiative and grace. This means that humans cannot initiate the eschatological events or realize their own salvation through revolutionary, Caligulian efforts. Augustine advocates a humble, expectant faith cloaked in mystery and animated by charity over an aggressive perfectionism bolstered by gnosis.[10]

The Augustinian position, then, avoids the pitfalls of fervent apocalypticism and revolutionary gnosis. Augustine postulates the idea of an absolute future that is coming from God, a future that we do not bring about and that lies at a radically indeterminate point in the future. For Augustine, this is the proper form of expectation in the final age of the world. To further mitigate any desire that Christians may feel for an immediate *eschaton*, Augustine emphasizes that the end of the *saeculum senescens* will be a terrifying time, especially for those who are alive to experience it: "May the evening of this [sixth] age not find us [while we live], if it has not already begun. This is the evening in which the Lord says, 'Do you think that the Son of Man will find faith on the earth when he comes?'"[11] Instead of elation, we should experience a "dark and mighty dread" of the approaching eschatological "sunset." Augustine warns that the Second Coming will bring "affliction as has never happened before" and final judgment.[12] Consequently, any fervent desire a Christian may feel for the *eschaton* should be mitigated by terror.[13]

In the late twentieth century, the deconstructionist Jacques Derrida provided a similar description of the hope and fear that accompanies messianic expectation:

> The Messiah is not simply the one, the other, that I am constantly waiting for. . . . [T]he Messiah might also be the one I expect even while I do not want him to come. There is the possibility that my relation to the Messiah is this: I would like him to come, I hope that he will come, that the other will come, as other, for that would be justice, peace, revolution—because in the concept of messianicity there is revolution—and, at the same time, I am scared. I do not want what I want and I would like the coming of the Messiah to be infinitely postponed, and there is desire in me. . . . [T]hat is the condition for me to go on asking questions and living. So there is some ambiguity in the messianic structure. We wait for something we would not like to wait for. That is another name for death.[14]

The idea of the "messiah" is most often associated with the "Abrahamic" traditions of Judaism, Christianity, and Islam—religions in which the faithful await the arrival of a savior to initiate the eschatological events. But Derrida does not identify the "messiah" with any one savior advocated by a particular Abrahamic "messianism." For Derrida, messianic expectation extends well beyond the Abrahamic faiths. According to him, the "messianic" is contained in the universal human experience of awaiting a "promise"—a promise of something to be said or of someone to come. Every awaited promise, no matter how ostensibly trivial, carries with it the expectation of "revolution," "peace," and "justice." In other words, all forms of future expectation are "messianic":

> The messianic structure is a universal structure. As soon as you address the other, as soon as you are open to the future, as soon as you

have a temporal experience of waiting for the future, of waiting for someone to come: that is the opening of experience. Someone is to come, is *now* to come. Justice and peace will have to do with this coming of the other, with the promise. Each time I open my mouth, I am promising something. When I speak to you, I am telling you that I promise to tell you something, to tell you the truth. . . . So the promise is not just one speech act among others; every speech act is fundamentally a promise. This universal structure of the promise, of the expectation of the future, for the coming, and the fact that this expectation of the coming has to do with justice—that is what I call the messianic structure.[15]

Derrida argues that this universal experience of the promise, and its intimation of justice and peace, is most clearly articulated in specific "messianisms," all of which promise some form of ultimate justice. However, the universal messianic structure is not to be identified with any one of these specific messianisms:

This messianic structure is not limited to what one calls messianisms, that is, Jewish, Christian, or Islamic messianism, to these determinant figures and forms of the Messiah. As soon as you reduce the messianic structure to messianism, then you are reducing the universality and this has important political consequences. Then you are accrediting one tradition among others and a notion of an elected people, of a given literal language, a given fundamentalism.[16]

Derrida makes a subtle distinction between the general "messianic structure" and particular "messianisms." The messianic, according to Derrida, is universal and open-ended; it does not ascertain a specific messiah, whereas specific messianisms do. In this sense, Derrida speaks of the messianic structure as "desert-like,"[17] as a vast expanse in which we wait for the messiah but in which, in John Caputo's words, "the flower of no determinable Messiah grows."[18]

This is not to say that there is no relation between the universal messianic structure and particular messianisms. Derrida hypothesizes that specific messianisms arise out of the general messianic desert—a desert that is the ontological condition for particular eschatological faiths. But he also hypothesizes that humans would not be able to articulate this desertlike experience if it were not for the arrival of specific historical messianisms.[19] He speculates

> that the events of revelation, the biblical traditions, the Jewish, Christian, and Islamic traditions, have been absolute events, irreducible events, which have unveiled this messianicity. We would not know what messianicity is without messianism. . . . In that case singular events would have unveiled or revealed these universal possibilities, and it is only on that condition that we can describe messianicity.[20]

Given that the advent of the Abrahamic faiths is "absolute," Derrida suggests that deconstructionists adopt a respectful, yet critical, approach to these religions while rejecting the specific dogmas that emerge within each tradition. He wants to salvage a general eschatological "spirit"—a "spirit" that, he argues, is not only essential for "justice," but is also inescapable in our daily experience. Derrida writes that "the messianic in general" is a "ghost which we cannot and ought not do without."[21]

Derrida claims he is searching for a "paradoxical way of contesting religious discourse in the name of a faith that cannot be simply mastered or domesticated or taught or logically understood, a faith that is paradoxical."[22] Such a "faith" is a "quasi-'messianism,'" a definite historical force like other messianisms, but one that lacks their doctrinal certainty and that exposes their contingencies, injustices, and inner contradictions.[23] Derrida also argues that deconstructionists should contest modern ideological messianisms, such as Communism, in the name of the messianic faith that animates them. Thus, he rejects rigid "Marxist doctrine" but seeks to retain the vague "messianic spirit" underlying Marx's critical writings.[24]

Derrida often refers to the general messianic promise as the promise of "the impossible." In a manner that echoes Caligula, Derrida claims that deconstruction is "constituted" in "the experience of the impossible."[25] The "impossible," for Derrida, is what he calls "absolute hospitality."[26] The coming of the messiah initiates the arrival of an impossible "democracy" in which every person is offered the gift of hospitality—care without conditions. In this "justice," no "other" is neglected due to expedient self-interest or calculations of efficiency on behalf of the state.[27] At the same time, there is a sober consciousness within deconstructive thinking that absolute hospitality can never be realized. In this way, Derrida radicalizes Augustine's conception of perpetual expectation in the old age of the world.[28] First, in Derrida's *eschaton,* everyone is saved. Second, the arrival of the messiah is not just radically indeterminate but infinitely postponed. The coming of the messiah for Derrida is not an actual historical event in the future or a "future present."[29] Rather, Derrida's "messianic" is structured by the general expectation of an "absolute future" that is always expected but never arrives.[30] He goes so far as to claim that if the messiah were to arrive, the deconstructionist should send him away.[31] There is ambiguity in Derrida's deconstructionist faith because it desires an eschatological fulfillment that it knows is impossible. At the same time, it does not want to see the absolute future realized even if it were possible. The actual arrival of the messiah would mean the end of life—life as constituted by struggle, questioning, desire, change, and injustice. This is why the messiah's arrival is another name for death.

In this manner, Derrida advocates a paradoxical faith that lives in the present but that is always aspiring for an impossible future it does not want. The impossible serves as a measure, revealing how far the present falls short of absolute hospitality. The deconstructionist fights for justice in the present by attempting to make politics as hospitable as possible while remaining pragmatically aware of the limits of politics. Accordingly, the messianic promise "produce[s] events" and "new effective forms of action, practice, organization, and so forth."[32] It is in light of the messianic promise that the deconstructionist works for "a new Enlightenment for the century to come."[33] At the same time, the deconstructionist is restrained from undertaking any absolute solutions because he is aware that absolute justice is beyond the limits of human action. The impossible, for Derrida, cannot—and ought not—be made possible.

———

I begin with this lengthy discussion of Augustine and Derrida because their accounts of eschatological faith apply directly to the problems that confront us when we approach Beckett's *Waiting for Godot* half a century after its first performance.

The situation in *Godot* is familiar to almost all students of twentieth-century literature. In Act 1, two tramps named Vladimir and Estragon wait by a tree in a desolate spot for a man named Godot who is supposed to arrive at sunset. The promise of Godot's arrival is something that fills both men with hope and fear. Two other men eventually pass by together: a slave named Lucky and his abusive master, Pozzo. Their appearance, however, does not occasion the arrival of Godot. Subsequently, a boy, who has a message from Godot, enters. The Boy announces that Godot will not arrive tonight but "surely tomorrow" (47). Night falls without Godot appearing on the stage. In Act 2, which takes place the "Next day. Same time. Same Place," the same sequence of events occurs (50). Vladimir and Estragon wait, Pozzo and Lucky pass by, and the Boy enters with a message proclaiming that Godot will not arrive until tomorrow. Once again, night falls without Godot's appearance; Vladimir and Estragon continue to wait for their elusive man.

The specific messianism referred to most frequently in *Waiting for Godot* is Christianity. Beckett once told Colin Duckworth, "Christianity is a mythology with which I am perfectly familiar, so I naturally use it."[34] It is clear that the spirit of Christianity haunts the world of Godot. There are scattered references throughout the play to Christ, the cross, the crucifixion, the two thieves, and the Gospels. There are also numerous cruciform images and patterns that appear onstage. The tree that stands upstage right implicitly suggests a crucifix.[35] When Pozzo and Lucky enter in Act 2, they collapse upon each other in a cruciform pattern (70).[36] Vladimir and Estragon at one point do an exercise called "the tree" in which they extend their arms horizontally to form a crucifix (70).[37]

Like Christians in Augustine's *saeculum senescens,* Vladimir and Estragon wait humbly for a transcendent savior who has come before and who will come again, but whose time of arrival is indeterminate and entirely dependent on his decision.[38] The play reveals, however, that Augustinian expectation has deteriorated into madness and impotence. Much of what Vladimir and Estragon do and say suggests a diminished Christian worldview. This is implied by the very name of the person they await.[39] The name "Godot" contains the word *God,* but Beckett adds the diminutive suffix *-ot,* suggesting that Godot is a diminished deity.[40] Godot and God are also linked in the play by the traditional image of an old divine patriarch. In Act 1, Lucky says that "God" has a "white beard"; in Act 2, the Boy claims that Godot also has a "white" beard (39; 83). Beckett himself never denied that the figure of Godot is suggestive of the

Christian God. However, he categorically denied that Godot is *only* an allegory for God or Christ's Second Coming. He always stressed that Godot
was not to be interpreted as a metaphor for a specific God, religion, philosophy, or ideology. He once said to Alec Reid, "The great success of
Waiting for Godot had arisen from a misunderstanding: critics and public alike were busy interpreting in allegorical or symbolic terms a play
which strove at all costs to avoid definition."[41] Beckett's attempt to avoid
definition can be seen in a comment he made to the American director Alan Schneider. When Schneider asked, "Who or what does Godot
mean?" Beckett is reported to have replied, "If I knew, I would have said
so in the play."[42]

In fact, the play *does* reveal the meaning of Godot. Ruby Cohn writes,
"Beckett's play tells us plainly who Godot is—the promise that is always
awaited and not fulfilled."[43] Despite Beckett's claim that he is trying to
avoid "definition" at all costs, the play has a certain degree of definition,
even if it is fairly broad in scope. *Waiting for Godot* contains a general
messianic definition. Godot is anything—a person, an idea, a hope, an
event, an ideology, a religion, a product, a technique, a god—that promises to bring a definitive end to present sufferings and create a radically
new condition. The play reveals the degree to which this promise affects
almost every aspect of contemporary human experience. Like Derrida,
Beckett presents the experience of a "promise" that never arrives but
that is always coming. Vladimir and Estragon wait for an indeterminate
savior whose arrival is infinitely postponed and whose actual appearance is not something they necessarily want. The promise of messianic
fulfillment, combined with the continual absence of this fulfillment, defines the central situation of the play. Furthermore, the play suggests,
like Derrida, that this situation is a constituent of human experience in
general. As Vladimir says to Estragon in Act 2, "All mankind is us" (73).
Several critics have noted the play's apparent universal applicability.[44]
In the very first review of *Godot*, Sylvain Zegel wrote that Vladimir and
Estragon "represent all humanity" and that Godot symbolizes "the ideal
and unattainable quest of all men."[45] Hugh Kenner similarly observes,
"The substance of the play, in short, is as common a human experience
as you can find. . . . The substance of the play is waiting, amid uncertainty."[46] Zegel and Kenner agree that Beckett's play tells us who Godot
is: the impossible promise that is always coming but that never arrives.

This is what gives *Godot* its broad messianic definition. In this sense, the play seems to illustrate what Derrida calls the universal "messianic structure" of human experience.

However, the common ground between Derrida and Beckett with regard to the messianic ends here. Beckett does not find anything redemptive or vital from within either messianism or the messianic. On the contrary, he indicates that the continual prevalence of the "messianic promise" within human experience is not leading to a "new Enlightenment" but to an unprecedented denigration of human thought and action. For Beckett, humans are trapped in an age of senility that has a different quality from Augustine's *saeculum senescens.*

Beckett's *Saeculum Senescens*

In *Waiting for Godot,* Beckett presents an Augustinian-based civilization in decline. The spiritual vitality that, for Augustine, characterizes messianic hope in the old age of the world has, in *Godot,* been devastated by ceaseless expectation. Vladimir says, "We wait. We are bored. . . . [W]e are bored to death" (74). Whereas Augustine used images such as "grains," "fruit-bearing trees" and "green plants" to describe all spiritual men consumed with messianic longing, Beckett presents a *saeculum senescens* of boredom, madness, and decay—an "age of senility" not characterized by energetic spiritual men and robust vegetation but by impotent geriatrics and a single skeletal tree.

The age of the characters is indicative of this geriatric motif. With the exception of the Boy who appears at the end of each act, all the characters are old men. Both Vladimir and Estragon claim that they have been together for about fifty years (49, 59).[47] Likewise, Pozzo claims that he took Lucky as a slave "nearly sixty years ago" (31). All the characters suffer from mental ailments typically associated with old age. They are continually confused and forgetful, and often have trouble recognizing people or things. The characters also suffer from physical ailments that are common in the elderly. Estragon has a sore foot, and Vladimir suffers from kidney and prostate problems that make urination difficult and laughing painful (10, 15–16). Pozzo has heart palpitations, and in Act 2 he loses his eyesight (27, 70). Lucky suffers from "goitre," a thyroid disease, which causes his eyes to bulge out of their sockets (25). He also babbles when he speaks in Act 1, like someone suffering from a form of dementia (39–40). By Act 2, Lucky loses his ability to speak altogether.

There are few humans inhabiting the world of *Godot*. Pozzo at one point tries to assure himself that the population has recently increased (31), but the evidence suggests otherwise. Humanity seems to be approaching extinction. We can only confirm the existence of four old men and a boy. But just as striking as the scarcity and age of the characters is the complete absence of women. There are no female characters in *Godot*. Consequently, there seems to be little chance of renewing the human race. There is one mention of the possibility of procreation, but it occurs in the midst of a consideration of suicide:

> ESTRAGON: What about hanging ourselves?
> VLADIMIR: Hmm. It might give us an erection.
> ESTRAGON: An erection!
> VLADIMIR: With all that follows. Where it falls mandrakes grow. That's why they shriek when you pull them up. Did you not know that?
> ESTRAGON: Let's hang ourselves immediately! (16)

Vladimir shows the fate of regeneration in a world where the female is dead. Impotent old men can only ejaculate by hanging themselves. Their spilt semen creates mandrakes, root plants shaped like humans. The only type of conception imagined is one that takes place without women, involves the death of men, and conceives shrieking simulations of human beings. All this suggests that the virile and procreative capacities of the human race have decayed irreparably.

The natural environment that surrounds the characters shows similar signs of deterioration. Pozzo says, "Indeed, all subsides. A great calm descends. Listen! Pan sleeps" (34).[48] Pan, the Greek god of flocks and the spirit of pastoral nature, is silent. The landscape is desolate and desertlike, covered by a "bog" that contributes to the prevailing sense of gloom (14). The sky is gray and overcast, and the temperature is cold (50). It is difficult for the characters to determine the season. Estragon suggests at one point that it is "spring" (59), but Pozzo claims there is a "touch of autumn in the air" (23). Lucky refers to "autumn, summer, winter, winter" but not to spring (39). Regardless of which season it is, there is little evidence of a springlike regeneration of nature.

Plant life consists almost entirely of root vegetables. Only carrots, turnips, and radishes are available for human consumption, yet even these are gradually being eradicated. By Act 2, there are no more carrots, and the radishes have turned black (19, 61). Other than these few remnants, there is little sign of any other plant life. The only distinct vegetation on the horizon is the tree that stands upstage. In Act 1, the tree is barren and appears to be dead. "No more weeping," Estragon says, implying the tree has been put out of its misery (13). But in Act 2 the weeping continues: the tree sprouts three leaves (50),[49] causing Vladimir to declare, "Everything's dead but this tree" (84). However, the few leaves that appear on the tree are more suggestive of old age and death than vitality and regeneration. Indeed, Estragon claims that the "dead" make a sound "like leaves" (55–56).

Everything about the setting suggests that the world has been struck by a recent cataclysm. But things have not always been this desolate. Both Vladimir and Estragon recollect a time when they harvested grapes in Macon country and the Rhône valley, two famous wine-growing regions in France. They recall that during those days the sun shone and the landscape was red (49, 55). Vladimir also remembers how he and Estragon were "presentable" back "in the nineties" or "around 1900" (10).[50] Currently they are vagabonds who live in a devastated world with ill-fitting clothes. Something catastrophic happened after the turn of the century. Vladimir says that back then, when they were presentable, they should have jumped "hand in hand from the top of the Eiffel Tower, among the first. . . . Now it's too late" (10). This implies that the dawn of the twentieth century heralded some form of collective suicide and that Vladimir and Estragon could have been "among the first" to die. Instead, they have survived, and now exist on the other side of this death event.

The sense of a dying world is also emphasized by the time of day. Both acts take place at sunset, the time when Godot is slated to appear. The arrival of night carries with it the expectation of something decisive, something that will mark the end the old world—much like Augustine's "sunset" that marks the end of the *saeculum senescens,* the sixth "day" of history (*CG* 16.24). The heightened expectation for night is evident in Vladimir, who impatiently cries, "Will night never come?" (31).[51]

When night suddenly falls at the end of each act it brings with it nothing new except the moon, which rises at the back of the stage and casts "pale light" on the darkened scene (48). Gradually, Vladimir's fervent expectation for night diminishes. When night arrives at the end of Act 1, Vladimir cries, "At last!" but he says nothing when night falls in Act 2 (48, 83).

The arrival of night in Act 1 does not bring relief or closure. The old age of the world continues the "next day" in Act 2, a day remarkably similar to the day before (50). The only difference is that things, in general, have deteriorated a bit further without actually dying. The approach toward death is asymptotic: everything is continually moving closer to annihilation, but nothing ever gets there.[52] Instead of reaching death or a culminating end point, the world is trapped in perpetual cycles of old age that get worse with each rotation. Night does not bring an end to the cycles; on the contrary, the downward spiral continues. Vladimir and Estragon are trapped in these cycles, which began long before the start of Act 1 and which will continue long after the end of Act 2:

> ESTRAGON: We came too soon [to meet Godot].
> VLADIMIR: It's always at nightfall.
> ESTRAGON: But night doesn't fall.
> VLADIMIR: It'll fall all of a sudden, like yesterday.
> ESTRAGON: Then it'll be night.
> VLADIMIR: Then we can go.
> ESTRAGON: Then it will be day again.
> (*Pause*)
> (*Despairing*) What'll we do, what'll we do! (64)

Antitheticals and Dualities: The Shape of *Godot*

The old age motif is accompanied by an emphasis on antithetical pairs. Bert O. States refers to this structural feature of *Godot* as the "shape of paradox"[53]—a stylistic form in which the assertion of one fact or the existence of one entity is immediately qualified by an opposing fact or entity. This paradoxical structure occurs in the play whenever two antithetical positions are presented next to each other in a symmetrical construction. For instance, almost every assertion in the play is either immediately qualified or contradicted:

ESTRAGON: I'm unhappy.
VLADIMIR: Not really! (46)

ESTRAGON: Another day done with.
VLADIMIR: Not yet. (52)

VLADIMIR : This is becoming really insignificant.
ESTRAGON: Not enough. (62)

ESTRAGON: I can't go on like this.
VLADIMIR: That's what you think. (85)

This overwhelming sense of qualification and contradiction leads to confusion and silence, since it is impossible for a character to make an irrefutable proclamation. Consider what Pozzo says in Act 1: "Let us not
speak ill of our generation. . . . Let us not speak well of it either. Let us
not speak of it at all" (31). Pozzo is trapped between wanting to bless his
contemporaries and wanting to curse them. In the end, he says nothing.

The prevalence of contradictory positions in *Godot* suggests duality,
and it is clear that Beckett has given his play a dualistic structure. Almost
everything in *Godot* comes in twos. The play is divided into two acts.[54]
There are two stationary set pieces on the stage: a tree and a stone.[55]
There are also two main sets of characters, both comprising two people:
Vladimir/Estragon and Pozzo/Lucky. Duality is likewise found in the
names of the characters. Vladimir and Estragon address each other by
two-syllable nicknames: Didi and Gogo. They never address one another
by their formal three-syllable names.[56] Vladimir also goes by the two-
syllable name "Albert," spoken by the Boy (45, 82). As well, the names
Pozzo, Lucky, and Godot are all composed of two syllables.

Most of the dualities in the play are antithetical. This is evident
in the way Beckett combines his pairs of characters, for each couple is
a mismatched combination of opposites. Let us first consider Vladimir
and Estragon. Vladimir is usually presented as tall and thin, Estragon as
short and stout.[57] Didi tends to move toward the tree located upstage
right, whereas Gogo is inclined toward the stone located downstage
left. This means that the lighter Didi is drawn toward an object that
tends skyward, whereas the heavier Gogo gravitates toward something
earthbound.[58] As a result, Vladimir spends much of the play looking up

at the sky, while Estragon tends to look down at the ground. The contrast between up and down is also suggested by the specific problems that each character has with his body and his wardrobe: Vladimir has "stinking breath," whereas Estragon has "stinking feet" (42); Vladimir has kidney and prostate ailments (16), whereas Estragon has a sore left foot (10); Vladimir is restless and tends to stand, whereas Estragon is lethargic and tends to sit; Vladimir has trouble finding a proper-fitting hat, whereas Estragon has trouble finding a proper-fitting pair of shoes. And though Vladimir chastises Estragon for "blaming on his boots the faults of his feet" (11), the same standard should be applied to Vladimir's hat problem. Thus the upward-tending Vladimir has a problem with his head, whereas the downward tending Estragon has a problem with his feet. These opposing problems are indicative of contrary temperaments. Vladimir tends to be cerebral, concerned with the elevated problems of the mind, whereas Estragon is largely motivated by his physical desires. Vladimir, in all his speculations and theorizations, never complains of hunger, and we never see him eat; Estragon repeatedly asks for food, and he actually eats on a couple of occasions. When Estragon is offered the rare delicacy of Pozzo's chicken bones, he gnaws on them ravenously and even belches in satisfaction (26–27). Estragon's name is French for the herb tarragon, which suggests food, as well as a vegetative attachment to the earth.[59] As we have seen, root vegetables are the only edible plants left in the world, and in Act 1 Estragon eats a carrot given to him by Vladimir (19). Even the food Estragon consumes tends toward the ground, not the sky.

Vladimir is a quasi-philosopher who conducts continual inquiries into his situation, whereas Estragon is a former poet who quotes W. B. Yeats and Percy B. Shelley (see 19, 48).[60] This combination of philosopher and poet evokes the traditional antagonism between philosophy and poetry. Vladimir, whose name is Russian for "ruler of the world," tries to conquer problems by using his head.[61] He is continually attempting to establish certainty about his situation through induction and theorizing. Estragon, on the other hand, is much less philosophically inclined; instead of struggling to arrive at certainties through meditative inquiry, he is prone to having daydreams and citing dead poets. His response to the situation is less speculative than Vladimir's; he seems to have arrived at a definite assessment of his condition.

This fundamental difference between Vladimir and Estragon is well illustrated in the first two lines of the play:

ESTRAGON: Nothing to be done.
VLADIMIR: I'm beginning to come round to that opinion. All my life I've tried to put it from me, saying, Vladimir, be reasonable, you haven't yet tried everything. And I resume the struggle. (9)

Vladimir continues to fight with his situation through his open-ended intellectual inquiries, whereas Estragon has generally given up and come to certain conclusions. As a result, Vladimir is more hopeful and obsessed with Godot's arrival; Estragon is more despondent and always forgets what they are waiting for. This is emphasized by a verbal exchange that occurs eight times between the two characters:

ESTRAGON: Let's go.
VLADIMIR: We can't.
ESTRAGON: Why not?
VLADIMIR: We're waiting for Godot.
ESTRAGON: (*Despairingly*) Ah yes! (13)[62]

Vladimir is usually the one who insists that they stay put. Estragon, on the other hand, continually asks to go, which may account for his nickname "Gogo."[63] Estragon also claims to "feel better alone." However, he "always come[s] crawling back" (53); he does not have the power to make a break from his partner, nor does he propose a viable alternative to waiting. This is indicative of a certain power dynamic between Vladimir and Estragon: Vladimir is the more domineering of the two. Estragon's general passivity and despondency makes him vulnerable, binding him even more tightly to his antithetical. He is, for example, beaten every night by a group of unspecified people ("they"), whereas Vladimir is subject to no such violence (9, 52–53). As well, Estragon cannot acquire food for himself; it is always Vladimir who finds whatever few vegetables are left (19, 61–62). Despite Estragon's desire to live independently, he clings to Vladimir for protection and sustenance. As he says to Didi, "Don't touch me! Don't question me! Don't speak to me! Stay with me!" (52).

There is, nevertheless, a relative degree of equality between Vladimir and Estragon. This is not the case with Pozzo and Lucky, whose antithetical natures are expressed in a master/slave relationship. Like Vladimir, Pozzo is the dominant partner. Pozzo, however, keeps his subordinate tied to him with a rope. In the first act, this rope is extremely long, allowing Lucky to reach midstage before Pozzo even appears (21). This suggests a strong connection between the two, as well as a large degree of distance. When he and Lucky enter they resemble a horse and carriage team, with Pozzo at one end holding the rope and Lucky at the other end tied around the neck. Pozzo cracks his whip and demands that they move "On"; Lucky ostensibly pulls his master forward while carrying a heavy bag, a picnic basket, a stool, and a greatcoat (21). When they stop to talk with Didi and Gogo, Pozzo continually shouts orders at Lucky and demeans him with names like "Hog" and "Pig." Pozzo's treatment of Lucky reflects one of the Italian meanings of his name, "cesspool."[64]

Pozzo and Lucky, like Didi and Gogo, have sharply contrasting demeanors and physical ailments. Pozzo is tempestuous and agitated, hardly able to sit for even a moment unless a stool is laid out for him.[65] This excitability mirrors his own erratic heart, which he says goes "pit-o-pat" whenever he smokes too much (27). Lucky, on the other hand, is a sagging narcolept who moves excruciatingly slow; his body is continually slouching toward the ground, and in both acts he collapses on the floor in exhaustion. This sense of fatigue is accentuated by Lucky's silence. Whereas Pozzo is constantly talking, Lucky speaks only once in the entire play (39–40).

The opposing dispositions of Pozzo and Lucky are indicative of their different occupations. Pozzo is a man of power, whose primary purpose is to dominate people, objects, and territory. He begins the play with more material possessions than any other character, including a whip, a watch, a pipe, a monocle, an overcoat, a bottle of wine, and a piece of chicken. Pozzo says he has a "manor" that contains several slaves and a Steinway piano (42). He even claims to own the land on which Vladimir and Estragon wait (22). Pozzo, however, is not charitable with his relative wealth. In Act 1, we see him drink the wine and eat the chicken "voraciously," but he does not offer anything to the other characters (24). His only courtesy is to allow Estragon to gnaw on the remaining chicken bones (26). By hoarding his possessions, Pozzo presents himself as a gentleman of wealth and good taste, far above the extreme poverty that surrounds him. But Pozzo is hardly a model of sophistication: his general demeanor is crude, and his bourgeois affectations are betrayed by lower-class tendencies, such as public burping and flatulence (26, 74). Beckett himself once referred to Pozzo as a "proletarian."[66]

Lucky, on the other hand, is a bourgeois intellectual with talents in the liberal arts. Pozzo informs us that Lucky can "dance, or sing, or recite, or think," though his ability to do these things is not as good as it was in the past (37). We find out that Lucky once knew an array of European dances. Lucky's current repertoire is much less extensive, and his choreography can only convey his sense of entrapment. When ordered by Pozzo to dance he performs "The Net," which begins with Lucky using his body to aspire to the heavens but ends with him slumped over the ground in defeat (37–38).[67] Even worse than Lucky's dancing is his thinking. Pozzo says that Lucky "used to think very prettily once, . . . Now . . . (*He shudders.*) So much the worse for me" (37). In Act 1, we see why Pozzo shudders at the very thought of Lucky's thinking. Lucky's hat is put on his head and Pozzo orders, "Think!" (38–39). Lucky obeys Pozzo's command and, like a machine under too much pressure, explodes with an onslaught of words. On first encounter, "Lucky's Think," as Beckett calls it,[68] seems like an irredeemable mess—a rambling soliloquy, punctuated by didactic reflections, pedantic words, and disturbing images. It also contains several "research tandems"—numerous references to imaginary scholars whom Lucky cites to support his own observations.[69] Overall, the Think reads like a nightmarish rough draft of an academic treatise. Nevertheless, it is apparent that Lucky is describing a world that, despite all intellectual and scientific advances, is caught in the grip of an unprecedented decline:

> as a result of the public works of Puncher and Wattmann it is established beyond all doubt that in view of the labours of Fartov and Belcher left unfinished for reasons unknown of Testew and Cunard left unfinished it is established what many deny that man in Possy of Testew and Cunard that man in Essy that man in short that man in brief in spite of the strides of alimentation and defecation wastes and pines wastes and pines and concurrently simultaneously what is more for reasons unknown in spite of the strides of physical culture . . .

> . . . and considering what is much more grave that in the light of
> the labours lost of Steinweg and Peterman it appears . . . that in the
> plains in the mountains by the seas by the rivers running water run-
> ning fire the air is the same and then the earth namely the air and
> then the earth in the great cold the great dark the air and the earth
> abode of stones in the great cold. (39–40)

This barrage of words, scholars, and horrific images does not stop until
Vladimir removes Lucky's hat. After that, we do not hear another word
from Lucky.

Lucky's deteriorating intellectual and cultural abilities are at the
mercy of Pozzo's rule. However, Lucky has not been forced into this
situation. He has deliberately submitted his bourgeois talents to the
whims of Pozzo's "proletarian" tyranny and does not want to be liberated. In fact, Lucky weeps when Pozzo announces that he will be sold
at a "fair" down the road (30). To forestall the possibility of being sold,
Lucky does everything he can to "impress" his master (29). Lucky depends on Pozzo's commands to give his life immediate purpose. It is
also clear that Pozzo is equally dependent on his partner. Pozzo can do
nothing for himself; Lucky must do everything for him. Without his slave,
Pozzo would be unable to survive. Pozzo also claims to have learned
"professional worries" about "beauty," "grace," and "truth" from Lucky—
topics that Pozzo claims were "beyond" his own "common" sensibilities (31). Throughout the play, Pozzo displays his education by allud-
ing to classical divinities such as Atlas, Japetos, and Pan (30, 34).[70] He
also recites soliloquies that evoke Greek and Shakespearean tragedy
but are, in actuality, grotesque abominations of tragic form. Take, for
instance, his "twilight monologue" in Act 1, where he reflects on the
setting sun:

> (*Lyrical*) An hour ago (*prosaic*) roughly (*lyrical*) after having poured
> forth ever since (*he hesitates, prosaic*) say ten o'clock in the morn-
> ing (*lyrical*) tirelessly torrents of red and white light it begins to
> lose its effulgence, to grow pale (*gesture of the two hands lapsing
> by stages*) pale, ever a little paler until (*dramatic pause, ample ges-
> ture of the two hands flung wide apart*) pppfff! finished! it comes
> to rest. But—(*hand raised in admonition*)—but behind this veil of
> gentleness and peace night is charging (*vibrantly*) and will burst

upon us (*snaps his fingers*) pop! like that! (*his inspiration leaves him*) just when we least expect it. (*Silence. Gloomily*) That's how it is on this bitch of an earth. (35)

Immediately after this, Pozzo asks Vladimir and Estragon to rate his performance on a scale of "Good? Fair? Middling? Poor? Positively bad?" (36). Regardless of what we think of his performance, Pozzo draws attention to the fact that he is performing, that he is a "ham" actor looking for applause, trying to give his dictatorship a touch of cultural sophistication. He appears, however, like a vulgar man with an education in the liberal arts. Lucky, it seems, was his only teacher.

Modes of Expectation and Salvation: Vladimir and Estragon's "Messianicity" versus Pozzo and Lucky's "Messianism"

Just as each couple is a mismatched combination of opposites, so both couples oppose each other with their general tendencies. Vladimir and Estragon rarely leave the stage;[71] Pozzo and Lucky make an entrance and an exit in each act. The former pair waits in one place, trapped in the single location, whereas the latter pair moves back and forth, enslaved to the road. This is indicative of two different orientations. Vladimir and Estragon are waiting for something to arrive; Pozzo and Lucky are traveling toward something. However, the "something" that Vladimir and Estragon await and Pozzo and Lucky seek is similar. Both couples desire some type of "salvation," but they employ different methods to get it. Vladimir and Estragon wait passively for a salvation that is mysterious, indeterminate, and uncertain; Pozzo and Lucky aggressively pursue a salvation that is apparent, well defined, and unequivocal. In Derrida's terminology, Vladimir and Estragon tend toward the "messianic," whereas Pozzo and Lucky tend toward "messianism."

First, consider Vladimir and Estragon. It is clear that Godot, whatever he might be, is a messianic figure who is expected to bring some type of deliverance:

VLADIMIR: We'll hang ourselves tomorrow. Unless Godot comes.
ESTRAGON: And if he comes?
VLADIMIR: We'll be saved. (85)

The promise of salvation brought by a superior power exerts a force that neither man can escape. They practice humility toward Godot instead of aggressively pursuing salvation by means of revolutionary actions:

> ESTRAGON: Where do we come in?
> VLADIMIR: Come in?
> ESTRAGON: Take your time.
> VLADIMIR: Come in? On our hands and knees?
> ESTRAGON: As bad as that?
> VLADIMIR: Your worship wishes to assert his prerogatives?
> ESTRAGON: We've no rights any more?
> VLADIMIR: You'd make me laugh, if it wasn't prohibited.
> ESTRAGON: We've lost our rights?
> VLADIMIR: We got rid of them. (18)

Even worse, they cannot hasten Godot's arrival with a definitive action of their own. All they can do is wait in one place and hope to be present when Godot appears. Their passive waiting has gradually become an inescapable habit, rendering them powerless to leave even if they wished. This impotence is expressed at the end of each act:

> VLADIMIR: Well? Shall we go?
> ESTRAGON: Yes, let's go.
>   (*They do not move. Silence.*) (85)[72]

For whatever reason, they are unable to "go." When Estragon asks if they are "tied," Vladimir responds, "Tied to Godot? What an idea! No question of it. For the moment" (20). The "moment," however, never ends. Given this overwhelming inertia and perpetual waiting, Estragon asks an obvious question: "And if he doesn't come?"

> VLADIMIR: We'll come back tomorrow.
> ESTRAGON: And then the day after tomorrow.
> VLADIMIR: Possibly.
> ESTRAGON: And so on.
> VLADIMIR: The point is—
> ESTRAGON: Until he comes.
> VLADIMIR: You're merciless. (13)

This merciless, never-ending expectation has not only caused profound stasis, but also extreme confusion and doubt. The only sure thing about Vladimir and Estragon's situation is that they are waiting. Vladimir says, "In this immense confusion one thing alone is clear. We are waiting for Godot to come— . . . Or for night to fall" (73). Other than this, "nothing is certain" (50).

There is assuredly nothing certain about their appointment with Godot. First, they are not sure if the man for whom they are waiting is actually named Godot:

> ESTRAGON: His name is Godot?
> VLADIMIR: I think so. (20)

Second, both tramps wonder if they are waiting in the right location. According to Vladimir, Godot said to wait "by the tree" (13). This would seem like a definite indicator of place, especially since there is no other vegetation to mark the landscape. However, Estragon wonders whether the tree is actually a "bush," to which Vladimir responds, "What are you insinuating? That we've come to the wrong place?" (13). They cannot determine in either act if they are waiting in the same spot as "yesterday" (13–14, 54, 58–61). Accompanying these confusions about space are doubts about time. Neither Vladimir or Estragon knows what day it is, nor do they know for sure what day Godot said he would arrive:

> ESTRAGON: You're sure it was this evening?
> VLADIMIR: What?
> ESTRAGON: That we were to wait.
> VLADIMIR: He said Saturday. (*Pause*) I think.
> ESTRAGON: You think.
> VLADIMIR: I must have made a note of it.
> ESTRAGON: But what Saturday? And is it Saturday? Is it not rather Sunday? Or Monday? Or Friday?
> VLADIMIR: It's not possible!
> ESTRAGON: Or Thursday?
> VLADIMIR: What'll we do? (14)

Finally, Vladimir and Estragon's confusions are aggravated by an indeterminate sense of what they want from Godot:

VLADIMIR: I'm curious to hear what he has to offer. Then we'll take it
or leave it.
ESTRAGON: What exactly did we ask him for?
VLADIMIR: Were you not there?
ESTRAGON: I can't have been listening.
VLADIMIR: Oh . . . nothing very definite.
ESTRAGON: A kind of prayer.
VLADIMIR: Precisely.
ESTRAGON: A vague supplication.
VLADIMIR: Exactly. (17)

It is unclear what Godot promises to bring. According to Estragon, Godot
"couldn't promise anything," and Vladimir claims that he "didn't say for
sure he'd come" (17, 13).

Everything about Godot and the situation is uncertain. Nevertheless, Godot is an indeterminate messiah who Vladimir says will "save"
them if he arrives. In this sense, Vladimir and Estragon's situation bears
an uncanny resemblance to Derrida's universal messianic structure. Derrida describes the "messianic" as "an experience open to the absolute future of what is coming, that is to say, a necessarily indeterminate, abstract,
desert-like experience that is confided, exposed, given up to its waiting
for the other and for the event."[73] Similarly, Vladimir and Estragon are exposed to the elements as they await a future event in a desertlike environment where nothing is certain. They have given up everything for
the arrival of someone who is always coming, someone indeterminate,
whose identity and modes are incomprehensible and who offers nothing definite except a vague promise of salvation.

In contrast to Vladimir's and Estragon's "messianic" condition, Pozzo
and Lucky try to actualize their own salvation through definite modes.
They do not have the patience for indeterminate messianic waiting; rather,
they seek absolute assurances in the present through their own revolutionary messianism. Lucky pursues a masochistic solution: he makes
Pozzo his immanent messiah and achieves an ironic salvation by damn-
ing himself to Pozzo's abuse. Like Vladimir and Estragon, Lucky gives
away his "rights" and "ties" himself to a savior, but he is literally tied to
a tangible tyrant instead of metaphorically attached to an absent messiah. By allowing himself to be dominated by an immediate force, Lucky

achieves a relative degree of existential security. He depends on Pozzo for direction—to tell him where to go and what to do. Unlike Vladimir and Estragon, who are gripped by painful uncertainty and excruciating expectation, Lucky knows what is expected of him and where he stands. He has, for the most part, no further hopes; this is why he is "lucky." Beckett himself once observed, "I suppose he is Lucky to have no more expectations."[74]

Yet Lucky's subservience is accompanied by an aggressive effort to achieve omniscience. Just as he desires a tyrant to give him certain commands, so he also wants knowledge that, in his words, is "beyond all doubt."[75] A careful look at Lucky's Think reveals that underneath its ostensible chaos is an organized structure. Lucky is trying to compose an encyclopedic account of everything, a total system of thought that will explain God, humanity, and the cosmos. The Think is divided into three parts: the first section deals with theology, the second with anthropology, and the third with nature. The Think ends with a recapitulation of the themes of the earlier parts.[76] But despite the encyclopedic breadth of the Think, Lucky does not achieve absolute knowledge. He repeats the phrase "for reasons unknown" more times than "beyond all doubt."[77]

Lucky deals with the present state of enlightened humanism in the second part of his Think. He claims to base his anthropological observations on the "labours left unfinished" by the "Acacacacademy of Anthropopopometry." The term "anthropometry" designates the science that measures the dimensions of humanity, in particular the human head (39). Given that Lucky stutters on the words *caca* and *popo*—childish French words for excrement and chamberpot[78]—it suggests that the stature of man has diminished to the level of waste. This is borne out by the "facts" Lucky states about the human condition. He deals with the present condition of the human body under the title "physical culture." He states "that man ... in spite of the strides of alimentation and defecation wastes and pines wastes and pines ... shrink[s] and dwindle[s] in spite of the tennis" (39–40). Regardless of the discovery of antibiotics ("penicilline and succedanea"), improvements in nutrition ("alimentation"), advancements in bowel regularity ("defecation"), and increased participation in "sports" ("tennis football running cycling swimming flying floating riding gliding"), humans continue to suffer and die (39). Science and exercise have been unable to realize bodily immortality.

Lucky also reports an astonishing diminution in humanity's intellectual capacities over the past two centuries:

> for reasons unknown but time will tell to shrink and dwindle I resume Fulham Clapham in a word the dead loss per caput since the death of Bishop Berkeley being to the tune of one inch four ounce per caput approximately by and large more or less to the nearest decimal good measure round figures (40)

Here, Lucky, as an anthropometrist, is concerned with the size of the human head, or "caput." According to Lucky's sources, heads have shrunk by approximately one inch, four ounces since the death of the English immaterialist George Berkeley (1685–1753). In the French version of *Godot,* Lucky refers to the French Enlightenment thinker François Voltaire (1694–1778).[79] By referring to Voltaire, Lucky suggests that the ability to reason and attain clear knowledge has declined since the Enlightenment, due to the shrinkage of the human mind. Berkeley, though a contemporary of Voltaire's, is not really an Enlightenment figure. Unlike his more empirically minded contemporaries, who sought knowledge of the outside world through observation, experiment, and induction, Berkeley, like the characters in *Godot,* could not establish correspondence between human mental states and an external world. He denied the commonsense assumption that there is an external world that we perceive through our senses and understand with our minds. Instead, he claimed that reality is fundamentally mental in nature; that is, our sensations and thoughts do not refer to an external world but are rather subjective mental states without an external referent. Berkeley did argue that we are real as mental subjects, and we could be certain of ourselves as perceiving entities, even if all our perceptions are subjective. As Estragon says, "We always find something . . . to give us the impression we exist" (62). In Berkeley's mind, we are essentially minds, which accounts for Lucky's reference to the big heads of Berkeley's day. Furthermore, Berkeley argued that in order *to* perceive we must *be* perceived, and this necessarily infers the existence of an infinite mind, or God.[80] It is from our own perception that Berkeley claimed we could be sure of God's actuality, for without his perception there would be no perception at all.[81] Lucky suggests, however, that trust in God and mental perception has deteriorated since Berkeley's death. The inability of the characters in *Godot* to express any certainty about time, place, people, or things is suggestive of a post-Enlightenment senility. Instead of gaining enlightened knowledge of the world, human beings have descended into a nightmarish version of Berkeley's subjective idealism, where they cannot communicate with each other or understand their experiences.

Vladimir and Estragon, like Lucky, are conscious of this end of "thinking." As Vladimir says, "We're in no danger of thinking any more" (57), but there is, in fact, something worse than not being able to think:

> VLADIMIR: What is terrible is to *have* thought.
> ESTRAGON: But did that ever happen to us?
> VLADIMIR: (*Looks out*) Where are all these corpses from?
> ESTRAGON: (*Looks out*) These skeletons.
> VLADIMIR: Tell me that.
> ESTRAGON: True.
> VLADIMIR: We must have thought a little.
> ESTRAGON: At the very beginning.
> VLADIMIR: A charnel house! A charnel house! (57, italics in original)

What is "terrible" is to be unable to think after the extraordinary achievements in modern thinking. All the characters exist in the aftermath of the Enlightenment and the absolute idealism of the eighteenth and nineteenth centuries. The encyclopedias and systems that promised either clarity or absolute knowledge have experientially outlived themselves; they are no longer persuasive. Though Estragon doubts that there ever really was "thought" in the first place, Vladimir directs him to the corpses proving that thinking really happened once upon a time. The encyclopedias and absolute ideas have produced corpses in both the intellectual and political realms; they have laid waste to both genuine reason and human beings. In the post-Enlightenment world, Vladimir and Estragon stare at the charnel house of ideas and realize that the promise of modern thought is both unfulfilled and impossible.

Nevertheless, these ideas—even as corpses—exert a certain power. Vladimir exclaims, "You can't help looking" (57). The characters gaze in horror at Lucky's Think—the rotting corpse of modern encyclopedic thought—and gape at the present state of academia, bogged down by pessimism, hypersophistication, pedantry, and ignorance. Though Lucky aspires to achieve Hegelian absoluteness, his all-encompassing Think actually incarnates indeterminacy and incompleteness. The final word of Lucky's Think is "unfinished," which not only stands in opposition to Christ's definitive statement "It is finished"[82] but also reveals that his intellectual labors are left undone (40, 39). Lucky's failed theoretical endeavor makes it clear that a historical moment has passed. Modern thought, for all its remarkable accomplishments, was unable to deliver the beatitude of absolute wisdom. Lucky now exists on the other side of this failure—a mad encyclopedist who has surrendered himself to an oppressive tyrant. His efforts culminate in mute ignorance rather than articulated omniscience. By Act 2, Lucky has gone "dumb"; indeed, he "can't even groan" (81).

Lucky's vain efforts to be all-knowing are complemented by Pozzo's futile attempts to be all-powerful. Whereas Lucky seeks salvation through omniscient masochism, Pozzo looks for deliverance through omnipotent sadism. In this way, Pozzo tries to rise above common human afflictions. Pozzo acknowledges, however, that there are limits to his domination. For example, he thinks it is a "disgrace" that the "road is free to all" (22), which suggests that he is not in complete control of the path he is on. Pozzo's impotence becomes increasingly evident as the play progresses. Of all the characters in *Godot,* Pozzo is the one who deteriorates the most. Over the course of Act 1 we see him lose some of his belongings, including his pipe and his watch (33, 42). In Act 2, all his possessions are gone. Bags that once contained food and drink are now filled with sand (80). Most devastating of all, Pozzo loses his eyesight and depends on Lucky to be his seeing-eye dog. Lucky's guidance is not particularly helpful. When Pozzo enters in Act 2, he collapses on top of Lucky and can only get up, much later in the act, with the assistance of Vladimir and Estragon. The character who remains standing for most of Act 1 lies helplessly on the ground for most of Act 2.

That Pozzo is constantly traveling along a road reveals he is not entirely satisfied with his present location. Despite the immediacy of his sadistic solution, he is strongly oriented toward the future, much like Vladimir and Estragon. Even Lucky, who has no real expectations, fears that something definitive might lie ahead, for he constantly repeats the phrase "time will tell" (39–40).[83] The relation between Pozzo and Lucky is a dim reflection of Hegel's master/slave dialectic in the *Phenomenology of Spirit,* in which the historical interaction of masters and slaves is interpreted as a necessary stage on the path toward freedom and absolute knowledge. Pozzo and Lucky, however, are proceeding toward greater enslavement and ignorance, even while they think they are moving toward a glorious consummation.

In Act 1, Pozzo forces Lucky to travel onward toward a "fair" that lies farther down the road (30). It is at this fair where Pozzo hopes to sell Lucky. In Beckett's French version of *Godot,* Pozzo refers to this fair as the "marché de Saint-Sauveur" (market of the Holy Savior).[84] Once again, the future is understood to offer some sort of salvation. Pozzo links this salvation with a definitive destination in the future and with the sale of his accursed companion. He can no longer stand the company of Lucky who "carries like a pig" (30). But when Pozzo returns with Lucky in Act 2 from the direction of the market, it is clear that he was unable to find a buyer.[85] The salvation that Pozzo was expecting down the road was not found. Lucky, on the other hand, got his wish; he wants his present enslavement to be his immanent *eschaton.*

Pozzo's progressive movement "onward" in Act 1 is inextricably linked to his concern about time. For Pozzo, the hands on the clock mark the developmental stages on the way to fulfillment. He does not want to consider Didi and Gogo's situation, in which progressive time has ceased and everything is trapped in an eternally recurring day. Upon hearing Vladimir's claim that "Time has stopped," Pozzo vehemently replies, "Don't you believe it, sir, don't you believe it. Whatever you like, but not that" (42). For Pozzo, knowing the time is an attribute of power. Throughout Act 1, he frequently checks his watch and asks for the time of day. The watch allows Pozzo to stay on his "schedule" as he marches "on" toward the market of salvation (34). Nevertheless, the consummation at the end of the road is constantly deferred; it acts as a regulative ideal that Pozzo moves toward incessantly. Pozzo does not actually desire the end of time; on the contrary, he desires time itself—time understood as the perpetual progress toward fulfillment. He wants to move closer to salvation, but he also dreads the *eschaton,* for that would mean the end of his habitual march "onward." This ambivalence regarding the future reveals a lingering "messianic" spirit in Pozzo's absolute "messianism." He wants linear time to continue forever without ever arriving at the timeless messianic age.

But when Pozzo loses his watch in Act 1, it is clear that time is stopping for him too. By the second act, the blind Pozzo has not only lost his perception of space but also his temporal sensibilities. Ironically, his entrance in Act 2 causes Vladimir to exclaim, "Time flows again already" (70). Pozzo is forced to correct Vladimir: "The blind have no notion of time. The things of time are hidden from them too." This contradicts the classic motif of blind seers who can, in Estragon's words, "see into the future" (78). Pozzo once thought he saw the future clearly and knew the end he was moving toward; now, he has no destination:

VLADIMIR: Where do you go from here?
POZZO: No concern of mine.
VLADIMIR: How changed you are. (80)

All visions of a future goal have been lost, along with any sense of progressive time moving toward a definitive end. Consequently, Pozzo has no patience for questions dealing with time (see 81). But notwithstanding Pozzo losing his sense of time and direction, he continues to march back and forth along the road with Lucky without ever arriving at anything. He cannot break his old habit.

Pozzo and Lucky's sadomasochistic messianism is clearly less desirable than Vladimir and Estragon's messianic waiting. At one point, Vladimir and Estragon try to "play at" being Pozzo and Lucky, but they cannot sustain it; Estragon leaves the stage in disgust (66). This suggests they are better off waiting for the arrival of a transcendent savior rather than actively seizing an immanent salvation through vehement aggression and fanatical subservience. Vladimir and Estragon's approach allows them to cultivate a relative degree of sanity and kindness in their dealings with each other. Consequently, they do not suffer as much, nor do they deteriorate as quickly, as Pozzo and Lucky.

Since Didi's and Gogo's lives are comparatively superior, it is tempting to argue that their messianic waiting is essential for goodness. Beckett, however, consistently undermines any inclination to celebrate or advocate their condition. Like Pozzo and Lucky, Vladimir and Estragon are trapped in habits from which they cannot escape. This ultimately devastates their ability to think and act in meaningful ways. Messianic expectation, Vladimir suggests, may initially appear to be a "reasonable" response to suffering and, for a period, might actually "beguile" the pain of existence. But as this expectation becomes perpetual and habitual, it becomes less persuasive, and thereby aggravates the very suffering it sought to ameliorate (see 73).

Throughout the play, Vladimir and Estragon dispute three possible responses to their suffering: they can leave, commit suicide, or stay put. The first two choices, if possible, might liberate them from their messianic habit. To leave would mean choosing to live without the expectation of Godot, but such a choice entails serious risks that neither character wants to take. Suicide, on the other hand, might seem a surer option, but they lack the resolution and the resources to kill themselves. At two points in the play they consider hanging themselves from the tree using Estragon's belt (16–17, 84–85). Both attempts are aborted when they realize that neither the branches on the tree nor the belt on Estragon's waist is strong enough to support their weight. They also cannot jump off the Eiffel Tower because, according to Vladimir, they would not be let up (10). But even if they could kill themselves, it would not solve their predicament. In Act 2, Vladimir and Estragon hear the "voices" of the "dead," who are as unfulfilled and restless as the living:

> VLADIMIR: To be dead is not enough for them.
> ESTRAGON: It is not sufficient. (56).

Death, it seems, cannot offer eternal peace, not even in the form of extinction or loss of consciousness. Like Shakespeare's Hamlet, it is the dread of something after death—something even worse than life—that makes Vladimir and Estragon bear their present ills rather than fly to others that they do not know.[86] Given the dangers involved with either leaving or committing suicide, Vladimir and Estragon decide to stay where they are, in a state of indecision and inactivity. Estragon says, "Don't let's do anything. It's safer" (17).

Instead of doing something, they look for diversions to alleviate their boredom. Sometimes they let themselves be entertained by the antics of Pozzo and Lucky.[87] At other times they amuse themselves with comic physical activity, as when they "do the tree," dance a waltz, or repeatedly exchange three hats between their two heads (70, 69, 65). They also pass the time with verbal squabbles, which are not so much substantive debates as rhetorical games. Estragon says at various points: "That's the idea, let's contradict one another," "let's ask each other questions," "let's abuse each other," seemingly aware that they are only clowning with their banter (57, 68). This physical and verbal comedy resembles the routines of Victorian music hall clowns and Hollywood tramps such as Charlie Chaplin, Buster Keaton, Laurel and Hardy, and the Marx Brothers. Beckett employs these comic elements not simply for a laugh but to emphasize the impotence and inactivity of those caught up in messianic expectation.

Despite Didi's and Gogo's constant bickering, their relationship is marked by occasional moments of tenderness. They embrace each other at two points in the play (21, 69). Furthermore, Vladimir offers Estragon food (19, 61), helps him with his boots (62–63), sings him to sleep (63), gives him his own coat (63), and comforts him after a nightmare (64). Undoubtedly, Vladimir and Estragon treat each other better than Pozzo and Lucky, but given the degree of cruelty and suffering between the latter, this is not necessarily a noteworthy achievement. Ceaseless waiting does not make Vladimir and Estragon stand out as paragons of excellence:

> VLADIMIR: . . . We are not saints, but we have kept our appointment. How many people can boast as much?
> ESTRAGON: Billions. (73)

Their faith in Godot is not exceptional. And if they are not justified by faith, they are certainly not redeemed by works. Though they try to alleviate suffering on a few occasions, there are many more when they either ignore the pain of others or intentionally cause harm. In his notebook for the 1975 Schiller-Theatre production of *Godot*, Beckett counts twenty-one moments in the play when Vladimir and Estragon are addressed by pleas for help. Of these twenty-one pleas, only four are answered with concrete gestures of assistance.[88]

For the most part, Vladimir and Estragon seem either indifferent to suffering or openly malicious. When the blind Pozzo screams for help on the ground, Vladimir and Estragon contemplate how they can take advantage of the situation and perhaps gain a "tangible return" (72). Estragon proposes that they give Pozzo a "good beating" and a "kick . . . in the crotch" (72, 76). Vladimir merely recognizes an abstract moral imperative in Pozzo's pleas rather than a direct personal appeal: "To all mankind they were addressed, those cries for help still ringing in our ears" (73). Vladimir does not offer Pozzo concrete assistance until he is offered money (74, 77). Indeed, before helping Pozzo, Vladimir strikes him, calling him a "bastard" and a "crablouse" (76). Similarly, Estragon kicks Lucky, but he ironically hurts himself in the attack (79).

Vladimir and Estragon also exhibit cruelty and indifference toward each other. At the start of the play, when Estragon says that his left foot is "swelling visibly," Vladimir is unaffected (11). At the end of the play, Vladimir's indifference remains. While Estragon howls in agony over his feet ("Ow! Ow! . . . My feet! Help me!"), Vladimir wonders, "Was I sleeping, while the others suffered?" (82). This is yet another instance of Vladimir's tendency to theorize about ethics while others request his immediate assistance. Estragon is likewise unsympathetic to Vladimir, deliberately aggravating Vladimir's kidney and prostate troubles by getting him to laugh (15). Estragon is also amused by Vladimir's painful attempts to urinate (15, 33).

It is not that Vladimir and Estragon have no power to help others or that their assistance is completely ineffective. The four times in the play that they respond to pleas of help make a difference, however slight. In Act 1, they help Lucky to his feet (41), and in Act 2, they do the same for Pozzo (77)—though the assistance in each case is fairly clumsy. Estragon also helps Pozzo sit in Act 1 (34). And the one time that Vladimir helps Estragon with his boots is the only time in the play that Estragon claims his condition is not entirely miserable. He says to Vladimir, "We don't manage too badly, eh Didi, between the two of us?" (62). Estragon even says that his boots fit better after this small bit of assistance—not perfectly, but good enough. These are small gestures of help, not eschatological transformations. They lead to momentary improvements, which is more than can be said of any consequence of waiting for Godot. However, the expectation of eschatological fulfillment has made such limited gestures seem unworthy.

Vladimir and Estragon suffer from a spiritual illness that does not destroy them as quickly as Pozzo and Lucky but that is a slower variety of the same disease. The expectation of something absolutely definitive, something promising salvation, has stripped all actions and experiences of their significance. The only significance is found in those things that indicate Godot's arrival. Such significations, however, are now increasingly difficult to find. The perpetual expectation of salvation, combined with the absence of definite signs indicating the savior, has made the situation unbearable.

The Saved and the Damned

The misery of the situation is aggravated by another factor. Vladimir and Estragon do not simply await salvation; their expectation of Godot is also intricately connected to the fear of judgment. They perceive Godot's arrival as a definitive end, bringing either reward or punishment, justification or denial, inclusion or exclusion, election or rejection, salvation or damnation.[89]

It is well known that Beckett had a lifelong interest in Dante's depictions of the final judgment in the *Divine Comedy*.[90] However, it is not Dante whom Beckett identifies as the source of the judgment motif in *Godot*. It is, rather, a mysterious "sentence" by Saint Augustine. When asked by Harold Hobson about the theme of salvation and damnation in *Godot*, Beckett responded:

> I am interested in the shape of ideas, even if I do not believe in them. There is a wonderful sentence in Augustine. I wish I could remember the Latin. It is even finer in Latin than in English. "Do not despair; one of the thieves was saved. Do not presume; one of the thieves was damned." That sentence has a wonderful shape. It is the shape that matters.[91]

The shape of Augustine's sentence serves as Beckett's model for the various dualities and antitheticals that I have examined in the play. It also reveals the antagonism and exclusivity within the very structure of the Christian apocalyptic promise. It signifies an absolute selection, not universal hospitality. In expectation of the *eschaton,* humans must live in the uncertainty of the final selection, in which hope is immediately qualified by fear. This, for Augustine, is the true shape of messianic experience in the *saeculum senescens,* and it is this shape that Beckett presents to us in *Godot*. In contrast to Augustine, however, Beckett presents it in all its late modern horror. The antithetical shape of apocalyptic expectation is, for Beckett, the "form that accommodates the mess," established by the fact the Beckett allows the shape to permeate almost everything in the play. He once explained, "One of Estragon's feet is blessed and the other is damned. The boot won't go on the foot that is damned, and it will go on the foot that is not. It is like the two thieves on the cross."[92] Thus when the curtain rises Estragon is found struggling with the boot of his damned left foot. Everything, no matter how mundane, is shaped by, and thereby made to suffer by, the final eschatological selection.

Each pair of characters in *Godot* is a dim reflection of the two thieves.[93] At first it seems that Vladimir and Pozzo are "saved" because they suffer a little less than their respective companions.[94] But as the play progresses, Vladimir and Pozzo's status as "saved" is undermined. By Act 2, the formerly blessed Pozzo is in misery, and the rope between him and Lucky is "much shorter" than in Act 1, suggesting that they have become more alike (70). Pozzo now responds to Estragon's calls of both "Abel" and "Cain": either name is appropriate since he is a man who has been both blessed and cursed by God. In this way, he is, in Estragon's words, "all humanity" (76). Furthermore, Vladimir, who is initially more optimistic than his accursed partner, becomes more despondent as the play progresses. Toward the end he says, "I can't go on" (82), echoing Estragon, who twice says, "I can't go on like this" (61, 85). Clearly, the differences between Vladimir and Estragon fade through time, making it difficult to determine which of them is more analogous to the saved thief.

The fear of Final Judgment, and the uncertainty regarding who is saved and who is damned, is evoked by Lucky at the very start of his Think. Lucky says:

> Given the existence as uttered forth in the public works of Puncher and Wattman of a personal God quaquaquaqua with white beard quaquaquaqua outside time without extension who from the heights of divine apathia divine athambia divine aphasia loves us dearly with some exceptions for reasons unknown but time will tell and suffers like the divine Miranda with those who for reasons unknown but time will tell are plunged in torment plunged in fire. (39)[95]

Lucky here describes a personal God who transcends space and time but who supposedly loves humanity and suffers with them. Lucky claims, however, that God is actually experienced differently; instead of divine benevolence, concern, and presence, humans experience God's insensitivity to suffering ("apathia"), imperturbability ("athambia"), and incommunicability ("aphasia"). Even if God were to make himself fully present to us, Lucky points out, there are—for "reasons unknown"—"exceptions" to his universal love. These exceptions will be "plunged in torment." In the meantime, humans are trapped within messianic uncertainty. Only "time will tell" which individuals are excluded from divine affection.

It is out of concern for the "exceptions" that Vladimir considers the story of the two thieves. At the beginning of the play, Vladimir provides a mangled rendition of Augustine's sentence:

> VLADIMIR: Our Saviour. Two thieves. One is supposed to have been saved and the other . . . (*he searches for the contrary of saved*) . . . damned.
> ESTRAGON: Saved from what?
> VLADIMIR: Hell. (12)[96]

Vladimir is comforted by the Gospel of Luke, which reports that one of the two thieves was delivered with Christ into paradise.[97] For Vladimir, the fifty-fifty chance of salvation suggested by Luke is "a reasonable percentage" (11). However, when Vladimir realizes that Luke's gospel is the only one in the New Testament to speak of a thief being saved, he begins to despair:

> how is it that of the four Evangelists, only one speaks of a thief being saved. The four of them were there—or thereabouts—and only one speaks of a thief being saved. . . . One out of four. Of the other three two don't mention any thieves at all and the third says that both of them abused him. (12)

In fact, things are worse than Vladimir claims: there are actually *two* gospel accounts that claim both thieves chided Jesus.[98] If one considers the Gospels as a whole, the odds of salvation are worse than fifty-fifty, for if both thieves abused Jesus, then, presumably, "the two of them must have been damned" (12). That would mean half the Gospels claim that both thieves were damned. Nevertheless, Vladimir's main argument is correct:

only one gospel speaks of a thief being saved. Vladimir fears that any comfort derived from this account in Luke is unwarranted:

> VLADIMIR: But one of the four says that one of the two was saved.
> ESTRAGON: Well? They don't agree, and that's all there is to it.
> VLADIMIR: But all four were there. And only one speaks of a thief being saved. Why believe him rather than the others?
> ESTRAGON: Who believes him?
> VLADIMIR: Everybody. It's the only version they know.
> ESTRAGON: People are bloody ignorant apes. (12)

Though Vladimir is initially anxious about the fifty-fifty chance of salvation, he becomes even more fearful of the possibility that neither thief was saved—a possibility that gets lost in the popularity of Luke's account. Once again, nothing is certain: the more Vladimir considers the story of the thieves, the more the "saved thief" becomes indistinguishable from his accursed partner. New Testament symbols cannot provide the certainty that Vladimir desires.

The motif of salvation and damnation evoked in Lucky's Think and in Vladimir's speculations about the Gospels is directly applicable to Vladimir's and Estragon's situation. Like Lucky's "God," who exists "outside time without extension" and who will judge all human beings, Vladimir and Estragon wait for a so-called Godot who never manifests himself in the space or time of the play and yet is expected to bring some type of judgment. The fear of judgment is linked to Godot's first coming. Vladimir and Estragon have vague memories of meeting Godot in the past, though the details are sketchy. The two tramps think they approached Godot with a "kind of prayer" and "vague supplication," which Godot said he would have to think over before "taking a decision" (18–19). They now wait for Godot's second coming in order to find out what that decision is. Regardless of what Godot decides, his judgment is expected to obliterate all the uncertainties of the present:

> VLADIMIR: Let's wait and see what he says.
> ESTRAGON: Who?
> VLADIMIR: Godot.
> ESTRAGON: Ah yes!
> VLADIMIR: Let's wait till we know exactly how we stand. (17)

There is an ominous tone to Vladimir's words, for the two tramps may be in bad standing with Godot. Nevertheless, Vladimir most often associates Godot with some type of salvation.

Vladimir understands salvation to be hospitality. He presumes that Godot will offer them everything that they currently lack, specifically, rest, comfort, and food. He says to Estragon, "Perhaps we'll sleep tonight in his loft. All snug and dry, our bellies full, in the hay. That's worth waiting for. No?" (19).[99] Given this expected hospitality, Vladimir fixates on the possibility that Godot is a savior, like those who concentrate exclusively on the saved thief in Luke's gospel. When Vladimir mistakenly thinks he hears Godot approaching in Act 2, he exclaims, "It's Godot! We're saved!" (67). But Estragon, in the same passage, shouts, "I'm accursed! . . . I'm in hell!" (66–67). An earlier suspected approach of Godot in Act 1 also gives Estragon "a fright" and even causes Vladimir to cower in fear (18). Godot evokes strong feelings of terror, but to stop waiting for him is even more fearful. When Estragon asks what would happen if they stopped waiting, Vladimir says, "He'd punish us" (84).

Vladimir hopes that he and Estragon will eventually sleep in Godot's loft with full bellies in the hay. The Boy who comes with a message from Godot at the end of Act 1 verifies some of Vladimir's expectations: he claims that he is fed by Godot and that he is allowed to sleep on a bed of "hay" in "the loft" (47–48). When pressed, the Boy confirms that Godot is "good" to him (47). This appears to validate Vladimir's expectation of complete hospitality: Godot will transform sleeplessness, pain, and hunger into rest, comfort, and satiation. But Godot's hospitality is limited. The Boy also says he has a "sick" brother who is "beaten" by Godot (83, 47). Here Beckett introduces a third pair of characters that, once again, reflects the two thieves: a healthy brother who is blessed by Godot and a sickly brother who is cursed. Each boy, it would appear, knows where he "stands."

The distinction between the blessed brother and the accursed brother begins to blur if we look carefully at everything the Boy tells Vladimir. The Boy reports that he looks after the "goats" at Godot's estate, whereas his brother looks after the "sheep" (47). There are at least two biblical allusions in this information. The first is to Genesis: the story of the two brothers, Cain and Abel, one who is cursed by God and the other who is blessed. In Genesis 4, Abel is a keeper of sheep whose animal sacrifice is accepted by God. Cain's fruit offering, on the other hand, is rejected by God for unknown reasons.[100] In *Godot,* by contrast, it is the sheep keeper who is rejected by his master. Beckett deliberately turns the image of the blessed "sheep" into an accursed symbol. His reversal is even more evident if we consider a passage from the New Testament. In Matthew 25:31–33, it is foretold that the "Son of Man" will "separate" the "sheep" from the "goats" when he comes to judge humanity.[101] The "goats," we are told, will be placed on God's left side and consigned to "eternal fire," whereas the "sheep" will be placed on the right and "blessed" with the heavenly "kingdom."[102] In *Godot,* this symbolism, once again, is reversed: the boy associated with the goats is rewarded, whereas the boy tending the sheep is beaten.[103]

Beckett deliberately alludes to traditional biblical symbols of blessings and curses in order to reverse their significance. Once again, the saved blurs into the damned. We discover that there is no certainty that Godot can offer any form of hospitality, even to those he prefers. The "saved" goat keeper testifies to this when he responds to Vladimir's inquiries:

> VLADIMIR: And why doesn't [Godot] beat you?
> BOY: I don't know, sir.
> VLADIMIR: He must be fond of you.
> BOY: I don't know, sir.
>   (*Silence*)
> VLADIMIR: Does he give you enough to eat?
>   (*The* BOY *hesitates*)
>   Does he feed you well?
> BOY: Fairly well, sir.
> VLADIMIR: You're not unhappy?
>   (*The* BOY *hesitates*)
>   Do you hear me?
> BOY: Yes sir.
> VLADIMIR: Well?
> BOY: I don't know, sir.
> VLADIMIR: You don't know if you're unhappy or not?
> BOY: No, sir.
> VLADIMIR: You're as bad as myself. (47–48)

The boy who is treated relatively well by Godot cannot confirm whether his master is "fond" of him, or if so, why. Regardless of which boy is actually preferred by Godot, it is clear that the life of the "saved" goat keeper is not free of suffering. For instance, the Boy admits that Godot feeds him "fairly well" but not very well (47). This does not bode well for Vladimir, who expects to receive a "full" stomach if Godot arrives (19). Even worse, the "saved" Boy cannot affirm whether he is happy or unhappy, causing Vladimir to exclaim, "You're as bad as myself." With this exclamation, Vladimir unintentionally implies that his own condition will not be improved if Godot arrives.

Godot's two boys are almost indistinguishable from Didi and Gogo. Like Vladimir, who ponders whether he is happy (47), the goat boy is uncertain about his own happiness (53–54), and like Estragon, who is abused every night by a group of men, the sheep boy is frequently beaten. Furthermore, if Didi and Gogo do not know where they "stand" with Godot, the same is true of the "saved" Boy, who appears at the end of each act. Indeed, it might not be the same boy who arrives in Act 1 and Act 2. In both acts, the "saved" Boy denies that it was he who came "yesterday" to deliver the message from Godot (46–47, 82). If it was not the "saved" Boy who came the day before, then it was his "damned" brother. Again, it is impossible to distinguish the saved from the damned, even when considering those who come from Godot's residence.

The information Vladimir receives from the Boy also reveals that there are two Godots. This is not surprising, given the dominance of pairs in the play. There is, first, the *Godot of faith,* the Godot whom Vladimir and Estragon *expect.* This Godot is thought to be extremely hospitable, but only to some. Vladimir generally lives in hope of such hospitality, whereas Estragon fears that he will be excluded from it. Nevertheless, if Vladimir and Estragon do not receive the hospitality they desire—or even if only one of them does—they will at least know where they stand with the Godot of faith, the Godot who is always coming, the Godot who inspires both hope and fear in the present. However, there is also the *real Godot,* the "historical" Godot, the Godot who is reported to us by the Boy. The real Godot cannot provide the certain judgment that Vladimir and Estragon expect, nor can he offer much hospitality, even to those whom he supposedly prefers. Consequently, the real Godot cannot bring a definitive end to the situation that presently plagues Vladimir and Estragon.

On the contrary, it seems that his arrival will only exacerbate the problems that Didi and Gogo already have.[104]

If the real Godot were to come, he would be like Pozzo. Pozzo exhibits a power over people and things that is similar to what we hear about Godot. Pozzo claims to have a "manor" full of slaves (42, 30), and given his treatment of Lucky we can see that, like Godot, he beats at least one of them. Since Pozzo is so noticeably similar, Vladimir and Estragon are confused about Pozzo's true identity. In both acts, the two tramps always mistake the impending approach of Pozzo for Godot (18–19, 66–68). At one point, Vladimir thinks he hears Godot "shout . . . at his horse," but what he hears is Pozzo shouting at Lucky (19).[105] The resemblance between what Gogo and Didi *expect* and what Pozzo and Lucky *are* is striking. The resemblance is so strong that Estragon wonders if Pozzo actually is Godot.[106] When Pozzo pronounces his own name, Estragon thinks he hears him say "Godot" (21). Despite Vladimir's assurances that Pozzo is most definitely not Godot, he is not entirely convinced:

> ESTRAGON: . . . Are you sure it wasn't him?
> VLADIMIR: Who?
> ESTRAGON: Godot.
> VLADIMIR: But who?
> ESTRAGON: Pozzo?
> VLADIMIR: Not at all! (*Less sure*) Not at all! (*Still less sure*) Not at all! (81)

Although Pozzo is like the man Vladimir and Estragon expect, he cannot offer them any definitive resolution or liberation. Initially, Pozzo and Lucky seem to embody lives of greater definition: they know exactly where they stand, however terrifying it may be. In Act 2, however, Pozzo and Lucky become less and less distinguishable from one another, much like Godot's two boys. Their condition looks remarkably similar to the uncertainty and suffering that the "real" Godot has to offer.

Perhaps more fearful than the "real" Godot is the Godot of "faith," the Godot who would tell Vladimir and Estragon exactly where they stand, the bringer of the decisive selection. Such a resolution might seem desirable to Vladimir at times, but anything that approaches this goal in the real world is horrific. With Pozzo and Lucky in Act 1, we see an approximation of what such a final selection would be like. They go the furthest toward realizing the eschatological promise of a final twofold division, a categorical and unchanging distinction between the saved and the damned. The "decision" that Vladimir and Estragon expect from Godot would result in a perfected version of what Pozzo and Lucky already experience: a complete separation between the blessed and the cursed, the flowers and the weeds, the pure and the impure. It would be terrifying to behold. Vladimir and Estragon thus wait for and desire something that is far more horrific than the bleak lives they live in the present.

Enough?

> But is it enough, that's what tortures me, is it enough?
> *Pozzo, in Act 1 (36)*

Beckett forces us to consider if any good can occur in the present if human life is structured by an illusory messianic promise of something that is always to come but which is likely to be undesirable even if it were to arrive. Unlike Derrida, Beckett does not simply link evil to specific religious or ideological messianisms. While it might be true that paradoxical messianic faith is preferable to the abuses of dogmatic messianisms, Beckett's criticism is radical: everything in *Godot* is corrupted by eschatological expectation, and thus any reconstituted Augustinianism, including Derrida's understanding of messianicity, is ultimately part of the same problem.

This disagreement between Beckett and Derrida results from a deeper disagreement concerning the nature of the messianic promise itself. In Derrida's heretical version of the messianic promise, everyone is saved. For Derrida, the messianic is characterized by the promise of an "absolute hospitality" offered to everyone. Yet even Derrida dreads the fulfillment of this end. He acknowledges that the perfect realization of hospitality—a complete apocatastasis—would be catastrophic; he is horrified of the very thing he desires. Beckett does not celebrate such "paradoxical" faith. For him, the dread that accompanies eschatological longing is an indication that we yearn for something undesirable. Traditionally, fear of the *eschaton* was symbolized by images of damnation. Beckett is haunted by the prevalence of damnation in the understandings of the eschatological traditions. For Beckett, the messianic is not, and never has been, structured by the promise of an "absolute hospitality"; on the contrary, there are almost always limits or "exceptions." Specific eschatological messianisms—be they apocalyptic, Gnostic, or secular—define themselves by how they define those who will be excluded from the final hospitality. This suggests that damnation is an essential component of the general messianic promise, not just a feature of specific messianisms. All will receive "justice," but only some will get hospitality. Beckett's "messianic," like Augustine's, is rooted in the expectation of a final twofold selection.[107]

Even if the messianic promise were to be reconstituted into a prophetic vision of universal salvation, it would still not cure what ails the characters in the play. *Godot* suggests that when we root our experience in the expectation of the impossible, even as a regulative ideal approached asymptotically, we desert the present. The perpetually absent *eschaton*, as Derrida points out, leads to a "desertification" of the world; we become trapped in a de-divinized wasteland, an "arid soil" where "the living figures of all the messiahs, whether they [are] announced, recognized, or still awaited," grow and pass away.[108] Beckett finds evil in the perpetual rise and fall of specific messiahs in a vast messianic desert. He suggests that our continued acceptance of the messianic promise, in any personal, political, or religious form, is what gives the modern experience of absurdity its uniquely catastrophic character. Every messianic expectation has been tried. The messianic has made us sick, distorting our perceptions of the present and causing us to desire an imaginary, and ultimately horrific, future.

The link between present sickness and messianic longing is established early in the play. Estragon observes that Vladimir always waits until "the last moment" to urinate. This is given a grand eschatological gloss by Vladimir:

> (*Musingly*) The last moment . . . (*He meditates.*) Hope deferred maketh the something sick, who said that? (10)

Vladimir's contemplation of "the last moment" leads to a mangled recitation of Proverbs 13:12: "Hope deferred makes the heart sick." Vladimir does not recall the biblical source of the quotation, and he forgets that it is the "heart" that becomes ill when hopes go unfulfilled. He also does not remember the second half of the verse: "but a desire fulfilled is a tree of life." The omission is significant: Vladimir is never satisfied with yearnings that can be fulfilled in the present. Instead, he desires Godot who, like the "last moment," destroys his heart. Vladimir wastes the potential of this life, with its limited rewards, because he yearns for something that is ultimately undesirable in any form. He waits next to a dying tree of unfulfilled desires in the middle of a desert instead of cultivating a tree of life.

The two tramps continue to wait because they are convinced that what they have is not enough. At one point, when Estragon is awakened from a dream, he makes a gesture toward the "universe" and asks, "This one is enough for you?" (15). Estragon dreams of a better place,[109] since nothing in this world, not even "nature," is sufficient:

> ESTRAGON: We should return resolutely towards Nature.
>   (*They turn to look quickly at the tree, then back front*)
> VLADIMIR: We've tried that.
> ESTRAGON: True. (58)

Nature has been devastated by the eschatological vision of purity. And even if nature were plentiful, it could not give Vladimir and Estragon what they want, since it cannot fulfill eschatological hopes or fears. What is more, nature is filled with its own horrors—horrors enough to cause a complete disenchantment with the cosmos.

The world is not enough—not enough for the living, but also not enough for the dead. Vladimir and Estragon discover this when they hear the mysterious "dead voices" that "murmur" and "rustle" around them:

> VLADIMIR: What do they say?
> ESTRAGON: They talk about their lives.
> VLADIMIR: To have lived is not enough for them.
> ESTRAGON: They have to talk about it.
> VLADIMIR: To be dead is not enough for them.
> ESTRAGON: It is not sufficient. (56)

In death there is neither eternal bliss nor peaceful extinction. The dead are compelled to keep talking and thinking; they are never fulfilled. Though

Vladimir claims that these voices "make a noise like wings" and "feathers," as if they were angels in paradise, he also says that they sound like "sand" and "ashes," which suggests a less elevated condition (55–56). It is as if the dead are trapped forever in purgatory, without the closure of paradise or hell. But the hints of an afterlife in *Godot* seem more pagan than Christian, resembling the Homeric Hades, a drab underworld of depressed souls. There is, however, a crucial difference between Beckett's afterworld and Homer's Hades: in the *Odyssey*, the soul of the dead Achilles still yearns for the joys of earthly existence, no matter how insignificant the particular life. Achilles tells Odysseus that he would rather live as a slave to a pauper than be a dead king over all the souls in Hades.[110] He desires life itself, regardless of how miserable. The souls in Beckett's land of the dead, by contrast, desire neither life nor death. In the absence of eschatological fulfillment, life and death are insufficient.

There is one character in *Waiting for Godot* who challenges us to accept this world as "enough." Strangely enough, it is Pozzo, who, in his final words of the play, berates Vladimir for continually asking "When?":

> Have you not done tormenting me with your accursed time! It's abominable! When! When! One day, is that not enough for you, one day like any other day, one day I went blind, one day we'll go deaf, one day we were born, one day we shall die, the same day, the same second, is that not enough for you? They give birth astride of a grave, the light gleams an instant, then it's night once more. (81)

Pozzo is furious at Vladimir for not accepting the cycle of life and death as enough. Each life is like a "day"—a day like "any other day"—and in the course of a day nothing definitive occurs to change the fact that people are born, live, and die. Asking "When?" about either past events or future *eschatons* is pointless. There are no absolute events in the past, and there are no absolute events in any real or hypothetical future.

Pozzo's blindness is accompanied by tragic insight, which might suggest a way out of ceaseless messianic expectation. But should Vladimir and Estragon embrace Pozzo's challenge and accept the world as enough? Beckett gives us reasons to be wary of this recommendation. First, it comes from Pozzo, the most despicable character in the play. Anything he says should be held in suspicion. Second, Pozzo's new understanding of life does not affect his actions; he continues in his old habits of abusing Lucky and marching down the road. He shouts "On!" immediately after his final soliloquy as if nothing has changed. It is his last utterance of the play, but it is also his first (81, 21), revealing that tragic insight has not changed his character in any significant way. Third, Pozzo might be feigning his blindness. Immediately after Pozzo's final soliloquy, Vladimir wonders if Pozzo is "really blind" (81). Yet again, nothing is certain: if Pozzo is faking his blindness, his final tragic soliloquy in Act 2 is every bit as pretentious as his feigned tragic monologues in Act 1. Fourth, it is important to consider that the character who goes the furthest toward living without hope is Lucky. If Vladimir and Estragon take Pozzo's advice and accept this world as enough, they may end up as powerless slaves — perhaps even as Pozzo's powerless slaves. In Homer's *Odyssey*, Achilles desires what Lucky has; he claims it is better than being a king of the dead. However, in the context of *Godot,* it is unclear whether being a shade in the underworld is worse than being the slave of a slave in the world.

Beckett forces us to consider whether it is desirable, or even possible, to live without messianic hope. We are compelled to ask: Is messianic expectation truly a universal structure within human experience that is inescapable, or is it something that gradually arose to prominence in human history and became habitual? If the latter is the case, then the idea of the "messianic" is a historical contingency, not an essential constituent of all human experience. Thus Vladimir and Estragon do not represent all humanity but rather humanity after twenty centuries of Judeo-Christian apocalyptic expectation. Beckett, however, does not turn, as does Camus, to traditions that offer possible alternatives to eschatological hope; nor does he search, as does Derrida, for redemptive features within the eschatological traditions. On the contrary, he suggests that neither option is desirable. His vision is terminal; it culminates in nothing but dead ends. For Beckett, the endeavor to redeem the messianic in any Augustinian or Derridian form is futile. Neither acceptance nor rejection of the messianic can adequately respond to the evil released in late modernity. There is nothing to be done about the mess, except perhaps to represent it accurately.

Epilogue

The Two "Nothings" of *Caligula* and *Waiting for Godot*

Rien

Nina Sjursen claims that the experience of absurdity in *Caligula* and *Waiting for Godot* engenders two "diametrically opposed" visions of humanity and action.[1] According to Sjursen, Camus's Caligula adopts a "solution of power" (*la solution de la puissance*); he tries to eliminate evil through sheer volition.[2] Beckett's Vladimir and Estragon, on the other hand, are paralyzed by evil; they adopt, or are adopted by, a solution of "powerlessness" (*l'impuissance*), waiting passively for Godot either to save or to damn them.[3] But Sjursen also argues that *Caligula* and *Godot* share a common theme: "nothing."

The word *nothing* (*rien*) is used repeatedly throughout both plays. Indeed, it is the first word attributed to Caligula, and it is the first word spoken in *Godot.* Sjursen claims that *Caligula* and *Godot* collectively end in "a double nothing" (*un double rien*).[4] Caligula holds the world to be nothing, and his revolutionary frenzy does not change this; in the end, he finds that he can do nothing to eliminate the given evils of existence. The characters in *Godot,* on the other hand, exist in the nothing of late Christian civilization. Beckett reveals that two thousand years of eschatological hopes—both passive and aggressive, apocalyptic and Gnostic, religious and secular—have culminated in disaster. There is "nothing to be done" within the confines of the eschatological. Everyone is powerless, even those who, like Pozzo, deify human power.

Despite the several differences between Caligula and the clowns of *Godot,* they are similar in desiring a final consummation, a fundamental utopian transformation of their present condition. However, imagined utopias are nothing; they cannot alleviate the sufferings of those who imagine them. When Vladimir asks the Boy, "What does he do, Mr. Godot?" the Boy responds, "He does nothing, sir" (83). Vladimir's utopia does not exist, nor will it do anything for him. The word *utopia* is often used to designate an ideal place. It literally means "no place"; and, more to the point, Camus writes, "utopia is that which is in contradiction with reality."[5] The phantasm of a utopia—either as a literal "future present" or as an imaginary regulative ideal—makes everything seem inadequate in comparison: real things that are good in themselves are, at best, experienced as insufficient, or, at worst, as evil. Such experiences tend to culminate in nothing—nothing in the sense of "nothing to be done," or nothing in the perception of the world as "nothing of value." This is the "double nothing," the twofold nihilism, that confronts us when we consider *Caligula* and *Waiting for Godot* together. Regardless of whether the eschatological "solution" is typified by the nihilistic power of Caligula or the powerless nihilism of Vladimir and Estragon, the expected consummation does not occur. The human condition remains unchanged, and if anything, worse. Ultimately, eschatological expectations only aggravate the very evils they attempt to transcend.

Misunderstandings and confusions regarding the nature of good and evil accompany such extreme expectations. Caligula misunderstands the nature of good and evil; Vladimir and Estragon suffer from both misunderstanding and confusion. Caligula creates an absolute distinction between the thoroughly evil world and the impossible, but such Gnostic dualism misrepresents the reality of both good and evil. Caligula cannot see the goods facing him *as* goods; everything in and of this world is evil, and, consequently, he commits the most extreme evils in attempting to realize impossible goodness. Vladimir and Estragon, similarly, misunderstand good and evil when they interpret Godot's arrival as the greatest good to be imagined. The presumed good they desire is actually a greater evil. On the other hand, Vladimir and Estragon do not dismiss the world out of hand as does Caligula. In the midst of their sufferings they continue to look for any significance given in their condition; however, they are confused about good and evil because they often misinterpret their sufferings as necessary evils on the way to an eschatological resolution. The world is teetering at the brink of oblivion, but it is not quite nothing—not yet. They find just enough messianic "significance" in their pain:

VLADIMIR: This is becoming really insignificant.
ESTRAGON: Not enough. (62)

Significance lies only in what signifies Godot, even though it is ironically the very expectation of Godot that strips the world of significance. In their most confused moments, Vladimir and Estragon, especially Vladimir, interpret meaninglessness and suffering as part of a process that is expediting the actualization of the good. In this sense, their understanding is identical to the apocalyptic account of history, which interprets all historical events—even the most horrific—as contributing to the realization of a final apotheosis. As we have seen, apocalyptic eschatology claims that everything is under the control of a divine or immanent historical power and that each event—no matter how ostensibly unjustifiable or meaningless—happens for a purpose. Such an account blurs the distinction between good and evil, for if anguish, malice, and insignificance are understood as necessities that realize utopia, then it is possible to perceive these "evils" as goods. This is what causes confusion.

According to Baudrillard, the indeterminacy of good and evil is itself a symptom of evil. He writes, "Good lies in the clear opposition between good and evil. Evil lies in the lack of any distinction between the two."[6] Good and evil lose their definition when it is claimed that one can somehow arise out of the other. More specifically, according to Baudrillard, it is evil to claim that good can come from evil:

Good is when Good comes out of Good, or Evil out of Evil. That is when there is order. Evil is when Evil comes out of Good, or Good out of Evil. That is when things are all wrong. It is as though the cells of the heart were producing liver cells. Every discrepancy between cause and effect is of the order of Evil.[7]

Waiting for Godot suggests that apocalyptic expectation aggravates the confusion of good and evil. This suggestion places apocalypticism within the "order of Evil" identified by Baudrillard.

Beyond Eschatology

We can, accordingly, read *Caligula* and *Godot* as absurdist works that elucidate the various nihilistic delusions of eschatological beliefs. For Camus, however, the absurd condition is not necessarily synonymous with nihilism. In *Sisyphus* he argues that genuine acceptance of the absurd gets us "beyond nihilism" (*MS* v). Awareness of the absurd for Camus is the realization of an irreconcilable antagonism between our utopian desires and the world as constituted. This antagonism, according to Camus, may be too harsh for some to bear and lead to suicide. It may also cause others, in the midst of their sufferings, to hope for another life—a life of universal harmony. Eschatological hope, like suicide, rests on the desire to get out of the absurd condition. Camus writes that a person animated by hope "live[s] not for life itself but for some great idea that will transcend it, refine it, give it a meaning, and betray it" (*MS* 7).

Given the tendencies in human beings toward either suicide or eschatology, Camus asks, "Does [life's] absurdity require one to escape it through hope or suicide"? (*MS* 7) Camus's answer to this is negative. He attempts to formulate an account of the truly absurd man who does not commit suicide or delude himself with unsubstantiated hopes but who chooses instead to live within a condition of rupture without the "consolation" of a future utopia (*MS* 44). According to Camus, nothing in our experience can verify the reality of a utopia that resolves the absurd. At the same time, Camus claims that this lack of verification cannot be interpreted "through an odd reasoning" as evidence of utopia (*MS* 24). The absurd man sticks to what is certain, and he is only certain of rupture without hope:

> [The absurd man] has forgotten how to hope. This hell of the present is his Kingdom at last. All problems recover their sharp edge. . . . The body, affection, creation, action, human nobility . . . resume their places in this mad world. . . . Hence, what [the absurd man] demands of himself is to live *solely* with what he knows, to accommodate himself to what is, and to bring in nothing that is not certain. He is told that nothing is. But this at least is a certainty. And it is with this that he is concerned: he wants to find out if it is possible to live without appeal. (*MS* 39; emphasis in original)[8]

A "greater life cannot mean for [the absurd man] another life" (*MS* 49). The important thing "is not to be cured, but to live with one's ailments" (*MS* 29). But this does not lead to despondency: "Being deprived of hope is not despairing. The flames of earth are surely worth celestial perfumes" (*MS* 67). For Camus, life is rendered more significant by the finality of death and by the absence of a future utopia; when there is nothing to look forward to, there is a stronger imperative to act and think meaningfully in the present. Such a hopeless existence, according to Camus, is vital and creative, defiant and realistic, erotic and tragic. Like Sisyphus in Homer's *Odyssey*, the absurd man continues to roll his rock toward the peak of the mountain without any hope that it will remain on top.[9] And yet Camus urges us to "imagine Sisyphus happy" in this "futile and hopeless labour" (*MS* 91, 88).[10]

It is possible to condemn Caligula's actions on the basis of this portrait of the absurd man. Caligula is not truly absurd insofar as he actually tries to escape from the absurd condition. In this sense, Caligula goes beyond what the absurd has revealed to him; he is, in the words of David Cook, "ignorant of the limitations implicit in the absurd."[11] However, as we have seen, Camus is ambivalent regarding Caligula's revolt against the absurd condition. He finds something praiseworthy in Caligula's refusal to acknowledge limitations. Consequently, Camus does not attempt to formulate a consistent account of virtue on the basis of absurd experience. In *Sisyphus*, he claims that "everything is permitted" for the absurd rebel, who can be "virtuous on a whim" (*MS* 50).

On the other hand, Camus condemns those who adopt a passive eschatological faith. For example, in *Sisyphus*, he criticizes the resigned hope of "existential" philosophers such as Chestov, Jaspers, Kierkegaard, Dostoevsky, and Kafka.[12] He claims that these writers suggest a way out of the absurd by interpreting human agonies and confusions as proof of an absolute happiness and an ultimate meaningfulness. These "existentialists," much like Vladimir and Estragon, "deify what crushes them and find reason to hope in what impoverishes them" (*MS* 24). According to Camus, nothing "logically prepares this reasoning." He refers to this reasoning as a "leap" since it attempts to vault from one particular condition to an opposing condition without any coherent justification. The "absurd becomes god" in the writings of Jaspers and Chestov, who show how the "inability to understand becomes the existence that illuminates everything" (*MS* 25). The same is true of Kierkegaard, who makes "the absurd the criterion of the other world, whereas it is simply a residue of the experience of this world" (*MS* 28). For Camus, the experience of the absurd should not be transformed into "eternity's springboard" (*MS* 26). When an existentialist makes such an unjustifiable leap, he integrates the absurd into a final solution and causes it to lose its essential characteristics, which are rupture, opposition, and incompleteness.

Whatever Camus's ambivalent feelings regarding Caligula, it is clear that the emperor is guilty of a similar "leap." Caligula hopes to cure all lacerations by exacerbating the lacerations of this world through crime. Similarly, Vladimir and Estragon hope that their extreme sufferings will eventually catapult them into a new condition without suffering. We can, therefore, interpret *Caligula* and *Waiting for Godot* as plays about different efforts to "leap" out of the absurd on the basis of the experience of the absurd. The more the characters attempt to resolve rupture through a leap, the more apparent rupture becomes; antagonism and suffering increase in direct proportion to the degree of eschatological hope.

However, the absurdist visions of *Caligula* and *Waiting for Godot* are also products of the eschatological understanding itself, for they present a de-divinized vision of the world inherited directly from eschatological symbolism. Camus and Beckett often presuppose an "either/or" eschatological worldview—a worldview that alleges meaning can only be found in an *eschaton* or in what indicates an *eschaton*. That is to say, *either* the world has a grand meaning with an eschatological resolution *or* it is entirely meaningless. Since neither Camus nor Beckett believes that there is an eschatological resolution to human suffering, they both accept, to varying degrees, that the world is inherently empty.

We can see this clearly in Camus's early writings. In *Sisyphus* and *Caligula*, he frequently presents the absurd struggle as a clear-cut dualistic battle between the heroic individual and the meaningless world. The absurd sets the individual "in opposition to all creation" (*MS* 38). In the process, Camus makes his own leap: he vaults from the absolute meaninglessness of life to the complete meaningfulness of human revolt. He writes, "It was previously a question of finding out whether or not life had to have a meaning to be lived. It now becomes clear, on the contrary, that it will be lived all the better if it has no meaning. . . .

[R]evolt gives life its value" (*MS* 40). But Camus, later catching himself, tried to arrive at a subtler understanding of revolt. In *The Rebel*, he provides an account of a rebel who perceives both ruptures and meanings in life. This is the rebel who rebels in the name of those things in the world that are inherently meaningful. However, even in *The Rebel* Camus continues to fall back on his earlier dualistic formulations when he suggests that true revolt is a fight with the entire cosmos. *Caligula* is similarly divided: on the one hand, it points to an understanding unmarked by any lingering eschatological residue; on the other, it tries to formulate this understanding within the eschatological assumption of the world's inherent emptiness.

Beckett, by contrast, finds nothing celebratory or heroic in the absurd condition. He suggests that if the world is as empty as Camus claims in *Sisyphus*, then it culminates in the pathetic characters of *Godot* and not the heroic rebels of Camus's imagination. There is no presentation of meaningful revolt in *Godot* because, for Beckett, the potentialities of revolt have been realized and exhausted.[13] The same is true of passive eschatological faith. Beckett does not try to salvage "the good" from within eschatological hope or attempt to redeem "the mess" that now accompanies this hope. On the contrary, the current mess is incompatible with anything that humans can imagine as relatively good. In this way, Beckett does not confuse good and evil, even as he brings this confusion to life on the stage. Instead, he paints a clear and uncompromising portrait of the absurd condition without making any eschatological leaps or tacitly defending certain types of messianic hopes.

But, again, this portrait is as much the product as it is the condemnation of eschatological de-divinization. Beckett accepts the de-divinized world that eschatological hopes have produced, even though he does not accept the hopes offered by any form of eschatology. Consequently, Beckett does not try to think his way outside of the eschatological framework, even while he criticizes it. He sometimes suggests that it is possible to live without eschatology, but he does not, like Camus, seriously intimate a viable, noneschatological alternative to the experience of meaninglessness. Though *Godot* is a greater aesthetic accomplishment than *Caligula*, it is, for better or worse, philosophically less ambitious. Like his characters, Beckett thinks he is powerless to escape the malaise created by centuries of eschatological expectation.

Thus neither Camus nor Beckett formulates a truly noneschatological understanding for the theatre: an understanding that sees meaningful ends *in* the world but no meaningful end *of* the world; meanings *in* history but no meaning *of* history; ruptures in the world but no single grand rupture between the world and human beings; goods and evils in perpetual struggle but no absolute Good and Evil in eschatological combat; particular evils breeding other evils but no supreme Good realizing itself through evil. Both *Caligula* and *Waiting for Godot* occasionally suggest such an account, but neither play is able to articulate it consistently.

PART TWO

Evil in
Renaissance Theatre

CHAPTER FOUR

Expediency and the Machiavel

Machiavelli and the Modern World

Machiavelli's *Mandragola* and Shakespeare's *Measure for Measure* are
two Renaissance comedies about a "bed-trick." The action of each play
concerns an illicit sexual encounter in which one partner is not aware of
the true identity of the other. In each case, the bed-trick is arranged in
such a way that it benefits the society as a whole, or appears to. Given
the fantastic nature of the bed-tricks and the ostensibly happy endings
of both plays, a reader might be tempted to dismiss *Mandragola* and *Measure for Measure* as amusing but unsubstantial works. Each play, however, deals with the expedient ethos, where calculations of efficiency and
effectiveness are granted the ultimate authority in determining social
purposes. This has direct bearing on our understanding of the late modern death event, which is characterized not only by an eschatological desire for utopia but also by a type of action that is justified by expediency.
In *Mandragola* and *Measure for Measure,* we see early modern expressions of this efficacious spirit—a spirit that would later dominate modern
politics.

On the surface, expediency seems to be the antithesis of eschatology.
The stereotypical "expedient type" is often characterized as living in
the "real world"—a person who is not given to flights of fancy or self-
destructiveness. Such a person is, thus, less likely to live in high expectation of an eschatological transformation. Instead, he is more likely to

accept evil as a constant feature of the human condition, both now and in the future. He might even be willing to commit evil when necessary if he thinks it can work to his advantage. Consider, for example, what is said in the Book of Ecclesiastes. The Ecclesiast does not wait for an *eschaton,* nor is he trying to realize one. He claims that humans are caught in never-ending cosmic and historical cycles wherein everything has its "season." God's blessings can only be received in this life, if at all.[1] And, as the following passage makes clear, God blesses those who use righteousness and wickedness in due measure:

> In my vain life I have seen everything; there are righteous people who perish in their righteousness, and there are wicked people who prolong their life in their evildoing. Do not be too righteous, and do not act too wise; why should you destroy yourself? Do not be too wicked, and do not be a fool; why should you die before your time? It is good that you should take hold of the one, without letting go of the other; for the one who fears God shall succeed with both. (Eccles. 7:15–18)

This teaching steers us away from Caligulian madness and *Godot*-like expectation. However, it is a disturbing lesson, as it suggests that we must compromise with evil to ensure a relative degree of worldly prosperity.

Such advice is usually not associated with the Bible; it is more often associated with Machiavelli. In *Mandragola,* the character Timoteo echoes Ecclesiastes: "Many times one comes to harm by being too easy-going and too good, as well as by being too wicked."[2] In *The Prince,* Machiavelli says something similar in his own voice: "A man who wants to make a profession of good in all regards must come to ruin among so many who are not good. Hence it is necessary to a prince, if he wants to maintain himself, to learn to be able not to be good" (P15).[3] Because of such advice, *The Prince* was placed on the Catholic Index of banned books;[4] Ecclesiastes, however, remains a canonical text for both Jews and Christians.

That "Machiavellian" advice is found in the Old Testament suggests Machiavelli's teachings are nothing new. This is somewhat surprising, given that Machiavelli is often associated with innovation and modern thinking. Many commentators have pointed to the disturbingly close relationship between Machiavelli and the beginning of modernity. Harvey

Mansfield writes, "We are . . . uneasily aware that Machiavelli was, to say the least, present at the origin of a revolution in morality, which can be defined loosely in our terms as a change from virtue protected by religion to self-interest justified by secularism. The revolution is known to us . . . as 'modernity.'"[5] But given that teachings resembling Machiavelli's were being expressed as far back as Ecclesiastes, what is it about Machiavelli that is "new" and "modern"?

Machiavelli proclaimed that he was driven by a "natural desire" to "find new modes and orders" that would "bring common benefit to everyone" (D 1. Pr.1).[6] Machiavelli's aspiration to improve the human condition by breaking from traditional religious understandings ("virtue protected by religion") and encouraging human ingenuity ("self-interest justified by secularism") would subsequently characterize the various efforts by philosophers, scientists, and rulers to exert greater control over politics and nature. Machiavelli might have fired the first shot in this revolution. As Mansfield writes, Machiavelli "began a project, later picked up and developed by other modern philosophers, for a permanent, irreversible improvement in human affairs establishing a new political regime."[7] Before the "Age of Reason," the "Enlightenment," modern natural science, modern technology, and modern social science, there is Machiavelli's political science, which teaches how rulers and regimes can realize their self-interest with remarkable success and command society with unprecedented power.

Mansfield's claim that Machiavelli started the modern project elaborates Leo Strauss's earlier proclamation that Machiavelli inaugurated the "first wave of modernity"—a wave with far-reaching consequences in the realms of the natural and social sciences. According to Strauss, Machiavelli's "spirit" initiated, on the one hand, a new approach to the natural world. "Nature" would no longer be understood as something that determines and limits human beings but as material that can be controlled and transformed through human ingenuity for the sake of comfortable self-preservation. Machiavelli's "spirit" also initiated, on the other hand, a new political understanding of "natural law" that would subsequently be expressed by Thomas Hobbes. After Machiavelli, the "law of nature" would no longer be understood as a constant measure by which humans comprehend their ethical duties but as the "right" of each individual to pursue his self-interest to the furthest extent possible. The human being, according to Machiavelli, has an acquisitive nature: "it is a very natural and ordinary thing to desire to acquire" (*P*3). Machiavelli, and the political philosophers who followed him, attempted to establish new regimes that better accommodated this acquisitive nature. This goes hand in hand with the desire to control the natural world through technology.[8]

Strauss claims that prior to Machiavelli humans believed they could obtain moral norms from a natural law imprinted in the cosmos. Thomas Aquinas, for example, argued that natural law was derived from God's eternal law and could be perceived through our "natural reason." Divine revelation, for Aquinas, must supplement natural reason for a full understanding; nevertheless, natural reason is sufficient for grasping the natural law and is thus adequate for distinguishing good from evil. Aquinas writes, "Natural reason, whereby we discern what is good and what is evil, which is the function of the natural law, is nothing else than an imprint on us of the Divine light. It is therefore evident that the natural law is nothing else than the rational creature's participation of the eternal law" (*ST* I–II, q. 91, a. 2). Machiavelli, unlike most of his contemporaries in the late medieval world, never uses the term "natural law" in his writings.[9] This curious absence is indicative of a radical shift in European thought—perhaps one initiated by Machiavelli himself. Strauss claims that after Machiavelli the world was increasingly perceived as inherently meaningless—as a thoroughly de-divinized realm without a permanent structure or order. In the modern self-understanding, ethical norms would no longer be derived from a "natural" cosmic order inherent in both the universe and human nature; instead, "order" would be understood to originate from human initiative alone. Nature and politics would be controlled through expedient modes of action, modes unrestrained by natural or eternal laws. In this new understanding, "justice" is no longer something that accords with natural order or a divine will; it is, rather, a product that emerges from humanity's "right" to assert itself and establish systems that allow for the expedient pursuit of acquisitions and self-preservation. This is the new natural law, the law through which human beings lift themselves out of the chaos that surrounds them. According to Strauss, it is how Machiavelli's desire to bring common benefit to everyone was expressed in modernity.

However, the twentieth century's death event shows that there has not been an "irreversible improvement in human affairs" in the half-millennium since Machiavelli. If Machiavelli, as Strauss and Mansfield suggest, is key to understanding the origin and essence of modernity, we must ask if his understanding of humanity and politics somehow facilitated these catastrophic events. This is not to suggest that Machiavelli is ultimately responsible for the death event. Nevertheless, his political philosophy may have encouraged a certain capacity within humanity, thus laying the foundation, not only for modern science and politics, but also for the expressions of evil that are unique to modernity.

Prudence and Cleverness: Expediency Defined

To understand Machiavellian "expediency," one might well distinguish it from Aristotle's account of "prudence." At the most general level, an "expedient" is whatever is advantageous. Any action that assists an individual or a group in achieving a desired goal is expedient. Expediency, when understood in this general sense, is not necessarily bad; each of us, every day, must take certain measures to ensure our personal and social well-being. For Aristotle, an expedient that realizes the good of society is politics in the highest sense. Aristotle writes that "the end of politics is the good for man" (*NE* 1.2, 1094b 6−7). The ability of a ruler, first, to deliberate on the best modes for realizing the good, and, second, to act on the basis of this deliberation, is Aristotle's definition of "prudence" or "practical wisdom" (*phronēsis*).[10]

In *The Nicomachean Ethics,* Aristotle claims that the "prudent" man is necessarily "morally virtuous"; that is, he is a person of good character whose soul is properly ordered and who avoids injustice in his dealings with others. For Aristotle, the morally virtuous man possesses characteristics such as courage, temperance, liberality, modesty, truthfulness, and justice—virtues that are essential in politics because they allow a person to perceive the ends in life that are good and worthy of pursuit. According to Aristotle, all humans are born with the natural capacity for moral virtue, but it can only be realized through proper habituation (*NE* 2.1, 1103a 14−1103b 25). The purpose of law is to inculcate good habits— that is, moral virtue—in citizens (*NE* 2.1, 1103b 2−5). A person who possesses moral virtue through proper habituation can then perceive the good through the "eye of the soul"—that is, through the "intelligence"

(*NE* 6.12, 1144a 30).[11] Prudence, however, is more than just the habitual practice of virtue. It is an "intellectual virtue" through which the morally virtuous man not only sees the goods in life but also knows how to realize them in practice. For Aristotle, the prudent man is both good and pragmatic; he is not an impractical ethicist or an amoral schemer. Aristotle writes, "It is impossible to be good in the full sense of the word without practical wisdom or to be a man of practical wisdom without moral excellence or virtue. . . . [I]t is also clear that no choice will be right without practical wisdom and [moral] virtue. For [moral] virtue determines the end, and practical wisdom makes us do what is conducive to the end" (*NE* 6.13, 1144b 30–33 and 1145a 3–6).

Aristotle also makes a crucial distinction between practical wisdom and mere "cleverness":

> There exists a capacity called "cleverness," which is the power to perform those steps which are conducive to a goal we have set for ourselves and to attain that goal. If the goal is noble, cleverness deserves praise; if the goal is base, cleverness is knavery. That is why men of practical wisdom are often described as "clever" or "knavish." But in fact this capacity alone is not practical wisdom, although practical wisdom does not exist without it. Without virtue or excellence, this eye of the soul, intelligence, does not acquire the characteristic of practical wisdom. . . . [W]hatever the true end may be, only a good man can judge it correctly. For wickedness distorts and causes us to be completely mistaken about the fundamental principles of action. Hence it is clear that a man cannot have practical wisdom unless he is good. (*NE* 6.12, 1144a 24–37)

Cleverness is a part of prudence but is not identical with it. Aristotle admits that some men are successful at achieving "base" goals through effective means. The "prudential" man, on the other hand, will only set good goals and realize them through good acts. Thus, according to Aristotle, it is possible to be wicked and clever but not wicked and prudent.

It is in the Aristotelian sense of "cleverness" that I will use the term "expediency" to describe a form of action that is concerned solely with what is effective in the pursuit of power but that is not necessarily concerned with realizing the good. In this sense, expediency is distinct from

Aristotelian prudence, which only makes pragmatic decisions in pursuit of the good. Of course, it is possible to argue that prudence in the Aristotelian sense does not exist. It could be said that the world, such as it is, does not allow a person—and particularly a political ruler—to avoid committing evil acts. A person must be prepared to employ wicked methods when necessary if he hopes to preserve himself and his state. This is Machiavelli's position: a person cannot always be morally virtuous because "human conditions do not permit it" (*P*15).

Machiavelli states that when choosing our methods we must deliberate on what is effective rather than imagine a type of goodness that is impossible to realize. He asks us to reject noneffectual falsehoods and accept what he calls the "effectual truth." In *The Prince*, Machiavelli writes:

> Since my intent is to write something useful to whoever understands it, it has appeared to me more fitting to go directly to the effectual truth of the thing than to the imagination of it. And many have imagined republics and principalities that have never been seen or known to exist in truth; for it is so far from how one lives to how one should live that he who lets go of what is done for what should be done learns his ruin rather than his preservation. For a man who wants to make a profession of good in all regards must come to ruin among so many who are not good. Hence, it is necessary to a prince, if he wants to maintain himself, to learn to be able not to be good, and to use this and not use it according to necessity. (*P*15)

Immediately following this passage, Machiavelli lists a number of dichotomous "qualities" that are traditionally held to be virtues and vices. The list includes liberality and niggardliness, mercy and cruelty, faithfulness and faithlessness, and chastity and lasciviousness. Contrary to Aristotle, Machiavelli claims that the prudent man employs both types of qualities, not just those held to be good (*P*15). For example, with regard to keeping promises, Machiavelli writes, "A prudent lord . . . cannot observe faith, nor should he, when such observance turns against him, and the causes that made him promise have been eliminated. And if all men were good, this teaching would not be good; but because they are wicked and do not observe faith with you, you also do not have to observe it with them" (*P*18). Thus Machiavelli advises the clever employment of dishonesty and dares to call it "prudence." For Aristotle, on the other hand, a genuinely prudent person is necessarily honest. In the *Nicomachean Ethics,* Aristotle celebrates the morally virtuous man who "is truthful in his speech and in his life simply because it is part of his character to be that kind of man. Such a man would seem to be honest (*epieikēs*). For a man who loves truth and who is truthful when nothing is at stake will be even more truthful when something is at stake. He will scrupulously avoid falsehood as being base" (*NE* 4.7, 1127b 1−7).[12] But for Machiavelli, it is precisely when something is at stake that a prudent person must be ready to break faith and lie. Machiavelli effectively rejects Aristotle's distinction between prudence and cleverness; whatever works, even if it is a vice, is prudent. Any prudent person who wants to preserve himself must "not depart from good, when possible, but know how to enter into evil, when forced by necessity" (*P* 18).

Machiavelli's frank speech about entering into evil is often said to have introduced a new type of intellectual inquiry that studies politics and the world as it is rather than as it ought to be. Some have claimed that Machiavelli was the first political thinker who refused to equate political excellence with moral goodness.[13] Machiavelli himself claims that his "useful" account of real "republics and principalities" is the reason why he "depart[s] from the orders of others" (*P* 15). In this sense, Machiavelli is modern because he describes the evils of politics with the objective eye of a value-neutral social scientist and without recourse to religious dogma or philosophical ethics. However, some scholars claim that Machiavelli's "realism" is "scarcely original."[14] Isaiah Berlin writes, "The fact that the wicked are seen to flourish or that immoral courses appear to pay, has never been very remote from the consciousness of mankind."[15] Clifford Orwin agrees with Berlin and claims that Machiavelli was not the first thinker to articulate the "discrepancy between thorough goodness and political success."[16] Berlin and Orwin both point out that the distinction between complete moral goodness and sheer political success is a central feature of Jewish, Christian, and classical thought.[17] Even Aristotle, who thinks it is possible and eminently desirable for good men to be politically successful, does not preclude the fact that wicked men often thrive in politics.[18] And insofar as Machiavelli emphasizes the inescapable evils of politics, he is firmly within the Christian tradition that stresses the inherent sinfulness of human beings and the corrupt nature of politics.[19]

Machiavelli is unique insofar as he suggests that "moral virtue," understood in either the Aristotelian or Christian sense, should have *no* bearing on how we act politically. Whether or not he thought morality should dictate how we act in private life is an issue I consider in *Mandragola.* Machiavelli certainly thinks that a regime must bear in mind what the majority of people *believe* is "moral," but rulers should not be restricted by the moral qualms of their subjects. For Machiavelli, politics should be driven by the "success ethic" alone. Even worse, Machiavelli does not just describe how evil can be used successfully; he advocates it. Wicked modes are not just the prerogative of unjust regimes and tyrannies; all rulers and all regimes must use them when necessary. Even a republic must use modes that are indistinguishable from those of a tyranny to secure power. Machiavelli claims that the "end of the republic is to enervate and to weaken all other bodies so as to increase its own body." The impulse of the republic toward expansion necessitates the oppression of surrounding territories. Machiavelli writes, "Of all hard servitudes, that is hardest that submits you to a republic" (*D* 2.3.4). Domestically, a republic must also conduct periodic executions that are "excessive and notable" so as to put "that terror and that fear" in citizens, a terror often experienced at the origins of regimes. Machiavelli refers to this "intrinsic prudence" in a republic as a turn "toward its beginnings" (*D* 3.1.1–3). In this account, Machiavelli is advocating the use of cruelty in a republic. Indeed, he calls it "prudence." It is difficult, then, to defend Machiavelli against the charge of promoting evil on the grounds that he might have preferred republics to tyrannies. Republics do unseemly things too, and so they should, according to Machiavelli.

While many before Machiavelli made a distinction between the highest morality and political success, very few—if any—openly advocated stooping to acts of evil to guarantee political advantages. Machiavelli denies that either Aristotelian prudence or moral Christian statesmanship can ensure political prosperity. But Machiavelli does not lament this fact or suffer from bad conscience; on the contrary, he seems to celebrate it, and suggests that politics will only reach its fullest potential if it is unhindered by traditional moral concerns. This explains why Machiavelli's name is associated with a particular way of doing politics. Strauss writes:

Machiavelli is the only political thinker whose name has come into common use for designating a kind of politics, which exists and will

continue to exist independently of his influence, a politics guided
exclusively by considerations of expediency, which uses all means,
fair or foul, iron or poison, for achieving its ends—its end being the
aggrandizement of one's country or fatherland—but also using the
fatherland in the service of the self-aggrandizement of the politician or statesman or one's party. But if this phenomenon is as old as
political society itself, why is it called after Machiavelli who thought
or wrote only a short while ago, about 500 years ago? Machiavelli
was the first publicly to defend it in books with his name on the title
pages. Machiavelli made it publicly defensible.[20]

Of course, Machiavelli's unique advocacy of well-used evils does not
tell us what, if anything, is unique in his advice. It may be true that no
one before Machiavelli used his own name to promote such unseemly
tactics, but if Machiavellian wisdom is, in Strauss's words, "as old as political society itself," then Machiavelli's thought is not uniquely "modern."
Nevertheless, Machiavelli's daring espousal of expediency, and his refusal to limit politics by Aristotelian and Christian understandings of
morality, is a starting point in the attempt to uncover the Machiavellian
"spirit" in modern evil. His full uniqueness will emerge in my discussion of
Mandragola.

Machiavelli and the British Monarchy

The British of the sixteenth and early seventeenth century were among
the first to perceive Machiavelli as a threat to traditional notions of morality and politics. Though Machiavelli died in 1527, it seems his spirit
haunted Britain long after his death. His name became synonymous with
the devil in England during the reign of Elizabeth I (1558–1603), the last
monarch of the Tudor dynasty, and throughout the reign of Elizabeth's
successor, James I (1603–25), the first king of the Stuart family. The Tu-
dors and Stuarts were deeply concerned with the question of political
"legitimacy"—of what gave a particular monarch the right to rule.[21] The
concern with legitimacy stemmed from the political struggles that consumed Britain at that time. Elizabeth and James were "Anglican" monarchs, but their rule was contested by both Catholics and radical Prot-

estants. To counter these attacks, Tudor and Stuart authorities not only took political measures against their enemies but also developed arguments concerning political legitimacy. These accounts stand in stark contrast to Machiavelli's open espousal of so-called Realpolitik. Legitimate power, according to Tudor and Stuart apologists, is not established through the clever use of force and fraud, as Machiavelli argues, but is rather the result of divine decree. Furthermore, success in politics is ultimately the result of holy discretion in the mind of the king, not the willingness of an ambitious type to do whatever is necessary for power.

Tudor authorities claimed that it was possible for a rightful monarch to rule in accord with Christian morality and be successful. They argued that a monarch possesses not only his own "natural body," or human physical body, but also a divine "mystical body," or "Political Body." It is the Body Politic that gives a monarch the legitimacy to rule and the ability to rule with divine discretion. In the language of English crown jurists, this was known as the doctrine of the King's Two Bodies. Edmund Plowden, an Elizabethan law apprentice, summarizes the main arguments of the Tudor jurists in his *Reports.* He writes that a monarch possesses a "Body natural" that is "subject to all Infirmities that come by Nature or Accident, to the Imbecility of Infancy or old Age, and like the Defects that happen to the natural Bodies of other People." The monarch also possesses a "Body politic" that "cannot be seen or handled, consisting of Policy and Government, and constituted for the Direction of the People and the Management of the public weal."[22] As opposed to the body natural, the body politic cannot be corrupted or killed; it is an immortal element bestowed on all rightful monarchs by God, giving them the ability to support the common good and punish all evildoers who would threaten it. In this sense, the rightful monarch is the natural embodiment of eternal law, possessing those Christian virtues necessary for good government. The "Body politic" also gives the king a "divine aura." Ernst Kantorowicz writes, "The body politic of kingship appears as a likeness of the 'holy spirites and angels,' because it represents, like the angels, the Immutable within Time."[23]

The doctrine of the King's Two Bodies reinforced the teaching that political order could embody Christian principles if a legitimate monarch was on the throne. As David Bevington writes, "Tudor defense of order was based . . . on the assumption that the monarch rules in accord with a divine plan . . . to which every just ruler is attuned. Political morality must be at one with religious morality."[24] Even Catholic and Protestant opponents of Elizabeth and James shared this basic assumption with the monarchs they opposed—that rightful rulers could govern in harmony with divine decree. An illegitimate ruler might emerge from time to time, but it was still possible for a legitimate monarch to govern successfully through Christian statesmanship.

It was widely perceived, however, that Machiavelli made a categorical distinction between politics and religious morality. Political "legitimacy," in Machiavelli's understanding, is not established by divine right but through clever political scheming; whoever can seize and maintain power, whatever the means, is legitimate. Tim Spiekerman writes:

> Machiavelli certainly recognizes the distinction between legitimate and illegitimate political authority, but he does not respect it: he teaches men with no claim to a kingdom how to become kings. The identification of legitimacy with force is really tantamount to denying the distinction between legitimacy and illegitimacy altogether. It is perhaps only a slight exaggeration to say that for Machiavelli, legitimate authority is not a special kind of authority, but authority pure and simple, however gotten and however used. The legitimate ruler, on this view, is the one in power, as well as the one who is strong enough or clever enough to topple him.[25]

Consequently, Machiavelli's writings were considered a threat, not only by Tudor and Stuart officials—who banned the publication of *The Prince* and the *Discourses*—but also by all sides of British politicoreligious struggle. It is clear, however, that Machiavelli's challenge to Tudor and Stuart understandings of authority, morality, and divine right intrigued the British public. Nowhere is this more apparent than in the drama of the period.

The Machiavel and the English Stage

In *Machiavelli and the Elizabethan Drama*, Edward Meyer finds 395 references to Machiavelli scattered throughout the dramatic works of Shakespeare and his contemporaries.[26] The overwhelming interest of the British in Machiavelli gave birth to the stage Machiavel, a character type personifying ruthlessness, villainy, and atheism. The first Machiavel of the English stage is the wealthy Jewish villain, Barabas, in Christopher Marlowe's tragedy, *The Jew of Malta* (c. 1589).[27] In the prologue to the play, the audience is addressed by "Machevill" himself, who says he has come to Britain to "present the tragedy of a Jew" whose "money was not got without my means." Machevill asks us to look favorably on Barabas: "grace as he deserves / And let him not be entertain'd the worse / Because he favours me."[28] From this moment on, English drama abounds with Machiavels who delight in trickery for the sake of power and acquisition. Mortimer in Marlowe's *Edward II*, Lorenzo in Kyd's *Spanish Tragedy*, Piero in Marston's *Antonio's Revenge*, Mosca in Jonson's *Volpone*, Bosola in Webster's *Duchess of Malfi*, and Vindice in Tourner's *Revenger's Tragedy* are just some examples. The most famous Machiavels of the English stage, however, are Shakespeare's: Gloucester in *Richard III*, Iago in *Othello*, and Edmund in *King Lear* are often cited as paradigms of this character type.

It has been argued that the stage Machiavel is derived from the older stock character "Vice" in medieval morality plays.[29] It was the role of "the Vice" to tempt a protagonist, who represents all humankind, into evil—to try to damn the soul of "Everyman." Vice would employ deceit and treachery to lead his victim astray. It was common for Vice to inform the audience of his diabolical intentions and to take delight in his own evil. But in the morality dramas, Vice's endeavors would consistently culminate in failure; the soul of the protagonist was always saved at the last moment.[30] The Machiavels of English Renaissance theatre have similar characteristics. These villains take delight in their schemes and are often quite comical in their private musings about their own wickedness. They are constantly trying to lead others astray to serve their own purposes. Furthermore, the Renaissance Machiavel is usually not successful in his efforts. One need only look at the fates of Richard III, Iago, and Edmund to see this motif played out in Shakespeare's plays. Like Vice, the Machiavel becomes too entangled in his own evil and is ultimately undermined. However, unlike Vice, the Machiavel is usually successful in destroying his victims. This is one of the decisive differences between medieval drama and Renaissance tragedy.

Whatever differences exist between the Machiavel and Vice, the link between them is strong.[31] But what is the relation between the Machiavel and his namesake? In general, scholars have tended to view the Machiavel as a vulgar rendering of Machiavelli. Their argument is usually based on the assumption that Machiavelli himself was not a teacher of evil but rather a misunderstood and unfairly maligned pragmatic political theorist. For example, Edward Meyer claims that Elizabethans distorted the maxims of Machiavelli "in a manner infinitely unjust" and that their understanding of Machiavelli "could not have been taken directly from the works of the great politician."[32] Meyer claims that Elizabethans formed their impression of Machiavelli through a dubious secondary source: the *Contre-Machiavel* of Innocent Gentillet, published in France in 1576 and available in an unpublished English manuscript translation in 1577.[33] In the *Contre-Machiavel,* Gentillet, a French Protestant, restates Machiavelli's central arguments and claims to refute them all. According to Meyer, the "Machiavellianism" criticized by Gentillet has little to do with Machiavelli himself. Given the derogatory account of Machiavelli contained in the *Contre-Machiavel,* along with the date of its initial circulation in Elizabethan England, Meyer claims that it is "perfectly evident that this was the book from which the dramatists drew" and that the book was "the source of all the Elizabethan misunderstanding."[34] He attempts to seal his argument by claiming that the Elizabethans did not have direct access to Machiavelli's most important writings. Though English translations of Machiavelli's *The Art of War* and *The Florentine Histories* were readily available,[35] *The Prince* and the *Discourses* were banned by Elizabethan and Stuart authorities, both civil and ecclesiastical. According to Meyer, Machiavelli's "weightiest writings" did not appear in English until Edward Dacres translated the *Discourses* in 1636 and *The Prince* in 1640—well after the height of Elizabethan and Jacobean theatre. If true, then it would have been extremely difficult for playwrights in Shakespeare's day to have direct access to Machiavelli's teachings.

Meyer's claim that the Elizabethans did not read Machiavelli and misrepresented him has had a major influence on scholars of Elizabethan theatre.[36] However, Meyer was mistaken when he argued that the Elizabethans had no access to Machiavelli's most important writings. In the 1930s, Napoleone Orsini, searching through the British Museum, found three separate Elizabethan English translations of *The Prince* and a complete translation of the *Discourses* (dated 1599) as well as two other unfinished ones.[37] The existence of these English manuscripts reveals that many Britons disregarded the official ban on Machiavelli's key writings. Indeed, unofficial manuscripts of Machiavelli in various languages were always in circulation throughout England during the Elizabethan period. *The Prince* could be found in a French edition as early as 1553, and seven Latin translations appeared between 1560 and 1622. An Elizabethan printer named John Wolfe defied the ban on Machiavelli and printed Italian editions of both *The Prince* and the *Discourses* in 1584 under the false inscription "Palermo." Margaret Scott points out, "These editions . . . were clearly produced at some risk to meet what must have been a considerable demand."[38] The demand was so great that, in addition to *The Prince* and *Discourses,* Wolfe printed Machiavelli's *The Art of War, Florentine Histories,* and *The Ass* between 1587 and 1588.[39]

It stands to reason that most Elizabethan dramatists would have turned to the English, Italian, French, and Latin editions of Machiavelli that were readily available rather than to a secondary source like the *Contre-Machiavel.* Indeed, it probably would have been easier for a dramatist to obtain copies of Machiavelli's original works than to acquire a copy of Gentillet.[40] There is no reason to suppose, then, that the Elizabethan dramatists depended solely on the *Contre-Machiavel* for their understanding of Machiavelli. On the contrary, it seems more likely that they were consulting Machiavelli himself. We can conclude that direct exposure to Machiavelli's writings was one of the primary factors behind the legend of the monstrous Machiavel in Renaissance England.

According to Scott, the Elizabethans had a clearer sense than we of just how radical Machiavelli is:

> There seems no doubt that the Elizabethans were correct in suggesting that the political counsel of Machiavelli was antagonistic to their religion and to their morality, and that the dramatists did nothing to distort Machiavelli's teaching when they showed the Machiavel, let loose in a God-centred world, as the natural enemy of true religion and Christian virtue.[41]

Nevertheless, even Scott argues that the Elizabethan playwrights were not always accurate in their representations of Machiavellian politics.[42]

The argument that the Elizabethans misrepresented Machiavelli is still widely accepted today. It is probably fair to say that in many cases the Machiavels are crude caricatures of Machiavelli's teachings. But this does not mean that the English playwrights were "infinitely unjust" to Machiavelli. They sensed what Leo Strauss would later describe with hindsight: Machiavelli was challenging established notions of what was possible and permissible, and, in the process, unleashing potentials that had previously been contained. The English playwrights were struggling to express this revolution. Some were better at expressing it than others. None was better than Shakespeare.

The Machiavel in *Measure for Measure* and *Mandragola*

We can be sure that Shakespeare knew of Machiavelli and fairly certain that he had access to Machiavelli's writings.[43] However, as Tim Spiekerman writes, "no direct evidence exists that Shakespeare read Machiavelli, or, if he did, that he was responding to him."[44] True as this may be, it is more likely that Shakespeare would have read Machiavelli, especially when so many of his contemporaries were doing so. But even if we assume that Shakespeare did not consult Machiavelli's texts, it is undeniable that he was concerned with the same sort of power politics that Machiavelli celebrates. Shakespeare's plays are filled with "Machiavellian" types who are unscrupulous in their pursuit of power. This is what Spiekerman calls the "deeper connection between Shakespeare and Machiavelli": both men "address the question of how political power is acquired and maintained" and "scrutinize the relation between morality, particularly Christian morality, and political practice."[45]

I argue that Shakespeare's *Measure for Measure* is a sophisticated theatrical rendering of Machiavellian politics and of the challenges it poses to classical and Christian ethics. Careful consideration of the play reveals that Shakespeare is presenting the fundamentals of Machiavellianism with unparalleled dramatic excellence. He does this through the character Duke Vincentio, a compelling and attractive ruler who, on close inspection, turns out to be a Machiavel unlike most other stage Machiavels. The Duke, contrary to the stereotypical Machiavel, never confesses to any malice; on the contrary, he presents himself as the paradigm of

Christian morality. He is also distinct from most other Machiavels in that he is entirely successful; indeed, his very name means "victory." But we should not let the Duke's triumph fool us: his very success might indicate that he is more Machiavellian than the so-called Machiavels. The Duke accomplishes what Shakespeare's Gloucester can only brag about: he "set[s] the murderous Machiavel to school."[46]

This is not to say that Shakespeare is an apologist for Machiavelli. If Shakespeare presents Machiavellian types onstage—even attractive Machiavels such as Vincentio—it does not necessarily mean that he countenances their behavior. As I argue, there is an implicit critique of Machiavellian politics in *Measure for Measure.* However, Shakespeare does not condemn Machiavelli in the manner of Gentillet's *Contre-Machiavel,* with a crude caricature and a moralistic retort. Shakespeare shows how the Machiavellian approach can be seductive, not because humans delight in the stratagems of evil characters, but because it is easy for us to mistake successful enterprises for the highest good. *Measure for Measure* tests us to see if our moral consciousness can withstand the seduction of Machiavellian effectiveness.

Well before Shakespeare and his contemporaries created their Machiavels in England, Machiavelli was creating his own for the Italian stage. In many respects, his villainous characters foreshadow the best diabolic creations of the English playwrights. Machiavelli's political writings have always eclipsed his artistic works, but he was involved in theatre throughout his life. His *Mandragola* stands as a crowning achievement of the Italian Renaissance stage. It might seem surprising to us that a political theorist would be interested in dramatic art. Nevertheless, theatre played a strategic role in Machiavelli's attempt to found a "new order." *Mandragola* was his most public attempt to steep his contemporaries in a new teaching. In this play, he presented the fundamentals of the "Machiavellian revolution" with great precision and humor. I consider it next, and then turn to Shakespeare's response to the revolution.

CHAPTER FIVE

Evil and Virtue in *Mandragola*

Machiavelli's Strategic Use of Comedy

Mandragola stands at the vanguard of a theatrical resurgence in early modernity. Machiavelli played a key role in the Italian rediscovery of Greek and Roman literature during the Renaissance. Like his contemporaries, Machiavelli was interested in classical works that had been neglected, suppressed, or lost during the Middle Ages. This effort led to a revival of ancient drama.[1] Published editions of Roman comedies by Terence and Plautus began to circulate in the late fifteenth century. Many of these plays were subsequently adapted or modified for the stage by Italian playwrights in the early sixteenth century, giving birth to a new theatrical genre, the *commedia erudita* (learned comedy), which borrowed stories from ancient Roman dramas and reconstituted them with contemporary Italian settings and dialects.[2] Italian drama at this time was generating innovations in dramaturgy, staging, performance, and content that would change the nature of European theatre in the following century, particularly in England, France, and Spain. The Italian rediscovery of classical theatre was the seminal event that marked the decline of medieval sacred drama and the revival of tragedy and comedy.[3] *Mandragola* is often cited as the greatest dramatic work to emerge from Italy during this period. Indeed, it is considered by many the best comedy in the Italian language.[4]

Machiavelli completed copies, translations, and adaptations of several Greek and Roman comedies throughout his life. His copy of Terence's

Eunuchus, probably completed in the early 1500s, exists in a Vatican manuscript.[5] He is reported to have adapted Plautus's *Aulularia,* but this has been difficult to verify as there are no surviving copies of the text.[6] Machiavelli's nephew and literary executor, Giuliano de'Ricci, also reported seeing a manuscript for a play titled *Le Machere* (The Masks), apparently written by Machiavelli in 1504 and loosely based on Aristophanes' *Clouds.* Ricci destroyed the play, however, because it criticized many prominent Florentine politicians and ecclesiastics who were still alive at that time.[7] *Andria* (c. 1517–20), *Mandragola* (c. 1504 or 1518–19), and *Clizia* (1524) are the only three plays by Machiavelli to have survived. *Andria* is a translation of Terence's play by the same name. *Clizia* is a close adaptation of Plautus's *Casina,* which is itself an adaptation of the Greek "new comedy" *Clerumenae* by Diphilus. Machiavelli acknowledges *Clizia*'s classical heritage in the prologue to the play, where he promises to present the "same case" (*medesimo caso*) that was presented in Athens many centuries ago.[8] The prologue to *Mandragola* promises the opposite. Machiavelli tells us that we will see a "new case" (*nuovo caso*)—one that recently occurred in Florence (Pr.).[9] *Mandragola,* as opposed to *Clizia,* is "new," but it also has a classical source. The plot is loosely based on Livy's account of the rape of Lucretia in his *History of Rome. Mandragola* is a nominal work of *commedia erudita* since it is adapted from a Roman historical work instead of an ancient comedy. However, Machiavelli takes extensive liberties with his source material, moving the play well beyond Livy. As a result, *Mandragola* is Machiavelli's only original play.

Mandragola's initial audience was relatively select. For the most part, works of *commedia erudita* were performed for Italian nobility in the courts and houses of rich families. These plays were funded and managed by private patrons for the entertainment of the political elite, not the common people.[10] Mera Flaumenhaft writes, "*Mandragola* is not intended directly to reach the public at large. But the particular coterie to whom the play is addressed is one whose attitudes and future actions will have the greatest effect on the wider community."[11] Despite its exclusive audience, *Mandragola* had a relative degree of popularity during Machiavelli's life; indeed, it was Machiavelli's most popular work while he lived. The play was performed numerous times to great acclaim for audiences in Florence and Venice and was produced in Rome at the court of Pope Leo X for a command performance in 1520. By the standards of sixteenth-century Italy, *Mandragola* was a resounding success.[12]

Mandragola is also one of the few works by Machiavelli that was published during his lifetime. Most scholars speculate that the play was written in 1519, around the time of its first performance.[13] A copy of the play exists in a codex of writings belonging to Duke Lorenzo de' Medici under the date and title, "Jhesus, 1519. Commedia Facta per Niccholò Machiavegli."[14] This manuscript, however, was not distributed in public. The first printed edition of the play intended for the public appeared under the title *Comedia di Callimaco: & di Lucretia*, with a cover depicting the centaur Chiron playing the violin. This edition is not dated, and it does not contain the name of a publisher. Even more surprising, Machiavelli's name does not appear on the cover. Sergio Bertelli concludes that *Mandragola* was "published anonymously during, we must suppose, the author's life. This is odd." It could be, as Bertelli suggests, that this printed edition was a pirated copy based on an earlier manuscript used for a performance and thus unapproved by Machiavelli for publication.[15] But it is also possible that Machiavelli wanted to remain semianonymous.

It seems that Machiavelli was reticent to publish anything under his own name. Besides *Mandragola*, the only works that Machiavelli published during his lifetime were *The First Decennial* and *The Art of War* — two texts that seem less shocking in comparison to some of his other political meditations.[16] Machiavelli chose not to publish the more important, and more infamous, *Prince* and *Discourses on Livy* — the two books that he says contain everything he knows.[17] He decided to distribute these works confidentially to specific individuals. *The Prince* was offered in private to Duke Lorenzo de' Medici. The *Discourses*, likewise, was a private gift from Machiavelli to his friends Zanobi Buondelmonti and Cosimo Rucellai. It seems that Machiavelli thought he could write about the harsh realities of politics to princes and young companions in private but not to the public at large. This suggests that Machiavelli kept *The Prince* and *Discourses* confidential for strategic purposes, given their controversial content. Harvey Mansfield writes, "One could assume that Machiavelli had to be more careful about challenging the morals and religion of his native country when he was alive to suffer the consequences of doing so. But he found a way around that difficulty by publishing . . . after his death."[18]

Mandragola has a decidedly "Machiavellian" flavor. Like the *Discourses* and *The Prince*, it seems to challenge the morality of Machiavelli's audience. In all three works, Machiavelli states that he is embarking on something radically new that could cause controversy and outrage. In the fifteenth chapter of the *Prince*, Machiavelli fears he might be "held presumptuous" because he will "depart from the orders of others" regarding political matters. Similarly, at the start of the *Discourses*, he claims he might anger "envious" men in his "dangerous" quest to discover "new modes and orders" because "men are more ready to blame than to praise the actions of others" (*D* 1. Pr.1). Finally, in the prologue to *Mandragola*, he says he expects his play to be poorly received because "everyone blames" and "speaks ill" of bold new works. These passages reveal Machiavelli's suspicion that each work is so revolutionary that people will be offended. However, it appears he thought that *Mandragola*—unlike the other two texts—was safe enough to publish in semianonymity during his lifetime and to present to larger groups of people in the theatre.

Machiavelli's decision to go public with *Mandragola* might have something to do with its genre. Unlike *The Prince* and *Discourses*, *Mandragola* is a comedy that ostensibly deals with the private realm, not politics. In the essay "A Dialogue on Language," Machiavelli writes that the "aim of a comedy is to hold up a mirror to domestic life . . . with expressions that excite laughter."[19] The subject matter of comedy is, thereby, less weighty than that of a serious political treatise. The prologue to *Mandragola* asserts that the play was written merely to "break your jaws with laughter." Though the "author" of the play would like to "seem grave and wise," we are asked to excuse him because "he has been cut off from showing with other undertakings other virtue"—an implicit reference to Machiavelli's banishment from politics.[20] Because of his unemployment, the author has decided to compose a comedy that is "light" and perhaps "not worthy" (Pr).

Machiavelli also emphasizes the "lightness" of comedy in the prologue to his later play *Clizia*. But here he suggests that comic triviality can somehow be beneficial to the audience:

Comedies were discovered in order to benefit and to delight the spectators. Truly it is a great benefit to any man and especially to a youth, to know the avarice of an old man, the passion of a lover, the tricks of a servant, the gluttony of a parasite, the misery of a pauper, the ambition of one who's rich, the flatteries of a whore, the untrustworthiness of all men. Comedies are full of such examples, and all these things can be presented with very great decency. But if one wants to delight, it is necessary to move the spectators to laughter, and this cannot be done if one keeps to grave and severe speech.[21]

Machiavelli does not explain what kind of "benefit" can be received from delighting in unseemly characters. It is clear, however, that the classic tradition of comedy allows Machiavelli to present immoral behavior in a lighthearted way without causing too much controversy. He can take liberties in comedy that he cannot take in other literary genres. Timothy Lukes writes, "The triviality and humour of the dramatic medium may have best suited Machiavelli's intentions—to relate truly revolutionary and immoral ideas without being labeled a gross revolutionary and atheist himself."[22] Machiavelli—if he is careful—can use comedy to attack the very foundations of classical and Christian ethics, while inciting his classically educated and Christian bred audience to laugh with approval. When the laughter stops, a serious teaching can be discerned with political ramifications. As Machiavelli writes in "Dialogue on Language," "The men who come eagerly to enjoy themselves [at a comedy], taste afterward the useful lesson that lay underneath."[23]

The genre of comedy also allows Machiavelli to distance himself from the evil things said and done on the stage because he is not saying or doing any of them.[24] In *Mandragola*, the characters do all the talking, whereas Machiavelli says nothing. Even the prologue to the play is spoken by a representative of Machiavelli; any direct reference to "the author" himself is anonymous and in the third person. This feature of *Mandragola* is different from *The Prince* and *Discourses*, in which Machiavelli gives teachings in his own voice that may be shocking to some. For example, in the *Prince*, Machiavelli writes, "A man who wants to make a profession of good in all regards must come to ruin among so many who are not good" (*P*15); in the *Discourses*, he similarly states that "goodness is not enough" (*D*3.30.1). These statements were left unpublished. In *Mandragola*, which was published and performed, the character Timoteo says, "Many times one comes to harm by being too easygoing and too-good" (4.6). Upstanding citizens, instead of being shocked, can laugh at this unseemly piece of advice because it is spoken by a corrupt character in a light comedy instead of by a political theorist in a serious treatise. And it is noteworthy that the *Art of War,* the only major political writing that Machiavelli published under his own name while he lived, is also a dramatic dialogue between characters, none of whom is named Machiavelli.

With this strategy, Machiavelli entertains the good, teaches the clever, and keeps himself out of controversy until after his death. *Mandragola* was obviously suitable enough for a pope, given that it was performed for Leo X at his request. But those who dare to look beneath the triviality of *Mandragola*—who consider what the play actually teaches when the laughter subsides—will find a "useful" lesson with revolutionary consequences.[25] It teaches certain "tricks" that might empower humans to overcome the vicissitudes of fortune, as suggested by the song that opens the play:

> because whoever deprives himself of pleasure,
> to live with anguish and with worries,
> doesn't know the tricks
> of the world, or by what ills
> and by what strange happenings
> all mortals are almost overwhelmed.

Mandragola reveals the tricks of the world to those who are willing to learn.

Ancient Virtue and the "New Case"

Machiavelli writes in the prologue that he wants us "to understand a new case born in this city." And yet despite Machiavelli's promise of something new, he appeals to the standard of something old.[26] He expects *Mandragola* to be poorly received because "the present age falls off from ancient virtue (*antica virtù*)," thereby suggesting that only those with ancient virtue will appreciate this radical new case (Pr). The simultaneous evocation of the "ancient" and the "new" in *Mandragola* is similar to the preface of book 1 of the *Discourses,* in which Machiavelli declares that he has "decided to take a path as yet untrodden by anyone" to find "new modes and orders." Then, in the next paragraph, he writes that he is studying Livy to revive the example of classical Rome since "no sign of that ancient virtue remains with us" (D1. Pr.1–2). Machiavelli, once again, associates the "new" with "ancient virtue"; the "path as yet untrodden by anyone" appears to have been well traveled by the ancients. We are left to wonder if Machiavelli is attempting to introduce something truly unique or merely reviving something old.

By "ancient virtue," Machiavelli is not referring to "Christian virtue," which looks to the biblical prescriptions contained in the Decalogue and the New Testament. In fact, Machiavelli does not use the term "Christian virtue" in any of his writings. By this omission, he implies that politics requires actions that go against the morality advocated by Jesus in the Sermon on the Mount.[27] Similarly, he never speaks of "Greek virtue" as elaborated by Plato and Aristotle.[28] He does, however, use the term "Roman virtue."[29] For Machiavelli, "ancient virtue" means "Roman virtue," and he turns to Livy's history of Rome as a compendium of this lost excellence.[30] True to the Latin word *virtus,* which originally denoted manliness, "ancient virtue" for Machiavelli refers to spiritedness, power, ability, and endurance—qualities that helped the Romans establish and enlarge their empire. In this sense, ancient virtue, as practiced by the Romans, was civic-minded; the "common good"—which is to say, the expansion of Rome—was realized through each individual's strength and fortitude. But ancient qualities such as power and civic-mindedness are, according to Machiavelli, conspicuously absent in Christian Europe. He blames the Christian religion itself for the decline of ancient virtue; he argues it has made the world weak and encouraged sectarian divisions.[31] In the *Discourses,* Machiavelli claims that the memory of ancient virtue was nearly eliminated when Christianity became the official religion of Rome. He writes that the "Christian sect" set about "burning the works of the poets and the historians, ruining images, and spoiling every other thing that might convey some sign of antiquity" (D 2.5.1). Unlike "Gentile" religious expressions, which placed the highest good "in greatness of spirit, strength of body, and all other things capable of making men very strong," Christianity "glorified humble and contemplative more than active men." Christian humility, according to Machiavelli, has "rendered the world weak" since "the collectivity of men, so as to go to paradise, think more of enduring their beatings than of avenging them." He concludes that the world has been "made effeminate"[32] due to "the cowardice of the men who have interpreted our religion according to idleness and not according to virtue" (*D* 2.2.2). Machiavelli desires a new interpretation that will encourage audacious human beings to conquer, rather than suffer, fortune.

It is clear that Machiavelli uses the term "ancient virtue" to both berate and motivate his contemporaries. He evokes the example of ancient Rome as a challenge, daring others to do something strong—even if it is merely writing a good comedy. In the prologue to *Mandragola,* Machiavelli expects that members of his Christian audience will condemn the play out of idleness rather than undertake the "labor," "strain," and "thousand discomforts" of writing comedies of their own. In other words, they are not manly enough to create something themselves, but they are idle enough to criticize those who do. This unwillingness to experience creative discomfort is, for Machiavelli, symptomatic of how far the "present age falls off from ancient virtue."

But Machiavelli does not just use the term "virtue" (*virtù*) in the sense of Roman virtue. Throughout his writings, the meaning tends to shift. Machiavelli has a tendency to call certain actions "virtuous" that, from either a Roman or a Christian perspective, could only be labeled "vices." Machiavelli's advocacy of "well-used" evils is well known (*P* 8); his tendency to speak of well-used evils as *virtuous* is less renowned, more troubling, and most radical.

Consider, for instance, Machiavelli's account of Agathocles the Sicilian in the eighth chapter of *The Prince*.[33] According to Machiavelli, Agathocles became king of Syracuse through a notorious series of crimes that should appal both good Romans and good Christians. Machiavelli writes, "One cannot call it virtue to kill one's citizens, betray one's friends, to be without faith, without mercy, without religion." Here, Machiavelli suggests that virtue—whether Roman or Christian—is categorically distinct from the sort of immoralities committed by Agathocles in ancient Syracuse.[34] However, in the next sentence, Machiavelli refers to the "*virtue* of Agathocles in entering into and escaping from dangers." And earlier in the same chapter, Machiavelli claims that Agathocles' "*crimes* were accompanied with such *virtue* of body and spirit" that he easily rose to the top of the military (*P* 8; my emphasis). Machiavelli seems to contradict himself: on the one hand, he says that Agathocles' crimes cannot be called virtuous; on the other, he says they are exemplary of virtue.[35]

Machiavelli's contradictory use of "virtue" is obviously intentional. He subtly suggests that the correct use of evil is virtuous, but then he takes back this suggestion.[36] He gives himself an alibi, lest he should ever be accused of saying evil is good under certain circumstances. His tendency to conflate virtue with certain forms of vice suggests that he is developing a new conception of human excellence—a conception that looks to the Romans for guidance but deviates from them in crucial respects. Though he often presents his understanding of "virtue" as a revival of "ancient virtue," a different teaching emerges when one carefully considers his writings. In the *Discourses*, Machiavelli does not just report the examples of virtue emulated by Livy; he frequently alters them in subtle, yet very significant, ways. According to Strauss, Machiavelli "consciously uses Livy for his non-Livian purposes,"[37] suggesting that Machiavelli is trying to refine the virtue of the very Romans who he claims should be emulated. Similarly, Harvey Mansfield and Nathan Tarcov write:

> [Machiavelli] praises ancient virtue in order to improve upon it. He wants to free it from inhibitions placed on it by writers such as those who inconsiderately blamed Hannibal's cruelty when in fact it was one of his infinite virtues (*P* 18; *D* 3.21.4, 40.1). . . . Ancient virtue, it turns out, needs a Machiavellian interpretation to ensure that it is reported correctly. Even Livy, who is not the type to enthuse and philosophize about ancient virtue, and who is treated with such reverence by Machiavelli, needs at least occasionally, and perhaps generally, to be set right. . . . The Machiavellian interpretation [of Livy] transforms ancient virtue into virtue proper, Machiavellian virtue.[38]

What is true of the *Discourses* is also true of *Mandragola*. As noted, the plot of *Mandragola* is derived from Livy's account of Lucretia, the legendary woman who stood as an exemplar of virtue for the Romans. But Machiavelli does not simply commemorate Lucretia's ancient virtue with a comic retelling of her tragic tale. Instead, he gives us a "new case" with a new "Lucrezia" who is markedly different from Livy's virtuous matron. *Mandragola*, in the words of the character Timoteo, is a "new sprout on the old" (5.6). Indeed, Machiavelli's critique of Livy in *Man-*

dragola is more obvious and direct than his critique in the *Discourses*. It is clear that Machiavelli is not simply trying to cure the weakness of Christian morality with ancient virtue. He is also attempting to remedy Roman *virtus* because it is not proficient enough at the "tricks of the world." True virtue—Machiavellian *virtù*—requires one to use vice in a way that Livy would have disapproved.

The Rape of Lucretia and the Mandrake Remedy

According to Livy, Lucretia was raped during the reign of the Roman king Tarquinius Superbus.[39] The rape was the result of a drunken dispute that occurred during the siege of Ardea (c. 509 B.C.E.). One night, during a break in the siege, a group of Roman noblemen got into a heated discussion over who had the most virtuous wife. Tarquinius Collantinus, a kinsman to the king, argued that his wife, Lucretia, exceeded all other Roman women. To prove it, he persuaded the men to return to Rome that night to put their spouses to the test. When the men arrived back at the capital unannounced, all their wives were discovered at a licentious party with young friends. The only exception was Lucretia, who was at home working with her servants. Collantinus won the contest for having the most virtuous wife; however, the sight of Lucretia's virtue and beauty incited the lust of Sextus Tarquin, the youngest son of the Roman king. A few days later Sextus secretly returned to Collantinus's residence and raped Lucretia.

The plot of *Mandragola* is initiated by a similar set of circumstances. At the start of the play we are introduced to an Italian expatriate named Callimaco Guadagni, who reports that while in Paris he was privy to an argument between a group of Florentine men concerning which country had the most beautiful women: Italy or France. One of the men, Cammillo Calfucci, argued that the refinement and beauty of his aunt "Lucrezia" in Florence was enough to redeem all Italian women. Cammillo's description of Lucrezia was so effective that it convinced Callimaco to travel to Florence to find her. When he arrives in Florence and sees Lucrezia, he discovers that her actual beauty and virtue exceed her reputation. Callimaco is now "burning with . . . a desire to be with her," though it will be difficult to get what he wants (1.1). He cannot honestly court Lucrezia because she is married to Nicia Calfucci, an old and wealthy doctor of laws (*dottore*). His only options, then, are rape or adultery. Callimaco will find his way into Lucrezia's bed before the play is finished, but he will employ different methods than Sextus. These new modes have markedly different results.

In Livy, Sextus uses force and coercion to entrap Lucretia. He bursts into her bedroom with a sword and threatens to kill her if she will not submit to his lust. When Lucretia adamantly refuses, Sextus goes one step further and threatens to punish her with everlasting disgrace. He tells Lucretia that he will murder her along with a male slave and place their bodies together in the same bed. He threatens to then tell the world that he killed the two of them when he caught them together in bed, thereby ensuring that Lucretia's name is forever dishonored. Upon hearing this threat, Lucretia reluctantly yields to Sextus's demands.

Sextus's actions have political consequences. The next day, Lucretia summons her father and her husband and asks them to come with trusted friends. Lucretia tells them that she was raped by Sextus and demands that they avenge the crime. But Lucretia also thinks she must take further action to protect her reputation and promote chastity among Roman women. Since she willingly yielded to Sextus, albeit under coercion, she is afraid that her action might serve as a convenient precedent for adulterous women to justify their behavior in the future, and thereby allow them to escape the Roman death penalty prescribed for infidelity. Lucretia says, "For my own part, though I acquit myself of the sin [of adultery], I do not absolve myself from punishment; not in time to come shall ever unchaste woman live through the example of Lucretia."[40] In front of the assembled men she stabs herself with a sword.

One of the men in the assembly is Lucius Junius Brutus, a companion of Lucretia's husband. Brutus is considered dimwitted and mute, but his idiocy is feigned so that the ruling family will not perceive him as a danger. Brutus is waiting for the right moment to avenge the deaths of his own father and brother, who were killed by King Tarquinius to obtain their wealth. The moment arrives with Lucretia's suicide: he withdraws the sword from Lucretia's side, and with vehement rhetoric—which appears miraculous after his feigned muteness—he inspires the men to revolt against the Tarquin "tyranny." Brutus takes Lucretia's body out in public, revealing to the people what Sextus has done and reminding them of the many abuses they have suffered. Brutus's actions and oratory inspire the people to rebel against the Tarquins. In the rebellion, they force the entire ruling family to leave Rome, including Sextus, who is later killed by "revengers of old quarrels."[41] With the defeat of the Tarquins, the Roman people decide to have no more kings: they install Brutus and Collatinus as the first consuls of the Roman republic. A new order is born.

Livy presents the rape of Lucretia as a brutal act that ultimately destroys Sextus and his entire family. Machiavelli's Callimaco, on the other hand, violates Lucrezia with methods that are less self-destructive than those of his Roman counterpart. Though impetuous like Sextus, Callimaco proceeds with more discretion. He does not barge into Lucrezia's bedchamber with threats and ultimatums; he tries instead to organize a conspiracy that will land him in Lucrezia's bed under more favorable conditions, and which might even allow him to obtain her unforced consent. However, Callimaco is aware that Lucrezia is not an openly licentious woman. Like her Roman namesake, Lucrezia stays at home with her servants and keeps away from "amusements" that usually delight young women her age. Callimaco says, "Her nature, which is extremely honest and in all ways alien to the things of love, makes war against me." Despite Lucrezia's resistance, Callimaco hopes to "change her nature" through seduction, not through physical attack or compulsion (1.1).

Callimaco is aware of three factors that might help him satisfy his desire. First, Lucrezia's husband, Nicia, is, according to Callimaco, "the simplest and most stupid man in Florence." Second, Nicia and Lucrezia have been unable to conceive a child after six years of marriage. Nicia blames Lucrezia for this problem, but—given Nicia's old age—the most likely cause is his own infertility or impotence, which has caused a rift in the marriage. Nicia is especially distressed about their inability to conceive and says he is "ready to do anything" (1.2). Third, and last, Callimaco is aware that Lucrezia's mother, Sostrata, is a woman of "good company" (*buona compagna*) or "easy virtue" (1.1). Sostrata does not have a husband, and we are not told that she is a widow. Lucrezia might be the product of an illicit affair.

These factors, then, will help Callimaco if he proceeds properly, but he cannot proceed alone. He uses his faithful servant Siro to perform menial tasks, and he hires Ligurio, a clever but unemployed marriage broker, to assist him. Ligurio, we are told, is "familiar" with Nicia and is trying to trick him into cuckoldry. He attempts to persuade Nicia to take his wife to the public baths outside Florence, which are apparently good for fertility. At least this is the reason offered by Ligurio. The real reason, of course, is to loosen Lucrezia's virtue. Callimaco reports that people "do nothing but party" at these places; in such a licentious environment, Callimaco hopes to woo Lucrezia with "pleasant amusement" and "magnificence" (1.1). But there are problems with this scheme. Ligurio has difficulty persuading Nicia to take his wife out of town. Ligurio is also aware that Callimaco's self-proclaimed "magnificence" might not be enough to win Lucrezia's affection in a bathhouse. As Ligurio points out, there could be other suitors at the baths who are "richer" and "more gracious" than Callimaco (1.3). In place of the bathhouse plan, Ligurio devises a new conspiracy designed more to trick Lucrezia out of her fidelity than to acquire her immediate consent. He concocts the mandrake remedy.

On Ligurio's advice, Callimaco pretends to be a doctor from the French royal court promoting a cure for infertility that worked for the king and queen of France. Callimaco tells Nicia that Lucrezia can easily be made pregnant if she takes a potion made from the mandrake root (*mandragola*). There is, however, a catch with this supposed cure: the first man to sleep with Lucrezia after she consumes the remedy will die of a venereal infection caused by mandrake poison. To ensure that Nicia is not killed, a man—unaware that Lucrezia is lethal—must be kidnapped and forced to have sex with her. Lucrezia will then become pregnant. As well, the poison from her body will be extracted into the body of the unknown suitor, thereby making her safe for future intercourse.

Nicia, impressed by Callimaco's apparent authority and diagnosis in Latin, eventually agrees to go ahead with this supposed cure (2.6). Of course, the entire remedy is a fraud, designed so that Callimaco will be the "unfortunate" man captured to impregnate Lucrezia. Eventually, the plan is realized. In Act 3, Lucrezia is persuaded by her confessor, Friar Timoteo, to undergo this cure for infertility. She consumes a bogus "mandrake" potion and waits in bed for her mysterious suitor (4.2). In Act 4, a disguised Callimaco is seized in a mock kidnapping and forced into Lucrezia's bedroom by Nicia himself. Under a medicinal pretense, Callimaco is finally in a position where he can demonstrate his "magnificence" to Lucrezia without violence or coercion. This he does, with beneficial consequences that are beyond his wildest imaginings. Lucrezia is so impressed by her first encounter with Callimaco that she wants more. After Callimaco reveals his true identity to her, the two of them decide to continue their illicit affair and get married after Nicia dies. In the meantime, all the characters assume that Lucrezia is pregnant — with a boy, no less. The play ends with everyone satisfied with what has taken place, especially Nicia, who offers Callimaco and Ligurio the key to his residence, effectively giving Callimaco unimpeded access to his wife. A new order is born.

It is obvious that none of the characters in *Mandragola* embody the Livian ideal of ancient virtue referred to in the prologue of the play. Some commentators conclude that *Mandragola* is a satire showing how far Renaissance Florentines have fallen from the ancient virtue of Lucretia and Brutus. Ronald L. Martinez writes, "*Mandragola* holds at its heart an etiological fable of the defection of ancient virtue. . . . [Livy's] tale of Lucretia, for Machiavelli the inception of a utopian ideal of civic virtue, gives the measure that permits *Mandragola* to be grasped as the etiology of dystopia."[42] But a close examination of *Mandragola* reveals that this argument is mistaken. Machiavelli, as I have already suggested, does not hold the Livian account of virtue as his "utopia." Qualities such as manliness, civic-mindedness, and chastity are not, as Livy would have us believe, inherently virtuous regardless of consequence. Machiavellian *virtù* is measured by effectiveness — by the ability to act in ways that ensure success regardless of what is required. With effectiveness as our measure, we must ask ourselves: Which character in *Mandragola* is the most "Machiavellian"? Answering this question is the key to understanding this play.

Callimaco: Ancient Virtue and Its Weaknesses

What is striking about the character Callimaco is that he embodies the qualities of Roman virtue that Machiavelli praises elsewhere: he is manly, powerful, virile, spirited, and enterprising. He possesses the youthful impetuousness that Machiavelli, in *The Prince*, says is necessary for conquering Lady Fortune:

> Fortune is a woman; and it is necessary, if one wants to hold her down, to beat her and strike her down. And one sees that she lets herself be won more by the impetuous than by those who proceed coldly. And so always, like a woman, she is the friend of the young,

because they are less cautious, more ferocious, and command her with more audacity. (*P* 25)

Machiavelli often argues that the strength and fortitude of the Romans allowed them to dominate fortune.[43] Similarly, Callimaco's audacity and spiritedness are effective tools for conquering Lucrezia, his Lady Fortune.[44] He does not use brute force, but his forceful nature is essential for acquiring what he wants. Callimaco's pursuit of sexual gratification might initially seem at odds with the austerity of Roman political *virtus.* Nevertheless, like the Roman republic, Callimaco's intentions are primarily expansionary: he wants to acquire another man's wife, just as the Romans sought to acquire other peoples' territories. Even Callimaco's name suggests a conquering spirit akin to Roman *virtus:* "Calli-maco" is formed from two Greek words, one meaning "noble" (*kalos*), the other meaning "battle" (*machê*); his last name, Guadagni, is Italian for "advantages," "profits," or "gains."[45]

We are informed of Callimaco's background in the first scene of the play. He was born in Italy but was sent to Paris when he was ten years old after his parents died. He is now thirty and has spent the past twenty years in Paris dividing his time between "studies," "pleasures," and "business." In other words, Callimaco has not dedicated a single moment of his life to either politics or warfare. He tells us that ten years ago, when he was twenty, he decided not to return home because King Charles VIII of France invaded Italy and nearly ruined the country.[46] This means that Callimaco, at a prime age for fighting, fought for neither the French nor the Italians. Callimaco's interests, it would seem, are primarily confined to the private realm. Nevertheless, like King Charles, Callimaco has moved from France into Italy to acquire something that is not rightfully his. His actions will also have consequences beyond the private realm, affecting Florentine society in a manner he did not originally intend.

Despite Callimaco's private concerns, he manifests a Roman attitude in his understanding of conquest, victory, and suicide. He likens his effort to seduce Lucezia to going into battle. He says that Lucrezia's austere nature "makes war against me" (1.1). He also asserts that he will either die or kill himself if he does not overcome Lucrezia's resistance (1.3, 4.1). In the context of the play, these references to death are humorous. Nevertheless, Callimaco expresses a central tenet of ancient Roman virtue: better death with honor than life with dishonor. In Livy, Lucretia commits suicide so that she will not be dishonored as an adulteress. In Callimaco's case, dishonor is not found in sexual licentiousness but in failing to seize what you set out to acquire. It is, for Callimaco, more "manly" to be killed or to kill yourself than to live with the shame of defeat. Such manliness is evident in Callimaco's understanding of divine punishment. In Act 4, he acknowledges that his desire to debauch Lucrezia might lead to his eternal damnation. But he also says to himself, "How many others are dead! And there are so many good men in hell! Are you ashamed to go there? Face your lot; flee evil, but, not being able to flee it, bear it like a man; don't prostrate yourself, don't degrade yourself like a woman" (4.1). Callimaco evokes the specter of damnation not to terrorize himself into repenting his sins but to strengthen his manly spirit. He transforms the Christian hell into an honorable place, akin to Homeric myths of the underworld or Dante's account of the first circle. For Callimaco, eternal damnation is a test of manliness.

Callimaco, then, is a Roman of the private realm; he is willing to face any adversity—even hellfire—if he can get new acquisitions. Sheer manliness, however, is not enough to ensure success. It occasionally becomes excessive, affecting Callimaco's ability to think clearly and making him prone to passionate outbursts. In 1.3, he exclaims that he will "die" if he cannot get Lucrezia and will do "anything" to satisfy his desire—even if it is "bestial, cruel, nefarious." Ligurio, when he hears Callimaco say these things, tells him to "curb such a rush of spirit (*animo*)" because it will undermine the entire enterprise. Callimaco is momentarily calmed by Ligurio's words, proving that he possesses enough discretion to let his unruly spirit be directed by someone else. However, he needs Ligurio's clearheadedness to be effective.[47] Conquering Lucrezia, and hence fortune, requires more than just ferocity. In *The Prince*, Machiavelli claims that it is good for a prince to be ferocious like a lion, but a prince must also be clever and deceptive like a fox if he is to be successful (see *P*18). In *Mandragola*, Ligurio makes Callimaco more "Machiavellian" by instructing him to use less of the ferocious lion and more of the deceptive fox. Callimaco is, thus, partially transformed from a haughty brute into a sly "pretender and dissembler" (*P*18). Throughout the course of the play, he takes on the personae of both a medical doctor and a hapless suitor, tricking both Nicia and Lucrezia with his disguises. Callimaco, it seems, has a natural talent for deception, but he depends on Ligurio's council to know how to use it. His Roman virtue always needs to be supplemented by something else to ensure success.

Nicia: Contemporary Weakness and Its Strengths

Lucrezia's husband, Nicia, is described by Ligurio as a man "of little prudence" (*di poco prudenzia*) and even "less spirit" (*di meno animo*) (1.3). He appears to embody all the qualities that Machiavelli criticizes in his Christian contemporaries. In contrast to Callimaco's youth, strength, spiritedness, and manliness, Nicia is old, weak, spiritless, and effeminate. As the song after the second act says, "Ambition does not press him, fear does not move him." Nicia desperately desires to have an heir to his fortune, but he appears to lack the intelligence, initiative, and fertility to do anything about it.

Throughout the play, Nicia's effeminacy is continually emphasized, in stark opposition to Callimaco's manliness. We are told that Nicia is governed by Lucrezia "in all things" (1.1); we see that he has a tremendous, and strikingly feminine, desire for a child (1.2); we hear him exclaim that he will cry womanly tears of "tenderness" (3.8); we see him carry a "little sword" underneath his cloak when setting out to capture Lucrezia's suitor (4.7); and, finally, we hear him boast of inspecting the suitor's body, including the genitalia, before allowing Callimaco to have intercourse with his wife (5.2). Regarding this last point, Nicia's inspection suggests homosexuality. He says to Ligurio, "You never saw finer flesh! White, soft, smooth" (5.2).

In the prologue, we are told that Nicia is a doctor of law who learned his trade from "Buethius" (*Buezio*), a misspelling of Boethius (*Boezio*), the Christian philosopher from the late classical period who, in *The Consolation of Philosophy,* celebrates the contemplative life over the political life.[48] Machiavelli misspells Boethius's name with *bue,* Italian for "ox." The implication is that philosophical men—and particularly Christian philosophers—are as servile as oxen.[49] Nicia appears to be the embodiment of Christian idleness. He has lived a contemplative life of sorts, and it seems to have distorted his understanding of the real world, leaving him idle and weak. Ligurio says to Nicia, "Someone like you, who stays in his study all day, understands those books, and doesn't know how to figure out the things of the world (*cose del mondo*)" (3.2). Worldly men like Callimaco and Ligurio easily lead Nicia astray by preying on his zealous desire for a child.

Ligurio tells us that Nicia is favored by "fortune," given that he is rich (by inheritance it would seem, though it is never made clear) and has a beautiful wife. But this good fortune is not related to any excellence on Nicia's part. His lack of virtue threatens both his marriage and his wealth: he cannot impregnate Lucrezia, and he claims to have no income ("not a hundred *lire,* not a hundred *grossi,* even!") because no one in Florence will hire him (2.3). Nicia, exactly like Machiavelli in the prologue, complains that his unemployment is due to the absence of virtue in contemporary Florence. He says, "In this city there are none who aren't shitsticks (*cacastecchi*); here they don't appreciate any *virtù*" (2.3). From all appearances, however, Nicia is not virtuous in any sense of the word. He is a vulgar man who, through wealth and education, has acquired the veneer of gentility. He tries to present himself as a true gentleman, representing the qualities of scholarship, law, and authority. His occasional use of French and Latin gives the appearance of sophistication but none of this is enough to hide his obvious crudeness, which is evident in his frequent use of profanities. The other characters often address Nicia by his official title, *dottore;* and Callimaco panders to Nicia's impression of himself, complementing the *dottore* as a man both "virtuous and good" (2.2). However, Nicia is clearly corrupt and hypocritical. He is willing to let a strange man sleep with his wife, and he participates in a conspiracy that, to his dim knowledge, results in the poisoning of another person. For this he expresses slight regret (see 5.2).

Nicia appears to be so base and so pathetic that we do not mind seeing him tricked by his younger, smarter, and stronger associates. But Nicia is not totally defeated at the end of the play: he is in some ways triumphant, as suggested by his name, which is derived from the Greek word for victory (*nikē*).[50] If Lucrezia is actually pregnant with a boy at the end of the play, then Nicia finally acquires the heir he wants. Nevertheless, he seems to be completely ignorant of how his "victory" was achieved. The mandrake remedy is a fraud: Lucrezia does not, in fact, consume a dangerous mandrake potion or any other fertility drug, nor is the man responsible for Lucrezia's assumed pregnancy actually poisoned. Nicia,

however, assures himself that his wife is pregnant and that her impregnator is dead (5.2); he appears oblivious of the fact that Callimaco is the
real impregnator who will return to Lucrezia's bedroom for future encounters. Callimaco has penetrated to the core of Nicia's household, acquiring governance over Lucrezia and threatening the posterity of the
Calfucci family name. By the end of the play, Lucrezia declares Callimaco
her "lord, master, and guide" (5.4). Ostensibly, Callimaco's ancient Roman
virtue defeats Nicia's contemporary Christian effeminacy.

Nicia appears to be the least Machiavellian character in the play. But
there is a disturbing possibility that he is, in fact, the most Machiavellian,
and perhaps the most like Machiavelli himself.[51] Machiavelli provides us
with several clues. Like Machiavelli, who "has been cut off / from showing with other undertakings other virtue" (Pr), Nicia is unemployed and
mostly shut out from political society; like Machiavelli, Nicia spends
his days reading and writing; like Machiavelli, Nicia finds he must cavort
with younger types to get anything done; and, like Machiavelli, Nicia attributes his unemployment to the lack of "virtue" in modern Florence
(2.3). There is even a strong resemblance between the name Nicia and
Machiavelli's first name, Niccolò.[52] It is possible, then, that Nicia is not as
stupid as he appears—that he is feigning his ineptitude so that no one
will suspect his motives, much like Brutus in Livy's account of the rape of
Lucretia. As a result, all the other characters in *Mandragola* think they
are taking advantage of Nicia, when it is in fact Nicia who is taking advantage of them. Like Brutus, Nicia uses Lucrezia's violation to serve his
own advantage and found a new order. But unlike Brutus, Nicia never
lets his true virtue be seen by others.[53] He remains an ostensible halfwit
to the end.

Nicia is faced with an inheritance problem at the start of the play:
he wants an heir to his estate but has not been able to get one after six
years of marriage (1.1). Consequently, he needs to find a younger man to
get Lucrezia pregnant under circumstances that are acceptable to both
himself and his wife. To arrange this, he hires the clever Ligurio. Though
it appears that Ligurio is primarily an agent of Callimaco, this is not spe-
cified. It may be that Ligurio is working primarily with Nicia to get Callimaco to sleep with Lucrezia.[54] If we presume that Nicia can see through
Callimaco's doctor impersonation and is aware that the phony doctor
desires Lucrezia, then it is clear that, from Nicia's perspective, Callimaco

is not a bad choice to be his wife's impregnator. Even if Nicia does not know Callimaco's true identity, he can nevertheless see that this man has what he wants. Callimaco seems virile, has had a good education (as attested by his language skills), and desires Lucrezia. Nicia hires Ligurio, then, to create the proper circumstances under which Lucrezia and Callimaco can procreate under the cloak of semirespectability and conceive an heir. Ligurio's first plan is to take Lucrezia to the bathhouses, but Nicia is, understandably, suspicious of this idea. The bathhouses are places of ill repute, and there is no guarantee that Lucrezia will relinquish her chastity in such an environment. Even if she does, she will not necessarily engage in sex with a suitor of Nicia's choice. It is Nicia's unwillingness to pursue the bathhouse remedy that causes Ligurio to come up with the mandrake solution. For this solution to work, Ligurio suggests they bring Lucrezia's confessor, Friar Timoteo, into the conspiracy— the only man who can persuade Lucrezia to consume the potion and sleep with a stranger. Timoteo will not only dispose Lucrezia toward this remedy; he will give the entire enterprise a religious sanctification as well. It is when Ligurio proposes Timoteo's involvement that Nicia consents fully to the new plan (2.6). Though it appears that Nicia is being taken in, he might actually be directing the way in which events proceed. He just lets others attend to the details.

Other actions by Nicia that initially appear ridiculous may in fact be the expedients of a clever mastermind. For instance, when Nicia examines Callimaco's body to make sure it is disease-free and sexually functional, he is exerting control over certain variables that otherwise he would not have. Through this inspection, Nicia assures himself that Lucrezia will not be made sick and that she stands a chance of being impregnated. And when Nicia gives Callimaco the key to his estate the following morning, it is not necessarily as dimwitted as it first appears. Lucrezia and Callimaco have slept together only once, and the "mandrake potion" is a fraud; Lucrezia might not be pregnant at all, let alone with a boy. Perhaps Nicia is fully aware of this. By giving Callimaco a key, Nicia encourages future sexual encounters to increase the odds of pregnancy. This also ensures that every sexual liaison between Lucrezia and Callimaco will take place on Nicia's estate, out of the public eye. There is even the suggestion that Nicia has acquired a new woman. In Act 5, he is noticeably friendly with his notorious mother-in-law, Sostrata; they now appear as an elderly couple (see 5.2, 5.5). Again, Nicia keeps everything under his control and gets what he wants. Perhaps Ligurio's comment to Nicia toward the end of the play is not as ironic as it first sounds: "With how much prudence you've managed this thing" (5.2).

Friar Timoteo's Reformation

The ambiguities surrounding Nicia raise serious questions about the true meaning of "strength" and "weakness" in Machiavelli's thought. Nicia seems, on first impression, to embody all the problems that Machiavelli is trying to remedy in his contemporaries. As a student of Boethius, Nicia ostensibly suffers from the weakness that afflicts Christian contemplatives. But even though it appears that Callimaco's Roman virility is triumphant over Nicia's Christian impotence, the reverse might be true. If so, it reflects a historical reality of which Machiavelli was undoubtedly aware. It was, after all, the supposedly weak and humble Christians who triumphed over pagan Rome at the end of the classical age, transforming the Roman Empire into the Holy Roman Empire. With Nicia, Machiavelli suggests that the ostensible weakness of Christians masks a subterranean cleverness that undermines the candid ferocity of Romans. Christianity conquered the world as it preached humility. Whatever Machiavelli's criticisms of Christianity, he does not dismiss the religion entirely.[55] It has proven itself an incredibly effective movement, even if the effects are not always to Machiavelli's liking. Machiavelli wants to introduce a new "spirit" that is in some sense derived from Christianity—a spirit that mixes the worldliness of the Romans with the clandestine tactics of the Christians and improves on both. In *Mandragola,* Friar Timoteo acts as religious adviser for this new spirit, though he may not be its most perfect embodiment.

In a letter to his friend Luigi Guicciardini, dated May 17, 1521, Machiavelli expressed the need for a new type of Christian friar:

> In truth, I know that I am at variance with the ideas of [Florentine] citizens, as I am in many other matters. They would like a preacher who would teach them the way to paradise, and I should like to find one who would teach them the way to go to the Devil. . . . For I be-

lieve that the following would be the true way to go to Paradise: learn the way to Hell in order to steer clear of it.[56]

In *Mandragola,* Timoteo seems to be this type of preacher. At one point, Lucrezia asks Timoteo, "What are you leading me to, Padre?" (3.11). In light of the passage above, we can see that he is leading her down the "way to Hell," showing her the earthly damnation of being an abandoned, childless widow. To avoid this, she must learn the way of Hell, and perhaps employ some of the Devil's own tricks. Timoteo practices the type of religion that Machiavelli thinks is lacking in his contemporaries: one that esteems success in this world through decisive—and perhaps unseemly—action rather than suffering in this world for the sake of the next.[57] But Timoteo is not a "pagan," nor is he cynically using the church as a mere means to achieve his "secular" ends. He understands himself as a reformer whose innovations are grounded in biblical precedent. His new gospel, however, comes at a price.

Timoteo is described in the prologue as an "ill-living friar" (*frate mal vissuto*), but his "ill-living" is not the sort normally associated with friars in Renaissance literature. He is not sexually licentious, nor is he given to fine clothes, luxury, or decadence. Furthermore, he is not cruel or sadistic.[58] His primary motivation is to acquire money. If he is paid handsomely, he is willing to sanctify things that, on first glance, appear sinful. But Timoteo does not desire money for his own personal fortune; on the contrary, all the evidence in the play suggests that he is trying to increase the wealth of the church. Though he seems to honor money above all else, his name is derived from the Greek name Timothy, which literally means "honor God" (*timē-theos*).[59] In the New Testament, there are two Pauline letters written to someone named Timothy.[60] In the first letter, Timothy is told that "the love of money is a root of all kinds of evil" (1 Tim. 6:10). But if the love of money causes evils, it is nevertheless a love that, in Timoteo's view, must be accepted if the church is to survive. For Timoteo, it is impossible to honor God if one does not honor money. His mission, therefore, is to increase the wealth of the church and bolster church attendance, even if this means countenancing acts that are traditionally deemed sinful. Timoteo is a deeply religious man, if by "religious" we mean someone who believes in God and who acts to support the church. Nothing in any of his soliloquies suggests that Timoteo is an

atheist or that he is using the church for ulterior motives. Since he finds
himself in a fallen world, he deems it necessary to compromise perfect
moral goodness to ensure the survival of the church. As he says, "Many
times one comes to harm by being too easy-going and too good, as well
as by being too wicked" (4.6). For Timoteo, wickedness and goodness
must be used in the right measure.

Like Machiavelli, Timoteo criticizes the church for breeding effeminacy. Timoteo's laity is composed mostly of superstitious women. When
we are first introduced to him in 3.3, Timoteo is having a discussion with
an unnamed "Donna" concerning the state of her dead husband's soul.
The donna breaks off her conversation with him because she sees another
woman who has some "thread" of hers.[61] Timoteo admits that he toler-
ates the annoyances of women because they are charitable in their dona-
tions (3.4). But he has a typically dismissive, and sexist, attitude toward
women. At one point he exclaims, "All women have few brains (*poco
cervella*)" (3.9). He later complains about the "few brains" of his fellow
friars (5.1), suggesting that the effeminacy of the laity has spread to the
clergy. Timoteo tries to correct this through his own reformation of the
church. He undertakes this reformation by providing a more worldly interpretation of Scripture and church dogma.

Ligurio senses that Timoteo is no dupe. He says to Nicia, "These *frati*
are cunning, astute; and it stands to reason, because they know our sins
and their own" (3.2). Ligurio also suspects that Timoteo is a religious
reformer who will sanctify any outrage—even adultery and incidental
homicide—if he is offered a handsome payment. But before asking Timoteo to participate in the mandrake plot, Ligurio decides to test his wickedness by asking him to legitimize a second trimester abortion. Ligurio tells
Timoteo a fallacious story concerning the young daughter of Nicia's
nephew Cammillo Calfucci. According to Ligurio, this girl was placed in
the care of a convent but is now four months pregnant, much to the em-
barrassment of the nunnery and the Calfucci family. Ligurio offers Timoteo three hundred ducats if he will convince the abbess of the convent to
administer a potion that will make the girl miscarry. Ligurio adds:

> Keep in mind, in doing this, how many goods will result from it; you
> maintain the honour of the convent, of the girl, of her relatives; you
> restore a daughter to her father; you satisfy Messer here [Nicia],

and so many of his relatives; you do as much charity as you can with these three hundred ducats; and on the other side, you don't offend anything but a piece of unborn flesh, without sense, which could be dispersed in a thousand ways; and I believe that good is that which does good to the most, and that by which the most are contented.

Timoteo responds, "So be it in the name of God. I'll do what you want, and may everything be done for God and for charity." Ligurio now knows that if Timoteo is willing to bless an abortion, then a lesser evil like adultery will be easy for the *frate* to facilitate for the right price. Ligurio says to Timoteo, "Now you seem to me that man of religion that I believed you were" (3.4).

In the midst of this suspicious discussion, Ligurio pretends to be called away for a moment, only to return with the "great news" that the girl in the abbey has miscarried on her own. An abortion will no longer be necessary. However, Ligurio calls Timoteo aside to tell him of another task, "less burdensome, less scandalous, more agreeable to us, more profitable to you" (3.6). Offstage, away from Nicia, Ligurio gives Timoteo the details of the mandrake plot and offers him money if he will convince Lucrezia to sleep with another man. Timoteo agrees to become an accomplice, aware that both Nicia and Callimaco are rich.

Timoteo thinks that persuading Lucrezia will be difficult because, in his words, she is both "wise and good." Nevertheless, he plans to "dupe her by her own goodness" (3.9). In Act 3, he tells Lucrezia that she can go through with the mandrake remedy and still maintain her chastity. Timoteo has a liberal interpretation of what constitutes "chastity." In the Christian tradition, it is generally held that chastity is practiced through either celibacy or marriage; one must either refuse to engage in sexual relations altogether or have sexual relations with one spouse. Lucrezia is a married woman. If she accepts the mandrake remedy, she will break the commandment against adultery and violate her chastity. But the mandrake remedy requires more: if Lucrezia has sexual intercourse after consuming the mandrake, she will sleep with a stranger who, in her understanding, will be poisoned, making her an accessory to murder. Indeed, she will be the murder weapon.[62] Lucrezia will thereby break the commandment against killing, at least at the level of intent. Notwithstanding these moral complications, Timoteo assures Lucrezia that it is proper for her to proceed. His counsel to her not only mitigates the apparent evil of the scheme but also transforms the entire remedy into something good. Though sleeping with a stranger, and killing him, may seem terrible, Timoteo tells her, it is not so bad when inspected closely:

> There are many things that from far away seem terrible, unbearable, strange, and when you get near them, they turn out to be humane, bearable, familiar; and so it is said that fears are worse than evils themselves; and this is one of those things. (3.11)

Timoteo persuades Lucrezia of the "humanity" of the mandrake remedy through a new interpretation of classical, biblical, and patristic texts that deal with the issue of chastity. One of the passages Timoteo cites is found in Livy's account of Lucretia. In Livy, the Roman men try to persuade Lucretia that she is not guilty of adultery since she did not *desire* to have sexual intercourse with her rapist. Guilt, according to these men, originates from a wicked intent, not from what happens to the body. Though Sextus violated her body, he did not violate her soul. They tell Lucretia that "it is the mind . . . that sins, not the body: and that where purpose has been wanting there is no guilt (*mentem peccare, non corpus, et unde consilium afuerit, culpam abesse*)."[63] Timoteo alludes to this statement directly in *Mandragola*. He tells Lucrezia that "the will is what sins, not the body (*la volontà è quella che pecca, non el corpo*)."[64] He assures her that since her intention is to have a child and please her husband, she can have sex with a stranger while still remaining chaste. So long as Lucrezia does not derive any pleasure from the act, her chastity is preserved. Timoteo says:

> As to the act, that it might be a sin, this is a fable, because the will is what sins, not the body; and what causes it to be a sin is displeasing to your husband—but you please him; taking pleasure in it—but you have no pleasure from it. Besides this, the end has to be looked to in all things; your end is to fill a seat in paradise, to make your husband happy.

To illustrate this point, the friar refers to Genesis 19:30–38. This passage recounts how Lot's two daughters were alone with their father shortly after the destruction of Sodom and Gomorrah, and they were afraid that no other man was alive to impregnate them. For two consecutive nights they made their father drunk and had sexual intercourse with him. Both daughters became pregnant. Timoteo argues that these daughters, "believing themselves alone in the world, lay with their father; and because their intention was good, they didn't sin" (3.11). Incest in this case was justifiable, according to Timoteo, because Lot's daughters intended to preserve the human race through their actions. He does not mention that the daughters' pregnancies actually started the lineages of the notorious Ammonite and Moabite nations.[65] Timoteo chooses to emphasize the positive instead, by pointing out the daughters' initial good intent. The moral that he derives from the story contradicts Lucrezia's earlier assertion that she would not pursue the mandrake remedy even if she "were the only woman remaining in the world and if human nature had to rise again from me" (3.10). Timoteo claims, on the contrary, that a good intention redeems any bodily outrage, even incest.

Timoteo's argument also draws on Saint Augustine's understanding of the body and the will. In an early section of *City of God,* Augustine discusses the rape of Christian women and asks whether they are guilty of any sin due to the violation of their bodies. His answer is that such women are innocent. He writes: "The consecrated body is the instrument of the consecrated will"; therefore, "the violence of another's lust cannot take away the chastity which is preserved by unwavering self-control" (*CG* 1.16, 1.18). These points are related to Augustine's major argument about original sin. According to Augustine, the body, as created by God, is not the origin of evil but rather the will disobedient to God.[66] It is the corrupt will that corrupts the body and not the corrupt body that corrupts the will. In *Mandragola,* we see Timoteo using parts of this doctrine to convince Lucrezia that sexual intercourse with a stranger need not burden her conscience if her will is pure.

There is another more direct source in Saint Augustine for Timoteo's argument. Timoteo tells Lucrezia that "to obey your husband in this case is as much a matter of conscience as eating meat on Wednesday, which is a sin that goes away with holy water" (3.11). The idea that she can relinquish her body to another man with the permission of her husband and commit, at worst, a venial sin is similar to Augustine's commentary about a sexual ransom in his *Commentary on the Lord's Sermon on the Mount.*[67]

In this text, Augustine tries to illuminate Saint Paul's pronouncement in 1 Corinthians that "the wife does not have authority over her own body but the husband does."[68] Augustine tells the story of a corrupt governor from Antioch named Acyndinus who informs one of his male subjects that he will be executed unless he pays a pound of gold owed to the public treasury. Unfortunately, the condemned man does not have the money. He does, however, have a beautiful wife. One day, the wife receives a message from a wealthy man who is desirous of her and who is aware of her husband's dire situation. The rich man offers to give her a pound of gold to pay off Acyndinus and, thereby, save her husband, if only "she would consent to have carnal intercourse with him for one night." Augustine continues:

> Bearing in mind that it was her husband, and not herself, who had authority over her body, she submitted the case to him and told him that she was willing to do this for his sake, provided that he wished thus to save his life in exchange for something which could be regarded as his own because her chastity belonged entirely to him as her husband, who therefore had dominion over her body. He thanked her and told her to comply; for, because her motive was entirely devoid of any lustful desire and was based exclusively on her great love for him and because he himself was consenting to her act and even ordering it, he did not even surmise that her act would be adulterous. The wife went to the mansion of the rich man and submitted to his lustful desires. But she yielded her body to her husband only, although he was now desirous of using it in order to save his life, and not in the usual manner of marital intercourse.[69]

Augustine tells the story to suggest that it is possible for a wife to have carnal relations with another man and *not* commit adultery. But this is possible only if three conditions are met: first, a wife can derive no physical enjoyment from the act; second, the purpose of the act must be to preserve "life"; and, third, the husband must consent. Since all of these conditions are met in this case, Augustine claims that the wife's actions are justified. He writes: "What that wife did at her husband's bidding becomes less repulsive to human feelings when the whole incident is explained: we do not experience the same loathing as we did at first."[70] We should recall that Timoteo also tells Lucrezia that many actions that appear "terrible, unbearable, strange" from "far away" are actually "humane, bearable, familiar" when "you get near them." Indeed Timoteo, like Augustine, argues that Lucrezia can sleep with another man and *not* violate her chastity if she meets three conditions: she must be free of lustful desire ("the will is what sins, not the body"); she must intend to continue life ("Here is a certain good, you . . . will acquire a soul for our Lord"); and she must have the bidding of her husband ("what causes it to be a sin is displeasing to your husband—but you please him") (3.11). These three conditions are identical to those laid out by Augustine. Lucrezia, like the wife in Augustine's story, meets all three. Timoteo—and, by extension, Machiavelli—appears to have consulted the *Commentary on the Lord's Sermon on the Mount* to make his argument.[71]

Timoteo also cites another Augustinian passage in his efforts to persuade Lucrezia. In *City of God,* Augustine claims that Roman Lucretia is innocent of any crime since she was raped against her will.[72] Given her innocence, Augustine is perplexed as to why she commits suicide and why she is considered an exemplar of virtue. For Augustine, Lucretia's suicide is not truly virtuous; on the contrary, it is equivalent to murder. He claims that no person can justifiably commit suicide, even if she has been raped. Furthermore, no woman is permitted to kill herself *before* she is raped in the fear that, despite herself, she may physically enjoy it. According to Augustine, women who kill themselves before they are raped abandon the *certain good* of preserving their life in fear of the *uncertain evil* of adultery. He writes, "Uncertain adultery in the future [is] preferable to certain homicide in the present" (*CG* 1.25).

In *Mandragola,* Timoteo uses this Augustinian reasoning to state his "general principle" of the conscience: "where there is a certain good and an uncertain evil, one should never leave that good for fear of that evil."[73] According to Timoteo, the certain good for Lucrezia is that she will become pregnant, thus acquiring "a soul for our Lord"; the uncertain evil is that the man who lies with Lucrezia might be fatally poisoned, though the friar assures her that "those who don't die are also found." Timoteo is, of course, aware that no one will die as a result of the mandrake conspiracy, but he cannot say this to Lucrezia; instead, he mitigates the likelihood that Lucrezia will actually kill someone. Since the possibility of murder is "uncertain," it should not stop her from proceeding. However, there is also the uncertain evil that Timoteo does not mention: Lucrezia might actually enjoy the sexual encounter against her better intentions. It is this uncertain evil that eventually takes place. But before Lucrezia has her sexual rendezvous, she presumes that she could never derive pleasure from such an act. Timoteo tactically supports this presumption in his counsel ("but you have no pleasure from it") and excludes it as a possible evil for her to consider (3.11). He also exaggerates the certainty of the "certain good" that will result from this remedy. There is, after all, no certainty that Lucrezia will become pregnant after only one sexual encounter.

On the basis of biblical, Livian, and Augustinian authority, Timoteo persuades Lucrezia to sleep with another man and possibly become an accessory to murder. He thinks he is duping Lucrezia with her own goodness. However, it is difficult to determine whether she is, in fact, duped or whether she lets herself *appear* to be duped. Perhaps Lucrezia is not the woman of "few brains" that Timoteo takes her to be.

Lucrezia and Machiavellian *Virtù*

Lucrezia is a woman of the private realm, a wife who avoids parties, attends church, and wants children. Many scholars have claimed that Machiavelli's advocacy of well-used evils applies to the political realm but not to the private realm where Lucrezia resides. Machiavelli, according to these commentators, thought it was possible—indeed, advisable—to practice moral virtue in private life.[74] If so, then Lucrezia at the start of the play is an example of the private moral virtue Machiavelli advocates for women. It is in the household and the cloister where, ostensibly, such a moral life can be lived, far away from the moral compromises required in politics. For example, Sebastian de Grazia writes:

> Although everyone is sinful, some classes of persons or certain areas of life may be less or more sinful than others. There are two important classes of persons we might consider who, although supposed like everyone else to be in some way a sinner, are presumed to lead a less sinful life and are protected and helped by the community to lead that life. These two classes are the clergy and the female sex. Both are kept away from certain areas of activity that overlap but

are distinct enough to be identified as commerce, politics, and war. As long as clerics and women keep off these zones they are at least in theory, inviolate.[75]

Grazia concludes that Machiavelli "supports the inviolable status of clergy and women. . . . Women and priests are protected and kept off the sinning ground of politics, commerce and war; others—citizens, subjects, soldiers, leaders—tread on it daily."[76] Similarly, Isaiah Berlin argues that Machiavelli invites humans "to choose either a good, virtuous private life, or a good, successful, social existence, but not both." Berlin claims that, for Machiavelli, private life operates according to a different "system of values." "Goodness," in private life, is based on moral virtue (however understood), whereas goodness in the public realm is based on "success" alone.[77] If Berlin and Grazia are correct, then Machiavelli actually disapproves of the private immoralities he presents in *Mandragola.* Timoteo is, thus, a corrupt priest who does not need to employ the tactics of princes. Lucrezia should, accordingly, reject Timoteo's interpretations of Livy, Augustine, and the Bible and embrace a more traditional account of virtue to secure her household.

However, in *Mandragola,* the private realm is not a categorically distinct moral sphere where different rules apply. It is, on the contrary, the political realm writ small. The "system of values" in the household, like that of politics, is measured by "success." Certainly the situation in *Mandragola* is comic, but the play has a serious political point—a point that is not supportive of moral virtue in the private realm. Furthermore, the actions of the characters in *Mandragola* have ramifications that extend beyond the household and affect the society at large, revealing that the distinction between public and private is by no means absolute for Machiavelli.[78] In *Mandragola,* the personal is political. Consequently, *Mandragola* is not a satire lamenting the extent to which modern Florentines have fallen from ancient or Christian virtue in their private lives; it is a fable that covertly advocates the "success ethic" in household affairs and reveals how this can have social benefits. Contrary to Grazia, Berlin, and others, Machiavelli measures "goodness" by the standard of success in both the political and the private realm.

This point is evident if we consider the character of Lucrezia in light of her classical and biblical precedents, as well as in association with

Machiavelli's comments about virtue and vice in *The Prince.* As her name suggests, "Madonna Lucrezia" is a Christianized version of the legendary Roman matron, combining the ancient virtue of Livy's Lucretia with the piety of the Virgin Mary.[79] Like both Lucretia and Mary, Machiavelli's Lucrezia contributes to the birth of a new order; but whereas the ancient Roman republic was conceived out of Lucretia's chastity and the Christian epoch out of Mary's piety, the order in *Mandragola* is generated out of Lucrezia's infidelity. Her licentiousness has a peculiarly modern cast. Lucrezia is not an adulteress who seeks sexual pleasure at any cost; she is, rather, a "shrewd" young woman who is willing to compromise her chastity if it ensures a certain kind of success.

The type of "virtue" Machiavelli advocates with his Lucrezia is markedly different from the virtue of Roman Lucretia. The Romans immortalized Lucretia because she insisted on killing herself in the name of chastity. For many ancient commentators, Lucretia's moral fortitude exemplifies manliness, or *virtus*. Ovid calls her a "matron of manly spirit" (*animi matrona virilis*), and Valerius Maximus claims that her "manly spirit" (*virilis animus*) was given a female body due to an error of Fortune.[80] But Machiavelli goes out of his way to tarnish the Roman Lucretia's reputation, not only indirectly in *Mandragola,* but also directly in the *Discourses.* According to Machiavelli, the Roman king Tarquin "was expelled not because his son Sextus had raped Lucretia, but because he had broken the laws of the kingdom and governed it tyrannically." The rape and suicide of Lucretia, Machiavelli claims, merely served as a convenient excuse for disgruntled subjects to rebel against the ruling family. Lucretia's suicide was not, according to Machiavelli, an indispensable factor in the republican revolution of Rome. With or without Lucretia, a revolt would have occurred. Machiavelli writes, "If the accident of Lucretia had not come, as soon as another had arisen it would have brought the same effect" (*D* 3.5.1). Thus, Machiavelli refuses to celebrate Lucretia as a paradigm of any sort of virtue; her case is merely an "accident," an opportunity for others. In *Mandragola,* Machiavelli takes his lack of respect for Lucretia even further by doing exactly what Lucretia killed herself to prevent: he uses her name to justify adultery.

Machiavelli's Lucrezia, like her Roman namesake, begins the play with a reputation for virtue—a reputation that spreads all the way to France. Her ancient virtue is supplemented by a hardy Christian faith.

Nicia tells us she prays every night, on her knees and in the cold, for four hours (2.6). We also learn that she refused the sexual advances of a friar in the Servi church, the place in which—so she was told—she would conceive miraculously through daily attendance (3.2, 3.10). Lucrezia seems to be austere and upright in everything; and this, along with her beauty, has made her famous. And yet, notwithstanding Lucrezia's reputation, there are several indications that she is not what she is reputed to be. The prologue to *Mandragola* refers to Lucrezia as a "shrewd" young woman (*Una giovane accorta*), not a virtuous matron. Ligurio also says that Lucrezia is "fit to govern a kingdom" (1.3), which, if Machiavelli's *Prince* is any indication, means she is ready to "enter into evil, when forced by necessity" (*P*18). Finally, her mother, Sostrata, is reputed to be a woman of easy virtue (1.1, 3.9), opening the possibility that Lucrezia has inherited some of her mother's characteristics.

Sostrata, when informed of the mandrake remedy, has a private discussion with her daughter regarding the options now available to her. Lucrezia could refuse the mandrake remedy and never get pregnant; but, Sostrata says, a woman with no children is "left like a beast, abandoned by everyone" once her husband dies (3.11). To avoid this fate, Sostrata advises Lucrezia to choose what, in her mind, is the lesser of two evils: to consume the mandrake potion and sleep with a strange man who will be poisoned. This choice is in accord with Sostrata's proclamation at the start of Act 3: "It's the duty of a prudent person to take the best among bad courses. If to have children, you have no other remedy, then you'll want to take this one" (3.1). Eventually Lucrezia accepts her mother's reasoning. And it only takes one afternoon to persuade Lucrezia of the merits of this undertaking. The rapidity with which she accepts the remedy suggests that she is not the exemplar of ancient and Christian virtue that she appears to be at the start of the play.[81]

Callimaco reports that after he and Lucrezia had their "pleasure" together, he revealed his true identity to her, offered to meet her in the future, and promised to marry her whenever "God did otherwise" with Nicia. Lucrezia—having "tasted" the difference between a "young lover" and an "old husband," and having also been offered a new husband in the future—accepts Callimaco's offer and ascribes the turn of events to divine providence. She is reported saying that only a "heavenly disposition" could have willed her to do what she otherwise would not have done. Lucrezia then decides to facilitate what "Heaven" has willed: she instructs Callimaco to attend church the next day to make Nicia his "close friend" or "godfather" (*compare*) (5.4). This advice, if heeded, will expedite any future infidelities, for Callimaco will be welcome to enter Nicia's household as a friend. The next morning, Nicia—still ostensibly mistaking Callimaco for a fertility expert—blesses him and gives him the key to the house (5.6). This allows the young lovers to, in Lucrezia's words, "come together at any time and without suspicion" (5.4).[82]

Lucrezia is not just "tricked" into compromising her chastity; she deliberately chooses to become a habitual adulteress—with all its attendant bodily pleasures—even after the mandrake trick is revealed to her. When Callimaco discloses his true identity to Lucrezia and divulges the conspiracy, she does not pray to God for forgiveness or consider committing suicide. She only utters "some sighs" and then makes new plans to meet with Callimaco (5.4). Lucrezia now wants to be an adulteress, which makes coercion on Callimaco's part unnecessary. In the process, she seems to undergo—or undertake—a change of nature. Even Nicia alludes to her transformation at the end, saying, "This morning it's just as if you were reborn" (5.5).

At the start of the play, Callimaco states that his intent is to "change [Lucrezia's] nature." By the end of the play, it is clear that Lucrezia has a nature that is predisposed toward change. Lucrezia is able to do what Machiavelli says is almost impossible: she is able to change her nature with the times so as not to be destroyed by changes in fortune.[83] In the *Prince,* Machiavelli writes that a ruler "needs to have a spirit disposed to change as the winds of fortune and variations of things command him." If he could always "change his nature with the times and with affairs, his fortune would not change" (*P*18). This "spirit," however, is difficult to attain, either because one "cannot deviate from what nature inclines him to or also because, when one has always flourished by walking on one path, he cannot be persuaded to depart from it" (*P*25). If the times require impetuousness, and a person is stubbornly cautious, disaster will inevitably result. Those who want to succeed cannot "remain obstinate in their modes" when "fortune varies" (*P*25). Lucrezia does not remain obstinate. The times require some degree of lasciviousness, and Lucrezia acts accordingly, demonstrating that her solemn nature is not as inflexible as it first appears.

Nicia informs us that Lucrezia has changed her nature at least once before. He says, "She used to be the sweetest person in the world, and the most easy-going" (3.2). She became austere only after she was harassed by a lecherous Servite friar. In retrospect, her change of nature from "easy-going" to severe was expedient, since she did not want to do anything foolhardy and thereby ruin her reputation forever. An ill-advised affair with a corrupt priest is a sure way to cause a scandal and disgrace her name. Furthermore, she became suspicious of her husband in the aftermath of the Servite affair. She says to Sostrata, "I've always feared that Messer Nicia's longing to have children would make us commit some error and, because of this, whenever he's spoken to me about something, I've been on guard and suspicious of it" (3.10). Nevertheless, she must change her modes if she hopes to continue acquiring advantages for herself. She forces her husband and his colleges to come up with an acceptable remedy—something that might require her to commit an infidelity while not compromising her reputation for moral virtue.

By going along with the mandrake plot, Lucrezia has the sanction and encouragement of everyone surrounding her. And since many people are involved with the conspiracy for their own reasons, they all have something to lose if they talk too much. As Timoteo says, "When a thing matters to many, many have to be careful about it" (4.6). Rumors of Lucrezia's infidelity are thus unlikely to spread beyond the inner circle of conspirators. Even more, her status is likely to be enhanced by her involvement. In the final scene, all the characters enter Timoteo's church to see Lucrezia blessed as a pregnant wife instead of condemned as a lecherous whore. Everyone knows that Lucrezia has just slept with another man; nevertheless, she is given public and religious sanctification for her deed. Lucrezia not only acquires what she wants—a talented lover, a future husband, and a child—but maintains and augments her chaste reputation.

Lucrezia's actions, of course, stand in direct contrast to classical understandings of chastity. For Livy, no person, under any circumstance, should commit adultery, regardless of what benefits can be procured. Livy celebrates Lucretia because she honored chastity for itself, not for what it could get her. Indeed, she killed herself to preserve this virtue in others. Similarly, Aristotle understands adultery as a case where "rightness and wrongness do not depend on committing it with the right woman at the right time and in the right manner, but the mere fact of committing such action at all is to do wrong." Aristotle places adultery in the same category as theft and murder, which are also things it is "impossible ever to do right" (*NE* 2.6.1107a 8–17).[84] For Machiavelli, however, adultery is something that can be done in the right way, at the right time, for the right reason, and with the right person.

To understand Lucrezia's breach of chastity, it is helpful to consider the fifteenth chapter of the *Prince*, in which Machiavelli lists chastity (*casto*) along with lasciviousness (*lascivo*) in the catalogue of antithetical "qualities" for which people are praised and blamed. Machiavelli states that one should not always pursue those qualities held to be virtuous (such as chastity, liberality, mercy, fidelity, religion) or categorically reject all those qualities held to be vices (such as lasciviousness, meanness, cruelty, infidelity, atheism). He continues:

> I know that everyone will confess that it would be a very laudable thing to find in a prince all of the above-mentioned qualities that are held good. But because he cannot have them, nor wholly observe them, since human conditions do not permit it, it is necessary for him to be so prudent as to know how to avoid the infamy of those vices that would take his state from him and to be on guard against those that do not, if that is possible; but if one cannot, one should not care about incurring the reputation of those vices without which it is difficult to save one's state; for if one considers everything well, one will find something *appears to be a virtue,* which if pursued would be one's ruin, and something else *appears to be vice,* which if pursued results in one's security and well-being. (*P* 15; my emphasis)

This passage, according to the political theorist Clifford Orwin, reveals Machiavelli's true originality; it is here that we can gauge the full extent to which Machiavelli "depart[s] from the orders of others." Machiavelli would not be unique if he simply affirmed a categorical distinction between genuine virtue and success at any cost—a distinction that Orwin claims "no political thinker has ever doubted." Machiavelli is original precisely because he denies this distinction altogether. For Machiavelli, whatever is conducive to success is "virtuous," regardless of whether it is held by others to be wicked. In the passage above there is, according to Orwin, "no gap between the demands of politics and the demands of virtue—between 'what is done' and 'what ought to be done'—but only between the demands of politics and what appears to be virtuous but is not. Whatever politics demands is virtuous."[85] Machiavelli places virtue and vice in the realm of ephemeral "appearances," which have no real content outside of what they can get you. Any "quality"—ostensibly moral or immoral—should be used if it can guarantee success; this, for Machiavelli, is true virtue. As Mansfield writes, "Virtue in [Machiavelli's] new meaning seems to be a prudent or well-taught combination of vice and virtue in the old meaning."[86]

Hence murder and adultery are not understood as "necessary evils" if they contribute to success; they are, rather, necessary goods if they have a beneficial effect. Machiavelli writes, "When the deed accuses . . . the effect excuses . . . ; and when the effect is good . . . it will always excuse the deed" (D 1.9.2).[87] Even more radically, Machiavelli says, "So let a prince win and maintain his state: the means will always be judged honourable, and will be praised by everyone" (P 18). It is not entirely correct to say that the end "justifies" the means—something Machiavelli never said. It is more precise to say that, for Machiavelli, the successful end renders the means virtuous.[88] By making well-used "evils" an aspect of virtue, good and evil are no longer moral opposites; they become indistinguishable as ethical categories. The only substantial distinction is between what is effective and what is not. The willingness to employ apparent evils in the right way and at the right time is the true measure of human "goodness"; virtue is not found in our ability to avoid such actions at all times. There are certain situations, such as Lucrezia's, in which it is truly virtuous to use the apparent "vice" of lasciviousness rather than the apparent "virtue" of chastity. And as *Mandragola* shows us, these situations do not just occur in politics, but in every sphere of human life.

Machiavelli does not liberate lasciviousness—or any other apparent vice—from all restraints, nor does he deny that morally virtuous behavior can sometimes be expedient. Lucrezia's primary purpose in committing adultery is not to receive sexual pleasure but to gain security for herself. Through her actions, she safeguards her future while avoiding the infamy of unrestrained licentiousness. But, Timoteo's arguments notwithstanding, she compromises a quality held to be good to get what she wants. She uses the "quality" of chastity only insofar as it is advantageous, and, when it is not, she changes the quality to suit the times. For

Machiavelli, this is the proper use of an apparent "virtue." Livy's Lucretia, in contrast, insists—to the point of suicide—that chastity is a virtue that must always be respected by herself and by other women. She thereby dies in the name of a quality that only appears to be virtuous at all times but in reality is not. For Machiavelli, chastity is not a good in itself regardless of consequence; rather, "virtue is as virtue gets."[89] Roman Lucretia might have ancient virtue, but she lacks Lucrezia's Machiavellian *virtù*.

Who Embodies "Machiavelli's Virtue"?

Despite the disparaging and outright sexist comments made by many of the male characters in *Mandragola,* it turns out that the best practitioner of Machiavellian virtue in the play is a woman. There is, however, another force in the play that is even more fundamental than Lucrezia to the success of the enterprise—a force of which she is only vaguely aware. This brings us to a crucial distinction that is hinted at by Machiavelli and which has been emphasized in the scholarship of Mansfield: the difference between "Machiavellian virtue" and "Machiavelli's virtue."[90] Though Lucrezia possesses the former, she is not completely cognizant of the latter.

Lucrezia credits divine providence for bringing about the circumstances in which the mandrake plot became possible. She is reported saying to Callimaco:

> Since your astuteness, my husband's stupidity, my mother's simplicity, and my confessor's wickedness have led me to do what I never would have done myself, I'm determined to judge that it comes from a heavenly disposition which has so willed; and I don't have it in me to reject what Heaven wills me to accept. (5.4)

Only a divine power could have orchestrated the qualities of every other character in the play to get her into bed with Callimaco. However, Lucrezia does not include Ligurio in her list of supporting characters, even though Ligurio is far more "astute" than Callimaco. In actuality, Ligurio might be the "heavenly disposition" who creates the perfect circumstances under which Lucrezia can relinquish her chastity. But if Ligurio is a heavenly disposition, then he is a divinity with Satanic qualities. The prologue describes him as the "darling of malice," and Timoteo calls him a "devil" (4.6).

Ligurio leaves nothing—or as little as possible—to chance. The entire conspiracy depends on his supervision and instruction. In the end, Ligurio's providence unfolds as he intends due to his superb management. Throughout, he acts like the immanent realization of divinity in a corrupt world. His self-divinization is suggested early in the play when he wonders how a stupid man like Nicia has ended up with a beautiful woman like Lucrezia. He says to himself, "It seems to me that proverb on marriages which says 'God makes men and they pair themselves off!' is rarely proven true" (1.3). Ligurio will see to it, if God will not and the people themselves cannot, that a shrewd woman like Lucrezia ends up with a better-qualified man like Callimaco. If he is successful, Ligurio will even oversee—in place of God—the making of another human being.

Ligurio is the only character who acknowledges that the mandrake plot is "evil" and entirely absent of God's involvement. In Act 4, when Callimaco exclaims he will "pray to God" for the "blessed" Timoteo, Ligurio responds, "Oh fine! As if God granted grace in evil things as well as good ones!" (4.2). All the other characters, to greater and lesser degrees, suspect some type of divine involvement, or so they say.[91] Ligurio, however, openly admits—in private—that he does not see divinity at work in these events. If there is a God, he is, for Ligurio, irrelevant. God has shown himself incompetent at pairing off humans, and divine grace cannot ensure success in a hostile world. It is incumbent, then, for someone to take the place of the absent God and bring evil to good account.

Ligurio does not exercise his abilities out in the open. Like Machiavelli, he is unemployed in his area of expertise and must beg for meals. He is described as a "parasite" and a "sponger" who feeds off the rich (Pr; 1.1); indeed, his primary motivation seems to be food. He makes himself the confidant of two wealthy patrons, Callimaco and Nicia, each of whom trust him with their secrets, employ him for services, and reward him with money and dinner. Though he obviously wants to eat, his ultimate intentions are not at all clear; what is more, his modes are inscrutable. Ligurio assures Callimaco that his own motives are not entirely selfish. He says, "Even if the profit I sense and hope for were not here, your blood is in accord with mine, and I desire for you to satisfy this desire of yours almost as much as you do yourself" (1.3). But Callimaco is right to be suspicious. Ligurio likes to frequent the circles of the wealthy and powerful; he is obviously working his way up the social ladder.

As a former marriage broker, Ligurio is an expert in household affairs, and, thus, the right man to fix the problem that animates the play. Ostensibly, he is hired to satisfy Callimaco's desire for Lucrezia. Ligurio is faced with a choice: either he can help Callimaco satisfy his lust at the expense of other people, or he can try to reconcile the various desires of the many characters so that everyone gets what he or she wants. Ligurio chooses the second course, apparently as a matter of principle. He says, "Good is that which does good to the most, and that by which the most are contented" (3.4). Like Machiavelli, who claims "to work, without any respect," for those things that bring "common benefit to everyone" (D1. Pr.1), Ligurio operates without respect for the commandment against adultery to realize the common good. Because of Ligurio's management, all of the conspirators acquire what they want: Callimaco gets Lucrezia; Nicia gets an heir; Sostrata gets a grandchild; Timoteo gets money; and Lucrezia gets a child, a lover, and a husband. Even the servant Siro is rewarded because Ligurio remembers him in the final scene ("Is there no man who remembers Siro?") (5.6). A temporary earthly paradise for all is established. As Sostrata exclaims, "Who wouldn't be happy?" (5.6). Moreover, no one is damned in Ligurio's providence; everyone is elected for momentary salvation. Callimaco says he "would be more blessed than the blessed, more sainted than the saints," if it were not for the fact that "death" and "time" will corrupt his happiness (5.4). Given the way the world is, things cannot get much better for Callimaco and his fellow conspirators. *Mandragola* celebrates the "common good" in this manner and honors those who can realize it. However, there is nothing inherently ethical or "altruistic" about Ligurio's quest to satisfy the community at large. In his pursuit of the "common good," he is looking out for himself, not obeying a moral imperative. He realizes that he can effectively secure his interests if he helps others secure theirs. Ligurio also does not insist that anyone be ethical in the process; instead, he encourages everyone to pursue his or her own acquisitive interests—but only under his leadership. By correctly managing their competing desires, he is able to control the society of the play.

Though it appears that Callimaco is the true prince of the new order at the end, it is by the grace of Ligurio's involvement that Callimaco is permitted to succeed. At the beginning of the play, Ligurio replaces Callimaco as captain of the enterprise by mysteriously introducing the mandrake remedy in place of the initial bathhouse scheme (1.3). From this point on, Ligurio manages the details of the conspiracy almost entirely by himself. He later says to the conspirators, "I'll be the captain and get the army in order for the battle" (4.9). Even Callimaco says to Siro, "Tonight you have to do everything Ligurio tells you, and imagine, when he commands you, that it's me" (4.5). Ligurio stays in charge by operating behind the scenes. He is the only character with full knowledge of all things at all times; the others are always kept in greater or lesser degrees of confusion. Furthermore, he is masterful at knowing how to manage the qualities of the various characters to ensure success. But even though Ligurio exercises extraordinary control, he leaves enough uncontrolled for the other characters to exercise their specific qualities with a sense of freedom: Callimaco uses his manliness; Nicia uses his (apparent) stupidity; Timoteo uses his religion; and Lucrezia uses her *virtù*. He also gives individual characters specific instructions, using their natures as necessity dictates.[92] The only character who Ligurio does not directly instruct is Lucrezia; nevertheless, he puts her in a position in which she is able to utilize her *virtù*, as he wishes, without instruction. Ligurio is aware that Lucrezia is "fit to govern a kingdom," and he is reasonably assured that she will act accordingly when put to the test (1.3). In this manner, Ligurio uses people's natures in accordance with the circumstances. He divides labor, gives everyone specific responsibilities, and promises certain rewards for complicity. And he succeeds.

If Ligurio is the true captain of the conspiracy, he is not acknowledged as such. At the end of the play, he is rewarded as an accomplice, not as a leader. Nicia acknowledges Callimaco—not Ligurio—as the "cause" of his happiness (5.6). Other men, like Nicia, Callimaco, and Timoteo, are more visible, but Ligurio's management lies behind the happiness of the new society. He lets others take credit for the founding, but he gets himself invited to their tables, at which he can advise and govern the apparent rulers. Ligurio is a hidden manager. Mansfield argues that hidden governance is a primary feature of Machiavelli's "new regime":

> Machiavelli proposed to replace [the classical] notion of direct government with indirect government carried on by a hidden power. Instead of ruling in open light, government would be 'management.'

Machiavelli speaks frequently of 'managing' (*maneggiare*) men in the up-to-date, business school sense of the term: ruling without seeming to.[93]

Ligurio seems to embody this notion in *Mandragola*. Indeed, he represents the possibility of an unprecedented degree of control over human affairs through the expedient management of human qualities.

But there is another possibility, one that we have already partly considered: it might be that underneath Ligurio's hidden management is the more covert governance of Nicia. Ligurio's supervision is what undoubtedly brings the play to its happy conclusion, but he is not the "first cause" that sets the play into motion; this honor goes to either Nicia or Callimaco. Though the plot of *Mandragola* seems to center on Callimaco's desire for Lucrezia, it may, in fact, center on Nicia's desire for a son. Perhaps it is Nicia, after all, who actually initiates the plot by looking for the best way to impregnate his wife. And Ligurio, as we have seen, is not just an agent of Callimaco but also, and perhaps primarily, an agent of Nicia.[94] In this sense, Ligurio is middle management, subordinate to Nicia's authority and perhaps not even aware of the degree to which he is subservient. Nicia's acquisitive purpose and clandestine leadership show through Ligurio's practical administration. Nicia's governance is thus more "spiritual" and less practical: he indicates the general direction that people must move and leaves them to work through the details. He steers while others paddle. And, perhaps most disturbing for us, Nicia's secret leadership is not only hidden from the other characters in the play, but also from the audience. Nicia tricks everyone. Ligurio, on the other hand, fools no one. Everyone, both onstage and in the audience, is certain he is a "devil."

Who is the most Machiavellian character in the play? It is the author himself, as incarnated in the secret management of Ligurio/Nicia. Machiavelli has persuaded us that everyone is a better or worse Machiavellian—that success alone is the ultimate criterion of human excellence, and that those who ensure success are the greatest human specimens. *Mandragola* not only presents Machiavellian *virtù*, as best exemplified by Lucrezia, but also "Machiavelli's own virtue,"[95] as exemplified by Ligurio and Nicia.[96] On careful analysis, it seems that Machiavelli has refracted himself into these two characters. Ligurio represents Machiavelli's more practical role as an

adviser to politicians, and Nicia represents his role as the spiritual founder
of a new world order that has subsequently come to be called "modernity." Like Ligurio, Machiavelli does not actually rule a kingdom or republic as do the men—and women—he advises. Like Nicia, Machiavelli has
an inheritance problem. He wants to create a new spiritual environment
in which men and women with *virtù* can thrive, but he needs to ensure
that his spirit does not die with him. In a manner akin to Nicia, Machiavelli is forced to procreate indirectly, through his writings and through
those who will teach his writings. Others will perform the actual pro-
creating, but those ambitious youths who accept his teaching will be his
children.[97] If Machiavelli is truly successful, we will all be his children to
some extent. His advocacy of the success ethic as the ultimate measure
of human excellence will be taught and accepted habitually, even by those
who have no ambition or who have never read Machiavelli.

Thus Machiavelli wants a new world of ostensible princes and hidden managers who are animated by his spirit—a spirit that liberates *virtù*
from the restraints imposed on it by classical ethics and Christian faith.
In this sense, Machiavelli's presence for moderns, like Jesus' presence
for Christians, grants humans a new dispensation with the potential to
change the world. And even though Machiavelli's governance is hidden
to most, his spirit works like divine providence, radiating through the
fortune-conquering actions of modern governors and managers. Mansfield writes:

> [Machiavelli's] virtue does not show. Nonetheless, he will be judged
> by the results that appear to all in broad daylight. Although his vir-
> tue *uses* others' virtue, it also *shows* in their virtue; their virtue is
> the effectual truth of his. His *animo,* in the sense of "mind" and "in-
> tent" as well as "spirit," is behind theirs animating them to think and
> act in, if not under, his direction. Machiavelli's *animo* replaces the
> impersonal Aristotelian *anima* (soul)—not to mention the personal
> God of Christianity—as the ground of human nature.[98]

If Mansfield's interpretation of Machiavelli is correct, then *Mandragola*
symbolically represents Machiavelli's effort to be the spirit behind a revolution in morality, a spirit that not only allows human beings to get away
with evils for the sake of effectiveness, but that also permits them to

perceive those apparent "evils" as higher goods if they bring benefit in the conquest of fortune. In the midst of this moral revolution, the old idea that God secretly governs human nature and history disappears. It is replaced by the modern notion of a strictly "human" spirit that enhances human nature and covertly manages affairs.

Perhaps a step backward is necessary. Perhaps it is too radical to claim that Machiavelli granted human beings a new dispensation that allows them to conquer fortune with unprecedented success and that renders all previous understandings of human excellence obsolete. Instead, it might be more accurate to say that he encouraged a certain potential in human nature that, subsequently, has come to dominate our modern self-understanding. Perhaps his "new order" is not as beneficial as he suggests. Nevertheless, there is no going back: any criticism of Machiavelli's new order must be done with as much astuteness as Machiavelli himself possessed. And so, we turn to Shakespeare.

CHAPTER SIX

The "Fantastical Duke of Dark Corners"

Shakespeare's *Measure for Measure*

The "Problem" of *Measure for Measure*

The title of *Measure for Measure* refers to Jesus' pronouncement in the three synoptic Gospels that "the measure you give will be the measure you get,"[1] the most famous occurring in the Sermon on the Mount:

> Do not judge, so that you may not be judged. For with the judgement you make you will be judged, and the measure you give will be the measure you get. (Matt. 7:1–2)

There are two related meanings of the word *measure*. It can refer to an action taken against someone, as when we speak of the "measures taken"; and it can also indicate a standard by which someone is judged. The phrase "measure for measure" suggests that if we punish someone for an evil he or she has committed, we should expect the same punishment if we commit the same evil. The phrase also suggests that the standard by which we judge someone should be the same standard by which we judge ourselves. If we are not prepared to do so, then we should "not judge." Taken out of context, the injunction "Do not judge, so that you may not be judged," appears to condemn any sort of judgment whatsoever. In Matthew, however, this command is immediately qualified by the sentences that follow:

Why do you see the speck in your neighbour's eye, but do not notice the log in your own eye? Or how can you say to your neighbour, "Let me take the speck out of your eye," when the log is in your own eye? You hypocrite, first take the log out of your own eye, and then you will see clearly to take the speck out of your neighbour's eye. (Matt. 7:3–5)

Jesus is not condemning judgment per se but rather hypocritical judgment. If we must judge others, then we must hold ourselves accountable to a strictly equitable moral measure.

In *Measure for Measure,* the character Angelo is put in a position where he must exercise judgment over others. Angelo is commissioned to govern a disorderly, lecherous city and return it to order through sound judgment and just punishment. He is made deputy of Vienna by the city's prince, Duke Vincentio, and must rule in the Duke's absence. During Angelo's tenure as deputy he becomes embroiled in a sexual impropriety. He insists, however, on executing another character for a similar indiscretion. Though Angelo presents himself as an "angel" in both name and deed, he dares to punish a citizen for a crime that he himself has committed. Thus he practices the type of hypocritical judgment that Jesus condemns. Duke Vincentio, when he learns of his deputy's indiscretions, takes it upon himself to reveal them. In this effort, the Duke is ostensibly guided by the ethic of the Sermon on the Mount. In his soliloquy at the end of Act 3, he says:

He who the sword of heaven will bear
Should be as holy as severe;
Pattern in himself to know,
Grace to stand, and virtue go;
More nor less to others paying
Than by self-offenses weighing.
Shame to him whose cruel striking
Kills for faults of his own liking!
Twice treble shame on Angelo,
To weed my vice and let his grow!
O, what may man within him hide,
Though angel on the outward side!

(3.2.254–65)

Vincentio will teach Angelo that he should take the log out of his own eye first before daring to condemn someone else.

In the end, however, the Duke does not execute Angelo. Instead of punishing him, he appears to forgive Angelo his sins. He also seems to restore order to Vienna without resorting to extraordinary cruelty. In sum, Vincentio appears to be the ideal Christian statesman advocated by Tudor and Stuart theorists, a stage version of the proper incarnation of the "Body politic" in a Christian monarch.[2] Vincentio rules by divine right because he is blessed with "power divine" (5.1.377), as Angelo himself comes to recognize.

Many scholars have interpreted Vincentio as an unambiguous allegory for the Christian God. In this sense, the play can be understood as a morality play revamped for the Jacobean stage.[3] But if it is a morality play, it has proven an unsatisfying one. *Measure for Measure* is often classified as a "problem play," and has drawn perplexed and conflicting responses from critics.[4] Some commentators have found the play problematic simply as a matter of taste. Samuel Coleridge, for instance, writes, "*Measure for Measure* is the single exception to the delightfulness of Shakespeare's plays. It is a hateful work."[5] Others have labeled *Measure for Measure* a "problem" because it is difficult to categorize simply as either a "comedy" or a "tragedy."[6] The first half of the play is dark and brooding, whereas the second half is largely comic in tone. Many have had difficulty reconciling these two parts in a way that makes stylistic or interpretive sense.[7] The "happy ending" is also problematic: it is abrupt and artificial, and it does not resolve the moral failings of the main characters adequately. Rosalind Miles concludes: "*Measure for Measure* remains an only partially successful play. It is not a fully satisfying emotional experience because it deprives us of the sense of harmony and completeness, even the harmony and completeness of a consistent ironic vision, which is the accompanying sensation of a great work."[8]

Others, however, have claimed that these objections on the basis of taste, categorization, or style do not really address the main problem of the play: *Measure for Measure* throws us into a world of moral ambiguity. Ernest Schanzer writes that *Measure for Measure* presents a "moral problem . . . in such a manner that we are unsure of our moral bearings, so that uncertain and divided responses to it in the minds of the audience are possible and even probable."[9] The moral ambivalence reported by Schanzer is pertinent to the Gospel morality evoked by the play. Harold Bloom claims that the ostensible Christian message of *Measure for Measure* is undermined if the play is carefully considered. He writes, "*Measure for Measure* . . . involves [Shakespeare's] audience in what I am compelled to call the dramatist's simultaneous invocation and evasion of Christian belief and Christian morals."[10]

The moral ambivalence reported by Schanzer and Bloom is reinforced if we consider the various sources that Shakespeare used to create *Measure for Measure.* As we have seen, the title of the play directs us to the Gospels. It is also clear that Shakespeare modeled the story of *Measure for Measure* on George Whetstone's play *Promos and Cassandra* (1578).[11] However, Shakespeare recasts *Promos and Cassandra* into something more Machiavellian. The political intrigue of *Measure for Measure* is based on an episode in the seventh chapter of Machiavelli's *Prince.* Shakespeare's Duke Vincentio bears a striking resemblance to one of Machiavelli's great heroes: Duke Valentino, better known as Cesare Borgia.[12] The similarities between Vincentio and Valentino are not exhausted by their names.[13] In *The Prince,* Machiavelli recounts how Borgia disciplined the province of Romagna:

> Since that province was quite full of robberies, quarrels, and every other kind of insolence, [Borgia] judged it necessary to give it good government, if he wanted to reduce it to peace and obedience to a kingly arm. So he put there Messer Remirro de Orco, a cruel and ready man, to whom he gave the fullest power. In a short time Remirro reduced it to peace and unity. . . . Then the duke [Borgia] judged that such excessive authority was not necessary, because he feared that it might become hateful; and he set up a civil court in the middle of the province, with a most excellent president. . . . And because he knew that past rigors had generated some hatred for Remirro, to purge the spirits of that people and to gain them entirely to himself, he wished to show that if any cruelty had been committed, this had not come from him but from the harsh nature of his minister. And having seized this opportunity, he had him placed one morning in the piazza as Cesena in two pieces, with a piece of wood and a bloody knife beside him. The ferocity of this spectacle left the people at once satisfied and stupefied. (*P* 7)

There is a remarkable similarity between this passage in *The Prince* and the situation in *Measure for Measure.* At the start of the play, Duke Vincentio, like Borgia, must contend with the lawlessness of the realm. The Duke knows that he will acquire a tyrannical reputation if he disciplines the city of Vienna by himself (1.3.34–43). To avoid the hatred of the people, he decides to commission Angelo—a man who, like Remirro, is renowned for his severity. Angelo is ordered by the Duke to enforce laws that have not been applied for many years. In the Duke's absence, Angelo brings the city to order and, as expected, becomes hated by the people. The Duke, in the meantime, does not actually leave Vienna but observes everything in disguise. When he relinquishes his disguise and "returns" to the city, he sets up a public court in which Angelo is disgraced. The effect of the Duke's actions leaves the people dazzled but eminently gratified.[14]

The parallels between Cesare Borgia and Duke Vincentio are uncomfortably obvious. There is, however, an important difference between the two princes: Vincentio, unlike Borgia, does not chop his deputy into two pieces. Vincentio's kinder approach seems to mitigate the excesses of politics with Christian virtue.[15] We shall see, however, that Vincentio's decision to keep Angelo alive is not as merciful as it first appears. It has much to do with circumstance, expediency, and diabolical intent, and little to do with Christian principle. Even without a bloody execution, Vincentio employs methods similar to those of Borgia and other Machiavellian heroes.

Norman Holland writes, "Interpretations of *Measure for Measure* that treat the Duke as a symbol of divine grace or the like must take into account his probable descent from Cesare Borgia."[16] With this observation, Holland identifies the most significant thing that makes *Measure for Measure* a problem play: the character who seems to incarnate the ideal of Christian statesmanship and who appears to serve as the moral measure of the other characters is, in reality, an excellent exemplar of Machiavellian politics. *Measure for Measure* is a Machiavellian comedy masquerading as a Christian morality play.

When considering the Duke, we should judge him by the same measure he uses to judge others. In the final act, the Duke warns the character Lucio: "Be perfect" (5.1.86). These words also echo the Sermon on the Mount, where Jesus proclaims, "Be perfect, therefore, as your heavenly Father is perfect" (Matt. 5:48). Human beings approach perfection, according to Jesus, when they love their enemies, turn the other cheek, forgive trespassers, practice charity, exercise mercy, avoid hypocrisy, make their intentions as pure as their actions, worship God with a sincere heart, and treat others as they themselves want to be treated.[17] Vincentio, like Jesus, demands this perfection of his subjects; however, he does not insist on it for himself. The Duke always operates outside the bounds of Christian morality. It is not just that he falls short of such moral perfection; he is its very antithesis.

In *Measure for Measure,* Shakespeare is both responding to the Machiavellian account of evil and testing our ability to perceive it. Put differently, Shakespeare gives us Machiavellian *virtù* in the guise of both Christian virtue and divine providence, and challenges us to see through it. Nothing in this play is exactly what it appears to be. Like Machiavellian politics, *Measure for Measure* is all about the manipulative use of appearances. Shakespeare, however, is not using appearances to keep his audience satisfied and stupefied, though this has been its effect on some. Instead, Shakespeare brings us face-to-face with the nature of Machiavellian *virtù* and challenges us to reflect on our willingness to accept the deceptions of Machiavellian politics.

The Duke's Plan

The word *evil* is most often used in *Measure for Measure* to refer to lechery.[18] Vienna, at the start of the play, is infected with sexual vice. Prostitutes and sexual diseases are everywhere, facilitated by the vast number of brothels in and around the city.[19] Throughout the play, we meet a number of characters who either work in or frequent these institutions: the pimp Pompey, the drunken Master Froth, the decadent "fantastic" Lucio, and the notorious Mistress Overdone, referred to by her customers as "Madam Mitigation" (1.2.43). We are also told of a prostitute named Kate Keepdown who has had an unwanted child by Lucio (3.2.193–97). The lechery laws that would normally restrain sexuality have not been enforced for many years. Consequently, the entire legal system is in disrepute. The last remaining practitioner of law enforcement among the common citizens is the dimwitted Constable Elbow. He is, however, incompetent at his job, demonstrating just how inept the city has become at applying its civic ordinances (see 2.1.41–272). Citizens like Pompey openly break the law without fear of punishment. The overwhelming lawlessness and sexual depravity of the city is accompanied by a striking absence of married couples. Vienna lacks stable family units in which to raise children. The decay of the family seems to have contributed to the general malaise of the city. The only married man we meet is, once again, Elbow, but even his pregnant wife has found her way into a brothel (see 2.1.69–105).

It is not that Vienna has no ordinances regarding lechery; as the Duke points out, there are "strict statutes and most biting laws" dealing with sex outside of marriage (1.3.19). At least two ordinances in Vienna's body of law deal with lechery: one bans all brothels; another demands that all lechers be executed. But these laws have not been applied for many years. The character Claudio claims that "nineteen zodiacs have gone round" since the laws were last applied; the Duke, on the other hand, claims that he has not enforced these laws for the past "fourteen years" (1.2.165; 1.3.21).[20] Regardless of how much time has passed, the Duke has decided to revive the laws. He claims, however, that he cannot initiate the process of reviving them himself because he has been called away on serious business. He must, therefore, appoint Angelo as his deputy and charge him with the unenviable task of law enforcement.

The first and only person whom Angelo chooses to execute is the young gentleman Claudio, who is charged with having sex outside of proper wedlock with a woman named Juliet. In 1.2, we see Claudio being led away to prison with Juliet, who is now pregnant with his child. Claudio does not protest that his arrest is unlawful; on the contrary, he says that it is "just" (1.2.123). However, Claudio is angry that he should be the only person charged with lechery after the law has been neglected for so many years (1.2.162–68). His only hope is that his sister, Isabella, might appeal to Angelo for clemency. He sends Lucio to inform her of the dire situation. In the meantime, Claudio is paraded before the city on his way to prison, restrained by the Provost and a host of officers. To the citizens of Vienna, Claudio is an unfortunate victim of a new tyranny gripping the city. Even the Provost who incarcerates Claudio claims he is only acting on Angelo's orders: "I do it not in evil disposition, / But from Lord Angelo by special charge" (1.2.118–19). The Provost suggests that Angelo is actually the person with the "evil disposition."

In fact, the city is caught between two evils: sexual vice, on the one hand, and severe laws, on the other. The citizens of Vienna are charged with the former evil; Angelo is charged with the latter. What goes unnoticed is that Duke Vincentio is ultimately responsible for both. If the laws regarding lechery are just, then the Duke should have enforced them. If these laws are unjust, then he should have changed them. When Vincentio took office, he either inherited these laws from a previous ruler or established them himself. Either way, he kept these laws in Vienna's official body of ordinances. He decided to make himself appear lenient by not applying them, effectively contrasting his mercy with the cruelty demanded by the laws. He would not have seemed merciful if he had enforced the laws—even if he had devised less extreme statutes and applied them strictly. Instead, he encouraged his citizens to become lecherous by not enforcing any laws. Now he must do something to stop the sexual chaos overwhelming the city while avoiding a tyrannical reputation for himself. So he charges Angelo to revive the laws. The Duke says to Friar Thomas:

> Sith 'twas my fault to give the people scope,
> 'Twould be my tyranny to strike and gall them
> For what I bid them do; for we bid this be done
> When evil deeds have their permissive pass
> And not the punishment. Therefore indeed, my father,
> I have on Angelo imposed the office,
> Who may, in the ambush of my name, strike home,
> And yet my nature never in the fight
> To do in slander.
>
> (1.3.34–43)

In this passage, the Duke openly admits—in private—that his charging of a deputy is an act of political expediency designed to keep himself loved by the people by deflecting all blame to another.

Angelo, as an acting deputy, has the authority to qualify the laws, but he must enforce them to some extent. He does not, like the Duke, have the power to change or revoke them. When the Duke commissions Angelo in the first scene, he makes Angelo's task sound less severe than it actually is. In front of his entire court, the Duke says to Angelo:

> Your scope is as mine own,
> So to enforce or qualify the laws
> As to your soul seems good.
> (1.1.65–67)

However, the Duke also hands Angelo a private commission in a sealed document, which Angelo goes off to read at the end of the scene (1.1.48, 77–84). It is in this letter that Angelo learns the "strength and nature" of his power (1.1.79–81). The content of the commission is never revealed, but we can be certain that it orders Angelo to emphasize law enforcement rather than law qualification. As we have seen, Vincentio admits that he has instructed Angelo to "strike home" (1.3.41).

But when we look at how Angelo actually rules, we find that he is true to the Duke's oral commission: he enforces *and* qualifies the laws. First, Angelo issues a proclamation closing down the poorer brothels in the suburbs. This order eventually leads to the arrest of pimps and prostitutes such as Pompey and Mistress Overdone, as well as to the incarceration of many customers who frequented the whorehouses (3.2.1–85, 184–202; 4.3.1–19). Pompey informs us, however, that the more upscale brothels in the city get to "stand for seed" (1.2.93–100). Angelo, we are told, has decided to keep the urban brothels open at the request of a "wise burgher" (1.2.100). Thus Angelo's strict proclamation to close the whorehouses is qualified by a high degree of leniency. Likewise, Angelo mitigates the law demanding capital punishment for all lechers. He could legally execute most of Vienna, given that lechery is so pervasive. Instead, he orders the execution of one man: Claudio. At no point in the play are we told that any other citizen is slated for execution for the crime of lechery. By executing Claudio alone, Angelo hopes to make an example of him and deter other citizens from committing the same crime (see 2.2.95–109).

Angelo also ensures that the laws are applied to each social class in due proportion. The closure of the suburban brothels affects only the lower classes. Accordingly, we see people such as Pompey and Mistress Overdone, as well as their former clients, arrested and taken to prison. The death penalty, on the other hand, affects only a single member of the upper class, Claudio, who, we are told, had a "most noble father" (2.1.7). In this manner, Angelo does not execute poor lechers, but he

212 | Evil in Renaissance Theatre

closes down their brothels and puts them in jail; he does not close down the whorehouses of the rich, but he orders the execution of a gentleman to serve as an example. This application of the laws is inconsistent, but at least it is balanced. Angelo's leniency goes unnoticed, however, and the people become desperate for the Duke to return. No matter how mercifully Angelo applies the laws, it is impossible for him to be loved by the people.

Two questions regarding the Duke's plan remain: Why does he choose this precise moment to revive the laws? and Why does he choose Angelo to be his deputy and not someone else?

The Duke's reasons for having the laws enforced are in part domestic, but these domestic concerns are not enough to explain the Duke's timing. Vienna has, presumably, been in dire straits for some time. If the Duke were truly concerned about sexual impropriety in his city, he would have dealt with it much earlier. In fact, the city's moral and social decay has served his political purposes up to now. By all accounts, everyone loves Vincentio. Though there is plenty of civil disobedience, there is not a hint of any internal political dissent. The reason the Duke is forced to take drastic action might have more to do with foreign matters than with internal problems. There are rumors throughout the city of an impending war. Lucio says, "If the Duke with the other dukes come not to composition with the King of Hungary, why then all the dukes fall upon the King" (1.2.1–3). If true, then the Duke is involved in a conspiracy that will potentially embroil Vienna in a rebellious war. Lucio also reveals that the gentlemen of the city are "in hand and hope of action" (1.4.51–52). Even Mistress Overdone complains that "the war" has been bad for business in her brothel (1.2.81). Lucio will later claim that the Duke has misled the public about a possible war. He says that the Duke's "givings-out were of an infinite distance / From his true-meant design" (1.4.54–55). But Lucio's subsequent behavior reveals that he has no idea what the Duke is up to politically. Vienna might actually be on the verge of war, though who the war will be against and how the Duke is preparing for it are a mystery to everyone, including Lucio. Even if war is not imminent, it appears that something major is about to occur in the near future that requires Vienna being brought to order.

Given that the city needs to be disciplined immediately, why does the Duke appoint Angelo and not somebody else? Vincentio says to Friar Thomas:

> Lord Angelo is precise,
> Stands at a guard with envy, scarce confesses
> That his blood flows or that his appetite
> Is more to bread than stone. Hence we shall see,
> If power change purpose, what our seemers be.
> (1.3.50–54)

The Duke senses that Angelo is a "seemer," a man who appears morally severe but is actually sexually depraved. For this reason, Vincentio says he wants to test Angelo to see if he will be corrupted by power. Justifying Angelo's commissioning in this way might appeal to a friar like Thomas, but it is hardly a good reason. It is unlikely that the Duke would throw the entire city into turmoil to test the moral character of one man, especially if a war is at hand. Even the Duke admits to Thomas that this is not his only reason for instating Angelo: "More reasons for this action / At our more leisure shall I render you" (1.3.48–49). However, we never hear these reasons. What is more, the reasons that we do hear are contradictory. Vincentio tells Thomas that he has commissioned Angelo to put an end to sexual corruption, and yet, at the same time, the Duke expects that Angelo's own sexual corruption will emerge once he is commissioned. If the Duke were truly concerned about the moral decay of his city, why would he appoint a man who is morally dubious? Vincentio could have appointed someone less suspicious, such as Lord Escalus, the Duke's "first in question" (1.1.47)—a man who, it seems, is untouched by scandal. The Duke, however, makes Escalus subordinate to Angelo. In addition, the Duke's private claim to Thomas that Angelo's virtue needs testing contradicts his public claim that Angelo's virtue is unquestionable. In the first scene, in front of lords and attendants, the Duke announces that he wants to *display* Angelo's virtue, not test it. He says to Angelo:

> There is a kind of character in thy life
> That to th' observer doth thy history
> Fully unfold. Thyself and thy belongings
> Are not thine own so proper as to waste
> Thyself upon thy virtues, they on thee.
> Heaven doth with us as we with torches do,
> Not light them for themselves; for if our virtues

Did not go forth of us, 'twere all alike
As if we had them not.

(1.1.28−36)[21]

When Angelo protests that a better "test" should be made of his "mettle" before he is made deputy, the Duke responds that no further examination is necessary (1.1.48−53).

In fact, Vincentio does not want to display or test Angelo's character. Rather, his primary intent is to disgrace Angelo irreparably. The Duke knows that Angelo is a troubled man, even before he commissions him.[22] He tells Thomas that Angelo's apparent moral austerity hides inherent corruption. What Vincentio does not tell Thomas—or the audience, until Act 3—is that he already knows a secret from Angelo's past. Many years ago, Angelo had a marriage "contract" with a woman named Mariana (3.1.217−18). Mariana's dowry was lost in a sea wreck before the wedding ceremony could take place. Angelo immediately broke off the engagement, citing the lost dowry as a reason, but also accusing Mariana of dishonorable behavior (3.1.210−32; also see 5.1.223−29). By all appearances, his treatment of Mariana was scandalous. The Duke is aware of how bad this looks, and he intends to use it against Angelo. It is clear that Vincentio was informed of Mariana's situation a long time ago, and he probably commissioned her to assist him before he commissioned Angelo.[23] Mariana wants revenge, but she is also—remarkably—still in love with Angelo. Her past sufferings and present feelings make her a valuable weapon for the Duke. He can employ her to revive memories of past wrongs and embroil Angelo in a new scandal. Before Angelo does a single thing wrong, the Duke co-opts Mariana and hides her outside the city on a moated grange called Saint Luke's. When we finally meet Mariana in Act 4, it is clear that she has been positioned at Saint Luke's all along, ready to be used at a moment's notice. That Mariana is on reserve reveals that Angelo has been set up right from the start. If Angelo makes one false move—as indeed he does—this will make it even easier for the Duke.

The Duke will be able to humiliate Angelo by linking his treatment of Mariana with Claudio's treatment of Juliet. The parallels between Angelo and Claudio are so obvious that it is likely Vincentio ordered Claudio's execution in his written commission (1.1.48, 79−81).[24] Like Angelo,

Claudio has not fulfilled a marriage "contract" due to a problem with a dowry. But in the case of Claudio there are numerous complicating factors. The circumstances surrounding Claudio's relation to Juliet are revealed as he is being led to prison. Claudio says to Lucio: "upon a true contract / I got possession of Julietta's bed . . . she is fast my wife / Save that we do the denunciation lack / Of outward order" (1.2.142–46). In other words, he and Juliet are bound by an official nuptial contract, but their marriage has not been validated by a Church ceremony.[25] Whatever the legal status of their "true contract," no one in the play, not even Claudio, argues that it is lawful for them to have sexual intercourse. Claudio and Juliet, it would seem, have deliberately broken the terms of the contract by entering into sexual relations before there was full "denunciation" in public.[26] Their sexual indiscretions are no longer secret since Juliet is obviously pregnant (1.2.152); indeed, her labor pains begin on the same day Claudio is arrested (2.2.18–19). Given her pregnancy, we must wonder why Claudio and Juliet have delayed their public vows. Claudio says they have done so in the hope that her family could be made agreeable to a "propagation" of her dowry (1.2.146–50). However, Claudio has not yet told her relatives that he is "contracted" to Juliet, nor has he approached them about the possibility of more money. Claudio says, "we thought it meet to hide our love / Till time had made them for us" (1.2.149–50). At least nine months have now gone by, and Claudio has done nothing.

The Duke knows that Claudio's treatment of Juliet appears better than Angelo's treatment of Mariana. Claudio is still nominally attached to his partner. Angelo, on the other hand, abandoned Mariana. But when we consider all the circumstances, it is clear that Claudio has been more callous and inconsiderate than Angelo. Angelo, for all his cruelty, at least made a complete break with Mariana when her dowry was lost, and he did not leave her pregnant. Claudio, on the other hand, has disgraced Juliet with a pregnancy out of wedlock while awaiting the possibility of an increased dowry. He has given every indication that he will abandon Juliet and the child if her dowry is not enhanced. In the meantime, Claudio has not even approached Juliet's relatives to discuss terms for an acceptable dower. Nothing Claudio says or does suggests that he desires Juliet for anything other than his convenience. We do not see Claudio speak to Juliet once in the entire play—this despite the fact that she accompanies him to prison during her labor. Claudio, however, commands greater public sympathy than Angelo. In the public eye, Angelo is incapable of desire, compassion, or love. Lucio says that Angelo is "a man whose blood / Is very snow broth" (1.4.57−58). Claudio, on the other hand, is perceived as an unfortunate lover. If he is executed on Angelo's orders, it will seem as if a cruel and unfeeling authority killed a passionate man merely for consummating his love.

Angelo's cruelty to Mariana, mixed with the severity of Claudio's execution, should allow the Duke to achieve his purposes. The Duke can use the parallels between Claudio and Angelo to humiliate the latter while bringing fear into the city through Claudio's execution. Even if Angelo does nothing illegal while in office, the Duke can use Angelo's scandalous past, as well as the hatred of the people toward him, to do anything he wants with the deputy—perhaps even kill him. We should not make the mistake of thinking that Angelo is disgraced at the end solely for the abuses he commits while in power. He is doomed before he commits a single indiscretion.

"Touching" Duke Vincentio

Vincentio can be gauged by keeping a particular piece of advice by Machiavelli in mind:

> [A prince] should appear all mercy, all faith, all honesty, all humanity, all religion. And nothing is more necessary to appear to have than this last quality. Men in general judge more by their eyes than by their hands, because seeing is given to everyone, touching to a few. Everyone sees how you appear, few touch what you are. (*P* 18)

In order for the Duke's plot to succeed, he must appear "all religion." Religion is immediately at hand for Vincentio: Vienna is the seat of the Holy Roman Empire. For most of the play Vincentio cloaks himself in the guise of Christian monasticism and enlists the support of the Church. If we are to "touch" the Duke, we must not be misled by the appearance of religion.

Vincentio fools everyone into thinking that he has left Vienna and put Angelo in charge. In fact, he does neither. After spreading false rumors about his whereabouts, the Duke retreats to a monastery within the city and covertly governs Vienna for the rest of the play (see 1.3.13−16). He asks Friar Thomas to supply him with a monk's habit and to instruct him on how to conduct himself "like a true friar" (1.3.48). In this manner, the Duke can "visit both prince and people" without being recognized (1.3.45). For most of the play, the Duke wanders around Vienna disguised. As the play progresses, it is easy to forget that the Duke is not a true friar. After 1.3, we do not see him in his own habit again until 4.5. Unless we continually remind ourselves that the Duke has no status as a religious counselor, we might actually be fooled into thinking that his concerns are somehow spiritual.

Vincentio's disguise symbolizes his quasi-supernatural power over the city. Like Christ, Vincentio disappears and leaves the people anxious for his second coming. Though he seems to be absent, he is still present, observing the trespasses of his subjects and peering into their souls. Though he lacks modern methods of surveillance such as video cameras and microphones, he nevertheless gathers intelligence about people as if he were using such technology. By bringing politics to bear on the inner souls of his citizens, he touches things traditionally beyond the reach of politics and uses what he sees for political effect. Vincentio examines the darkest recesses of other people, but no one examines him.

Since we in the audience, unlike most of the characters, are cognizant of the Duke's disguise, we are immediately misled into thinking that we know all his secrets. In fact, we know hardly anything about Vincentio. He does not, for instance, use soliloquies to make us privy to his political goals; indeed, he hardly soliloquizes at all.[27] Most of what we know about the Duke is gathered from what he says to other characters, but his words are untrustworthy. Almost everything he says is either a lie or a half-truth, and if he does utter a truth, its purpose is to mislead. True to Machiavelli's injunction, the Duke does not let anyone touch who he is.

Though no one touches the Duke, he is reputed to be many things by many people. Some believe the Duke to be a recluse who prefers the quiet contemplative life to the tumultuous public life. Vincentio fosters this impression of himself by pronouncing his disdain for large crowds and his impatience with politics. He says to Angelo and the rest of his court in the first scene:

> I love the people
> But do not like to stage me to their eyes;
> Though it do well, I do not relish well
> Their loud applause and "aves" vehement,
> Nor do I think the man of safe discretion
> That does affect it.
>
> $(1.1.68-73)$

Later, he says to Friar Thomas:

> My holy sir, none better knows than you
> How I have ever loved the life removed
> And held in idle price to haunt assemblies
> Where youth and cost witless bravery keeps.
>
> $(1.3.7-10)$

His words to Thomas reveal that he has retreated to the monastery on previous occasions to escape his public duties. He makes it appear as if his contemplative disposition is to blame for his political negligence.

However, Lucio claims that "the old fantastical Duke of dark corners" has used his private life for activities other than spiritual contemplation $(4.3.156-57)$. These activities are "a secret" to those who believe "the Duke to be wise" but are well known to those in other circles $(3.2.131-34)$. Lucio describes the Duke as a voracious lecher who has "crotchets in him"—an unrepentant "woodman" prone to every type of sexual excess and disposed to "eat mutton on Fridays" $(3.2.124, 175; 4.3.162)$. When Lucio makes these accusations, he is not aware that he is speaking to the Duke himself in disguise. Vincentio will later charge Lucio with "slanders" $(5.1.530)$, but these slanders are partially confirmed by Friar Thomas. Thomas asks the Duke before the start of 1.3 if he is using the monastery to hide an illicit sexual affair. We do not hear the Friar ask this question, but we do hear the Duke's response:

> No, holy Father, throw away that thought;
> Believe not that the dribbling dart of love
> Can pierce a complete bosom. Why I desire thee
> To give me secret harbor hath a purpose

More grave and wrinkled than the aims and ends
Of burning youth.

(1.3.1–6)

The Friar's concern is revealing, especially since the Duke has retreated to
the monastery before. Perhaps the Duke, in his "burning youth," used it
as a private brothel. Given that the Duke is a bachelor who has ruled
Vienna for at least fourteen years, it is highly unlikely that he has remained
celibate all this time (see 1.3.21).

Notwithstanding Lucio and Thomas, the majority of subjects hold
the Duke to be "wise," especially Lord Escalus. Vincentio, while in disguise, asks Escalus to describe the "disposition" and "pleasure" of the
Duke (3.2.225–26, 229). Escalus, unlike Lucio, gives the politically correct response. He says that the Duke is "a gentleman of all temperance"
who "contended especially to know himself" (3.2.227–28, 232). If Escalus is to be believed, the Duke lives in accord with the ancient Delphic
injunctions: "nothing to excess" and "know thyself." Escalus also claims
that Vincentio's Greek virtue is perfected by Christian charity. According to Escalus, the Duke would rather see "another merry than merry at
anything which professed to make him rejoice" (3.2.229–32).

Notwithstanding Escalus's claims, most of what the Duke says contradicts both Greek philosophy and Christian dogma. Consider, for example, his counsel to Claudio in Act 3. The Duke, acting as a spiritual adviser, prepares Claudio's soul for death by providing an account of a
de-divinized world:

Be absolute for death. Either death or life
Shall thereby be the sweeter. Reason thus with life:
If I do lose thee, I do lose a thing
That none but fools would keep. A breath thou art,
Servile to all the skyey influences
That dost this habitation where thou keep'st
Hourly afflict. Merely, thou art death's fool
For him thou labor'st by thy flight to shun,
And yet runn'st toward him still. Thou art not noble,
For all th' accommodations that thou bear'st
Are nursed by baseness. Thou'rt by no means valiant,

For thou dost fear the soft and tender fork
Of a poor worm. Thy best of rest is sleep,
And that thou oft provok'st, yet grossly fear'st
Thy death, which is no more. Thou art not thyself,
For thou exists on many a thousand grains
That issue out of dust. Happy thou art not,
For what thou hast not, still thou striv'st to get,
And what thou hast, forget'st. Thou art not certain,
For thy complexion shifts to strange effects,
After the moon. If thou art rich, thou'rt poor,
For, like an ass whose back with ingots bows,
Thou bear'st thy heavy riches but a journey,
And death unloads thee. Friend hast thou none,
For thine own bowels which do call thee sire,
The mere effusion of thy proper loins,
Do curse the gout, serpigo, and the rheum
For ending thee no sooner. Thou hast nor youth nor age,
But as it were an after-dinner's sleep
Dreaming on both, for all thy blessèd youth
Becomes as agèd and doth beg the alms
Of palsied eld; and, when thou art old and rich,
Thou hast neither heat, affection, limb, nor beauty
To make thy riches pleasant. What's yet in this
That bears the name of life? Yet in this life
Lie hid more thousand deaths; yet death we fear,
That makes these odds all even.

(3.1.5−41)

Vincentio, dressed as a Christian monk, does not mention the most fundamental Christian teachings on hope, faith, love, repentance, resurrection, and salvation. The Duke's expressed purpose is to kill any "hope" in Claudio (see 3.1.1−6). Death, according to Vincentio, is preferable to life, not because we enter God's kingdom, but because we fall into everlasting sleep. Eternal sleep is better than living in a world where humans are victims of nature; where nobility is "nursed by baseness"; where friendship is absent; where children are mere "effusion"; where offspring want their parents dead; where the young are poor; where the old are sick; and where no one is happy.

Since Vincentio's counsel ignores basic Christian dogmas, it is often interpreted as evidence of the Duke's "pagan" or philosophical approach to life.[28] Many scholars have argued that the Duke is trying to comfort Claudio on the basis of reason instead of Christian revelation. And yet it is revealing that the one character in *Measure for Measure* who lives according to Vincentio's advice is not a virtuous philosopher but a drunken murderer named Barnardine. Barnardine is in prison awaiting execution. The Provost characterizes Barnardine as a "man that apprehends death no more dreadfully but as a drunken sleep—careless, reckless, and fearless of what's past, present, or to come; insensible of mortality, and desperately mortal" (4.2.143–46). Barnardine is so wretched that even Vincentio is horrified when he meets him. He describes Barnardine as "Unfit to live or die. . . . A creature unprepared, unmeet for death; / And to transport him in the mind he is / Were damnable" (4.3.64, 67–69). However, it is precisely Barnardine's state of mind that Vincentio recommends for Claudio, which suggests that the Duke is preparing Claudio's soul for damnation. It also reveals that only an indifferent killer could accept the Duke's counsel without qualification. It is not that there is nothing true in what the Duke says. It is, however, dangerously incomplete.[29] And moreover, the Duke does not accept his own advice. In a godless world, the best activity for him is not apathetic sleep but the quest for power.

The Duke's dark soul is revealed in another conversation with Escalus. Escalus—not aware that he is speaking with Vincentio—asks him, "What news abroad i' the world?" (3.2.216). The Duke responds:

> None, but that there is so great a fever on goodness that the dissolution of it must cure it. Novelty is only in request, and, as it is, as dangerous to be aged in any kind of course as it is virtuous to be constant in any undertaking. There is scarce truth enough alive to make societies secure, but security enough to make fellowships accursed. Much upon this riddle runs the wisdom of the world. This news is old enough, yet it is every day's news. (3.2.217–25)

These reflections on the nature of politics reveal that the Duke is not so much an ancient philosopher as he is a Machiavellian sage. The Duke expresses no concern for justice, friendship, virtue, or the good. Indeed, Vincentio claims that "goodness" is so sick that we should perform euthanasia ("dissolution") on it and put it out of its misery. Since there is

222 | Evil in Renaissance Theatre

no measure of moral virtue in the world, we need not be "constant" or principled; as the Duke says, constancy might be called "virtuous," but it is "dangerous" for those in politics. Since "novelty" is the only thing people truly desire, the good must be compromised to satisfy this demand. In accord with Machiavelli, Vincentio argues that one must change with the times rather than be "aged in any kind of course." As well, the Duke claims there is not enough trust (or "truth") in the world to bind people together in justice and friendship. Instead, humans must be forced into collectives and restrained by law ("security"). Such a society makes "fellowships accursed," but it is the only society possible.

Whatever "truths" are contained in the Duke's reflections, and however complete they might be from a Machiavellian perspective, they are deficient from the standpoint of ancient political philosophy. We must not be misled into thinking that the Duke has genuine philosophic or spiritual interests. Though he dispenses advice freely in prison, he is not there to inculcate virtue or provide comfort; rather, he is there in the disguise of "a true friar" to spy on "both prince and people" (1.3.48, 45). The prison is perhaps the best place for him to ensure that Angelo is "striking home" with severity. He does not visit the prison to mitigate Angelo's cruel governance with Christian mercy. On the contrary, he wants to see that arrests are taking place and to verify that someone is slated for execution. Subsequent events should not distort our understanding of why he goes to the prison in the first place. When the Duke first enters the prison in 2.3 and learns that Claudio is scheduled for execution, he takes no steps to intervene (2.3.10–16). He tells Juliet that Claudio "must die tomorrow" (2.3.38). Shortly afterward, he tells Claudio to relinquish any hope of a pardon and be "absolute for death" (3.1.1–5). Of course, he could unveil himself immediately or take other steps to revoke the death sentence. He does not do this because, at this point in the play, he wants Claudio dead.

The imperative for Claudio's execution changes when the Duke learns what Angelo has done. Hidden from sight, he overhears Isabella, Claudio's sister, tell her brother that Angelo has offered a possible reprieve: if Isabella agrees to sleep with Angelo, then Angelo, in exchange, will revoke Claudio's execution (3.1.44–155). Vincentio decides to intervene on Claudio's behalf only after he learns this information, not before. Despite appearances, he does not intervene because he is outraged by what Angelo has done; on the contrary, he had always hoped that Angelo would embroil himself in a new scandal such as this. Vincentio can now devise a plan that will more effectively disgrace the deputy and dazzle the Viennese. He also has a new and powerful weapon in his arsenal: Isabella.

The Problem of Isabella

Isabella is, ostensibly, a nun. She is certainly dressed in robes that proclaim her as such. The Provost describes her as "a very virtuous maid, / And to be shortly of a sisterhood, / If not already" (2.2.23–25). She enters the Order of Saint Clare on the same morning that Claudio is arrested (see 1.2.174–75). Lucio arrives at the convent to inform Isabella of the impending execution and to ask her to plead to Angelo for clemency. When she arrives at Angelo's court in 2.2, Angelo has already decided to execute Claudio "by nine tomorrow morning" and has given the Provost specific instructions to carry out the deed (2.1.33–4; 2.2.6–20). Isabella proceeds to question Angelo about his decision. Ostensibly, what we see in 2.2 is a struggle between a man who represents the "letter of the law" and a nun who represents the "spirit." None of Isabella's arguments are successful until she asks Angelo to consider whether he has lecherous desires that are similar to those of her brother (2.2.144). If so, Angelo should temper the law with mercy, for otherwise he will judge hypocritically:

> authority, though it err like others,
> Hath yet a kind of medicine in itself
> That skins the vice o' the top. Go to your bosom;
> Knock there, and ask your heart what it doth know
> That's like my brother's fault. If it confess
> A natural guiltiness such as his,
> Let it not sound a thought upon your tongue
> Against my brother's life.
>
> (2.2.139–46)

Angelo, unlike Isabella, makes a clear distinction between action and intent when applying the law. He tells Escalus: "'Tis one thing to be tempted . . . / Another thing to fall" (2.1.17–18). Angelo thinks it is not hypocritical for him to judge those who commit lechery, even if he has lecherous desires of his own (2.1.27–27). So long as he does not act on his "natural guiltiness," he is qualified to administer punishment to those who do. However, Isabella's arguments and appearance affect him strangely. He agrees to reconsider his decision and asks her to return tomorrow.

At the end of 2.2, Angelo admits to himself that he has become desirous of Isabella:

> What, do I love her,
> That I desire to hear her speak again
> And feast upon her eyes?
>   (2.2.184–86)

Isabella returns in 2.4 to find out what Angelo has decided. After a long and psychologically complex discussion, Angelo confesses his desire.

> ANGELO: Plainly conceive, I love you.
> ISABELLA: My brother did love Juliet,
> And you tell me he must die for 't.
> ANGELO: He shall not, Isabel, if you give me love.
>   (2.4.142–45)

The possibility of a plea bargain emerges at this point, but Angelo's terms are not clear. He does not initially propose that Isabella give her "body" in exchange for Claudio's life; he proposes instead that she give him "love," which might mean more than just sex.[30] However, as Angelo admits, such "untaught love / Must needs appear offense" (2.4.29–30). Even if Angelo is sincere in his "love," his proposal is coercive, foolish, and illegal. Isabella spurns Angelo's "love" and threatens to tell the entire city:

> Ha! Little honour to be much believed,
> And most pernicious purpose! Seeming, seeming!
> I will proclaim thee, Angelo, look for 't!
> Sign me a present pardon for my brother,
> Or with an outstretched throat I'll tell the world aloud
> What man thou art.
>   (2.4.150–55)

Angelo, in response, decides to "give [his] sensual race the rein" (2.4.160–61) and makes the following offer: "Redeem thy brother, / By yielding up thy *body* to my will" (2.4.164–65; my emphasis). It is at this point that Angelo speaks unambiguously of sparing Claudio's life in exchange for a one-night sexual encounter. He tells her to return the next day to say if she will accept the offer.

Isabella decides not to tell any civic authorities about what has happened. She is deterred by Angelo's claim that no one would believe her if she made her accusation public (2.4.155–60). Instead, she visits Claudio to tell him he must die. When Isabella arrives at the prison, the Duke is pretending to be Claudio's spiritual counselor. The Duke quickly hides himself so that he can overhear what she will say to her brother. When Claudio learns from Isabella that there is now an opportunity to avoid execution, he loses his resolve to die and begs his sister to accept Angelo's offer. Like Timoteo in Machiavelli's *Mandragola* and Augustine in *Commentary on the Lord's Sermon on the Mount*, Claudio argues that it is not sinful for a woman to have illicit sex if it is necessary to save a life:

> Sweet sister, let me live.
> What sin you do to save a brother's life,
> Nature dispenses with the deed so far
> That it becomes a virtue.
> (3.1.135–8)[31]

As reprehensible as Claudio might be, his request is understandable given that his life is at stake. Isabella's response, however, is vitriolic:

> O you beast!
> O faithless coward! O dishonest wretch!
> Wilt thou be made a man out of my vice?
> Is 't not a kind of incest, to take life
> From thine own sister's shame? What should I think?
> Heaven shield my mother played my father fair!
> For such a warped slip of wilderness
> Ne'er issued from his blood. Take my defiance,
> Die, perish! Might but my bending down

Reprieve thee from thy fate, it should proceed.
I'll pray a thousand prayers for thy death,
No word to save thee. . . .
                    O, fie, fie, fie!
Thy sin's not accidental, but a trade.
Mercy to thee would prove itself a bawd;
'Tis best that thou diest quickly.
                    (3.1.138–49, 150–53)[32]

Isabella never says another word to her brother for the rest of the play.

Isabella's rebuke of Claudio seems to go too far, notwithstanding the sympathy we may feel for her situation and the disgust we may have for Claudio. Her diatribe might be understandable if she had suffered physical abuse or sexual assault at the hands of Angelo, but no such event has taken place. Angelo presented Isabella with an offer; he did not rape her. Isabella's rebuke is even more incomprehensible when we compare it to her earlier pleas for Claudio's life. She now says that Claudio deserves to die, right to his face, and in her nun's habit. Every word jars our sensibilities. The Duke, however, is pleased by what he hears—and sees. Unbeknownst to Isabella, Vincentio is watching her and listening to what she says. In less than forty-eight hours, he will ask her to be his wife. The two of them have much in common. Isabella, as it turns out, is a false monastic like the Duke. She might not use her disguise with the same degree of self-awareness, but she nevertheless uses the appearance of Christian piety to mislead those around her. The Duke recognizes his affinity with Isabella and knows that she can serve both his political and his sexual objectives.

Isabella's rebuke of her brother is the most obvious clue that she is not what she appears to be, but there are indications that she is not a true nun from the first moment we meet her. We are introduced to her in 1.4 during her first morning in the nunnery. She is beginning her novitiate, and a nun named Francisca is teaching her the rules of the sisterhood. At this point, Isabella has not been in the convent for more than a few hours, and it is questionable whether her official period of probation has even begun. She certainly has not taken any formal vows to enter the sisterhood. Francisca informs us that Isabella is "yet unsworn" (1.4.9). Nevertheless, for the rest of the play, Isabella roams around Vienna dressed as a nun and convinces everyone that she is a genuine renunciant.

Her motivations for wanting to enter the nunnery are mysterious. Given that most of the women in Vienna are either fornicatresses or prostitutes, a convent is one place where she can preserve her honor.[33] Perhaps Isabella wants to flee the chaos of the city and escape to a realm where ordinances are upheld with extreme severity. Her first words of the play, however, are puzzling. After hearing the strict rules of the convent, she asks Francisca, "And have you nuns no farther privileges?" Her query does not imply that nuns have too many privileges, but too few. Francisca responds to Isabella's question by asking, "Are not these large enough?" Isabella is then forced to backtrack and claim that she speaks not of desiring more liberties but of "wishing a more strict restraint" (1.4.1–4). Her initial question, however, suggests that she is not happy with the extent of privileges granted to nuns. Francisca will, in fact, inform her of even further restrictions. When Lucio arrives to speak with Isabella, Francisca describes the rules concerning her future interactions with men. For the moment, Isabella can speak to Lucio without any restrictions because she has not yet taken her vows. But once Isabella has "vowed," she will not be able speak with a man except in the presence of a mother superior. Then, whenever she does address a man, she must not show her face to him, or, if she does show her face, she must not speak to him (1.4.7–13). These rules are important for Isabella because they will put restraints on her most significant talent: *being seen by* and *speaking to* men simultaneously. Claudio tells Lucio in 1.2:

> in [Isabella's] youth
> There is a prone and speechless dialect
> Such as move men; besides, she hath prosperous art
> When she will play with reason and discourse,
> And well she can persuade.
>
> (1.2.179–83)

Like the Duke, Isabella can dazzle men with appearances and rhetoric. This is why Claudio requests Isabella's assistance in the first place. True to Claudio's description, Isabella is able to stupefy Angelo with her speech and her beauty, so much so that Angelo expresses a desire to talk with her and look in her eyes (2.2.185–86). But if she enters the Order of Saint Clare she will not be able to affect men in this way because her interactions will be monitored and restricted. Even before she meets Angelo,

Isabella probably realizes it is not in her best interest to become a nun. When she departs from the convent to speak to Angelo, it appears that she is taking a momentary leave of absence (1.4.86–88). In fact, she never sets foot in the nunnery again.

True to Claudio's description, Isabella can "play with reason and discourse" to make whatever argument she wants. She contradicts herself continually, but she still manages to look as if she is arguing on the basis of principle. For instance, she tells Francisca that she desires the strictest restraints possible to uphold Christian virtue, but afterward she criticizes Angelo for being too strict. When she speaks with Angelo, her words, for the most part, evoke the New Testament ethic of forgiveness and mercy (see 2.2.64–70, 78–84, 104), but she says many things that are curious, and even shocking—statements that stand in marked contrast to her elevated Christian rhetoric. She tends to intersperse her Gospel-based platitudes with Roman sentiments. At one point, she criticizes Angelo's stern leadership with the following observation:

> Could great men thunder
> As Jove himself does, Jove would never be quiet,
> For every pelting, petty officer
> Would use his heaven for thunder,
> Nothing but thunder!
>
> (2.2.115–19)

Isabella evokes the highest Roman deity—"Jove," or Jupiter—instead of the only Christian God.[34] If Isabella were a sworn nun and forced to speak in the presence of a mother superior, she would certainly be censured. Indeed, her rhetoric frequently suggests a greater love of pagan Rome than Holy Rome.[35] Qualities such as honor, rank, and manliness seem to mean more to her than faith, hope, and charity. Her understanding of Roman virtue, however, is as distorted as her understanding of Christian piety. Isabella's odd concern with social rank emerges during her first conversation with Angelo. In her defense of Claudio, she proposes an inverted Roman ethic in which social rank is the measure of greatness rather than greatness the measure of social rank. Even worse, she argues that the "great" do not need to live within the same moral limits prescribed for lesser human beings:

We cannot weigh our brother with ourself.
Great men may jest with saints; 'tis wit in them,
But in the less foul profanation. . . .
That in the captain's but a choleric word
Which in the soldier is flat blasphemy.

(2.2.131–33; 135–36)

At first, Isabella implies that Angelo should not judge Claudio by the same extreme measure with which he judges himself. But then she suggests that men of higher rank (such as Claudio) should be granted indulgences that are not permitted to men in lower stations. Either way, different human beings should be measured by different moral standards—some more stringent, some less stringent. Isabella contradicts the Gospel imperative evoked by the title of the play. Even Lucio is shocked that a nun would utter such profane words ("Art advised o' that?" [2.2.137]).

Isabella continues to say surprising things. Toward the end of her first encounter with Angelo, she offers to "bribe" him so that he will pardon Claudio (2.2.151). This comment shocks everyone in the room. When pressed by Angelo ("How? Bribe me?"), Isabella is forced—as she was with Francisca—to backtrack and misrepresent herself. She claims that by "bribe" she did not mean money but rather "prayers" from "fasting maids whose minds are dedicate / To nothing temporal" (2.2.152–61).[36] According to Isabella, the sisters of the nunnery—"sisters" whom Isabella barely knows and will never see again—will pray for Angelo if he saves Claudio. Her slip concerning a "bribe," however, is indicative of Isabella's intent. She is not arguing with Angelo on moral principle, but rather using her looks and rhetoric to "bribe" him into pardoning Claudio.

When Isabella speaks of a bribe in 2.2, both the Provost and Lucio overhear what she says.[37] Her rhetoric is even more provocative when there are no witnesses. When she returns to Angelo in 2.4, no one else is present. Though it goes unmentioned in the play, she in fact returns to Angelo on the *same day* as her first encounter with the deputy in 2.2—perhaps mere moments later. She does this despite Angelo's request that she return "tomorrow" (2.2.161).[38] But why would Isabella return to Angelo on the same day? First of all, Claudio's execution is scheduled to occur "by nine tomorrow"—at latest (2.1.34).[39] If she returns "any time 'fore noon" tomorrow, as Angelo requests (2.2.167), it may be too late;

Angelo might proceed with the execution in spite of her pleas. Therefore, it is imperative for her to return immediately. Second, and more provocatively, if she returns immediately she can "bribe" Angelo in private. Lucio and the Provost have left Angelo's residence and she knows the deputy is alone. She may not have this advantage if she returns tomorrow. She is also aware that she has had an immediate effect on Angelo. It is advisable, then, for her to continue to press him before the effect wears off. She will now say things in private that she otherwise might not say, and encourage Angelo to do things that he otherwise might not do. Angelo can only proposition Isabella in private, and Isabella can only entrap him when no one else is present. Isabella, however, gets more than she bargained for.

Initially, Angelo presents the possibility of a sexual ransom as a hypothesis. He asks Isabella: "which had you rather, that the most just law / Now took your brother's life, or, to redeem him, / Give up your body to such sweet uncleanness / As she that he hath stained" (2.4.52–55). When Angelo asks this question he is not making an actual offer to Isabella just yet; rather, he asks her to undertake a hypothetical consideration. After a long and complicated discussion, Isabella finally answers that she would never yield her body to shame, no matter what was at stake. And yet when she makes this claim, she employs an image of herself that is both sexually provocative and sadomasochistic:

> were I under the terms of death,
> Th' impression of keen whips I'd wear as rubies,
> And strip myself to death as to a bed
> That longing have been sick for, ere I'd yield
> My body up to shame.
>   (2.4.100–104)[40]

Isabella's words are, to say the least, suggestive. Moments later, Angelo propositions Isabella directly. At this point, Isabella has achieved her objective: she has entrapped Angelo, and she threatens to tell the city. But her threat does not seem to affect Angelo ("Who will believe thee Isabel?"), and she decides not to go public (2.4.156).

Notwithstanding all her curious tactics and provocative comments, Isabella presents herself as an austere Roman matron who has supplemented her virtue with Christian faith—a Lucretia in nun's clothing. Most people, including Angelo, are taken in by this appearance. The Duke, on the other hand, is not. In his first discussion with Isabella, he asks her to participate in a morally dubious conspiracy. Immediately after her tirade against Claudio, Vincentio comes forward and proposes the "bed-trick," which will require Isabella's participation, as well as the participation of Angelo's former fiancée Mariana. The Duke asks Isabella to return to Angelo immediately and set a time to meet with him for the sexual encounter. Mariana will then disguise herself in Isabella's habit and go in her place. In the darkness of night, Mariana will lie with Angelo. Afterward, Angelo will think he had sex with Isabella and pardon Claudio.

Despite the sexual indiscretion entailed by the bed-trick, Vincentio reassures Isabella of the plan's beneficence: "by this, is your brother saved, your honour untainted, the poor Mariana advantaged, and the corrupt deputy scaled. . . . If you think well to carry this as you may, the doubleness of the benefit defends the deceit from reproof" (3.1.254–60). But deceit is only one of the evils that the bed-trick entails. The entire plot is designed to entrap a public official. Furthermore, the bed-trick does not stop Angelo's corrupt bargain but facilitates it: Angelo will commit lechery, albeit not with the woman he intends. Finally, the bed-trick will compromise Mariana's chastity, given that she is not actually married to Angelo. The Duke claims that the sexual encounter is "no sin" because Mariana is Angelo's wife on a "precontract" (4.1.71–72). However, the precontract was rendered null and void at least five years before, when Mariana's dowry was lost (see 5.1.223–31). Angelo's separation from Mariana on the basis of the lost dowry was harsh but legal. Mariana has no title to him now; any sexual encounter between her and Angelo is criminal.[41]

Thus the Duke asks Isabella to participate in a plot that is both illegal and immoral. Before the Duke proposed the bed-trick, Isabella was faced with a number of hard options. First, she could have accepted Angelo's terrible bargain by agreeing to relinquish her body to save Claudio's life. Though repugnant, this choice could be defended as a virtuous one. She chose not to pursue it. As a second alternative, she could have refused Angelo because there was nothing guaranteeing that he would honor his end of the bargain. Such an objection, as it turns out, would have been prudent. However, she did not raise it. Finally, as a third course, Isabella could have told "the world aloud" about Angelo's offer as she had originally threatened to do. She would have risked public disgrace if she pursued this option, for people might not have believed her. Rather than take this risk, she chose to stay quiet. Instead of taking any step that would entail either compromising her chastity or public humiliation, Isabella chose to visit the prison to tell Claudio he must die. And she was more than willing to let him die, until she learns that Claudio might be saved by a bed-trick that will leave her own "honour untainted" and "much please the absent Duke" (3.1.255, 205–6).

Isabella immediately agrees to participate in the Duke's plan (3.1.261–62). In fact, the Duke has her arrange the entire bed-trick herself. Isabella returns to Angelo *that* day—once again disregarding his request to return "tomorrow"—and tells him that she will yield her body in return for Claudio's life. This, of course, is a lie, for Isabella will do no such thing. The audience does not see Isabella's third encounter with Angelo, in which she knowingly entraps a public official, but we know that she successfully beguiles him. Angelo, we are informed, tells her to meet him in an enclosed garden at his residence at midnight (4.1.28–35). Isabella, after her third meeting with Angelo, then goes to Mariana's abode at Saint Luke's to share the news with the Duke. It is then Isabella, not the Duke, who convinces Mariana to disguise herself as a nun and have sexual intercourse with Angelo that night. Earlier in the play, the Duke had told Isabella that *he* would dispose Mariana toward the bed-trick: "The maid [Mariana] will I frame and make fit for [Angelo's] attempt" (3.1.257–58). But when Isabella arrives at Saint Luke's, the Duke says to her, "I have not yet made known to Mariana / A word of this" (4.1.48–49). Isabella, without being asked, persuades Mariana herself to commit an unseemly crime, but this discussion takes place offstage. Once again, we do not see Isabella in a morally questionable act. Shakespeare, it seems, is testing our ability to comprehend Isabella's corruption by intentionally leaving two important scenes out of the play.

Isabella's easy acceptance of, and eager participation in, the Duke's bed-trick undermines any status she might have as an exemplar of Roman virtue or Christian piety. We should recall that Lucretia—the paradigmatic Roman matron—killed herself to ensure that women did not cite her as a precedent to justify their own sexual indiscretions. Isabella, in contrast, is immediately willing to compromise the chastity of another woman to preserve her own.[42] She even allows her nun's robes to be used in a lecherous act. Though Isabella accuses Angelo of "Seeming, seeming," we find that Isabella is herself a "seemer" with a "most pernicious purpose" (2.4.151). Like the Duke, she is amenable to Machiavellian *virtù*, using whatever appearances are necessary to fulfill her ends and employing others in unseemly tasks to enhance her reputation.

Changing the Modes with the Times

The most "seeming" and "pernicious" character in *Measure for Measure* is the Duke. The second half of the play is taken up with the Duke's clandestine tactics and nefarious schemes. The primary purpose of his activities is to bring Vienna to order while keeping himself loved and feared. He must change his modes with the times to achieve this end. As we have seen, he thinks it is "dangerous to be aged in any kind of course" (3.2.219–20). The seemingly effortless manner in which he changes his plans and gains control over volatile situations creates the illusion of total control, but he is not in control of every variable. He conquers fortune through his uncanny ability to respond successfully to unexpected circumstances. To understand the fine points of the Duke's actions in the last two acts, it is necessary for my discussion to become less thematic and more technical. Vincentio does not want us to ponder these intricacies because they reveal his malicious intent and ruin the desired effect. The devil, as we shall see, is truly in the details.

When the Duke starts out, he is fully prepared to disgrace Angelo in some way or other. Angelo's reputed cruelty, his treatment of Mariana, and his similarities with Claudio will be enough for the Duke to destroy him. But things go better than expected for the Duke when he learns that Angelo has propositioned Isabella. The Duke immediately devises the bed-trick. Though Vincentio speaks of the bed-trick as "craft against vice" (3.2.270), the Duke's craft actually encourages Angelo's vice. Vincentio, we must remember, can unveil himself at any moment and stop Angelo; however, he would deny himself the luxury of having incriminating evidence against his deputy. Once again, the Duke does not inform the audience of the details, but there are numerous ways in which Angelo is rendered criminally culpable by the bed-trick. If the bed-trick proceeds as planned, Angelo will have sex with Mariana while thinking it is Isabella and then pardon Claudio. But if Angelo revokes Claudio's death sentence, he will in fact be guilty of disobeying the Duke's orders. We must recall that Angelo has been commissioned to "strike home," and it is probably criminal for Angelo to grant Claudio an unwarranted reprieve. The Duke can thus use the reprieve to suggest that Angelo was bribed, and employ Mariana and Isabella to accuse the deputy of lechery. Angelo will thus be exposed to the public as a corrupt, hypocritical lecher who is guilty of a capital offense.

With this plan, Vincentio will never need to reveal his friar disguise in public and thereby implicate himself. He will have the hard evidence of Claudio's reprieve. Isabella and Mariana can say to the city that a friar — who has mysteriously disappeared — encouraged them to entrap Angelo; nevertheless, responsibility for the bed-trick will lie with them.[43] Vincentio can pardon the two women and use them as witnesses to prove Angelo was bribed. There might even be physical evidence of Angelo's lechery if Mariana becomes pregnant. The Duke can then have Angelo executed instead of Claudio, which would cause celebration throughout the city, as well as some fear. If Mariana protests Angelo's execution, the Duke can save Angelo and execute someone else entirely — perhaps Lucio. The Duke has a number of options open to him. All of them are played out to some degree in the final act.

It is shortly after midnight when the Duke enters the prison in 4.2 (see 4.2.64, 71), and the sexual encounter between Angelo and Mariana has just taken place. The Duke expects the Provost to receive a letter from Angelo at any moment revoking Claudio's death sentence. Vincentio wants to be present when the letter arrives so that he can seize it as evidence against Angelo. He arrives at the prison with a concealed letter of his own bearing the Duke's official seal and announcing his return to the city within two days (see 4.2.198). He intends to send the letter to someone immediately after Claudio is pardoned. Once Claudio's reprieve is in his hands, the Duke possesses the incriminating evidence he needs to destroy Angelo. He can then take the necessary steps to remove his friar disguise in secret and "return" to Vienna.

The Duke assumes that Angelo will actually pardon Claudio. This assumption, as it turns out, is wrong, and it is Vincentio's only mistake in the entire play. The pardon never arrives. The letter Angelo actually sends to the Provost demands that Claudio be beheaded at four o'clock in the morning[44] and that the head be delivered immediately to his residence. Angelo also orders that Barnardine be executed at noon. That Angelo does not send a reprieve makes it harder for the Duke, because Angelo is still carrying out his duties as commissioned. The Duke cannot charge Angelo with granting an illegal reprieve, nor can he accuse him of accepting a bribe.

Vincentio is forced to change his plans. He can still proceed against Angelo without legal evidence. In fact, Angelo's refusal to honor the terms of the bed-trick looks worse for him—far worse than if he had actually honored his promise to repeal Claudio's death sentence. It appears as if Angelo did not keep his promise to Isabella and proceeded cruelly with the execution. It remains in Vincentio's best interest, nevertheless, to save Claudio, who still is slated for beheading in four hours. The Duke must quickly put a stop to the scheduled execution but encourage everyone to believe that the execution actually took place. The public will be furious when it is disclosed that Angelo reneged on his promise to pardon Claudio. Vincentio can then use this anger to do what he wants with Angelo, and later further please the people by revealing that Claudio is still alive.

This new plot has the potential to be overwhelmingly effective, but it is also the hardest to realize. Without evidence of a bribe, there is only the allegation of sexual impropriety. It will be Angelo's word against Mariana's and Isabella's concerning whether any illicit sex took place. For his plan to work, Vincentio must let everyone know that he has personally observed Angelo's wrongdoings in disguise. In other words, the Duke will be required to reveal his disguise in public, after which Angelo will be forced to confess. There are risks involved with this strategy, for it will show that the Duke was part of a conspiracy. But once the full extent of Angelo's depravity is revealed and the deputy admits his wrongdoings, any criticisms of the Duke will be muted. Furthermore, no one will raise any questions if Vincentio can bring Claudio back from the dead.

The Duke asks the Provost to execute Barnardine in Claudio's place and hide Claudio away; he also asks him to send Barnardine's head to Angelo as a substitute for Claudio's. The Provost initially rejects this, since it would require him to disobey Angelo's orders. Given the Provost's reluctance, Vincentio is forced to improvise yet again by revealing the letter in his pocket to a person, and in a manner, that he did not originally

intend (4.2.191–94). He gives it to the Provost, who sees the Duke's official seal on the letter; the Provost now assumes that the friar is an agent
of the Duke, and he reads in the letter that Vincentio will return in two
days. The Provost is thus persuaded to behead Barnardine in place of
Claudio, then shave Barnardine's head so that it will pass unrecognized
by Angelo. However, the plan changes four hours later, just as Barnardine
is about to be executed. The Provost learns that a prisoner named Ragozine, who looks strikingly like Claudio, has died of natural causes. The
Provost suggests that they send Ragozine's head to Angelo instead of Barnardine's. The Duke agrees to this, more because Ragozine bears a close
resemblance to Claudio than out of any concern for Barnardine. Vincentio also convinces the Provost to delay Barnardine's scheduled execution.
The Duke's reasons for sparing Barnardine are mysterious, but perhaps
he has thought of a role the murderer can serve in the future.

Vincentio's final plan is thereby set in motion: Claudio and Barnardine are both hidden away, and Ragozine's head is delivered to Angelo.
Isabella then arrives at the prison to find out if her brother was pardoned. The Duke lies to Isabella to abet her fury and co-opt her into the
new scheme: he tells her that Angelo did not honor his promise and that
Claudio was killed. When Isabella is given the false report, she exclaims
(while still in her religious habit): "O, I will to [Angelo] and pluck out his
eyes!" (4.3.119). The Duke suggests that he has a new plan to redeem the
situation, but he does not tell Isabella what it is. He simply repeats his
refrain about consequences:

> If you can pace your wisdom
> In that good path that I would wish it go,
> And you shall have your bosom on this wretch,
> Grace of the Duke, revenges to your heart,
> And general honour.
> $\qquad\qquad\qquad\qquad$ (4.3.132–36)

Once again, the Duke appeals to Isabella's desire for honor and revenge,
to which she replies, "I am directed by you" (4.3.136).

Vincentio, still in his friar's disguise, gives Isabella the assurance that
his monastery is in league with the Duke and that the Duke will return
tomorrow (4.3.127–27).[45] He asks Isabella to deliver a letter to a certain
Friar Peter and then to accompany Peter to Mariana's house, where there

will be a meeting that night. Isabella, Mariana, and Peter will be directed
by the disguised Duke on how to accuse Angelo (see 4.3.137–43). In 4.6,
which takes place the following morning, we learn some of what was said
at that meeting:

> ISABELLA: To speak so indirectly I am loath.
> I would say the truth, but to accuse him [Angelo] so,
> That is your part. Yet I am advised to do it,
> He [the Duke] says, to veil full purpose.
> MARIANA: Be ruled by him [the Duke].
> ISABELLA: Besides, he [the Duke] tells me that, if peradventure
> He [the Duke] speak against me on the adverse side,
> I should not think it strange, for 'tis a physic
> That's bitter to sweet end.
>
> (4.6.1–8)[46]

This discussion reveals the degree of control that the Duke has in the last
act. Almost everything is scripted. Isabella has been instructed to bear
false witness against Angelo in public and has been warned that the Duke
will pretend to chastise her. Mariana, in her role, will accuse Angelo directly. The Duke justifies this spectacle of false accusations and feigned
reprimands as "bitter" medicine for a "sweet end." What the women do
not know is that the Duke has not yet finished composing his play. There
will come a point at which the women will run out of lines, and yet the
show will continue. How the play ends depends on how the women
improvise.

Deus ex Machina: The Duke's Final Judgment

> So whenever you give alms, do not sound a trumpet before you, as the
> hypocrites do in the synagogues and in the streets, so that they may be
> praised by others. Truly I tell you, they have received their reward.
> —Matt. 6:2

The Duke reenters the city with trumpets blasting (4.6.12). Up to this
point in the play he has governed his realm like a hidden god. Now, deus
ex machina, Vincentio returns to set things straight and establish his rule

in the open. His second coming is accompanied by pomp and pageantry. He has arranged for the people of Vienna to meet him at the city gates when he returns, where he is flanked by attendants named Valencius, Rowland, Crassus, Flavius, and Varrius—names that suggest nobility and whose presence enhances the splendor of the Duke's arrival (4.5.6–12). We should recall, however, that Vincentio had claimed to hate spectacles and crowds (see 1.1.68–73; 1.3.7–10). In fact, everything he does throughout the play is designed to create the extravaganza we see in Act 5.[47] The final act is not an official ceremony in which due process is observed but a dazzling show trial that simulates the Final Judgment. Vincentio appears to his people as "power divine."

When the Duke arrives at the city gates, he greets Angelo and gives him praise. Isabella, as scripted, emerges from the crowd and charges Angelo with having violated her chastity and reneging on his promise to free Claudio. The Duke greets Isabella's charges with feigned scorn and disbelief. Friar Peter then comes forward to deliver his scripted lines, and he introduces Mariana. Mariana proceeds to accuse Angelo of having slept with her while thinking he was sleeping with Isabella. Angelo denies every accusation raised against him, and Vincentio promptly dismisses the charges. The women's accusations appear like the work of an unlawful conspiracy, which, in fact, they are. Angelo tries to use this to his advantage, claiming that the women are "instruments of some more mightier member" (5.1.245). The Duke immediately sends for "Friar Lodowick," the monastic who is reported to have "set the women on" (5.1.258). When Isabella speaks the name "Lodowick" in public in Act 5 (5.1.130), this is the first time we discover that Vincentio went by a pseudonym when disguised as a friar. The likelihood is that the Duke had not used this false name all along. Up to Act 5, he remained more mysterious by not announcing a name; now he is forced to use a pseudonym because he must appear before the entire city as a friar. The name was probably invented the night before and scripted for Isabella to say in public.[48] After demanding that "Lodowick" be sent for, Vincentio then commissions Escalus to judge the affair and exits the stage without offering an explanation (5.1.262–68). Of course, the Duke uses this opportunity to disguise himself. He is forced to assume his costume one last time because he must reveal to Angelo—and all of Vienna—that *he* is the mysterious friar who has secretly governed the city. Angelo will not confess until he knows that the Duke has observed his trespasses.

Vincentio reenters the stage disguised as Lodowick and appears before Escalus. Vincentio's responses to Escalus's questions are so evasive and insulting that Escalus is whipped into a frenzy: "Take him hence. To th' rack with him! We'll touse you / Joint by joint" (5.1.319–20). Merciful Escalus, unknowingly, orders the torture of the Duke. Now the Duke has something against everyone—even his most dedicated servant—and he chooses this moment to reveal "Lodowick's" true identity. Lucio pulls off the friar's hood to uncover the Duke. With this unveiling, it is now clear that the Duke has observed all the sins in his city and is about to judge everyone. It is not just Angelo who stands accused; every character is guilty of something. Vincentio immediately pardons Escalus for demanding that the Duke be tortured, but his forgiveness occurs only after he has made his merciful minister feel guilty. This pattern is repeated throughout the rest of Act 5; the Duke will, at some point, judge and "forgive" each major character.

The majority of the act is taken up with the judgment of Angelo. It is Angelo who likens the Duke to God:

> O my dread lord,
> I should be guiltier than my guiltiness
> To think I can be undiscernible,
> When I perceive Your Grace, like power divine,
> Hath looked upon my passes.
> (5.1.374–78)

The Duke's unveiling has the desired effect. Standing in the presence of the Godlike Vincentio, Angelo confesses his guilt in front of the entire city before the Duke has raised a single charge against him. Vincentio does not immediately condemn Angelo. Instead, he sends Angelo off to be married to Mariana. It is only when Angelo returns to the stage as a married man that Vincentio finally charges him with anything. He says to Isabella and all of Vienna:

> But as [Angelo] adjudged your brother—
> Being criminal, in double violation
> Of sacred chastity and of promise breach
> Thereon dependent, for your brother's life—
> The very mercy of the law cries out

Most audible, even from his proper tongue,
"An Angelo for Claudio, death for death!"
Haste still pays haste, and leisure answers leisure;
Like doth quit like, and measure still for measure.

(5.1.411–19)

The Duke condemns Angelo to death for committing a "double violation": (1) violating "sacred chastity" and (2) "promise breach" causing Claudio's death. In fact, neither of the Duke's charges stands up when examined carefully.

Angelo cannot be legally charged with "promise breach" on the grounds that he did not abide by the terms of his compact with Isabella. First, his agreement with her has no legal standing. On the contrary, if Angelo had kept his "promise," he would have been legally charged with accepting a bribe. Second, even if the compact were legally binding, Angelo would still be innocent. Isabella did not honor her end of the bargain either: she sent Mariana in her place, which means that the required ransom was not paid for Claudio's life. Isabella is thus guilty of "promise breach." Assuming that the compact was binding in some way, Angelo was under no obligation to spare Claudio since Isabella did not do her part.

With regard to the Duke's accusation of violating "sacred chastity," Angelo is one sense guilty and in another sense innocent. Angelo is guilty of lechery because he has had sex with Mariana outside of wedlock, but even here there are mitigating circumstances. Angelo was entrapped by a sex-for-profit conspiracy. If Angelo is guilty of committing lechery, then Mariana, Isabella, and the Duke are guilty of arranging and facilitating it. From the standpoint of the lechery laws, Angelo is a client, Mariana is a prostitute, Isabella is a madam, and the Duke is a pimp. Any guilt on Angelo's part implicates the others. For this reason, the Duke orders the immediate marriage of Angelo and Mariana, to make it seem as if Mariana was merely having sex with her husband. Of course, the Duke never claims that Angelo violated Mariana's "sacred chastity." Instead, he suggests that it was Isabella's chastity that was disgraced. However, Angelo is, at most, guilty of committing lechery with Isabella in his mind. And if Angelo is guilty of having sexual thoughts about a nun, then so is the Duke, who is moments away from proposing marriage to Isabella.

When everything is considered, the charges raised against Angelo either have no legal standing or implicate others. There is one illegality that is Angelo's alone: he offered to pardon Claudio in exchange for Isabella's maidenhead. The Duke, however, never charges Angelo with proposing a bribe. On the contrary, the Duke reprimands Angelo for *not* following through on his illegal offer.

Of course, Angelo is guilty of numerous sins if we judge him according to his intentions. In Act 4, Angelo expresses his own horror of what he thinks he has done:

> This deed unshapes me quite, make me unpregnant
> And dull to all proceedings. A deflowered maid,
> And by an eminent body that enforced
> The law against it. . . .
>   [Claudio] should have lived,
> Save that his riotous youth, with dangerous sense,
> Might in the times to come have ta'en revenge,
> By so receiving a dishonored life
> With ransom of such shame. Would yet he had lived!
>   (4.4.20–23, 28–32)

Angelo confesses that he ordered Claudio's execution to stop him from revenging his sister's honor. A murderous intent is revealed: Angelo insisted on Claudio's beheading for a personal reason, not because he was administering the law. Nevertheless, Angelo's sin still remains at the level of intent. Even if Claudio's execution had gone ahead, it could not be used as legal evidence against him. At most, Angelo is guilty of murdering Claudio in his mind.

Surprisingly, Isabella defends Angelo on exactly these grounds in her final words of the play. She pleads to the Duke to spare Angelo's life:

> Look, if it please you, on this man [Angelo] condemned
> As if my brother lived. I partly think
> A due sincerity governed his deeds,
> Till he did look on me. Since it is so,
> Let him not die. My brother had but justice.
> In that he did the thing for which he died.

For Angelo,
His act did not o'ertake his bad intent,
And must be buried but as an intent
That perished by the way. Thoughts are no subjects,
Intents but merely thoughts.

(5.1.452−62)

Before considering Isabella's intentions, it must be said that most of what she says in this passage is true. She argues that even if Angelo had lecherous or murderous intentions, it would be unjust to execute him for these alone. By carrying out the execution, Angelo was acting within the law: Claudio's death sentence was legal ("but justice") because Claudio actually committed a crime, not just in his mind, but in his actions. Angelo's crimes, for the most part, were committed in his "thoughts." She reminds the Duke that worldly political leaders cannot—or at least, should not—condemn people for their thoughts ("Thoughts are no subjects"). The Duke, however, chooses to transgress worldly limits. Like God, he judges another man as if action and intent are equivalent. In the Sermon on the Mount, Jesus proclaims:

> You have heard that it was said to those of ancient times, "You shall not commit murder"; and "whoever murders shall be liable to judgement." But I say to you that if you are angry with a brother or sister, you will be liable to judgement. . . . You have heard that it was said, "You shall not commit adultery." But I say to you that everyone who looks at a woman with lust has already committed adultery with her in his heart. (Matt. 5: 21−22, 27−78)

God holds committed sins and intended sins as equal in his Final Judgment, but it is simply untenable for worldly courts to hold action and intent as equal in their proceedings against criminals. The desire to commit a crime—even if it can be proven—does not deserve as great a punishment as actually committing one. There is, then, some degree of truth to Isabella's earlier claim that the things "set down so in heaven" are not always practicable "in earth" (2.4.50).[49] But the Duke transforms his earthly court into a heavenly council. He sentences Angelo to death for intending to murder Claudio and for disgracing Isabella in his mind. Unless Mariana protests, Vincentio might actually intend to follow through with Angelo's execution. No one else in Vienna will defend Angelo, and most would be pleased to see him killed.

The Duke's decision to execute Angelo certainly surprises Mariana, who is likely working without a script at this point. She proceeds to demonstrate genuine affection for her new husband by pleading for his life. The Duke, denying her appeal, offers her Angelo's estate as a widow's inheritance. She refuses this offer and insists that Angelo live to be her spouse (5.1.430–43). Vincentio, once again, rejects her plea. Mariana is then forced to ask Isabella to plead on her behalf. Isabella, at this point, gives her final speech in defense of Angelo, which I have examined above (5.1.451–62). Her words appear charitable, but we must consider the context in which they are spoken, as well as Isabella's intentions. Before she addresses the Duke, she is in a situation where she can either insist on revenge (thereby ignoring Mariana's pleas) or plead for mercy. It would seem that at this point she is working without a script as well. Given that she is still in her novice's outfit and that all of Vienna is watching, it would appear saintly for her to defend Angelo—a man who ordered her brother's execution and who tried to violate her chastity. She thereby proceeds to mount a compelling defense of Angelo. Her argument, however, contradicts some of her previous statements in defense of Claudio. In Act 2, she had held Angelo accountable for his intentions, essentially equating action and intent. She had argued that Angelo—like all men—was guilty of lecherous thoughts; therefore, he could not justifiably execute Claudio for committing lechery (see 2.2.139–46). Now Isabella, in her final speech, argues the opposite: Angelo, she claims, should *not* be held accountable for his "thoughts," whereas Claudio received "justice" because "he *did* the thing for which he died" (5.1.457; my emphasis). In this manner, she tries to prevent Angelo's death using the same argument that Angelo had used in Act 2 to justify Claudio's execution: the law, Angelo had said, punishes those who "fall," not those who are merely "tempted" (see 2.1.17–31). Isabella now appears to accept this argument, but her advocacy of this position has nothing to do with principle or clear reasoning. She continues to "play with reason and discourse" right to the end of the play, using whatever argument she thinks will work in a given situation to get what she wants.

Vincentio refuses to pardon Angelo on Isabella's request. He is intent, it seems, on emphasizing his cruelty so as to put some fear into the citizens. At this point, the Provost emerges from the jail with Claudio and Barnardine. Claudio is unveiled before everyone. With the revelation that Claudio is alive, the Duke, in effect, performs a resurrection, and his redemption begins to take effect. He proceeds to do something untenable in both worldly law and Christian eschatology: he forgives everyone, or at least he appears to. In the end, no one is punished for either their actions or their thoughts. But in fact, the quality of Vincentio's mercy is strained. The absence of bloodshed at the end of *Measure for Measure* is not evidence of the Duke's benevolence. In some cases, his mercy is worse than death.

When the Duke forgives his subjects, it is often not clear what he is forgiving them for. In almost every case, the Duke himself instigated the "sin" he absolves. For example, he pardons Escalus for unknowingly threatening him with torture, but it was the Duke himself who provoked this outburst while in disguise (5.1.369). He forgives the Provost for "Th' offense" of not executing Claudio as commissioned, even though the Duke ordered this offense himself (5.1.541–45). He forgives Isabella for having "pained" his "unknown sovereignty," even though she actually helped him achieve his purposes (5.1.393–95). But the Duke's most disturbing show of "mercy" is toward Barnardine, who he releases from prison (5.1.493–97). Nothing justifies this decision, given that Barnardine is a convicted and unrepentant murderer. The Duke's action has the aura of supernatural redemption, especially given that he had earlier been willing to condemn Barnardine to eternal damnation (see 4.3.67–69). Vincentio's apparent grace should not fool us. He puts Barnardine in the care of Friar Peter, the man who is perhaps the Duke's closest confidant and who we know is a conspirator in the Duke's nefarious schemes. Perhaps Vincentio has some future employment in mind for Barnardine. It may help the Duke to have killers in the ranks, especially if he plans to lead the city to war.

The Duke also forgives Angelo, but in this case his forgiveness looks more like damnation. He pardons Angelo with the words "your evil quits you well," and he orders him to stay married to Mariana (5.1.507–8). However, at two points in Act 5, Angelo asks to be executed (5.1.381–82, 487–88). In his last words of the play, Angelo says, "I crave death more willingly than mercy. / 'Tis my deserving, and I do entreat it" (5.1.487–88).[50] The Duke will not honor Angelo's request; instead, he demands that Angelo remain married to a woman he does not love. Even worse, Angelo will live to see the marriage of Isabella and the Duke—a psychological torment that Vincentio undoubtedly intends. Even though the Duke appears merciful when he rescinds the death sentence, he gives his former deputy a punishment worse than death—at least in the deputy's mind.[51]

The man who Vincentio initially says he "cannot pardon" is Lucio. Though Lucio is guilty of lechery and of siring a bastard child with Kate Keepdown, the Duke actually punishes him for "slanders." He orders that Lucio be wedded to Kate and then "whipped and hanged" (5.1.524). Lucio, surprisingly, does not plead for his life; he only asks that he not be married to a whore (5.1.525–26). Like Angelo, Lucio thinks that marriage is "worse than hanging" (5.1.368). Vincentio, in a supposed show of mercy, cancels the order for Lucio's torture and execution, but he insists on Lucio's marriage to Kate (5.1.529–32). Once again, the Duke orders a punishment that from the subject's perspective is worse than death; as Lucio says in his final words: "Marrying a punk, my lord, is pressing to death, whipping, and hanging" (5.1.533–34).

Finally, as the Duke is pronouncing final judgment on everyone else, he proposes marriage to Isabella. Whereas Angelo's desire for a nun seemed perverse, the Duke makes his own longing seem respectable. His first proposal to Isabella is a command: "*Give* me your hand and *say* you will be mine" (5.1.503, my emphasis). His second proposal is an offer: "if you'll a willing ear incline, / What's mine is yours and what is yours is mine" (5.1.547–48). Regardless of whether the Duke is commanding or offering, he understands marriage in terms of acquisition. The Duke's first proposal treats Isabella as a possession that must submit to his will. His second proposal echoes Jesus' statement in the Gospel of John: "All mine are yours, and yours are mine" (John 17:10)[52]—apropos, perhaps, since the Duke is proposing to a bride of Christ. But in Vincentio's mouth these words suggest economic and sexual transactions. Nowhere does he, like Angelo, express a desire to "speak" to Isabella and look in her eyes; nowhere does he, like Angelo, confess his "love" for Isabella. Unlike Angelo, the Duke remains in firm control of his desires, and he uses them to fulfill his political objectives. The Duke also makes his proposals in public, putting Isabella in a difficult position. Whereas Angelo, even at his worst, left Isabella with a choice, the Duke does not. Everyone in

Vienna is watching, and it would be foolhardy for Isabella to refuse the Duke's proposal, especially after he saved her brother from execution. With tactics such as these, the Duke shows himself more effective than Angelo at seducing a nun.

Given that Vincentio has a divine aura, his proposal to Isabella does not seem blasphemous. Symbolically, the Duke asks Isabella to break her marriage with Jesus and become engaged to Christ's replacement.[53] Even the friars in the play—Thomas and Peter—have switched their allegiance to the new incarnate Lord. But Isabella says nothing after the Duke proposes to her. Her silence is mysterious. Perhaps she thinks it is unseemly for her to accept his proposal in public while wearing an outfit that proclaims sexual abstinence. Nevertheless, it is unlikely that she will return to the Order of Saint Clare. By marrying the Duke, she will finally receive the honor she has always craved.

With his proposal to Isabella, the Duke seems to have realized all his purposes. In fact, his providence is still unfolding. It is clear that the Duke has something else in store. He announces: "So, bring us to our palace, where we'll show / What's yet behind that's meet you all should know" (5.1.549–50). There is something "yet behind," or "still to come." The Duke has more surprises in store, but only *some* things will be told to the Viennese. We in the audience do not get to hear any of these things because the play ends. Perhaps the Duke, in full regalia and surrounded by noblemen, will announce that Vienna is going to war against the king of Hungary. Or he might announce something else entirely. Regardless, something major is on the horizon for the city of Vienna.[54] We never get to hear the real reason Vincentio needed to bring the city to order at this moment in time.

Vincentio's Theodicy

[E]very good tree bears good fruit and every bad tree bears bad fruit.
A good tree cannot bear bad fruit, nor can a bad tree bear good fruit.
—Matt. 7:17–18

If we do as the title of the play suggests and measure each character by the same standard, we find that most if not all of the characters are con-

demnable. Everything seems to indicate that Angelo is the true Machiavel of *Measure for Measure*. Isabella says to the Duke:

> even so may Angelo,
> In all his dressings, characts, titles, forms,
> Be an archvillain. Believe it, royal Prince,
> If he be less, he's nothing; but he's more,
> Had I more name for badness.
>   (5.1.58–62)

But when we cut through the lies, distortions, and appearances propagated by the Duke and Isabella, we find that Angelo is not necessarily
the most villainous character in the play. Indeed, much of Angelo's evil,
either real or imaginary, is facilitated by the same characters who condemn him. Angelo is simply a pawn in the Duke's game. It is Vincentio
who covertly sanctions and promotes every immorality in the play. Ultimately, it is Vincentio, in "all his dressings, characts, titles, forms," who is
the true "archvillain," not Angelo.

Some might argue that the Duke has a good purpose because order,
marriage, and civility return to Vienna as a result of his efforts. This claim,
however, is weak. Notwithstanding the appearance of a resolution, the
new order at the end is problematic. True to his political philosophy, Vincentio creates a society in which there is "security enough to make fellowships accursed" but not enough goodness to make fellowships blessed
(3.2.222–23). Orderliness returns to Vienna, but it is as undesirable as the
anarchy that plagues the city at the start. The Duke has used illegal and
immoral means to discipline the city, and he is perhaps about to drag his
citizens into an unjust war. It is true, however, that the Duke reestablishes
marriage as an institution. He does this by ordering the unions of Angelo
and Mariana, Lucio and Kate, and Claudio and Juliet. He sets an example
by arranging his own marriage to Isabella. To produce these marriages, he
must drag people out of brothels and convents where, respectively, licentiousness and celibacy are celebrated instead of matrimony. Marriage will
now be the norm of the city, not the exception. Nevertheless, the Duke has
allowed his citizens to neglect marriage for so long that he must now force
people into partnerships against their will. Angelo, Lucio, and Claudio are
not in love with their respective spouses, and, as a result, the nuptials at

the end are entirely unsatisfactory. So too is the general appearance of harmony. The silence between Isabella and Claudio in the final moments of the play testifies to this. It would, of course, be appropriate for a "nun" like Isabella to try to reconcile with Claudio, especially after thinking he was dead, but she does not make a single gesture toward her brother (5.1.501). In the Sermon on the Mount, Jesus says, "If you insult a brother or sister, you will be liable to the council; and if you say, 'You fool,' you will be liable to the hell of fire. . . . [B]e reconciled to your brother or sister" (Matt. 5:22, 24). Isabella's last words to her brother are spoken in Act 3: "Mercy to thee would prove itself a bawd; / 'Tis best that thou diest quickly" (3.1.152–53). She never takes these words back.

The unsatisfying conclusion of *Measure for Measure* suggests that the play moves from one relatively evil condition at the start to another at the end, with the Duke at the helm all along. Vienna starts off as a city infected with lawlessness and lechery; it ends up as a coercive regime founded on criminality, corruption, and fraud. But even if we grant that Vienna is truly rehabilitated, does it justify the Duke's tactics? Harry V. Jaffa argues that it does: "The returned Duke, like a returned Christ, has brought good out of evil, in the process of revealing himself."[55] Jaffa goes on to say:

> The Duke, in his disguise, plays the role of Providence, and thereby makes the otherwise implausible become plausible. God may permit evil, because God can bring good out of evil. Men may not do evil that good may come to pass, in part because there is no assurance that the good they intend will actually come to pass. Where the evil is certain and the good uncertain, to have the ends justify the means is unreasonable and impermissible. . . . We accept the legitimacy of the illicit means embodied in the bed-trick, because the Duke's presence assures success. The Duke here presents a practical example of what Machiavelli in the *Prince* meant by the conquest of fortune or chance. The tyrannical reputation of the Duke will be avoided, but his actual means are not for that reason less outside the bounds of morality. Because of his indirect and invisible government, however, they *seem* to be moral.[56]

Jaffa uses an argument traditionally offered as an answer to the "theodicy question" and applies it to Machiavellian politics. Christian theodicy attempts to reconcile God's beneficence, omniscience, and omnipotence with the fact of evil. In Christian doctrine, God is not the source of evil, but he uses the evil of others to realize the greatest good. His omnipotence ensures final victory. Humans, on the other hand, are not permitted to use evil strategically because we are not assured of success. We must accept that it is impossible for us to bear good fruit from bad trees. Machiavelli, of course, teaches otherwise. He effectively politicizes Christian theodicy when he claims that success can be guaranteed, more or less, if humans are willing to employ a sufficient amount of what appears to be "evil." Jaffa claims that only God and true Machiavellian princes are allowed to use "evil" since only they are assured of success. *Measure for Measure* reveals what politics looks like when a prince proceeds like God. Machiavellian politics can even "seem to be moral."

Some might argue that *Measure for Measure* should not be studied as a commentary on theodicy or as a gritty portrayal of Realpolitik. The play is, after all, "just a comedy,"[57] and a fantastic one at that. One of the reasons the play is such a problem is its inextricable combination of the real and the fantastic. On the one hand, the play depicts the real-world intricacies of power politics; on the other, it ends with an incredible resolution that has the aura of divine providence. However, this unsettling mixture is not a stylistic shortcoming on Shakespeare's part. It is, rather, indicative of Shakespeare's critique of Machiavellian *virtù*. The Godlike control that Machiavelli promised over politics is here shown to be both criminal and fantastic. However, the attempt to master politics through extraordinary administration and moral confusion is very real. Duke Vincentio is Shakespeare's symbol of modern politics. *Measure for Measure* does not depict a prudential statesman trying to approximate the good. It presents a clever Duke who actualizes a pseudo-eschaton through well-used evils and, in so doing, appears to be the standard of morality.

It may be true that politics, by its very nature, necessitates immoral acts and choosing the lesser evil. Vincentio goes much further than this. He perpetrates evil beyond what is necessary and then dares to call such surplus immorality good. Undoubtedly, his tactics are remarkably effective. But "effectiveness" outside of the Machiavellian universe is not synonymous with the good. If we are uncomfortable with the Duke's politics, then we must consider if there is a genuinely good and politically effective type of virtue that humans can, and should, aspire to. On the basis of Aristotle's distinction between "prudence" and "cleverness," it might be possible to develop an account of politics in which goods and evils are not reduced to mere appearances. In this way, we might arrive at a politically astute understanding of human excellence that is distinct from Machiavellian *virtù* but that also remains uncompromisingly realistic. Such an understanding would recognize the reality of the good, the ineradicable nature of evil, and the folly of confusing the two.

Epilogue

Machiavellianism and Providence

The Reign of Efficacy

Mandragola and *Measure for Measure* both present a particular dispensation: the urge to administrate human affairs with complete efficacy. They also reveal the effect this ethos has on our sense of moral responsibility. Moral categories are neutralized "once the calculation of efficiency has been awarded supreme authority in deciding political purposes."[1] The movement to give "supreme authority" to efficacy was initiated by Machiavelli in the early sixteenth century. It would express itself more radically in the bureaucracies of late modernity. Bureaucracies, with their inherent drive to find effective "solutions," are perhaps the most extreme instance of the reign of efficacy. *Mandragola* and *Measure for Measure* do not present the genocidal capacities of bureaucratic systems, nor do they depict corporations peopled by banal office workers. They do, however, portray organized conspiracies that operate according to an ethos of unadulterated expediency. Bureaucracies can thus be understood as Machiavellian business taken to its logical extreme: they aim to conquer fortune by replacing ethical scruples with efficacious concern, intoxicating people with grand designs, and offering rewards for complicity. They also require innovative executives and managers who can direct the cooperative, who can maintain effectiveness, who can adapt to change, and who can "think outside the box." Such leaders equate "necessity" with the good,[2] and will do whatever it takes to succeed.

Machiavelli's decision to give supreme authority to considerations of expediency helped initiate the modern project and is part of what defines modernity. Machiavelli is not "modern" because he claimed that people must do bad things to succeed in a hostile world. He is "modern" because he claimed that whatever is conducive to human success *is* good—including those things that appear to be "evil."

Machiavelli's Augustinian Inheritance

Machiavelli's insistence that both "good" and "evil" be used in due proportion to acquire power distinguishes him from irrational extremists. T. S. Eliot writes, "Machiavelli was no fanatic; he merely observed the truth about humanity. The world of human motives which he depicts is true— that is to say, it is humanity without the addition of superhuman grace."[3] Machiavelli claims that human nature, left on its own, is constituted by overweening pride, by an insatiable desire for ownership, and by a totalizing impulse to control all that exists. He writes: "Nature has created men so that they are able to desire everything and are unable to attain everything" (*D* 1.37.1). Though no single person can acquire everything, honor is given to those who acquire more than others:

> It is a very natural and ordinary thing to desire to acquire, and always, when men do it who can, they will be praised or not blamed; but when they cannot, and want to do it anyway, here lie the error and the blame. (*P* 3)

Excellence in politics is measured by the ability of a principality or republic to acquire what it desires. The same is true in private life. *Mandragola* and *Measure for Measure* depict such public and private "excellence."

Machiavelli's account of human motivation and political association in a Godless world is similar to Augustine's. According to Augustine, justice cannot be realized in a society lacking Christian faith.[4] Such groups are indistinguishable from gangs of thieves—much like the conspirators in *Mandragola*. In *City of God*, Augustine writes:

> Remove justice and what are kingdoms but gangs of criminals on a large scale? What are criminal gangs but petty kingdoms? A gang

is a group of men under the command of a leader, bound by a compact of association, in which the plunder is divided according to an
agreed convention. (*CG* 4.5)

The classical idea of justice as that which gives each person his due is, for
Augustine, reduced to dividing the spoils of criminal conquest. Virtue is
accordingly the ability to seize these spoils in the first place through the
expedient use of force and fraud. Giuseppe Prezzolini writes, "Augustine
had pronounced a judgement about politics and about political communi-
ties which does not differ essentially from Machiavelli's, although it was,
of course, supplemented by the vision of a hereafter that is altogether absent in Machiavelli."[5]

Prezzolini's argument supports Eliot's point that Machiavelli simply
subtracts the Christian notion of "superhuman grace" and accepts the
political world that remains. The remainder, however, is not politics as
understood by either Greeks or Romans. Machiavelli, despite appearances, does not ultimately advise us to return to "pagan" ways. For Machiavelli, the Aristotelian and Livian attempts to define "virtue" as something related to acquisition, but not reducible to successful acquisition
alone, are misguided and mistaken; such efforts simply whitewash or
distort the essential acquisitive drive of *virtù* in a world without God.
Machiavelli accepts Christian dogmas regarding the full extent of human
depravity and demonstrates how Greek and Roman notions of virtue
are false in light of these teachings; at the same time he rejects the belief
in divine grace and develops an account of "virtue" based on Christian
notions of fallen humanity alone. Aristotle or Livy might respond, in defense of their own accounts of virtue, that Christianity has effectively
stacked the deck—that rejecting Christian teachings does not necessarily result in the account of *virtù* offered by Machiavelli. There may, in
fact, be ways of thinking about human nature, excellence, and politics
that are not somehow derived from the Christian eschatological vision.
But Machiavelli, notwithstanding his turn to the ancient Romans, was
not an ancient. Though he advises princes to exercise political judgment
without the influence of Christian eschatology, he accepts the Christian
teaching of what the world is like without the *eschaton*. It is not just an
imperfect world, but a radically fallen world, where all human impulses
are inherently vile, where good and evil are mere appearances used
to acquire power, and where there is no genuine moral virtue. Such a

worldview is not Greek or Roman but Christian—a Christianity without supernatural transcendence.

Machiavelli suggests that a human force can fill the supernatural void. There actually is "superhuman grace" in Machiavelli's world: it emanates from the world-immanent manager, not from the world-transcendent God. Machiavelli intimates the possibility of a superior princely intelligence realizing the common "good" through his own acquisitive interests and the interests of others.[6] The princely manager becomes the source of order in a de-divinized world. Such management may not lead to an everlasting utopia, but it does facilitate unprecedented control over politics.

But is it possible for a governor to found a regime that can last forever? In the *Discourses,* Machiavelli postulates the idea of a "perpetual republic"—a republic in which fortune has been conquered definitively. The perpetual republic is not without any hardship, but it is one in which there is a remedy for each new threat. As Mansfield argues, Machiavelli seems somewhat ambivalent about the possibility of a concrete political regime ever being perpetual. He first denies the possibility, saying "it is impossible to order a perpetual republic, because its ruin is caused through a thousand unexpected ways" (*D* 3.17.1); but he later affirms the possibility, saying, "if a republic were so happy that it often had one who with his example might renew the laws, and not only restrain it from running into ruin but pull it back, it would be perpetual" (*D* 3.22.3). Machiavelli's apparent conflicting thoughts on the issue are resolved if we consider them in light of Augustine. Augustine argued that no earthly regime is eternal; mundane history—the history of the City of Man—is essentially the rise and fall of regimes with no inherent providential significance. However, the Church, as the earthly representative of the eternal City of God, survives the fluctuations of political fortune. While individual regimes rise and fall—including Christian regimes—the Church, in some form or other, remains.[7] But something similar could be said of modernity: notwithstanding the rise and fall of specific modern regimes, modernity—understood as the faith in human self-sufficiency and unmitigated expediency—continues, even if it is occasionally necessary to "renew the laws" by which modernity operates. In this sense, the "perpetual republic," according to Mansfield, is Machiavelli's republic, or what we call modernity. If Machiavelli intends his "perpetual republic" to be a genuine possibility, it is not best understood as a concrete regime that conducts wars, taxes people, establishes laws, and so on. Rather, it is a secular analogue of Augustine's City of God—a particular ethos that survives the rise and fall of various polities, and, in this way, conquers fortune. The Machiavellian spirit, like the Christian Holy Spirit, tries to introduce a new dispensation—a new virtue—into history permanently. Just as the Church survives the fluctuations that afflict Christian regimes, so the spirit of Machiavelli continues regardless of the fate of individual Machiavellian polities.[8] Human beings, after Machiavelli, will habitually give supreme authority to considerations of expediency, even if they have never read Machiavelli. They will frequently fall short of this measure when they are reckless or allow moral considerations to intrude on their deliberations. Nevertheless, *virtù* is a constant measure that humans can turn to when they confront fortune.

The tragedy of inevitable political decay is thus alleviated by the comedy of an eternal republic. And Machiavelli subtly suggests that he is the "one" who can pull the perpetual republic back from ruin. Whenever specific modern polities lose their effectiveness, or whenever there is lack of confidence in the modern project as a whole, it is necessary to return "toward beginnings"[9]—in this case, toward the beginning initiated by Machiavelli. It is Machiavelli who, ultimately, bestows superhuman grace in a Godless world.

Providence in a De-Divinized World

Machiavelli himself and his managerial progeny acquire what Voegelin calls "human-divine heroic proportions" in a world where "the Christian, transcendental order of existence [has] become a dead letter."[10] Machiavelli "divinizes" the human quality that brings success in the world. His account of *virtù* as a force that works through the qualities of good and evil to reach a greater good is, in fact, a reconstitution of Christian providence. Machiavelli postulates the idea of a superior *human* intelligence who—like God—works behind appearances, using whatever means necessary to realize his desired end. In Augustine's words, God's ability to "turn to good account the good and the evil alike" is transferred by Machiavelli to humans (*CG* 14.27). In this sense, Machiavelli's *virtù* resonates—albeit heretically—with the very Christian apocalypticism that it seems to reject. Once again, it is not antithetical to Christianity but derivative.

Both *Mandragola* and *Measure for Measure* intentionally evoke the aura of providential unfolding. It is not simply that the Machiavels in these plays use religion to serve their purposes. It is, rather, that "providence" takes a secular, human form that is derived from, and intermingled with, its religious source. We are presented with two superior administrators: Ligurio and Vincentio. Like God, they secretly manage the conditions in which people—knowingly or unknowingly—can be wicked for the common good. Ligurio and Vincentio show us how a covert Machiavellian manager bears an uncanny resemblance to the apocalyptic God of Christian faith. Of course, from the Christian perspective, the attempt to imitate God's ability to bring good out of evil is blasphemous; only God possesses such expediency. Furthermore, Christian symbols reveal a transcendental dimension to life that cannot be expressed adequately by secular analogues. Augustine's "City of God" may be represented in this world by the Church, but its full realization is deferred to an atemporal future. Machiavelli's administrative republic is intended to be realized in the temporal present, but, from the Augustinian perspective, it will inevitably encounter resistance from the reality it is attempting to conquer. Complete management of this world is impossible—a point suggested by the fantastic conclusion of *Measure for Measure.* Vincentio's administration is just too perfect; underneath the Duke's artificial republic is a darker reality that only a transcendental God could truly conquer.

Measure for Measure, when read carefully, seems to present us with this Christian critique of Machiavelli. The "intermittent immanence of Godhead,"[11] as symbolized by Vincentio, is presented as an undesirable phenomenon. However, Shakespeare's implicit critique of the Duke—and, by extension, Machiavelli—also affects how we understand providential conceptions of God. If the Machiavellian manager bears an uncanny resemblance to God, it is also true to say that such a God bears an uncomfortable similarity to a Machiavellian prince. "Gods," according to Voegelin, are symbols that "stand for forces . . . experienced in the soul of man."[12] Through Vincentio, Shakespeare reveals that the Christian God is a symbol of a perfect expedient force. But *Measure for Measure* provokes us to consider if such perfect expediency, as experienced in the human soul, is equivalent to perfect goodness.

As we discovered in the discussion of apocalyptic eschatology in *Waiting for Godot,* providential belief can aggravate the indeterminacy of good and evil. Wickedness and suffering, which would commonly be called evil, are understood as necessary expedients fulfilling God's plan. Notwithstanding Augustine's claim that evil does not come from God and is solely the responsibility of human beings and fallen angels, the providential understanding explicitly equates divine necessity with supreme goodness. In the apocalyptic melodrama, everything—good and evil—is assigned a role in God's providence, including the fall of angels and human beings. God creates Satan and Adam knowing that they will commit evil, but he is also cognizant that their sins will help to actualize the greatest good in the end: the Christian *eschaton.* Augustine writes, "God, when he created the Devil, was without doubt well aware of his future wickedness, and had foreseen the good that he himself would bring out of that evil." Thus "God turns evil choices to good use," whereas humans and demons, through their "evil choices," make "wrong use of [the] good natures" God has given them (*CG* 11.17).

Just as God sets up Satan and Adam to make wrong use of the goodness they have been granted, so Vincentio sets up Angelo—his own fallen "angel"—to misuse the power he has been given. Vincentio is aware of Angelo's inclinations, and foresees the good that he can bring out of them. Similarly, Ligurio uses the wickedness of those around him to realize his own purposes and create a common happiness. It is other people who make wicked choices; Vincentio and Ligurio simply turn these evil choices to good use. Vincentio, Ligurio, and God are all one or two steps removed from the evil through which they work, but they all operate according to the principle of evil as defined by Baudrillard: "Evil is when Evil comes out of Good or Good out of Evil. That is when things are all wrong."[13]

There are those who will insist that the divine use of evil is absolutely good, for it contributes to a beneficent end. This belief is a commonplace. Augustine writes:

> For the Omnipotent God . . . would not allow any evil in his works, unless in his omnipotence and goodness, as the Supreme Good, he is able to bring forth good out of evil.[14]

Similarly, Aquinas writes:

Since God, then, provides universally for all being, it belongs to His providence to permit certain defects in particular effects, that the perfect good of the universe may not be hindered; for if all evil were prevented, much good would be absent from the universe. (*ST,* I, q. 22, a. 2, ad 2ᵐ)

Finally, consider Martin Luther:

God works evil in us (that is, by means of us) not through God's own fault, but by reason of our own defect. We being evil by nature, and God being God, when he impels us to act by His own acting upon us according to the nature of his omnipotence, good though He is in Himself, He cannot but do evil by our evil instrumentally; although, according to His wisdom, He makes good use of this evil for His own glory and for our salvation.

Thus God, finding Satan's will evil, not creating it so (it became so by Satan's sinning and God's withdrawing), carries it along by His own operation and moves it where He wills.[15]

Machiavelli tries to justify human instrumentality with similar arguments. He implicitly asks: If God can realize good through evil, and still be called beneficent, why cannot humans realize good through evil and still be called virtuous?

Shakespeare understands this type of reasoning well. Through *Measure for Measure,* he reveals the Christian providential essence of Machiavellian *virtù,* or, conversely, the Machiavellian nature of Christian providence. It might be, as Christian doctrine informs us, that God's providence is inscrutable and not to be imitated by mortals. But insofar as we can understand it, such a God looks uncomfortably similar to a Machiavellian archetype. Shakespeare presents us with an irony: the human force that most closely resembles the beneficent God of Christian faith is the maleficent prince of Machiavellian politics. What is most horrible to behold in this world is what is most like the absolute good of Christian doctrine. Shakespeare's portrayal of such a profound moral confusion in *Measure for Measure* reveals why modernity tends toward totalitarianism.

Conclusion

Modern Theatre and the Tragic Vision

The Inseparability and Incompatibility of Good and Evil

Caligula, Waiting for Godot, Mandragola, and *Measure for Measure* collectively reveal the eschatological and expedient impulses that have allowed evil to flourish in the modern world. On first glance, eschatology and expediency appear to be opposites. Each presents itself as the corrective for the other: so-called Machiavellian Realpolitik seems to remedy the utopian fantasies of eschatology, whereas eschatological faith seems to counteract the so-called spiritual emptiness of expedient politics. But on closer examination, expediency and eschatology are not as antithetical as they first appear. Machiavelli's suggestion that it is virtuous to use "evils" instrumentally is derived from Christian apocalypticism. Insofar as the Machiavellian and Christian teachings agree that a superior being can work through evil to realize a greater good, there is no difference between expediency and apocalyptic eschatology. Furthermore, twentieth-century totalitarianism has revealed that the eschatological and expedient impulses can be compatible. The efficient use of genocide is deemed a virtue if it facilitates the realization of an absolute purity. Camus writes that a "mixture of Machiavellianism and Augustinism in fact explains twentieth century rebellion; no more audacious expression can be given to the nihilism of the times" (*R* 95).[1]

And there is a further issue. In late modernity, "reason" has largely been reduced to empiricism, technique, and instrumentality, whereas

259

there is little trust that we can speak reasonably about ethics or the good life. "Values," it is thought, are subjective and cannot be rationally justified, whereas genuine reason is concerned with empirical "facts" and the expedient pursuit of acquisitions. This reduction of reason to pure observation and technique creates a void of meaning that is often filled by radical eschatological aspirations, be they secular or religious. Technical reason and instrumentality are then employed in the service of these aspirations, with the disastrous results that are considered here. In this manner, sheer expediency and radical eschatology are two sides of the same worldview and serve to nurture each other.

The eschatological imagination has not always reduced reason to sheer instrumentality. On the contrary, rational discussion of the good life is a central feature of the Jewish, Christian, and Islamic traditions. All three Abrahamic faiths have, at various points, drawn from Greek political philosophy, which helped to moderate any radical eschatological inclinations of their respective faiths. But with the dominance of instrumental reason in late modernity, and with the eclipsing of the Greek tragic and philosophical traditions, the more excessive aspects of Abrahamic eschatology were allowed to proliferate in all their secular and religious permutations.

In the shadow of the "death event," the politics and aesthetics of eschatology and expediency are no longer tenable. The four plays I have examined prompt us to consider alternative responses to evil. *Caligula* and *Waiting for Godot* suggest that we move beyond the dream of an "end of evil," no matter whether the end is understood as a concrete historical event or as a regulative ideal toward which we perpetually move. These plays also reveal the curious tendency of evil to flourish, both when we actively try to exterminate it and, to a lesser extent, when we passively wait for its future extermination. Jean Baudrillard has recently developed this point:

> It is not by expurgating evil that we liberate good. Worse, by liberating good, we also liberate evil. . . . It is the inseparability of good and evil which constitutes our true equilibrium, our true balance. We ought not to entertain the illusion that we might separate the two, that we might cultivate good and happiness in a pure state and expel evil and sorrow as wastes.[2]

The utopian hope for a perfect state is, in Baudrillard's words, a "terroristic dream."[3] Our "equilibrium" consists in recognizing the inseparability of good and evil. On this point, Machiavelli is in agreement with Baudrillard, and shares his criticisms of the eschatological desire for purity.[4] But to say that good and evil are inseparable is not equivalent to saying they are compatible. Machiavelli and Baudrillard part ways on this issue of compatibility. Baudrillard writes, "The real problem is precisely the strangeness, the imperviousness of Good and Evil to each other, which means there is no reconciling, no superseding them, and thus no ethical solution to the problem of their opposition."[5] Nor, for that matter, is there an unethical solution to the antagonism of good and evil; evil is too erratic to cooperate with, or be transfigured into, the good. *Mandragola* and *Measure for Measure,* on the other hand, deal with the possibility that good and evil can work together—indeed, that immoralities can be transfigured into superior goods when successfully employed. Machiavelli affirms the ethos, but Shakespeare, in accord with Baudrillard, implicitly denies that good and evil are compatible. In *Measure for Measure,* evil does not cooperate with the good, nor is it transformed into a greater good; evil simply changes from one form to another.

By this account, evil is superfluity; it cannot be co-opted, exterminated, synthesized, or legitimized under the auspices of expedient or eschatological benevolence. It is not true, then, to say that all actualities, including suffering and malice, "happen for a reason"—that is to say, for a "good" reason. Contra Hegel, it is wrong to say "what is rational is actual and what is actual is rational";[6] certain realities—suffering, wickedness, calamity—cannot be subsumed by rationality. To claim that the great slaughters and catastrophes of history are a part of a rational process leading to a decisive improvement in human affairs—Hegel's "cunning of reason"[7]—whitewashes the experience of evil. In actuality, evil is impossible to integrate completely in a comprehensive providence because it is essentially excess. This understanding of evil is offered by Emmanuel Levinas:

> In evil's malignancy, it is excess. Though the notion of excess evokes from the first the quantitative idea of intensity—by its degree of surpassing all measure—evil is excess in its very quiddity. Here is a very important remark: evil is not excess because suffering can be strong

and thus go beyond what is bearable. The rupture with the normal and the normative, with order, with synthesis, with the world, already constitutes its qualitative essence. Suffering, as suffering, is but a concrete and quasi-sensible manifestation of the nonintegratable, or the unjustifiable. The "quality" of evil is this *non-integratableness* itself, if we may use such a term.[8]

The essential superfluity of evil means it cannot be utilized or purified by any "dialectical" force that presents itself as a higher good. Evil is "pure incompatibility":[9] as a principle of antagonism and destruction, it refuses to play the role assigned to it by a providential God, a Machiavellian manager, or a historical dialectic.[10] If malice and suffering are interpreted as expedients in the hand of a greater good, then the distinction between good and evil becomes radically indeterminate, creating the potential for extreme imbalance, confusion, and catastrophe.

Baudrillard writes, "The notion that [Good and Evil] might be separated out from one another is pure fantasy, and it is even more utopian to think in terms of reconciling them."[11] In place of such naïveté, Baudrillard urges us to accept that good and evil "are at once both irreducible to each other and inextricably interrelated."[12] There is a twofold benefit to this understanding. On the one hand, the inseparability of good and evil rules out the possibility of utopia or of a completely justified power; on the other, the incompatibility of good and evil means that evil cannot be utilized by the good. To try to escape the simultaneous inseparability and incompatibility of good and evil is to seek a solution. And, as we have seen, "solutions" aggravate evil's destructive capabilities. If we accept this as a general principle, we think and act outside of eschatological and expedient presumptions.

Camus, Beckett, and Shakespeare have varying degrees of success in their efforts to escape from the excesses wrought by eschatology and expediency. All three playwrights—each in his own way—direct us toward a tragic vision of the world, which lies outside of the eschatological and expedient frameworks I have discussed. This vision is linked to the birth of theatre itself in Greece, and is integral to its aesthetic. It is best, then, to conclude by considering tragic theatre, and contrast it with alternative types of drama that are associated with the excesses considered in this study.

Nietzsche's "Real Paganism" and the Tragic Vision of Evil

In *Human, All Too Human,* Nietzsche argues that the Greeks recognized a primal violence in the world and human nature that could be limited but not exterminated. They accorded evil a wary respect—a respect that is unfathomable to Christian and post-Christian eschatology. They showed their respect through various festivals and cults. Nietzsche writes:

> Perhaps nothing astonishes the observer of the Greek world more than when he discovers that from time to time the Greeks made as it were a festival of all their passions and evil natural inclinations and even instituted a kind of official order of proceedings in the cele-bration of what was all-too-human in them: this constitutes the real paganism of their world, uncomprehended by and incomprehen-sible to Christianity, which has always despised and combated it with the greatest severity.—They took this all-too-human to be in-escapable and, instead of reviling it, preferred to accord it a kind of right of the second rank through regulating it within the usages of society and religion: indeed, everything in man possessing *power* they called divine and inscribed it on the walls of their Heaven. They do not repudiate the natural drive that finds expression in the evil qualities but regulate it and, as soon as they have discovered sufficient prescriptive measures to provide these wild waters with the least harmful means of channeling and out-flow, confine them to definite cults and days. . . . Where did the Greeks acquire this free-dom, this sense for the actual? Perhaps from Homer and the poets before him; for it is precisely the poets, whose natures are not com-monly the most sagacious or judicious, who possess by way of com-pensation a joy in the actual and active *of every kind* and have no desire to deny even evil altogether: they are satisfied if it keeps it-self within bounds and refrains from wholesale slaughter or inner subversion.[13]

In this passage, Nietzsche celebrates aesthetic and political forms that rec-ognize the inseparability and incompatibility of good and evil. Good and evil are distinct in substantial ways—they are not mere appearances—but they must be thought together. This "regard for all human actuality" is what characterizes Homer and the other Greek poets. They do not deny those impulses that Christianity declared sinful but present them symbolically as divine powers that must, to some extent, be honoured. The legislators of the Greek polis allowed violent and disruptive drives to be expressed on "definite cults and days." The purpose of these sacrificial and ecstatic festivals was not to cause evil but to achieve an uneasy equilibrium—to live with, and limit, the barbaric elements that could not be annihilated or reasoned with. Any civilization that denies these "all-too-human" features is deluded about the extent to which it can control evil; indeed, the effort to eliminate the "barbaric" completely is much more likely to perpetuate "wholesale slaughter and inner subversion," which the Greek legislators and poets hoped to contain.

Nietzsche's description of the Greek response to evil in *Human, All Too Human* is perhaps too functionalist to account for evil's superfluous essence adequately. When Nietzsche speaks of evil being "accommodated" and "regulated" through a "system of procedures" that allows frenzied passions to purge themselves in specific cults and festivals, he comes perilously close to making evil a managerial problem—much like Machiavelli, who similarly proposed that evil should be expressed in the right way and at the right time. As Baudrillard and Levinas argue, evil cannot be completely "accommodated"; it will disrupt any society, no matter how well balanced and accommodating it is of the "barbaric." This deficiency in Nietzsche's account, however, does not alter its central insights. The Greeks did not expect, or desire, a final extermination of evil; they strove to establish aesthetic, cultic, and political forms that would recognize, honour, and limit the destructiveness of evil. Furthermore, many of the "passions" celebrated in these festivals—"passions" defined as essentially evil in Christian doctrine—were not understood by the Greeks as such. Dionysian intoxication, for instance, was one of life's greatest goods when kept within certain limits; it was only an evil when taken to excess.

The City Dionysia is a primary example of an Athenian festival that not only allowed for the expression of ecstatic, Dionysian passions, but that also presented evil's superfluity in stark, uncompromising terms. The annual celebration had, on the one hand, a carnivalesque atmosphere, featuring costumes, drinking, parades, sacrifices, and ritual phalluses; on the other hand, the tragedies performed at the festival offered the Athenians sober depictions of evil.[14] As Nietzsche describes it in *The Birth of Tragedy,* tragedy—both as a festival and as an aesthetic form—was a combination of "Dionysian" and "Apollonian" impulses, encompassing the ecstatic and the reflective, the drunken and the sober.[15]

Understood in this way, the City Dionysia was not only a public cult permitting the momentary discharge of ecstatic energies. It was also a medium that encouraged theoretical reflection about the nature of evil and the limits of human endeavor. Whatever the purgative use-value of the tragic festival—whether "purging" is understood as the "moderate discharge" of disruptive passions (Nietzsche) or as the *catharsis* of pity and fear that occurs when watching a tragedy (Aristotle)—the tragedies themselves provided a forum in which the Athenians could contemplate human possibilities and limitations. The City Dionysia forced the Athenians to confront the essential superfluity of evil and deliberate on the best response. Voegelin claims that the "great problem" examined by the Greek tragedians is "the morass of demonic evil surrounding the island of order."[16] For Voegelin, it is the tragedies of Aeschylus that best reveal how to create "a shining bulwark of order in a very disorderly world."[17] He writes:

> It was the greatness of Aeschylus that he understood the order of Dike [justice] in society as a precarious incarnation of divine order, as a passing realization wrung from the forces of disorder through tragic action by sacrifices and risks, and—even if momentarily successful—under the shadow that ultimately will envelop it.[18]

In the Aeschylean vision—and, indeed, the Greek tragic vision as a whole—there is no transcendent or immanent utopia; there are limits to what any endeavor can accomplish; all accomplishments will eventually be destroyed; good is always accompanied by something bad; heroic suffering does not indicate eternal salvation; death is final. The central concern in tragedy is how to live *with* evil and limit its destructiveness, but there is no technique, therapy, or political program that can guarantee that evil will always remain within prescribed limits. Even men and women of relatively good moral character are often destroyed in tragedy by unfortunate circumstances beyond their control.[19] Still, humans are not completely helpless all the time. Whatever given evils the gods are responsible for, humans, through their own folly, make things worse. The tragedies of Aeschylus, Sophocles, and Euripides—whatever their differences—show us what excesses to avoid.

For Camus, the tragic account is a sane response to the various excesses of the twentieth century. It is not, however, a final solution to the experience of evil. As Camus writes in his notebooks, "Tragedy is not a solution."[20] No human or divine force in a tragedy can entirely separate good from evil, which means that no single power is depicted as absolutely just, or, for that matter, absolutely evil. On the contrary, each character in a tragedy has a certain amount of both good and bad. This means that the moral conflicts presented in tragedy are not struggles between absolute right and wrong. In this way, tragedy, for Camus, is categorically distinct from "melodrama":

> The forces confronting each other in tragedy are equally legitimate, equally justified. In melodramas or dramas, on the other hand, only one force is legitimate. In other words, tragedy is ambiguous and drama simple-minded. In the former, each force is at the same time both good and bad. In the latter, one is good and the other evil (which is why, in our day and age, propaganda plays are nothing but the resurrection of melodrama). Antigone is right, but Creon is not wrong. Similarly, Prometheus is both just and unjust, and Zeus who pitilessly oppresses him also has right on his side. Melodrama could thus be summed up by saying: "Only one is just and justifiable," while the perfect tragic formula would be: "All can be justified, no one is just." This is why the chorus in classical tragedies generally advises prudence. For the chorus knows that up to a certain limit everyone is right and that the person who, from blindness or passion, oversteps this limit is heading for catastrophe if he persists in his desire to assert a right he thinks he alone possesses. The constant theme of classical tragedy, therefore, is the limit that must not be transgressed. On either side of this limit equally legitimate forces meet in quivering and endless confrontation. To make a mistake about this limit, to try to destroy the balance, is to perish. . . . The ideal tragedy . . . and especially Greek tragedy, is first and foremost tension, since it is a conflict, in a frenzied immobility, between two powers, each of which wears the double mask of good and evil.[21]

Camus perhaps overstates his case when he suggests that the forces in Greek tragedy are *equally* legitimate, *equally* justified. Certain forces in a tragedy may be more justified than others. But Camus is correct to claim that no agent, be it a god or a human, is absolutely just in tragedy. It is precisely when an agent exaggerates the goodness of his cause and the evil of another—when he becomes "melodramatic"—that a limit is crossed and disorder results. Tragedy does not indicate a resolution or purification through a single force; instead, it proposes a delicate balance between impure forces, such as the resolution that occurs between Orestes and the Furies at the end of the *Oresteia*. Aeschylus points to an uneasy equilibrium between guilty parties, not a final solution to the problem of evil.

The tragic sensibility, broadly understood, is also not confined to the tragic genre per se. The ancient comedies of Aristophanes offer an understanding of evil that is similar to that of the tragedies, insofar as no one is absolutely good, and yet the world is threatened with chaos. In the case of Greek comedy, tragic experience is revealed by evoking laughter rather than pity and fear. It also reveals, through ridiculous characters and situations, what excesses to avoid. As Camus has argued, the antithesis of tragedy is not comedy but melodrama. For Camus, any play that presents a completely justifiable person, faith, doctrine, or ideology is a form of melodrama, regardless of whether the play triggers laughter, horror, or tears.

Melodrama is not just found in the popular entertainment that goes by this name: it is in the ideological plays and agit-prop spectacles of the twentieth century, as well as in the Christian morality dramas and pageant plays of the Middle Ages. According to Camus, the Christian mystery plays are not tragic because they present God as absolutely beneficent and totally legitimate. "The divine order" in Christian drama "cannot be called into question."[22] Such dramas inculcate the notion that there is a completely justifiable providence that is moving humanity toward a final resolution. For Camus, the antagonism between tragedy and Christian doctrine is what "explains the silence of tragedy" in medieval Christendom up to the Renaissance.[23] Christianity does not accept the notion that evil may stem, in part, from God. But in Greek tragedy everything—even a god—has some evil within it. In Sophocles' *Philoctetes,* the title character says, "How can I reckon the score, how can I praise / when praising

Heaven I find the Gods are bad?"[24] It is certainly true, as Homer's Zeus points out, that humans exaggerate the degree to which the gods are to blame for evil. Nevertheless, the gods are at least partially responsible for human suffering and wickedness.[25] Consequently, no divine force can purify the world.

Melodramatic and Alchemical Theatre

The Greek experience of evil was central to the creation of theatre itself. Camus points out, however, that the tragic vision of evil has stayed mostly to the margins of Western civilization, flourishing only during the ancient Greek and Renaissance periods. Indeed, many prominent dramatists and dramatic theorists in the modern West have challenged the tragic response to evil. Consider, for instance, Bertolt Brecht, one of the most influential playwrights and theatrical theorists of the twentieth century. Brecht's "epic theatre" is, by Camus's definition, melodramatic. His plays contain conflict, but in the form of class struggle interpreted from a Marxist perspective, and in which there is an absolutely justified force. This conflict is intended by Brecht to reveal the historical process of "dialectical materialism"—a secular providence that Marxists believe is moving humanity toward a classless society. Brecht writes that the theatre of dialectical materialism "treats social situations as processes" in order to "unearth society's laws of motion." By pointing out the "inconsistencies" that underlie social struggle, the audience sees how these inconsistencies can be overcome.[26] While watching an "epic" play, with its specific "alienation" techniques, people are encouraged to use their reason rather than rely on feelings.[27] In this manner, the audience's senses and emotions are not overwhelmed; the audience is detached— or alienated—from the action onstage so that they can reflect. Through detached observation, they are made aware that the tragic social conflicts presented in Brechtian drama can be completely resolved (under the proper conditions) through innovation and revolution. Brecht wants the audience to leave the theatre deliberating on how to overcome the tragic condition through the proper measures.[28]

Consider, for example, the conclusion of Brecht's *Good Person of Szechwan*. At the end of this play, the gods abandon the heroine Shen

Teh, the "good person" of the title. A "Player," who acts as a chorus, then appears to apologize to the audience for the sad ending. The Player, however, informs the audience that this is not the real end of the story and that the audience should not "forget the rest." It is up to the audience to transcend the tragic universe of the play though decisive action:

> But what would you suggest?
> What is your answer? Nothing's been arranged.
> Should men be better? Should the world be changed?
> Or just the gods? Or ought there to be none?
> We for our part feel well and truly done.
> There's only one solution that we know:
> That you should now consider as you go
> What sort of measures you would recommend
> To help good people to a happy end.
> Ladies and gentlemen, in you we trust:
> There must be happy endings, must, must, must![29]

In this passage, we get a clear glimpse of Brecht's melodramatic approach. Revolutionary forces that fight on behalf of "good people" can overcome what appears to be implacable fortune. Human nature, the world, and the gods, can be changed or destroyed, since "nothing's been arranged"— nothing, that is, except for the providential forces of dialectical materialism. Those who serve this process through the correct use of violence are completely justified. Revolutionary activism is the "one solution" that the audience must accept if they are to ensure "happy endings" for all "good people."

Brechtian and Christian melodrama are similar in their expectation that the human condition will undergo a final transfiguration. In both cases, an absolutely justifiable force is expected to perform some kind of decisive renovation, purging certain impure elements and purifying others through a cataclysmic chain of events. Theatre becomes a site in which to bring about the transformation. Just as the medieval Corpus Christi pageants were epic renderings of biblical history, from Creation to the Final Judgment, so Brecht sought to condense the history of social struggle in his epic theatre, which depicts "man as a process" moving toward consummation.[30] In both cases, the story ends with the triumph of the absolute good—something that is either presented explicitly on-stage, as in the depictions of resurrection and Final Judgment in the medieval pageants, or directly indicated as a reality of the future, as in Brecht's epics.

The expectation that theatre can somehow promote a cataclysmic revolution, and anticipate a purified future state, is not uncommon in twentieth-century theatrical theory. Antonin Artaud, like Brecht, is one of the prominent theorists of modern theatre, and he also understood theatre to be revolutionary. In *The Theatre and Its Double,* Artaud speaks of the "alchemical" nature of theatre. Just as the Alchemist's Stone is said magically to turn base matter into gold, so theatre can affect a similar transformation at the "spiritual" level. The "theatrical operation of making gold," according to Artaud, unleashes intense conflict. This volatility evokes "an absolute and abstract purity" that "resolve[s] or even annihilates every conflict."[31]

The Artaudian vision of theatre has several qualities that distinguish it from Brecht's Marxist epics. Artaud seeks to create a theatre where the audience is immersed, not detached, from the performance. He claims that the theatrical event is a microcosm of life, which, according to Artaud, is "cruelty"—a word he uses in the "Gnostic sense" to describe a cosmos constituted by an "implacable necessity."[32] He writes: "In the manifested world . . . evil is the permanent law."[33] In response to this "law," Artaud proposes a "theatre of cruelty," in which symbolizations of evil are central. As he writes, "the theatre is the time of evil, the triumph of dark powers."[34] The theatre of cruelty would represent the evil of the cosmos through theatricality itself; that is, through the correct employment of elements specific to the theatrical event, such as sound, color, gesture, movement, dance, staging, and festivity. In this way, he argues for a theatre that is not tied to literary texts. He wants to expunge the memorized scripts—what he sarcastically calls the "masterpieces"—from contemporary theatre and encourage the performance of nontextually based spectacles.[35] Exactly what Artaud has in mind has always been a matter of debate. However, he claims that theatre should be a "total spectacle" that "attack[s] the spectator's sensibility on all sides."[36] Instead of the audience gazing distantly on staged productions of written texts—thereby privileging both the "eye" and the written word—Artaud wants the audience to have all their senses assaulted in a nontextually based spectaculum. Theatre, like life, will provide the audience with constant shocks.

To create this type of theatre, Artaud looks to archaic, non-Western forms of performance and ritual that he claims were spectacular and nontextual,[37] but he gives them a modern Western spin. He looks to theatre not just as a contained site in which ecstatic energies are released, or as a medium in which suffering is represented, but as a locale of eschatological transformation. Artaud postulates a theatre of revolution, of transgression, and of ultimate liberation—a spectacle that will erupt beyond the theatre and unleash its virulence within a staid society. In this way, Artaud likens theatre to a plague, as something that perpetrates a complete disaster in order to effect a total purification. He writes:

> The theatre, like the plague, is in the image of this carnage and this essential separation. It releases conflicts, disengages powers, liberates possibilities, and if these possibilities and these powers are dark, it is the fault not of the plague nor of the theatre, but of life. . . . The theatre like the plague is a crisis which is resolved by death or cure. And the plague is a superior disease because it is a total crisis after which nothing remains except death or an extreme purification. Similarly the theatre is a disease because it is the supreme equilibrium which cannot be achieved without destruction.[38]

All the vestiges of the eschatological mindset—the melodramatic sorting myth, the desire for cataclysm, the dream of purification—are expressed through a peculiar theatrical messianism. Artaud goes so far as to describe the plague of theatre as "an avenging scourge, a redeeming epidemic."[39] Like Caligula, he claims that evil will consume itself and make way for absolute purity if humans surrender to the violent impulses of creation.[40] Unleashing cruelty creates a "whirlwind that devours the darkness"; gradually the "kernel of evil [becomes] ever more condensed, and ever more consumed."[41] In the end, the "cruelty that molds the features of the created world" will be obliterated "at the supreme instant."[42] The theatre of cruelty will play a central role in this Gnostic cataclysm. The Artaudian spectacle is the local of metastasis, the symbolic matrix of absolute transfiguration.

Artaud's theatre, like Brecht's, exemplifies a revolutionary tendency that is characteristic of much of the theatre of the twentieth century. Though the various forms of revolutionary theatre are disparate, and often at odds with each other, most of them use theatre to actualize what the Polish director Tadeusz Kantor calls a "new reality."[43] Kantor's notion of an "impossible theatre," Augusto Boal's "Theatre of the Oppressed," the futurist theatre of Filippo Marinetti, Emilio Settimelli, and Bruno Corra, the theatrical "happenings" of the 1960s, and the various "theatres of the left" fostered by Brecht, Vsevolod Meyerhold, Erwin Piscator, and Dario Fo—all of these theatrical avant-gardes are driven by the expectation of a revolutionary transformation, be it political, technological, or spiritual. Whatever their ideological and aesthetic differences, they are all "alchemical" in some form. Thus theatre has not always been a remedy for the excesses we have examined in this study. On the contrary, it is often only symptomatic.

Art and Politics in the New World Disorder

Of the theatrical works discussed in this study, only *Mandrogola* promotes a type of alchemy. The very title of *Mandragola* suggests its dubious chemistry. The play offers a transfiguring remedy—not one that will turn sterility into fertility, or base matter into gold, but one that will transfigure apparent evils into superior goods. It is true that Machiavelli's alchemy is mostly free of utopianism. Nevertheless, his intent is revolutionary because he thinks that fortune, in general, can be conquered by clever human agents. As Strauss writes, "There is no tragedy in Machiavelli."[44] But the other three plays studied here ultimately reject expedient and eschatological alchemy, and, to various degrees, embody a tragic outlook.

Is there any chance that the tragic understanding can somehow take root in contemporary societies and have cultural impact? Camus himself was skeptical of this during his own life, and, as Beckett reveals, human beings after the "death event" are simply resuscitating and revamping previous forms of eschatology. If Beckett's account is accurate, our present situation is not a genuine break from modern excesses but rather a necrophilic reconstitution of old eschatological hopes and expedient pursuits. Certainly the idea that art should embody and promote cataclysmic transfiguration persists into the twenty-first century. A striking statement of this understanding was offered by the German avant-garde composer Karlheinz Stockhausen. Days after the terrorist attacks against the United States on September 11, 2001, Stockhausen dared to connect contemporary terrorist violence with modern artistic performance. He was particularly impressed by the theatricality of the 9/11 attacks. As he pointed out, the nineteen hijackers rehearsed their single performance for years and achieved maximum impact by striking buildings that were symbolic of Western economic and military dominance. The attackers were themselves driven by an Islamist eschatological vision, lashing out at a global order that they perceived as Satanic. Their desire was to initiate a global cataclysm, out of which they believed Islam would ultimately emerge triumphant. Despite their wish to return to a premodern form of Islam, they used thoroughly modern technological means to carry out an attack that they knew would be witnessed around the world through the mass media. The attack was staged *for* the global television networks, but not *by* them, and this infusion of reality through the virtual media was intended to have an apocalyptic effect. As the world watched the twin towers of the World Trade Center collapse — two citadels of global capitalism — it appeared as if the Western order itself was collapsing. The magnitude and effectiveness of the terrorist's "performance" was not lost on Stockhausen:

> What happened there [on September 11] is, of course — and now you are going to have to readjust your brains — the greatest work of art that there has ever been. That minds [Geister] should carry out something like that in an act that we in music could never dream of doing: that people could rehearse like crazy for ten years, totally fanatically, for a concert and then die. Just try and imagine what happened there. Those are people who are so concentrated on the one performance and then 5000 people are blown to resurrection in one moment. I couldn't do that. In comparison to that, we composers are nothing.[45]

Stockhausen's comments caused outrage, but they are significant insofar as they exemplify the cataclysmic inclination within certain types of modern art. Artists, for Stockhausen, are cowardly terrorists with apocalyptic ambitions; art and eschatological violence unite. This is why the 9/11 event is, for Stockhausen, the greatest work of art ever performed. As Christopher Baum notes, Stockhausen "intimates that only terrorist acts of this dimension can attain to what art in modernist terms set itself as a task."[46] Clearly, Stockhausen's understanding of performance resonates with Artaud's theatre of cruelty. Indeed, Baudrillard observes how the spectacle of apocalyptic terrorism is "our theatre of cruelty, the only one we have left."[47]

If the residue of alchemical art remains with us in the twenty-first century, it is also true that politics continues to be consumed by eschatological ambitions. A revamped eschatological messianism, along with a fortune-conquering Machiavellianism, fuels the contemporary Western fetish for globalization and technological innovation. With the defeat of Communism in Eastern Europe and Russia, the more radical eschatological tendencies of Western capitalist democracies were unleashed. A secular evangelical fervor emerged in the West, proclaiming that history had finally arrived at its *eschaton* and that the world was approaching unity. Francis Fukuyama famously declared in 1989 that we had reached the "end of history": the eschatological events were occurring in our lifetime, and they were culminating in a "universal and homogeneous state" that would be politically democratic and economically capitalist.[48] This secular process currently goes by the name "globalization," which advocates claim is transforming the world through the spread of free markets, technology, democracy, and human rights. The guarantor of this new world order is the United States, which remains the world's sole superpower.

Not all humanity, however, is sympathetic to this Western-based world project, and terrorist resistance is emerging—often with its own eschatological self-understanding. The 9/11 attacks stand as a striking example of this resistance. But according to Robert Jay Lifton, these strikes, in turn, encouraged a more radical apocalyptic ethos in the United States. Lifton argues that the feelings of shock, pain, humiliation, and vulnerability experienced by Americans on 9/11 led to an angry determination on the part of American leadership not simply to contain terrorism but to make the United States an omnipotent world power—a power that exerts maximum global control in order to, in President Bush's words, "rid the world of evil."[49] Lifton refers to this drive for global dominance as "superpower syndrome," and he claims that the desire to assert unlimited control is nothing less than an "apocalyptic confrontation" with the world. In this manner, there is what Lifton calls an "apocalyptic contagion" at work in the current war on terror. Eschatological violence is begetting more eschatological violence with no clear end in sight.[50] Lifton writes, "Islamist and American leaders seem to act in concert. That is, each, in its excess, nurtures the apocalypticism of the other, resulting in a malignant synergy."[51]

It is certainly clear that the geopolitical situation at the start of the twenty-first century is rife with tragedy. In among all of these competing eschatologies, with their attendant violence, it is difficult for the tragic voice to be heard. It is imperative, then, for the contemporary tragic artist to separate himself from the current expressions of radical eschatology and Machiavellianism. Dreams of catastrophic purifications or fortune-conquering saviors do not animate the tragic mind, even though the tragic artist must reveal the nature of these dreams in his work. As we have seen in this study, *Measure for Measure* and *Waiting for Godot* stand as preeminent examples of what can be accomplished in theatre when the defeat or assimilation of evil is not assumed.

The primary question of these concluding reflections is whether a new tragic art can emerge today that has a broad-based cultural impact. The present politicocultural situation might have to play itself out before we can speak again of a tragic renaissance, for tragic circumstances do not necessarily give birth to tragic art. Nevertheless, the stress of our times might eventually produce a new tragic sensibility—a sensibility that is acutely aware that there are no absolute solutions to our current political and moral dilemmas. There are only tough choices, which often entail compromise or choosing the lesser evil.[52] This turn towards tragedy should not be understood as defeatist or despairing. Rather, it should be seen as an effort to gain lucid awareness of our current situation— an effort to understand the limits of politics, the indelible nature of violence, our inescapable mortality, and the need for prudence. A revived tragic ethos will mean relinquishing all eschatological dreams, regardless of whether they are of cataclysmic destruction, universal consensus, uninhibited markets, or global democracy. Tragic recognition might provide us instead with a more realistic assessment of our political and artistic responsibilities.

NOTES

Preface: Revaluating Modernity

1. For an account of the imprecise use of "Manichaeism" as applied to President Bush, see Richard J. Bernstein, *The Abuse of Evil: The Corruption of Politics and Religions since 9/11* (Cambridge: Polity Press, 2005), 48–49, 117–18.

2. This ultimatum was given during President Bush's speech to a joint session of Congress on September 20, 2001.

3. President Bush stated this ambition during a speech delivered at the memorial service on September 14, 2001, at the National Cathedral in Washington, D.C. He said, "Our responsibility to history is already clear: to answer these attacks and rid the world of evil."

4. See Robert Jay Lifton, *Superpower Syndrome: America's Apocalyptic Confrontation with the World* (New York: Thunder's Mouth Press/Nation Books, 2003).

5. Susan Neiman, *Evil in Modern Thought: An Alternative History of Philosophy* (Princeton: Princeton University Press, 2002), 2.

6. Joan Copjec, ed., *Radical Evil* (London: Verso, 1996), xviii; emphasis in original.

7. Edith Wyschogrod, *Spirit in Ashes: Hegel, Heidegger, and Man-Made Mass Death* (New Haven: Yale University Press, 1985), xii; emphasis in original.

8. See Zygmunt Bauman, "A Century of Camps?" in *The Bauman Reader*, ed. Peter Beilharz (Malden: Blackwell, 2001), 267. The essay originally appeared in Bauman, *Life in Fragments: Essays in Postmodern Morality* (Oxford: Blackwell, 1995).

Introduction

1. 1.32–34. The translation is by Richmond Lattimore in *The Odyssey of Homer* (New York: Harper Perennial, 1965).

2. Nietzsche points out in the *Genealogy of Morals* 2.23 that Zeus understands "recklessness" in the sense of "'foolishness,' 'folly,' a little 'disturbance in the head'" (*Basic Writings of Nietzsche*, ed. and trans. Walter Kaufmann [New York: Modern Library, 1992], 530).

3. Martin Southwold, "Buddhism and Evil," in *The Anthropology of Evil*, ed. David Parkin (Cambridge, Mass.: Blackwell, 1985), 131. Several other anthropologists in the same anthology support Southwold's point. Alan Macfarlane writes that "we still use 'evil' in the strong sense, for instance, to describe the Nazi holocaust, mass torture, sadistic crimes"; however, in other senses, the word has become "obsolete" (57–58, n. 1). David Pocock claims that people rarely use the term "evil" today precisely because "it has acquired added strength in relatively recent times" (55).

4. Southwold, "Buddhism and Evil," 132.

5. Southwold's primary intention is to make a categorical distinction between "monotheistic" notions of "evil" and Buddhist notions of "dukkha" (suffering, dis-ease). He is uncomfortable with the monotheistic account of "evil" because, he claims, it gives rise to uncompromising, militaristic attitudes that cause intolerance ("Buddhism and Evil," 132, 139–40). He concludes that Buddhism lacks a conception of evil in the Western monotheistic sense of "sin" and that this is perhaps preferable (134). Southwold's account, however, is somewhat ambivalent: on the one hand, he wants to move beyond the Western understanding of evil; on the other, he feels that this understanding is appropriate when discussing the Holocaust and other extreme atrocities.

6. See Neiman, *Evil in Modern Thought*, 18–57.

7. Jean-Jacques Rousseau, *Emile or On Education*, trans. Allan Bloom (New York: Basic Books, 1979).

8. "Letter from J. J. Rousseau to M. de Voltaire, 18 August 1756," in *The Discourses and Other Early Political Writings*, ed. and trans. Victor Gourevitch (New York: Cambridge University Press, 1997), 234.

9. See Neiman, *Evil in Modern Thought*, 2–4, 8.

10. 7.3.5. All quotations from the *Confessions* are taken from the translation by Henry Chadwick (Oxford: Oxford University Press, 1991).

11. See *CG* 11.17.

12. We might ask: Why would God allow angels and humans to fall into evil? Augustine's answer is twofold. First, if God did not allow the possibility for angels and humans to sin, they would not have free will. God wants his created subjects to love him freely out of their own volition, not out of coercion. Better that humans and angels exist as free but potentially wicked agents than as automatons with no potential for sin. See *CG* 5.9, 22.1. Second, God is using angelic and human sin to realize an even greater good: the final triumph of the Kingdom of God. The fall into sin is part of God's providential design, leading to eternal life for some and eternal damnation for others. See *CG* 14.27.

13. *Confessions*, 7.3.5.

14. As Paul writes, "The wages of sin is death" (Rom. 6:23).

15. See Gen. 2–3. For Augustine's interpretation of Adam's sin and its consequences, see *CG* 14.10–27.

16. See *CG* 14.1.

17. Immanuel Kant, *Religion within the Limits of Reason Alone*, trans. Theodore M. Greene and Hoyt H. Hudson (New York: Harper Torchbooks, 1960), 28; emphasis in original.

18. Ibid., 24.

19. Immanuel Kant, *Foundations of the Metaphysics of Morals*, trans. Lewis White Beck (New York: Macmillan, 1990), 38 (2.421).

20. Kant, *Religion within the Limits*, 25.

21. Ibid., 24; emphasis in original.

22. Nietzsche, *Genealogy of Morals*, 1.17; *Basic Writings of Nietzsche*, ed. and trans. Kaufmann, 491.

23. Parkin, Introduction to his *Anthropology of Evil*. Parkin writes:

> In a number of languages, such as those of Bantu Africa . . . or Balinese . . . [,] some terms translatable as bad or evil . . . have a sense of physically rotten, misshapen, and ugly. Among the Piaroa Indians of Venezuela . . . evil powers of madness are semantically linked to ugliness and dirt. . . . *Tamas,* in the Hindu texts[,] . . . refers at root to inert and benighted lethargy, that is, to something not properly alive and yet capable of being activated as evil. This and many other terms in other societies, rendered by us as evil or bad, denote blackness, obscurity, and unfulfillment. . . . We may also speculate that, in the 'concrete' languages of early man, it would be failed harvests and depleted forests and jungles, ravaged by flood or burnt by sun and drought, or the decaying corpses of animals and people that might strike him as 'bad'. The very concept of 'bad death', such as through accidents and homicide, many cases of which have been gathered by anthropologists from all over the world, refers to a human exit that was ill-timed and so failed to satisfy the normal expectations associated with natural death. (7)

24. Ibid., 15.

25. St. Augustine had a similar notion of evil as deprivation. In *City of God*, he writes, "'evil' is merely a name for the privation of good" (11.22). However, Augustine understood all privation to proceed exclusively from human sin.

26. David Parkin writes, "*Ra* [in Hebrew] meant worthless, unclean, and thence bad, ugly and even sad. Other terms were used later to refer to the breaking of the covenant with God and variously denoted disorder through such root notions as 'falling short of a target', 'breaking of a relationship, or rebelliousness', and 'twisting, making crooked or wrong'" (*Anthropology of Evil*, 7). For various uses of the word *ra*, see Jer. 4.6, Amos 3.6, Mic. 2.3, Eccles. 1.13, Job 2.10. God is frequently presented in the Old Testament as being the source of *ra*. This is evident in Isa. 45:6–7: "I am the LORD, and there is no other. I form light and create darkness. I make weal and create woe (*ra*); I the LORD do all these things."

27. Paul Ricoeur, *The Symbolism of Evil*, trans. Emerson Buchanan (Boston: Beacon Press, 1969), 27. Ricoeur also claims that the Adamic myth of Gen. 2–3 reveals

that the "origin of evil is in an ancestor of the human race." The story of Adam's "deviation" shows the "radical origin of evil distinct from the primordial origin of the goodness of things" (233). In this sense, Ricoeur's interpretation of the Eden story is similar to Augustine's.

28. C. Fred Alford, *What Evil Means to Us* (Ithaca: Cornell University Press, 1997), 62.

29. Jean Baudrillard, *Paroxysm*, trans. Chris Turner (London: Verso, 1998), 25.

30. See Jean Baudrillard, *The Transparency of Evil: Essays on Extreme Phenomena*, trans. James Benedict (London: Verso, 1993), 106–7; and *Impossible Exchange*, trans. Chris Turner (London: Verso, 2001), 96–97. That said, Baudrillard continues to speak of evil as an "agent" (*Paroxysm*, 25). This suggests that he has retained a demonic conception of evil—of a superhuman agency behind the disasters and confusions that afflict humans in this world. Baudrillard himself confesses that his understanding of evil is similar to ancient and medieval gnosis. As he says in *Paroxysm*, "I wouldn't have minded being Manichaean, heretical, and Gnostic" (46). In another interview, Baudrillard announces, "I am almost Manichean" (Mike Gane, ed., *Baudrillard Live: Selected Interviews* [London: Routledge, 1993], 176). Be that as it may, there is an important distinction between Baudrillard and Manichaeanism: Baudrillard insists that evil can never be exterminated or entirely separated from the good, whereas Manichaean doctrine lives in expectation of a final separation of good and evil. This is a crucial difference.

31. C. Fred Alford, *Think No Evil: Korean Values in the Age of Globalization* (Ithaca: Cornell University Press, 1999), 25.

32. Alford, *What Evil Means to Us*, 18. That said, Alford insists that he does not want to equate evil with the term "bad," for if "evil is anything and everything bad, then it is nothing" (18). However, with the "commensurable" instances of evil listed above, Alford makes evil a very general category. It is difficult to articulate a categorical distinction between "evil" and "bad" based on Alford's discussion. It is perhaps best to speak of kinds and degrees of evil.

33. Ibid., 2–3.

34. Ibid., 3.

35. Ibid., 58. Alford uses Melanie Klein's term "paranoid-schizoid" to refer to this desire to do harm to others in the attempt to purge dread:

> From this perspective, evil is a paranoid-schizoid attempt to evacuate the formless dread by giving it form via violent intrusion into another. . . . Destroying the other, we destroy our dread (or so the fantasy goes). . . . This process applies not just to physical violence but to the cutting remark, the hurtful gesture, and perhaps even the purposeful neglect of the humanity of others, as though some must lose their humanity for others to possess it. (43–44)

In other words, we lash out at dread by making others feel dreadful. Through such actions, we become dread so that we may not be its victim (see 3).

36. Baudrillard, *Transparency of Evil*, 107.

37. The only notable exception is Rousseau. In his *Letter to M. d'Alembert on the Theatre*, Rousseau argues that theatre is detrimental to the formation of moral character. Theatre, according to Rousseau, evokes moral sentiments for the purpose of distracting audiences with diversionary entertainments that excite their emotions disproportionately and cultivate a taste for extravagance.

38. See Voltaire's *Mahomet, ou le Fanatisme*, or Diderot's *Le Père de Famille*.

39. J. Peter Euben, *Tragedy of Political Theory: The Road Not Taken* (Princeton: Princeton University Press, 1990), 56.

40. Eric Voegelin, *New Science of Politics: An Introduction* (Chicago: University of Chicago Press, 1952), 73.

41. Christian Meier, *The Political Art of Greek Tragedy*, trans. Andrew Webber (Baltimore: Johns Hopkins University Press, 1993), 43.

42. See *Poetics*, 1449b27–28. Also see *Politics*, 1342a.

43. "On the Future of Tragedy" appears in Albert Camus, *Lyrical and Critical Essays*, ed. Philip Thody, trans. Ellen Conroy Kennedy (New York: Vintage Books, 1970), 295–310.

44. Ibid., 296.

45. Ibid., 298.

46. John Orr, *Tragic Drama and Modern Society: Studies in the Social and Literary Theory of Drama from 1870 to the Present* (London: Macmillan, 1981), xi.

47. There are many scholars, however, who argue that Roman theatre possesses its own inherent excellence. See Erich Segal, *Roman Laughter: The Comedy of Plautus* (Cambridge, Mass.: Harvard University Press, 1968); A. J. Boyle, *Tragic Seneca: An Essay in the Theatrical Tradition* (London: Routledge, 1997).

48. See Camus's account of Christian theatre in "On the Future of Tragedy," 296–97, 303.

49. Ibid., 306.

50. Ibid., 296.

51. Boyle argues that Senecan tragedy in ancient Rome also developed during a period of social turbulence similar to that of the Renaissance: "Late Julio-Claudian Rome and Renaissance Europe were societies undergoing momentous social change and, in some cases, on the verge of dissolution. . . . [O]ne of the hallmarks of Senecan and Renaissance tragedy is to function as a site within culture where the inadequacies and contradictions of culture may be contested. . . . [T]heatricality appears most obvious at times of great social stress" (*Tragic Seneca*, 211–12).

52. Meier writes, "The Athens of the fifth century, the era of tragedy, was an exuberant and disconcerting city, a city in extreme ferment" (*The Political Art of Greek Tragedy*, 8).

53. See C. Fred Alford, *The Psychoanalytic Theory of Greek Tragedy* (New Haven: Yale University Press, 1994), 29.

54. Lines 675–6. The translation is by David Grene in *The Complete Greek Tragedies, Volume 2: Sophocles,* 2d ed. ed. David Grene and Richmond Lattimore (Chicago: University of Chicago Press, 1991).

55. Alford, *Psychoanalytic Theory of Greek Tragedy,* 60.

56. Mera Flaumenhaft, *The Civic Spectacle: Essays on Drama and Community* (Lanham: Rowman and Littlefield, 1994), 74.

57. Euben, *The Tragedy of Political Theory,* 146.

58. See Flaumenhaft, *The Civic Spectacle,* 58.

59. Euben, *The Tragedy of Political Theory,* 145–46.

60. See lines 278–86, 379–86, 770–75.

61. Alford, *Psychoanalytic Theory of Greek Tragedy,* 47.

62. See Martin Esslin, *The Theatre of the Absurd* (London: Penguin Books, 1961), 23–25.

63. Patrice Pavis, *Dictionary of the Theatre: Terms, Concepts, and Analysis,* trans. Christine Shantz (Toronto: University of Toronto Press, 1998), 2.

64. Eugène Ionesco, *Notes and Counternotes: Writings on the Theatre by Eugène Ionesco,* trans. Donald Watson (New York: Grove Press, 1964), 92; emphasis in original.

65. Ibid., 110–11.

66. Zygmunt Bauman, *Modernity and the Holocaust* (Ithaca: Cornell University Press, 1989), 90.

67. Wyschogrod, *Spirit in Ashes,* 15.

68. Ibid., x.

69. I occasionally refer to the original French to correct Anthony Bowers's translation of *The Rebel* (New York: Vintage International, 1956). These changes are bracketed and explained in footnotes. I have used the version of *L'Homme révolté* contained in *Essais,* ed. Roger Quilliot and Louis Faucon (Paris: Gallimard, Bibliothèque de la Pléiade, 1965).

70. See Hannah Arendt, *Eichmann in Jerusalem: A Report on the Banality of Evil* (New York: Viking Press, 1965). Also see Arendt's illuminating comments about the "banality of evil" in the introduction to *The Life of the Mind* (San Diego: Harcourt Brace Jovanovich, 1978), 3–5.

71. See Camus's account of Communist totalitarianism in *The Rebel,* 226–45.

72. Bauman, *Modernity and the Holocaust,* 90.

73. Ibid., 89.

74. Ibid., 98.

75. Ibid.

76. Ibid., 102.

77. This is not a universal truth in all modern genocides. For example, in the Rwandan genocide, most of the Hutu killers were forced to confront their Tutsis victims face-to-face. The preferred method of murder was hacking people with machetes. With these crude means, the Hutu majority was able to kill about

800,000 Tutsis in just three months. For a vivid account, see Philip Gourevitch, *We Wish to Inform You That Tomorrow We Will Be Killed with Our Families: Stories from Rwanda* (New York: Picador, 1999). From all appearances, it is easy to mistake the Rwandan genocide as an instance of mass passionate crime. Gourevitch says that it is "tempting" in this case "to play with theories of collective madness, mob mania, a fever of hatred erupted into a mass crime of passion, and to imagine the blind orgy of the mob, with each member killing one or two people" (17). But Gourevitch points out that such theories of passionate evil in Rwanda are wrong: the Rwandan genocide was the product of modern social engineering and rational calculation on the part of the Hutu government. The entire event was organized by a bureaucracy charged with overseeing the extermination of Tutsis. Furthermore, the killers themselves were not constantly filled with rage and perverse pleasure as they carried out the slaughter; on the contrary, they experienced their killing as hard and tedious. Gourevitch writes, "The rallying cry to the killers during the genocide was 'Do your work!' And I saw that it *was* work, this butchery; hard work." He points out that "hundreds of thousands of Hutus had worked as killers in regular shifts. There was always the next victim, and the next. What sustained them, beyond the frenzy of the first attack, through the plain physical exhaustion and the mess of it?" (17). This low-tech, face-to-face method proved very efficient. It "was the most efficient mass killing since the atomic bombings of Hiroshima and Nagasaki" (3). It was also short lived: the genocide could not sustain itself after a few months.

78. Bauman, *Modernity and the Holocaust,* 105, 106. This is not to say that all bureaucracies are genocidal. Bauman argues, however, that every bureaucracy is designed in such a way as to seek an "optimal solution" and to shelter most employees within the bureaucracy from directly encountering the harmful effects that these so-called solutions create. According to Bauman, we should not suffer from the illusion that modern bureaucracies are morally neutral instruments that can be used for either good or evil. On the contrary, they contain an inherent ethos that seeks optimum technical solutions regardless of the human cost:

> Bureaucracy is not merely a tool, which can be used with equal facility at one time for cruel and morally contemptible, at another for deeply human purposes. Even if it does move in any direction in which it is pushed, bureaucracy is more like a loaded dice. It has a logic and a momentum of its own. It renders some solutions more, and others solutions less, probable. . . . Bureaucracy is programmed to seek the optimal solution. It is programmed to measure the optimum in such terms as would not distinguish between one human object and another, or between human and inhuman objects. What matters is the efficiency and lowering of costs of their processing. (104)

This reveals that bureaucracies have an innate utopian tendency to obliterate every questionable element—real or imagined—that stands in the way of perfect functioning.

79. Ibid., 116.
80. Ibid., 101.
81. Ibid., 98.
82. This was one of the conclusions of Stanley Milgram's famous obedience experiments. See Stanley Milgram, "Some Conditions of Obedience and Disobedience to Authority," in *The Individual in a Social World* (Reading: Addison-Wesley, 1977), 120–21.
83. Bauman, *Modernity and the Holocaust,* 91.
84. Ibid,; emphasis in original.
85. Ibid., 106.
86. In brackets I have corrected Bower's translation of Camus's French. See Camus, *Essais,* 413. Bower translates "devant des crimes si candides, la conscience pouvait être ferme, et le jugement clair" as "the mind did not reel before such unabashed crimes, and judgement remained unclouded." He also translates "l'amour de l'homme" as "philanthropy."
87. Albert Camus, "Neither Victims nor Executioners," in *Between Hell and Reason: Essays from the Resistance Newspaper "Combat," 1944–1947,* trans. Alexandre de Gramont (Hanover: Wesleyan University Press, 1991), 121.
88. For an account of utopianism in modern theatre, see Dragan Klaiç, *Plot of the Future: Utopia and Dystopia in Modern Drama* (Ann Arbor: University of Michigan Press, 1991).
89. Leo Strauss, *Thoughts on Machiavelli* (Chicago: University of Chicago Press, 1958), 9.
90. See Leo Strauss, "The Three Waves of Modernity," in *An Introduction to Political Philosophy: Ten Essays by Leo Strauss,* ed. Hilail Gildin (Detroit: Wayne State University Press, 1989), 83–89.
91. Bauman, *Modernity and the Holocaust,* 116.
92. The four plays I am studying are *written* texts. Hence my approach to them is literary, which is to say that I provide a careful examination of what is written on the page. Certainly, the "theatricality" of these plays—that is, their nonliterary elements, such as sound, gesture, movement, space, and spectacle—will be considered. Nevertheless, all these plays display a traditional concern with writing; they are not spectacle. As a result, my analysis will privilege "theatre"—understood as the fusion of public performance and literary script—over sheer theatricality.

Chapter One. Eschatology and the Absurd

1. See Esslin, *Theatre of the Absurd,* 23.
2. See *MS* 10.
3. Samuel Beckett, *Disjecta: Miscellaneous Writings and a Dramatic Fragment,* ed. Ruby Cohn (New York: Grove Press), 70.

4. Ibid.

5. These letters were written to Tom MacGreevy. Portions of them appear in James Knowlson, *Damned to Fame: The Life of Samuel Beckett* (New York: Touchstone, 1996), 187–88.

6. See Knowlson's commentary in *Damned to Fame*, 181.

7. Tom Driver, "Beckett by the Madeleine," *Columbia University Forum* 4, no. 3 (Summer 1961): 22–23.

8. See Esslin, *Theatre of the Absurd*, 25.

9. Camus, "Three Interviews," in *Lyrical and Critical Essays*, 345.

10. See Esslin, *Theatre of the Absurd*, 24.

11. E. Freeman, "Camus, Suetonius, and the Caligula Myth," *Symposium* 24, no. 3 (Fall 1970): 230.

12. Esslin, *Theatre of the Absurd*, 24.

13. Albert Camus, "Author's Preface," in *Caligula and Three Other Plays*, trans. Justin O'Brien (New York: Vintage Books, 1958), v–vi.

14. Esslin, *Theatre of the Absurd*, 24.

15. Ibid., 25, emphasis in original. Esslin's point is supported by Patrice Pavis, who writes, "The plays of Camus and Sarte (*Caligula, le Malentendu, Huis clos*), do not meet any of the formal criteria of the absurd, even though their characters are its philosophic spokesmen" (*Dictionary of the Theatre*, 2).

16. Driver, "Beckett by the Madeleine," 22–23.

17. Samuel Beckett, "Dante . . . Bruno. Vico . . . Joyce," in *Our Exagmination Round His Factification for Incamination of Work in Progress* (Paris: Shakespeare and Co., 1929; reprint, London: Faber and Faber, 1961), 14 (page reference is to reprint edition; emphasis in original). Beckett is referring specifically to Joyce's "Work in Progress," which would later be published as *Finnegans Wake*.

18. Israel Shenker, "Moody Man of Letters," *New York Times*, 6 May 1956, sec. 2, p. 3.

19. Walter Schmithals, *The Apocalyptic Movement: Introduction and Interpretation*, trans. John E. Steely (Nashville: Abingdon Press, 1975), 106. Schmithals contends that these two categories of eschatology are not absolutely distinct and often overlap (see 95).

20. Wyschogrod, *Spirit in Ashes*, 41, 43.

21. See Caroline Walker Bynum and Paul Freedman, eds., *Last Things: Death and the Apocalypse in the Middle Ages* (Philadelphia: University of Pennsylvania Press, 2000), 1.

22. See Aristotle's discussion of *telos*, virtue, and happiness in *NE* 1.1–2, 7.1097a15–1098a19.

23. It was probably first used in 1804 by Karl Gottlieb Bretschneider. See G. Filoramo, "Eschatology," in *Encyclopedia of the Early Church*, 2 vols., ed. Angelo Di Bernardino, trans. Adrian Walford (New York: Oxford University Press, 1992), 1:284–86.

24. Bernard McGinn, John J. Collins, and Stephen J. Stein in *The Encyclopedia of Apocalypticism, Volume I: The Origins of Apocalypticism in Judaism and Christianity,* ed. John J. Collins (New York: Continuum, 1999), viii–ix.

25. Norman Cohn, *Cosmos, Chaos, and the World to Come: The Ancient Roots of Apocalyptic Faith* (New Haven: Yale University Press, 1993), preface (n.p.).

26. Ibid., 227.

27. Ibid., 27–30.

28. Ibid., 55–56, 140. For an account of the Greek underworld, see book 11 of Homer's *Odyssey.*

29. There are many ancient beliefs that the present world will be destroyed and then re-created. As Mircea Eliade points out, Indian mythology speaks of an "eternal creation, deterioration, destruction, and recreation of the Universe," but "for India there is no final End of the World properly speaking" (*Myth and Reality,* trans. Willard R. Trask [New York: Harper Torchbooks, 1963], 62–63). Furthermore, Indian myths do not claim that all evil elements will be purged in a new creation. New worlds emerge, but they remain imperfect mixtures of cosmos and chaos, purity and impurity; there is no once and for all triumph of order over disorder. Consequently, both humans and the gods must defend order (*dharma*) in each new creation. Eliade points out that the ultimate end for humans in "Indian theory" is not found in the new creation but in the condition that exists beyond the perpetual cycles of destruction and creation. He writes, "man does not want this eternal re-creation, his goal is to escape from the cosmic cycle" (62).

30. It is important, however, that we do not claim Zoroaster introduced an entirely new mythology that had never been thought of before. It is possible that myths about a coming cataclysm, in which the world is either destroyed or renewed and where all evil is purged, have existed from the earliest times independent of Zoroastrian influence. We can, however, say with some certainty that such myths were uncommon in the ancient world. In *Myth and Reality,* Eliade finds vague traces of eschatological expectation in certain "primitive" myths, such as those told by the Andaman Islanders, the Kai of New Guina, the Namolut and Aurepik peoples of the Caroline Islands, and the various indigenous tribes of North and South America (54–60). With many of these myths, however, Eliade claims that "it is not clear if the End is final" (57), or even if the "End" is "in the past or in the future" (56). He argues that most ancient stories of a cosmic cataclysm refer to the past, and may suggest perpetual cycles of destruction and renewal but not a final end (54–55). He concludes, "Myths referring to an end to come are curiously scarce amongst primitives" (55).

31. Cohn, *Cosmos, Chaos and the World to Come,* 227–28.

32. Ibid., 141–62.

33. Ibid., 163–93.

34. Ibid., 194–211.

35. Voegelin, *New Science of Politics,* 107.

36. See Eric Voegelin, *The Ecumenic Age*, vol. 4 of *Order and History* (Baton Rouge: Louisiana State University Press, 1974), 8–11. Here Voegelin describes how myths of intracosmic gods were gradually replaced by symbols of a world transcendent "Beyond."

37. See Cohn, *Cosmos, Chaos and the World to Come*, 20–22.

38. Ibid., 22.

39. The following discussion of apocalypticism and Gnosticism is primarily based on Schmithals, *The Apocalyptic Movement*; and Hans Jonas, *The Gnostic Religion: The Message of the Alien God and the Beginnings of Christianity*, 2d ed., rev. (Boston: Beacon Press, 1963).

40. See Schmithals, *The Apocalyptic Movement*, 100.

41. Ibid., 98, 101–2.

42. Ibid., 104.

43. Dan. 12:1–3; Rev. 20–21:8. Also see Paul's account of resurrection in 1 Cor.15.

44. See Jonas, *The Gnostic Religion*, 42–43.

45. See Schmithals, *The Apocalyptic Movement*, 92–93.

46. Jonas, *The Gnostic Religion*, 42.

47. Ibid., 44.

48. See Schmithals, *The Apocalyptic Movement*, 90–92, 103.

49. See Jonas, *The Gnostic Religion*, 45.

50. Ibid., 45.

51. Ibid., 45–46.

52. Schmithals, *The Apocalyptic Movement*, 98.

53. Ibid., 106.

54. Bernard McGinn, "Introduction: John's Apocalypse and the Apocalyptic Mentality," in *The Apocalypse in the Middle Ages*, ed. Richard K. Emmerson and Bernard McGinn (Ithaca: Cornell University Press, 1992), 8.

55. Augustine quotes Ps. 11:2. Also see *CG* 14.11.

56. Voegelin, *New Science of Politics*, 119.

57. Wyschogrod, *Spirit in Ashes*, 46.

58. Lifton, *Superpower Syndrome*, 21, 26–29.

59. Bauman, *Modernity and the Holocaust*, 92–93.

60. Voegelin, *New Science of Politics*, 126.

61. Wyschogrod, *Spirit in Ashes*, 44. There are, however, some variations of this sorting myth. For example, it is possible for an eschatological myth to claim that evil will be defeated through a process of reconciliation, assimilation, and synthesization. In this sense, the process of salvation is a procedure that gradually transforms or accommodates all impurities and incorporates them into a larger harmonious totality. In this type of eschatology, there is a hope that all will be saved. Historically, such apocatastatic eschatologies have been rare. Some of the heretical speculations of Origen, for instance, are considered apocatastatic. Apocatastasis

and "Origenism" in general, were condemned as anathema by the Second Council of Constantinople in 553.

62. Ibid., 43.

63. Ibid., 46.

Chapter 2. The Gnostic Caesar

For this chapter, I use the English translation of *Caligula* by Stuart Gilbert in *Caligula and Three Other Plays*, 1–74. All references are indicated by page numbers in parentheses. Gilbert's translation is based on the first French edition of *Caligula* published in *Le Malentendu suivi de Caligula* (Paris: Librairie Gallimard, 1944). Camus would later revise the play, first in 1947 and again in 1958. The final 1958 French edition is available in *Théâtre, Récits, Nouvelles*, comp. and ed. Roger Quilliot (Paris: Éditions Gallimard, 1962), 3–108. I refer to this French edition not only to consider Camus's subsequent modifications of the play but also occasionally to correct Gilbert's English translation. My corrections appear in brackets and are explained in notes.

1. Claude K. Abraham writes, "*Caligula* is to the theatre what *Le Mythe de Sisyphe* is to the philosophic essay. . . . *Caligula* is Camus' theatre of the absurd" ("*Caligula*: Drama of Revolt or Drama of Deception?" *Modern Drama*, 5, no. 4 [February 1963]: 451). Similarly, David Sprintzen writes, "[*Caligula*] was completed in the early 1940s, contemporaneously with *The Myth* and *The Stranger*, and properly forms an integral part of Camus's 'first series' on the absurd" (*Camus: A Critical Examination* [Philadelphia: Temple University Press, 1988], 66).

2. David Cook describes this tension within the absurd man as a conflict between "epistemology" and "ontology." Epistemologically, the absurd man knows that life is ultimately unreasonable; ontologically, however, the absurd man strives for complete reason. See David Cook, "Albert Camus' *Caligula*: The Metaphysics of an Emperor," in *Domination*, ed. Alkis Kontos (Toronto: University of Toronto Press, 1975), 201–9.

3. See Cook, "Albert Camus' *Caligula*," 202–3.

4. Camus also refers to it as "metaphysical crime" (*MS* 80).

5. Camus, *Essais*, 1268.

6. Camus writes, "C'est le mal qui obsède les gnostiques" (*Essais*, 1268).

7. Camus titles one section of *Christian Metaphysics* "Les Thèmes de la Solution Gnostique" (*Essais*, 1252). According to Camus, the four main themes of the "Gnostic solution" are (1) the problem of evil, (2) redemption, (3) the theory of intermediaries between God and the world, and (4) the idea of God as ineffable and incommunicable (ibid.).

8. Camus, *Essais*, 1257. Camus makes this comment when discussing the gnostic Marcion, who, according to Camus, desired to see the universe destroyed. Camus claims that Maricon's attitude resonates with a modern sensibility.

9. Paul Archambault, *Camus' Hellenic Sources* (Chapel Hill: University of North Carolina Press, 1972), 113–14.

10. Camus, "Author's Preface," vi.

11. Albert Sonnenfeld, "Albert Camus as Dramatist: The Sources of His Failure," *Tulane Drama Review* 5, no. 4 (June 1961): 106.

12. Pavis, *Dictionary of the Theatre,* 2.

13. Quoted and translated by Sonnenfeld in "Albert Camus as Dramatist," 111.

14. Ibid., 113.

15. For discussions of how Camus has used and altered Suetonius, see Walter A. Strauss, "*Caligula*: Ancient Sources and Modern Parallels," *Comparative Literature* 3, no. 2 (Spring 1951): 160–73; Freeman, "Camus, Suetonius, and the Caligula Myth," 230–42.

16. Suetonius, 4.9.1. I use J. C. Rolfe's translation of Suetonius in the Loeb Classical Library edition (Cambridge, Mass.: Harvard University Press, 1914).

17. It was a custom in Rome, before Caligula, to deify emperors after they died. This honor was bestowed on both Caesar and Augustus. The empire, at this early stage in its history, retained enough of a republican sensibility to delay the full deification of the living emperor—at least in the capital, Rome. Augustus, for example, was forced to assume the appearance of a republican magistrate. However, there was mounting pressure to divinize the emperor and give him a godly aura. Eric Voegelin writes, "The deification of the living emperor evolved in fits and starts. Caius Caligula insisted on his personal divinity; Claudius reverted to the Augustan tradition; Nero followed him in the earlier part of his reign but later identified himself with the sun god; Domitian (81–96) seems to have been the first emperor who in the later part of his reign preferred the address *Dominus et Deus* (Master and God)" (*History of Political Ideas,* Vol. 1: *Hellenism, Rome, and Early Christianity,* ed. Athanasios Moulakis, vol. 19 of *The Collected Works of Eric Voegelin* [Columbia: University of Missouri Press, 1997], 191). For a historical discussion of Caligula's demand to be recognized as a god and how this was addressed by the Romans, see Anthony A. Barrett, *Caligula: The Corruption of Power* (New Haven: Yale University Press, 1989), 140–53. Barrett writes, "The sources show that . . . obsequious courtiers fell over themselves in addressing [Caligula] in terms appropriate to a divine figure, and it was by a decree in the senate that a temple was formally devoted to his cult or that of his *genius.* That Caligula did nothing to discourage this behaviour, unlike Augustus or even Nero in similar circumstances, is no credit to him, but it is hardly a sign of madness" (153).

18. Suetonius, 4.22.2.

19. Ibid., 4.22.1.

20. Ibid., 4.37.2–3; my emphasis. In Latin, the italicized portion reads "tam efficere concupiscebat quam quod posse effici negaretur." Robert Graves, like Rolfe, uses the word *impossible* in his translation of this sentence. See Suetonius, *The Twelve Caesars,* trans. Robert Graves, rev. trans. Michael Grant (London: Penguin Books, 1979), 172. It cannot be said with absolute certainty that this passage is

290 | Notes to Pages 54–60

the source of Camus's decision to use the term "l'impossible" to describe Caligula's passion. Henri Ailloud's 1932 French translation, which Camus probably used, speaks of Caligula's passion to do the "irréalisable." See *Suétone: Vies des Douze Césars II*, 4th ed., trans. Henri Ailloud (Paris: Société d'Édition "Les Belles Lettres," 1967), 91. Camus might have translated Suetonius on his own. Like most educated Europeans of his day, he knew some Latin. See Oliver Todd, *Albert Camus: A Life*, trans. Benjamin Ivry (New York: Alfred A. Knopf, 1997), 13.

21. The titles of Camus's essays alone—such as *The Myth of Sisyphus*, "The Minotaur," "Prometheus in the Underworld," "Helen's Exile," and the proposed *Myth of Nemesis*—indicate his enormous debt to Greek mythology.

22. Camus, "The New Mediterranean Culture," in *Lyrical and Critical Essays*, 190.

23. Ibid., 193.

24. Ibid.

25. Camus claimed that the character Caligula was not a symbolic representation of Hitler or any other totalitarian leader. Germaine Bree reports that in 1943 Camus said *Caligula* was originally conceived as a "drama of the mind, outside all contingencies," but that "events have given it a meaning which it did not originally have" ("Camus' *Caligula*: Evolution of a Play," *Symposium* 12 [1958]: 44). There is little doubt, however, that Camus is responding to immediate realities in Europe.

26. Camus, "Helen's Exile," in *Lyrical and Critical Essays*, 150.

27. Ibid.

28. See *R* 245–46, 250, 298, 300.

29. Camus himself would attempt to present the bureaucratic banality of totalitarianism in his later, and much less successful, play *State of Siege*.

30. This definition of nihilism occurs in the context of a discussion of Nietzsche.

31. Camus, *Théâtre, Récits, Nouvelles*, 15. Gilbert translates *raisonnable* as "lucid" (8).

32. In French, Caligula says he wants "l'immortalité" (Camus, *Théâtre, Récits, Nouvelles*, 15). Gilbert translates this as "eternal life" (8).

33. Gilbert's complete translation of this passage reads, "Suppose the moon were brought here, everything would be different. . . . Then the impossible would become possible, in a flash the Great Change come, and all things be transfigured." This is an inaccurate rendering of Camus's French. The brackets indicate where I have changed Gilbert's translation. See Camus, *Théâtre, Récits, Nouvelles*, 75.

34. Camus, *Théâtre, Récits, Nouvelles*, 78.

35. Ibid., 58.

36. Jonas, *The Gnostic Religion*, 46.

37. Jonas writes, "The Archons collectively rule over the world. . . . Their tyrannical world rule is called *heimarmene*, universal Fate, a concept taken over from astrology but now tinged with the gnostic anti-cosmic spirit" (*The Gnostic Religion*, 43).

38. Jonas, *The Gnostic Religion*, 46.

39. Ibid.

40. Camus, *Théâtre, Récits, Nouvelles*, 16.

41. In French, Caligula says "leur métier ridicule" (Camus, *Théâtre, Récits, Nouvelles*, 67). Gilbert translates this as "their [i.e., the gods'] absurd parts" (43). It is important to be precise in this regard, given the significance of the word *absurd* in Camus's thought. There is another passage in which Gilbert uses the word *absurd* where it does not occur in French. In Act 3, Gilbert has Cherea say that most men "resent living in a world where the most preposterous fancy may at any moment become reality, and the absurd transfix their lives, like a dagger in the heart" (51). The French reads, "Ils sont incapables de vivre dans un univers où la pensée la plus bizarre peut en une seconde entrer dans la réalité—où, la plupart du temps, elle y entre, comme un couteau dans un cœur" (Camus, *Théâtre, Récits, Nouvelles*, 77). Gilbert also translates Caligula using the word *absurd* in another passage (29). This is a correct translation of Camus's 1944 edition of *Caligula*. However, Camus replaced the word *absurde* with *ennuyeux* (tedious) in his revision of the play. See Camus, *Théâtre, Récits, Nouvelles*, 46, 1762.

42. Camus, "Author's Preface," v.

43. Ibid., vi; my emphasis.

44. In French, Caesonia speaks of "la seule révolution définitive de ce monde" (Camus, *Théâtre, Récits, Nouvelles*, 53). Gilbert translates the word *définitive*, which literally means "final" or "definitive," as "real" (33).

45. For commentary on Gnostic readings of Christ's mission and crucifixion, see Jonas, *The Gnostic Religion*, 137–40, 228–31.

46. See Matt. 26:36–46; Mark 14:32–42; Luke 22:39–46.

47. Caligula says, "Hélicon! Hélicon! Rien! rien encore" (Camus, *Théâtre, Récits, Nouvelles*, 108). Gilbert does not include "Helicon, Helicon" in his translation (see 73). Jesus' "My God, my God, why have you forsaken me?" occurs in Mark 15:34 and Matt. 27:45.

48. See Camus's description of this possibility in *MS* 48.

49. See Suetonius, 4.58.4.

50. Archambault, *Camus' Hellenic Sources*, 113–14.

51. Fred Willhoite writes, "[*Caligula*] can be interpreted, without distortion, I believe, as a premonition of Camus's mature views on revolt" (*Beyond Nihilism* [Baton Rouge: Louisiana State University Press, 1968], 48). Similarly, John Cruickshank writes, "Readers of *L'Homme révolté* will find *Caligula* particularly interesting because it contains an imaginative projection of various ideas more fully explained and discussed in the later essay" (*Albert Camus and the Literature of Revolt* [New York: Oxford University Press, 1960], 198).

52. According to Camus, this awareness of limits is derived, in part, from "nature." Camus speaks of a form of rebellion based on what he calls "solar thought"— a Mediterranean sensitivity to beauty in the universe (*R* 300). Despite natural afflictions, the Greeks did not anticipate or endeavor to actualize a transfiguration of the cosmos. Camus claims that, on the contrary, the Greeks derived notions of

moderation, balance, and harmony from their contemplation of beauty in the surrounding universe. This beauty is maintained when each element is constrained within certain limits. Crossing these limits destroys equilibrium. See Camus's reflections in *R* 298–300 and in "Helen's Exile," 148–53.

53. Camus, "Helen's Exile," 152.

54. Camus, "On the Future of Tragedy," 302–3.

55. Albert Camus, *Carnets: 1942–1951*, trans. Philip Thody (London: Hamish Hamilton, 1966), 120.

56. Ibid., 83; emphasis in original. In brackets I have altered Thody's translation. Thody translates "C'est une histoire de chrétiens" as "It's a Christian kind of business." For the French text, see Albert Camus, *Carnets II: Janvier 1942–Mars 1951* (n.p.: Éditions Gallimard, 1964), 164.

57. Cherea uses the words *vénères* and *profond* (Camus, *Théâtre, Récits, Nouvelles*, 83, 34). Gilbert translates these words as "sacred" (56, 21).

58. This translation is mine. The French reads "il faut bien plaider pour ce monde, si nous voulons y vivre" (Camus, *Théâtre, Récits, Nouvelles*, 25). Gilbert translates this as "since this world is the only one we have, why not plead its case" (14).

59. The French reads "contre une grande idée dont la victorire signifierait la fin du monde" (Camus, *Théâtre, Récits, Nouvelles*, 34). Gilbert translates *la fin du monde* as "the end of everything" (21).

60. The French reads "jusqu'à nier l'homme et le monde" (Camus, *Théâtre, Récits, Nouvelles*, 34). Gilbert translates this as "counts mankind, and the world we know, for nothing" (21).

61. Camus was not always consistent in this regard. He also refers to true rebels as "innocent murderers" (*R* 297).

62. Camus, "Neither Victims nor Executioners," 120–21.

63. In the 1944 version of *Caligula*, Scipio does not actually leave Rome. Instead, he reappears in the final scene as one of Caligula's assassins. The English edition retains the stage direction that has Scipio lead the assassins into Caligula's chamber (73). But given Scipio's earlier announcement that he is leaving Rome (67) and his claim that he can "never again take anybody's side" (56), his participation in the assassination does not make dramatic sense. In the 1958 edition of *Caligula*, Camus took Scipio out of the final scene. See Camus, *Théâtre, Récits, Nouvelles* 108, 1771.

64. Camus, "Neither Victims nor Executioners," 122.

65. On this point, it is interesting to note that Camus, for all his criticisms of Gnosticism, was drawn to the thought of Simone Weil, the twentieth-century French mystic whose writings often display a Gnostic attitude. Weil, as is well known, believed that God is absent from this world and that God's spiritual realm is infinitely distant from our own universe. Weil also had an obsessive desire for purity, to the point where she often neglected her physical health. She starved herself to death in 1943. Camus became familiar with her writings after her death, and he was responsible for publishing several of her works in his *Espoir* series. He was

particularly interested in Weil's account of the proletariat's inhuman working conditions and her meditations on our "duties towards mankind" contained in her book *The Need for Roots*. This had a major influence on Camus's account of oppression and rebellion in *The Rebel*. However, as Oliver Todd notes, Camus was "less drawn to her penchant for unhappiness, and her premature death from anorexia was disturbing" (*Albert Camus: A Life*, 291).

66. I. H. Walker, "The Composition of *Caligula*," *Symposium* 20, no. 3 (Fall 1966): 268.

67. Albert Camus, *Carnets 1935–1942*, trans. Philip Thody (London: Hamish Hamilton, 1963), 16.

68. These manuscripts are printed in Camus, *Théâtre, Récits, Nouvelles* 1744–71. For an account of these drafts, see Walker, "The Composition of *Caligula*," 264–65, 271–74. Walker points out that Camus became increasingly critical of Caligula with each manuscript. The main argument of Walker's essay is to contest Camus's claim that he wrote *Caligula* in 1938 (see Camus, "Author's Preface," v). Walker claims that Camus decided to write a play about Caligula in 1937. However, Camus composed several drafts over many years before he completed the first published edition of *Caligula* in 1944. Walker states that Camus, "for polemical purposes[,] . . . was prepared to exaggerate the degree of completion which *Caligula* had undergone by 1938" (274). He argues that Camus did this to counter those critics who accused him of being a "populariser" of Sartre's "existentialism." Sartre published his novel *Nausea* in 1938 and later published his theoretical work *Being and Nothingness* in 1943. Walker contends that Camus insisted on *Caligula*'s 1938 composition date to imply that he had formulated his own account of the absurd before, and independent of, Sartre's major publications.

69. This passage is in Camus, *Théâtre, Récits, Nouvelles*, 18. The translation is mine.

70. Ibid., 35. Gilbert translates this as "a philosophy that's logical from start to finish" (21).

71. In the 1944 edition of *Caligula*, the original French reads "Je te comprends et je t'approuve." See Camus, *Théâtre, Récits, Nouvelles*, 1765.

72. Ibid., 79.

73. Ronald D. Srigley, "Albert Camus' Political Philosophy," unpublished manuscript (2007), 71–144.

74. The examples Camus gives of "true rebellion" also appear to contradict some of his other statements. His models of true revolt in *The Rebel* are the 1905 Russian revolutionaries led by Ivan Kaliayev, who assassinated Grand Duke Sergei (see *R* 164–73). Camus's play *The Just Assassins* is based on the rebellion of Kaliayev and his comrades. In this play, Camus has Kaliayev assert, "When we kill, we're killing so as to build up a world in which there will be no more killing. We consent to being criminals so that at last the innocent, and only they, will inherit the earth" (Camus, *Caligula and Three Other Plays*, 245). Kaliayev's aspirations are similar to Caligula's, and yet Camus does not criticize Kaliayev's passion for a world where

murder no longer exists. On the contrary, Camus writes, "My admiration for my heroes, Kaliayev and Dora, *is complete*" ("Author's Preface," x; my emphasis). We
should recall that Camus, in his essay "Neither Victims nor Executioners," says that
he is not "so crazy" as to want "a world where murder no longer exists," but that he
more modestly desires a world where "murder is no longer legitimized" (120–21).
This is contrary to Kaliayev's aspirations in *The Just Assassins*.

75. This has been noted by scholars such as Fred Willhoite, who claims that
the murderous excesses of metaphysical revolt "does not mean that metaphysical
rebellion is in itself evil and to be suppressed. Camus admired and participated in
its essential impulse, which is the struggle against death and suffering. . . . The aims
of metaphysical rebellion are noble, but the process of its unfolding is too often
marked by tragedy" (*Beyond Nihilism*, 108). Similarly, Sprintzen writes, "If a metaphysical revolution is clearly impossible, the passion motivating it may nonetheless express significant human needs that must be addressed and worked through"
(*Camus: A Critical Examination*, 68).

76. Srigley, "Albert Camus's Political Philosophy," 75.

77. Camus, "Author's Preface," vi.

78. Camus claims that the Caesarian has defeated the Promethean in the mod-
ern world. He writes that the modern rebel "is no longer Prometheus, he is Caesar.
The real, the eternal Prometheus has now assumed the aspect of one of his victims"
(*R* 245).

79. Srigley, "Albert Camus's Political Philosophy," 76.

Chapter 3. Messianism and the Age of Senility

In this chapter I use the revised text of *Waiting for Godot* contained in *The Theatrical Notebooks of Samuel Beckett*, vol. 1: *Waiting for Godot*, ed. Dougald McMillan
and James Knowlson (New York: Grove Press, 1993). All references to the revised
text are indicated by page numbers in parentheses. McMillan and Knowlson write
that the revised text "is based on Samuel Beckett's own direction of *Warten auf
Godot* at the Schiller-Theatre in Berlin in March 1975, on two English-language
adaptations of that production and on the various annotated scripts and notebooks
that were prepared for these three productions" (3). According to McMillan and
Knowlson, Beckett approved the publication of the revised English text before his
death in 1989 (v). The revised text contains several important alterations of Beckett's original French version (*En attendant Godot* [Paris: Éditions de Minuit, 1952])
and his initial English translation (*Waiting for Godot* [New York: Grove Press, 1954]).
I note some of these significant revisions where applicable. The McMillan and
Knowlson volume also contains Beckett's notebook for the 1975 Schiller-Theatre
production of *Godot*, as well as an introduction and textual notes by the editors for
the revised text. I refer to these in notes.

1. All quotations from Augustine's *Two Books on Genesis against the Manichees* are taken from *The Fathers of the Church*, vol. 84, ed. Thomas P. Halton, trans. Roland J. Teske (Washington, D.C.: Catholic University of America, 1991). For the Latin text, I refer to *De Genesis Contra Manichaeos* in *Sancti Augustini Opera*, vol. 91, ed. Dorothea Weber (Wien: Österreichischen Akademie der Wissenschaften, 1998).

2. See Augustine, *Two Books on Genesis*, 1.23.35–40. Augustine also discusses these ages in a number of his other writings. For example, see *CG* 10.14, 16.24 and 43, 22.30; *The First Catechetical Instruction*, 22.39; *Eighty Three Different Questions*, 58.2, 64.2; and *Of True Religion*, 26.48–49, 27.50.

3. See Gen. 2:1–3.

4. Augustine, *Two Books on Genesis*, 1.23.41.

5. For a commentary on the *saeculum senescens*, see Eric Voegelin, *Collected Works*, vol. 19, 211–12.

6. Augustine, *Two Books on Genesis*, 1.23.40.

7. Ibid.

8. Ibid., 1.24.42. Also see Augustine, *Eighty Three Different Questions*, 58.2.

9. For a historical account of the personal and political excesses that fervent millennial expectations can cause, see Norman Cohn, *The Pursuit of the Millennium* (New York: Oxford University Press, 1957).

10. See especially Augustine's criticisms of the Manichaeans in *On the Morals of the Manichaeans* and *Concerning the Nature of Good, against the Manichaeans*. Both works are found in vol. 4 of *The Writings against the Manichaeans and against the Donatists, Nicene and Post-Nicene Fathers of the Christian Church*, ed. Philip Schaff (Grand Rapids: Eerdmans, 1956), 65–89, 347–65.

11. Augustine, *Two Books on Genesis*, 1.23.41. Augustine quotes Luke 18:8.

12. Augustine, *CG* 16.24.

13. See Augustine's speculations about the end of the world and final judgment in *CG* 20–22.

14. John D. Caputo, *Deconstruction in a Nutshell: A Conversation with Jacques Derrida* (New York: Fordham University Press, 1997), 25.

15. Ibid., 22–23; emphasis in original.

16. Ibid., 23.

17. Jacques Derrida, *Specters of Marx: The State of Debt, the Work of Mourning, and the New International*, trans. Peggy Kamuf (New York: Routledge, 1994), 90.

18. Caputo, *Deconstruction in a Nutshell*, 172.

19. Derrida confesses that he oscillates between these two hypotheses. See Caputo, *Deconstruction in a Nutshell*, 24. He also claims that these two hypotheses are not mutually exclusive. See Derrida, *Specters of Marx*, 168. Also see Caputo's commentary in his *Deconstruction in a Nutshell*, 170.

20. Caputo, *Deconstruction in a Nutshell*, 23–24.

21. Derrida, *Specters of Marx*, 168.

22. Caputo, *Deconstruction in a Nutshell*, 21–22.

23. Derrida, *Specters of Marx*, 168.

24. Ibid., 88, 90.

25. Ibid., 89. Caputo writes, "Deconstruction is the relentless pursuit of *the* impossible," and "Deconstruction is a passion for justice, for the impossible" (*Deconstruction in a Nutshell*, 32, 173; emphasis in original).

26. Derrida, *Specters of Marx*, 168.

27. Derrida says, "Justice and gift should go beyond calculation. This does not mean that we should not calculate. . . . But there is a point or limit beyond which calculation must fail, and we must recognize that. What I tried to think or suggest is a concept of the political and of democracy that would be compatible with, that could be articulated with, these impossible notions of the gift and justice" (Caputo, *Deconstruction in a Nutshell*, 19).

28. This might be intentional. Derrida confesses to his own "love and admiration for St. Augustine." Derrida goes so far as to announce that there is a "love story and a deconstruction" between himself and the bishop of Hippo (Caputo, *Deconstruction in a Nutshell*, 21).

29. Caputo, *Deconstruction in a Nutshell*, 24.

30. Derrida, *Specters of Marx*, 90.

31. Caputo, *Deconstruction in a Nutshell*, 24–25.

32. Derrida, *Specters of Marx*, 89.

33. Ibid., 90.

34. Colin Duckworth, Introduction to his *Samuel Beckett: En attendant Godot* (London: George G. Harrap, 1966), lvii.

35. Beckett himself was not entirely adverse to this suggestion. See Anthony Cronin, *Samuel Beckett: The Last Modernist* (London: Flamingo, 1996), 582.

36. See Beckett's diagram of this in Beryl S. Fletcher and John Fletcher, *A Student's Guide to the Plays of Samuel Beckett* (London: Faber and Faber, 1985), 73.

37. See the full description of the "tree" exercise in McMillan and Knowlson, *Theatrical Notebooks*, 1:161. The characters also evoke the image of Christ and the two thieves with their bodies. In Act 1, Vladimir and Estragon support Lucky on both his left and right sides while he extends his arms around them in cruciform fashion (41). In Act 2, this same pose is struck with Pozzo (77–78). In the original English version, Pozzo wonders whether Didi and Gogo are "highwaymen" (i.e., thieves) (Beckett, *Waiting for Godot*, 97). Beckett took out Pozzo's reference to "highwaymen" in the revised text, along with some of the surrounding dialogue. See *Waiting for Godot*, 165–67.

38. The parallels between Augustine's *saeculum senescens* and the situation in *Waiting for Godot* was first suggested to me by Zdravko Planinc during a lecture he presented at McMaster University in summer 1995.

39. Beckett never completely acknowledged his source for the name "Godot." According to Roger Blin, the first director of the play, Beckett claimed that "Godot"

was suggested by the words for boot in French, *godillot* or *godasse*. This may be related to Estragon's boots, which figure prominently in the play. See John Fletcher, "Roger Blin at Work," *Modern Drama* 8, no. 4 (February 1966): 407. If this is the true source of the name, then "Godot," like "Caligula," literally denotes a boot. However, Beckett continually changed his account of the source of the name. He playfully suggested to Hugh Kenner that he derived the name from a French racing cyclist in the early fifties named Godeau. He also told his friend Con Leventhal about an event he experienced on the corner of the rue Godot le Mauroy, a haunt of prostitutes in Paris. When a prostitute tried unsuccessfully to solicit Beckett's patronage, she sarcastically asked if he was waiting for Godot. For Kenner's and Leventhal's speculations about the source of the name "Godot," see Cronin, *Samuel Beckett: The Last Modernist*, 393. Cronin himself suggests that the name "Godot" could possibly have been derived from Nietzsche's *Gott ist tod* (God is dead).

40. Beckett insisted that emphasis be placed on the first syllable (*God*-ot) rather than the second. See McMillan and Knowlson, *Theatrical Notebooks*, 1:87. Also see Cronin, *Samuel Beckett: The Last Modernist*, 394.

41. Alec Reid, *All I Can Manage, More than I Could: An Approach to the Plays of Samuel Beckett* (Dublin: Dolmen Press, 1968), 65.

42. Alan Schneider, "Waiting for Beckett: A Personal Chronicle," in *Casebook on Waiting for Godot*, ed. Ruby Cohn (New York: Grove Press, 1967), 55. This article was originally published in the *Chelsea Review*, no. 2 (September 1958). It has also been reported that Beckett encouraged Schneider to make a list of over a hundred possibilities as to who or what Godot might be. See McMillan and Knowlson, *Theatrical Notebooks*, 1:87.

43. Ruby Cohn, *Back to Beckett* (Princeton: Princeton University Press, 1973), 132.

44. Universality is often cited as one of the defining features of the theatre of the absurd. Patrice Pavis, for instance, writes that absurdist theatre is characterized by an "ahistorical" structure in which "Man is a timeless abstraction" stripped of any link to time or place. See Pavis, *Dictionary of the Theatre*, 1.

45. Sylvain Zegel, "At the Théâtre de Babylon: *Waiting for Godot* by Samuel Beckett," trans. Ruby Cohn, in *Casebook on Waiting for Godot*, 12. The review originally appeared in *La Libération*, January 7, 1953.

46. Hugh Kenner, *A Reader's Guide to Samuel Beckett* (Syracuse: Syracuse University Press, 1996), 32.

47. Pozzo estimates that Vladimir and Estragon are "Sixty" or "Seventy" (27).

48. This sense of a "great calm" is accentuated by Estragon who says, "Calm . . . calm . . . The English say cawm" (15). By using an English accent, Estragon draws out the length of the word to suggest something greater than momentary tranquility.

49. In Beckett's original French edition, the tree in Act 2 is "couvert de feuilles" (covered in leaves) (Beckett, *En attendant Godot*, 95). In the original English edition, the tree "has four or five leaves" (Beckett, *Waiting for Godot*, 62). In the revised text,

which is based on Beckett's own directions, the tree has only three leaves. McMillan and Knowlson argue that the three leaves "implicitly . . . echo the theme of Christ and the two thieves" (*Theatrical Notebooks*, 1:145).

50. The phrase "vers 1900" is used in Beckett's original French edition (*En attendant Godot*, 13).

51. Later, Vladimir says, "We are waiting for Godot to come . . . or for night to fall" (73).

52. This is noted by Darko Suvin in "Preparing for Godot—or the Purgatory of Individualism," in *Casebook on Waiting for Godot*, 129. Survin's article was originally published in *Tulane Drama Review* 11, no. 4 (Summer 1967).

53. Bert O. States, *Shape of Paradox: An Essay on "Waiting for Godot"* (Berkeley: University of California Press, 1978).

54. Beckett himself alluded to the crucial importance of *Godot*'s two-act structure: "One act would have been too little, and three acts would have been too much" (Shenker, "Moody Man of Letters," 3).

55. In the original French and English versions, Estragon sits on a "terre," or mound, of earth (Beckett, *En attendant Godot*, 11; and *Waiting for Godot*, 2). However, Beckett wanted a "stone" to be used in every production he was associated with. McMillan and Knowlson write, "Beckett insisted on a stone in order to represent 'animal, vegetable, mineral'" (*Theatrical Notebooks* 1:89).

56. Vladimir refers to himself as "Vladimir" in Act 1 (9). In Act 2, he utters the name "Estragon" while speaking to himself (82).

57. This is how Beckett tended to cast these characters in any production with which he was involved. See McMillan and Knowlson, *Theatrical Notebooks*, 1:87. In the actual text, Vladimir claims he is heavier than Estragon, though he is not entirely certain (16–17).

58. According to Walter Asmus, Beckett said, "Estragon is on the ground; he belongs to the stone. Vladimir is light; he is oriented towards the sky. He belongs to the tree" (Walter Asmus, "Beckett Directs Godot," *Theatre Quarterly* 5, no. 19 [1975]: 21).

59. See Eugene Webb, *The Plays of Samuel Beckett* (Seattle: University of Washington Press, 1972), 27.

60. Estragon uses the phrase, "The wind in the reeds," which is a possible allusion to Yeats's collection of poems, *The Wind among the Reeds*. It might also refer to Christ's words in Matthew 11:7: "A reed shaken by the wind." The reference to Shelley occurs at the end of Act 1 when Estragon says to the moon, "Pale for weariness. . . . Of climbing heaven and gazing on the likes of us" (48). These words are taken from Shelley's poem "To the Moon": "Art thou pale for weariness / Of climbing heaven and gazing on the earth." See McMillan and Knowlson, *Theatrical Notebooks*, 1:108, 144. The issue of Estragon's former employment (or unemployment) as a poet occurs toward the beginning of the play. Vladimir says, "You should have been a poet," to which Estragon responds, "I was. (*Gesture towards his rags.*) Isn't that obvious?" (11).

61. Webb, *Plays of Samuel Beckett,* 144 n. 2. Webb notes that the name "Vladimir" was made famous by St. Vladimir (d. 1015) who consolidated the Russian state at Kiev and imposed Christianity on its people.

62. The same exchange occurs on pp. 44, 61, 64, 71, and 77. Two variations occur on pp. 19 and 84. See Beckett's note of this in McMillan and Knowlson, *Theatrical Notebooks,* 1:347. Estragon also says to himself, "Let's go. (*Half rises.*) We can't. (*Sits again.*) Ah yes!" (81). It should be noted that there is only one time in the play when Estragon reminds Vladimir that they are "waiting for Godot" (see 78–79).

63. There is one moment when the opposite occurs. Vladimir says, "Let's go," to which Estragon responds, "So soon?" (27). Shortly after this, Vladimir says "Let's go" again (35).

64. See Webb, *Plays of Samuel Beckett,* 144 n. 3.

65. Even then, sitting is extremely difficult for Pozzo. At one point Pozzo must be compelled to sit by Estragon. He remains seated for only three words (34).

66. See McMillan and Knowlson, *Theatrical Notebooks,* 1:116.

67. McMillan and Knowlson write, "Lucky's dance in [the] Schiller [production] was a structured image of aspiration leading to failure" (*Theatrical Notebooks,* 1:129).

68. Beckett uses the phrase in his notebook for the Schiller-Theatre production (McMillan and Knowlson, *Theatrical Notebooks,* 1:179, 291–99).

69. Beckett uses the phrase "research tandems" in his Schiller-Theatre production notebook to refer to Lucky's scholarly sources (McMillan and Knowlson, *Theatrical Notebooks,* 1:295). Many of the scholars whom Lucky cites have names that evoke something either sexual or scatological, such as *Teste*w, *Cun*ard, *Fart*ov, *Belche*r, *Peter*man.

70. In the original French and English versions Pozzo says, "Atlas, son of Jupiter." (Beckett, *En attendant Godot,* 50; and *Waiting for Godot,* 30). In Hesiod, however, Atlas is the son of Japetos (*Theogony,* 507–9). According to McMillan and Knowlson, Beckett replaced Jupiter with Japetos during rehearsals for the Schiller-Theatre production on the recommendation of Ruby Cohn. They note that Beckett, in making this correction, "actively avoided leaving Pozzo in error" (McMillan and Knowlson, *Theatrical Notebooks,* 1:120).

71. In the original French and English versions, Beckett had Vladimir enter the stage by himself at the start of Act 2, followed a little later by Estragon (*En attendant Godot,* 95–97; and *Waiting for Godot,* 62–63). In the revised text, however, the two of them are onstage immediately when the curtain rises (50). This not only emphasizes the inseparability of Vladimir and Estragon but also the degree to which they are rooted in one place. There are a few moments in the play when they actually exit the stage, but they are never gone for very long (see 15, 33, 66–67).

72. The same dialogue occurs at the end of Act 1, but the speakers are reversed (50).

73. Derrida, *Specters of Marx*, 90.

74. Duckworth, "Introduction," lxiii.

75. Lucky uses this phrase twice in his Think. The phrase "who can doubt it" also occurs twice (39–40).

76. In his notebook for the Schiller-Theatre production, Beckett divided Lucky's Think into three main parts, under the headings "Indifferent Heaven," "Dwindling Man," and "Earth abode of stones." He also identifies a "cadenza" at the end of the third section in which Lucky reiterates the themes of his Think. The "Indifferent Heaven" section extends from Lucky saying "Better than nothing" to where he says "but not so fast"; "Dwindling Man" extends from "What is more" to "waste and pine"; "Earth abode of stones" extends from "And considering" to "the facts are there but"; and finally, the "cadenza" extends from "time will tell I resume" to "unfinished." See McMillan and Knowlson, *Theatrical Notebooks*, 1:291.

77. Lucky says "for reasons unknown" nine times throughout his Think. "Beyond all doubt" only occurs twice (39–40).

78. See McMillan and Knowlson, *Theatrical Notebooks*, 1:134.

79. Beckett, *En attendant Godot*, 73. In the Schiller-Theatre production, Beckett had Lucky mention the German neoclassicist Johann Christoph Gottsched (1700–1766). Like Voltaire, Gottsched is associated with the Enlightenment. See McMillan and Knowlson, *Theatrical Notebooks*, 1:135.

80. As Berkeley claims, through his character Philonous: "For philosophers, though they acknowledge all corporeal beings to be perceived by God, yet they attribute to them an absolute subsistence distinct from their being perceived by any mind whatever, which I do not. Besides, is there no difference between saying, *there is a God, therefore he perceives all things:* and saying, *sensible things do really exist: and if they exist, they are necessarily perceived by an infinite mind: therefore there is an infinite mind, or God.* This furnishes you with a direct and immediate demonstration, for a most evident principle, of the *being of a God*" (George Berkeley, *Three Dialogues between Hylas and Philonous*, ed. Jonathan Dancy [Oxford: Oxford University Press, 1998], 98 [2.212], emphasis in original).

81. Estragon, while doing his "tree" exercise, asks, "Do you think God sees me?" (70).

82. John 19:30.

83. He says it four times during his "Think."

84. Beckett, *En attendant Godot*, 51. McMillan and Knowlson write that this allusion to "Saint Sauveur" adds "yet another to the many religious associations found in the original text of the play." They also point out that the "rue Saint-Sauveur in Paris's 2ème arrondissement has . . . a certain reputation as a haunt of prostitutes!" (McMillan and Knowlson, *Theatrical Notebooks*, 1:120). This suggests that the salvation Pozzo seeks is analogous to a squalid red-light district. The link between prostitution and the characters' desires is implied in other passages. In Act 2, Vladimir asks the Boy whether Godot has a "fair," "black," or "red" beard (83),

recalling Estragon's joke in Act 1 about the "fair," "dark," and "red-haired" prostitutes (15). This suggests that Godot is an imaginary whore who can perform eschatological favors. As we have seen, one of Beckett's few acknowledged sources for the name "Godot" comes from rue Godot le Mauroy, another area in Paris renowned for its prostitutes.

85. In Act 1, Pozzo and Lucky enter from upstage right and exit upstage left (21, 43–44). In Act 2, they enter from the left and exit on the right (70, 80–81).

86. Shakespeare, *Hamlet*, 3.1.79–83. Vladimir alludes to *Hamlet* 3.1.57 when he asks, "What are we doing here, *that* is the question" (73).

87. Vladimir assures Estragon that this helps pass the time more "rapidly" (44).

88. Of the rest, fourteen are ignored, one is aborted, one is answered on condition, and the status of another is unknown. See Beckett's notebook for the Schiller-Theatre production in McMillan and Knowlson, *Theatrical Notebooks*, 1:355.

89. During rehearsals for a production of *Godot* at the Gate Theatre in Dublin, Beckett is quoted saying that Vladimir and Estragon wait for "salvation or whatever" (Cronin, *Samuel Beckett: The Last Modernist*, 582).

90. See Knowlson, *Damned to Fame*, 67–68.

91. Harold Hobson, "Samuel Beckett, Dramatist of the Year," in *International Theatre Annual*, no. 1 (London: John Calder, 1956), 153. No scholar has ever been able to locate the source of the quotation that Beckett attributes to Augustine, leading to speculation that it is apocryphal. States directs us to a sentence by Augustine that is strikingly similar: "Let the good man fear lest he perish through pride; let the evil man not despair (*desperet*) of his many wicked acts" (*The Shape of Paradox*, 3 n. 4). The sentence is found in Augustine, "De Symbolo ad Catechumenos," *Patrologiae Latina*, vol. 40, ed. J. P. Migne (Paris, 1945), col. 646.

92. Hobson, "Samuel Beckett, Dramatist of the Year," 153. Contrary to what Beckett says in this quotation, Estragon is not trying to put his left boot on. When the play begins, he is struggling to take it off (9).

93. See States, *The Shape of Paradox*, 1–3.

94. Pozzo says, "I might just as well have been in [Lucky's] shoes and he in mine. If chance had not fated otherwise. To each his due" (30).

95. In this passage, Lucky twice says "quaquaquaqua." *Qua* means "in the capacity of" or "by virtue of being," and Pozzo, like his teacher, says "Qua sky" (35). Clearly, Lucky has a pedantic fascination with the term. But Lucky is actually trying to say "quaversalis" (in the capacity of being universal). During rehearsals for the Schiller-Theatre production in Berlin, Beckett is reported to have said, " It concerns a god who turns himself in all directions at the same time. Lucky wants to say 'quaquaquaquaversalis' but he can't bring it out. He says instead only quaquaquaqua" (Asmus, "Beckett Directs Godot," 22).

96. Immediately after this, Vladimir corrects Estragon by saying that the "Saviour" did not save the thieves from "hell" but from "death" (12). Vladimir is not exactly sure what they were saved from.

97. See Luke 23:39–43.

98. See Mark 15:27, 32; and Matt. 27:38, 44. The Gospel of John does not say that Jesus was crucified with "thieves," but it does mention that he was crucified between "two others" (John 19:18). One can only speculate whether Beckett intended Vladimir to be wrong about the Gospels. It is certainly true that Vladimir's memory of the Bible is eroding. At another point in the play he tries to quote Proverbs 33:12, but he forgets the quotation and the source ("Hope deferred maketh the something sick, who said that?" [10]). In the passage above concerning the thieves, it would surely be more devastating for Vladimir to remember that in *two* of the four Gospels both thieves are presumably damned.

99. This crucial passage occurs in the original French version of *Godot* (Beckett, *En attendant Godot*, 30) but not in Beckett's original English translation. It is not known whether Beckett intentionally omitted these lines or if it was an oversight committed by Beckett or someone else in preparation for the first English edition. When revising the play with director Walter Asmus, Beckett restored the missing passage to the English text. See McMillan and Knowlson, *Theatrical Notebooks*, 1:xv–xvi, 108–9.

100. Gen. 4:1–5.

101. Beckett's reference to Matthew 25 is identified by Ruby Cohn in *Back to Beckett*, 130.

102. Matt. 25:31–34, 41. For an Old Testament account of "goats" bearing punishment for the sins of people, see Lev. 16:6–10, 15–22.

103. This reversal of the symbolism in Matthew 25 is discussed by Kristin Morrison in *Canters and Chronicles: The Use of Narrative in the Plays of Samuel Beckett and Harold Pinter* (Chicago: University of Chicago Press, 1983), 21–22.

104. Duckworth writes, "What the tramps expect from Godot—which is extremely vague—and what he may in fact be capable of, could be very different indeed. We should not, therefore, be surprised if he is a personification of evil" (Duckworth, "Introduction," lxi–lxii).

105. Again, Vladimir uses biblical images to describe Godot's second coming. This idea of Godot shouting at his horse evokes the image of Christ in Revelation 19:11–16, returning on a "white horse" and shouting a "sword" from his mouth to "strike down" the sinful.

106. Beckett denied that Godot could be identified as Pozzo. When asked by Duckworth, "Is Pozzo Godot?" Beckett replied, "No. It is implied in the text, but it's not true" (Duckworth, "Introduction," lx). The significance of Beckett's implication is the point.

107. Derrida does not explicitly deal with this notion of the damned within the messianic, but he suggests that the concept of an elected people is an unfortunate aspect of messianism. See Caputo, *Deconstruction in a Nutshell*, 23.

108. Derrida, *Specters of Marx*, 168. The term "desertification" is used by Caputo in *Decontruction in a Nutshell*, 172.

109. Estragon falls asleep three times in the play and has a dream in each instance. His dreams are not a consistent source of comfort. The status of his first dream in Act 1 is uncertain (15), but he has a nightmare of falling from a height in Act 2 (64). Only once does he dream of happiness (81). See Beckett's note on "Estragon's sleeps" in McMillan and Knowlson, *Theatrical Notebooks*, 1:311.

110. Homer, *Odyssey*, 11.487–91.

Epilogue I. The Two "Nothings" of *Caligula* and *Waiting for Godot*

1. Nina Sjursen, "La puissance et l'impuissance: Dialogue entre *Caligula* et *En attendant Godot*," in *Camus et le Théâtre*, ed. Jacqueline Lévi-Valensi (Paris: Imec Éditions, 1992), 83–84.

2. Ibid., 92.

3. Ibid., 89.

4. Ibid., 84.

5. Camus, "Neither Victims nor Executioners," 121.

6. Baudrillard, *Paroxysm*, 25.

7. Jean Baudrillard, *The Perfect Crime,* trans. Chris Turner (London: Verso, 1996), 67.

8. Justin O'Brien, in his English translation of *Sisyphus*, italicizes the words "*without appeal*." In the original French, Camus does not italicize "sans appel" (*Essais*, 137).

9. Homer, *Odyssey*, 11.593–600.

10. Camus overstates the case when he writes, "[Sisyphus] too concludes that all is well" (*MS* 91). If "all is well," then there would be no rupture, and hence no Sisyphean task.

11. Cook, "Albert Camus' *Caligula*," 203.

12. See *MS* 24–38, 81–83, 92–102.

13. See Sjursen, "La puissance et l'impuissance," 85.

Chapter 4. Expediency and the Machiavel

1. See Eccles. 3:1–8; 9:1–10.

2. Niccolò Machiavelli, *Mandragola*, trans. Mera J. Flaumenhaft (Prospect Heights: Waveland Press, 1981), Act 4, scene 6.

3. All references to *The Prince* indicate chapter number.

4. Silvia Ruffo-Fiore writes, "Even though *The Prince* had originally appeared with Pope Clement VII's imprimatur, in 1559 Pope Paul IV placed it on the Index, where it remained until 1890. In 1562 the Council of Trent confirmed his papal edict" (Silvia Ruffo-Fiore, *Niccolò Machiavelli* [Boston: Twayne Publishers,

1982], 132). Machiavelli did not live to see his work placed on the Index. Indeed, he did not live to see the publication of *The Prince*, which occurred in 1532, five years after his death.

5. Harvey Mansfield, *Machiavelli's Virtue* (Chicago: University of Chicago Press, 1996), 7–8.

6. All references to the *Discourses* indicate book number, chapter number or preface (Pr), and paragraph number.

7. Mansfield, *Machiavelli's Virtue*, 109.

8. See Strauss, "The Three Waves of Modernity," 87–89. Also see Roger D. Masters, *Machiavelli, Leonardo, and the Science of Power* (Notre Dame: University of Notre Dame Press, 1996).

9. See Mansfield, *Machiavelli's Virtue*, 296.

10. For Aristotle's extended account of prudence as an "intellectual virtue," and how it is distinct from "intelligence" and "theoretical wisdom," see *NE* 6.5 and 6.8–13. In *The Politics,* Aristotle claims that prudence is a virtue that only a ruler can possess (see 3.5, 1277b 25–32).

11. Also see *NE* 6.6.

12. Aristotle uses the term *epieikēs* to describe the person who is equitable and fair in his dealings with others (see *NE* 5.10) According to Aristotle, this stems from a general "truthfulness" (*alētheia*) in character (see *NE* 4.7). When such a person practices fairness in politics, he realizes the virtue of "justice."

13. See Allan Gilbert, *Machiavelli's Prince and Its Forerunners* (Durham: Duke University Press, 1968), 77–83; Sydney Anglo, *Machiavelli: A Dissection* (London: Victor Gollancz, 1969), 71–73, 189–90.

14. Isaiah Berlin, "The Originality of Machiavelli," in *Studies on Machiavelli,* ed. Myron P. Gilmore (Florence: G. C. Sansoni, 1972), 162.

15. Ibid., 150.

16. Clifford Orwin, "Machiavelli's Unchristian Charity," *American Political Science Review* 72 (1978): 1218.

17. Berlin writes: "The Bible, Herodotus, Thucydides, Plato, Aristotle—to take only some of the fundamental works of western culture—the characters of Jacob or Joshua or David, Samuel's advice to Saul, Thucydides' Melian dialogue or his account of at least one ferocious but rescinded Athenian resolution, the philosophies of Thrasymachus and Callicles [in Plato], Aristotle's advice to tyrants in *The Politics,* Carneades' speeches to the Roman Senate as described by Cicero, Augustine's view of the secular state from one vantage point, and Marsilio's from another—all of these had cast enough light on political realities to shock the credulous and naive out of uncritical idealism" (Berlin, "The Originality of Machiavelli," 150). Orwin writes, "There would not have been, as is so often assumed, anything new in the discovery of a wide discrepancy between the purest goodness and the qualities most conducive to political success. . . . We need only consider the impact of the fates of Socrates and Christ upon the traditions that sprang from them in order to see that this 'Machiavellian' insight had defined the central moral problem with

which Machiavelli's predecessors had wrestled" (Orwin, "Machiavelli's Unchristian Charity," 1218).

18. See especially Aristotle's account of how tyrants can best preserve themselves in the *Politics* 5.10–11.

19. See Giuseppe Prezzolini, "The Christian Roots of Machiavelli's Moral Pessimism," *Review of National Literatures* 1, no. 1 (Spring 1970): 26–37.

20. Leo Strauss, "Niccolo Machiavelli," in *History of Political Philosophy,* 3d ed., ed. Leo Strauss and Joseph Cropsey (Chicago: University of Chicago Press, 1987), 297.

21. For a discussion of the various issues surrounding "legitimacy," see Tim Spiekerman, *Shakespeare's Political Realism: The English History Plays* (Albany: State University of New York Press, 2001), 17–24.

22. Quoted in Ernst H. Kantorowicz, *The King's Two Bodies: A Study in Mediaeval Political Theology* (Princeton: Princeton University Press, 1957), 7.

23. Ibid., 8.

24. David Bevington, Introduction to *The Complete Works of Shakespeare,* 4th ed., ed. David Bevington (New York: Longman, 1997), xxii.

25. Spiekerman, *Shakespeare's Political Realism,* 23.

26. Edward Meyer, *Machiavelli and the Elizabethan Drama* (Weimar: Litterarhistorische Forschungen, 1897), xi. There is an extensive body of literature on Machiavelli and the Elizabethans. See Mario Praz, "Machiavelli and the Elizabethans," *Proceedings of the British Academy* 13 (1928): 49–97; Irving Ribner, "The Significance of Gentillet's *Contre-Machiavel,*" *Modern Language Quarterly* 10 (1949): 177–87, and "Marlow and Machiavelli," *Comparative Literature* 6 (1954): 348–56; Antonio D'Andrea, "Studies on Machiavelli and His Reputation in the Sixteenth Century: I, Marlowe's Prologue to *The Jew of Malta,*" *Medieval and Renaissance Studies* 5 (1960): 214–48; Felix Raab, *The English Face of Machiavelli* (London: Routledge & Kegan Paul, 1964); Christopher Morris, "Machiavelli's Reputation in Tudor England," *Il pensiero politico* 2 (1969): 416–33; N. W. Bawcutt, "Some Elizabethan Allusions to Machiavelli," *English Miscellany* 20 (1969): 53–74; Daniel C. Boughner, *The Devil's Disciple: Ben Jonson's Debt to Machiavelli* (New York: Philosophical Library, 1978); Margaret Scott, "Machiavelli and the Machiavel," *Renaissance Drama* 15 (1984): 147–74.

27. See Meyer, *Machiavelli and the Elizabethan Drama,* 30.

28. Christopher Marlowe, *The Jew of Malta,* prologue, lines 29–30, 32, 33–35. I have used the edition of the play contained in Marlowe, *The Complete Plays,* ed. J. B. Steane (London: Penguin Books, 1969).

29. See Bernard Spivack, *Shakespeare and the Allegory of Evil* (New York: Columbia University Press, 1958), 374–75.

30. For an account of the main features of the morality drama and the role of Vice, see Spivack, *Shakespeare and the Allegory of Evil,* 96–150.

31. It has also been argued that there is a strong affinity between the Machiavel and the Senecan tyrant of ancient Roman tragedy. See Praz, "Machiavelli and the Elizabethans," 49–97.

32. Meyer, *Machiavelli and the Elizabethan Drama*, ix.

33. Innocent Gentillet, *A Discourse upon the Meanes of Wel Governing and Maintaining in Good Peace a Kingdom*, trans. Simon Patericke (London, 1602).

34. Meyer, *Machiavelli and the Elizabethan Drama*, x.

35. See ibid., 3.

36. For example, Spivack implicitly accepts Meyer's argument when he writes, "The [Elizabethan] age was aware of Machiavellianism before it was aware of Machiavelli" (*Shakespeare and the Allegory of Evil*, 376).

37. See Napoleone Orsini, "Machiavelli's *Discourses*: A MSS Translation of 1599," *Times Literary Supplement* 10 (October 1936): 820; and "Elizabethan Manuscript Translations of Machiavelli's *Prince*," *Journal of the Warburg and Courtauld Institutes* 1 (1937–38): 166–69. Also see Hardin Craig, ed., *Machiavelli's Prince: An Elizabethan Translation* (Chapel Hill: University of North Carolina Press, 1944), v–xxxii.

38. Scott, "Machiavelli and the Machiavel," 150.

39. For accounts of John Wolfe's publication of Machiavelli's works, see A. Gerber, "All of the Five Fictitious Italian Editions of the Writings of Machiavelli and Three of Those of Pietro Aretino, Printed by John Wolfe of London (1584–88)," *Modern Language Notes* 22 (1907): 129–35; and L. Goldberg, "A Note on John Wolfe, Elizabethan Printer," *Historical Studies: Australia and New Zealand* 7, no. 25 (1955): 55–61.

40. See Scott, "Machiavelli and the Machiavel," 151.

41. Ibid., 164.

42. Ibid., 172.

43. There are three references to Machiavelli in Shakespeare's plays: *1 Henry VI*, 4.4.74; *3 Henry VI*, 3.2.193; *The Merry Wives of Windsor* 3.1.96.

44. Spiekerman, *Shakespeare's Political Realism*, 156.

45. Spiekerman writes, "The list of Shakespearean characters who have been called, by one critic or another, 'Machiavellian,' is extensive: Aaron, Iago, Edmund, Octavius, Cassius, Macbeth, Claudio, Faulconbridge, Henry IV, Henry V, Richard III. Whether a particular 'Machiavellian' character is true to type or a mere caricature, and whether Shakespeare admires or disdains him, is debatable in each case" (*Shakespeare's Political Realism*, 25).

46. Shakespeare, *3 Henry VI*, 3.2.193.

Chapter 5. Evil and Virtue in *Mandragola*

In this chapter I use Mera J. Flaumenhaft's translation of *Mandragola*. I refer to act and scene numbers in parentheses. The prologue to the play is referred to with the abbreviation Pr. in parentheses. For the Italian, I use the edition of *Mandragola* contained in Niccolò Machiavelli, Machiavelli, *Il teatro e gli scritti letterari*, ed. Franco Gaeta (Milan: Feltrinelli, 1965), 53–112.

1. For surveys of Renaissance Italian theatre, see Marvin T. Herrick, *Italian Comedy in the Renaissance* (Urbana: University of Illinois Press, 1960) and *Italian Tragedy in the Renaissance* (Urbana: University of Illinois Press, 1965); Douglas Radcliff-Ulmstead, *The Birth of Modern Comedy in Renaissance Italy* (Chicago: University of Chicago Press, 1969).

2. For commentaries on the *commedia erudita,* see Herrick, *Italian Comedy in the Renaissance,* 60–164; Radcliff-Ulmstead, *The Birth of Modern Comedy,* 59–155.

3. Herrick writes, "The beginnings of modern tragedy . . . were in Latin and in Italy, the cradle of all the modern arts" (Herrick, *Italian Tragedy in the Renaissance,* 4). Radcliff-Ulmstead writes, "Italian playwrights turned to Roman antiquity to find a dramatic technique, but they combined literary traditions and contemporary reality of their own country to create a comic theatre that helped determine the course of modern European drama" (Radcliff-Ulmstead, *The Birth of Modern Comedy,* 243).

4. Laura Richards writes that *Mandragola* is "generally considered to be the finest comedy of the Italian Renaissance" (Machiavelli, Niccolo, in *The Cambridge Guide to the Theatre,* ed. Martin Banham, rev. ed. [Cambridge: Cambridge University Press, 1992], 603). Bruce Penman writes that Machiavelli is "the author of what is generally considered to be the best comedy in the Italian language—*The Mandragola*" (*Five Italian Renaissance Comedies,* ed. Bruce Penman [Harmondsworth: Penguin Books, 1978], 13). Samuel Beckett shared this high regard for *Mandragola.* Kay Boyle recounts how in 1930 Beckett "wanted to make me understand that [*Mandragola*] was the most powerful play in the Italian language" (Boyle, "All Mankind Is Us," in *Samuel Beckett: A Collection of Criticism,* ed. Ruby Cohn [New York: McGraw-Hill, 1975], 16). James Knowlson reports that "Beckett was still 'boosting' *Mandragola* to a German director, Eggers-Kastner, in Munich in 1937" (Knowlson, *Damned to Fame,* 639 n. 83).

5. See Sergio Bertelli, "When Did Machiavelli Write *Mandragola?*" *Renaissance Quarterly* 24 (1971): 324.

6. See James B. Atkinson, "An Essay on Machiavelli and Comedy," in *The Comedies of Machiavelli,* ed. and trans. David Sices and James B. Atkinson (Hanover: University Press of New England, 1985), 3.

7. See Bertelli, "When Did Machiavelli Write *Mandragola,*" 324.

8. Niccolò Machiavelli, *Clizia,* trans. Daniel T. Gallagher (Prospect Heights: Waveland Press, 1996), Pr. For the Italian, I use the edition of *Clizia* contained in Machiavelli, *Il teatro e gli scritti letterari,* 113–66.

9. See Mera Flaumenhaft, "The Comic Remedy in Private Spectacle: Machiavelli's *Mandragola,*" in her *Civic Spectacle,* 86–88. An earlier version of this article appears in *Interpretation: A Journal of Political Philosophy* 7, no. 2 (1978), 33–74.

10. This is distinct from the *commedia dell'arte* which emerged in northern Italy toward the middle of the sixteenth century. *Commedia dell'arte* was performed by professional acting companies who mounted improvised comedies in

both public piazzas and private courts. See Herrick, *Italian Comedy in the Renaissance*, 210–27. For a survey of the *commedia dell'arte*, see Kenneth Richards and Laura Richards, *The Commedia dell'Arte: A Documentary History* (Oxford: Blackwell, 1990).

11. Flaumenhaft, *The Civic Spectacle*, 108; emphasis in original.

12. James Atkinson writes, "The record of performances indicates that the play's reputation spread widely and developed quickly throughout Renaissance Italy" (Atkinson, "An Essay on Machiavelli and Comedy," 15).

13. See Bertelli, "When Did Machiavelli Write Mandragola," 326; and Atkinson, "An Essay on Machiavelli and Comedy," 13–15. Bertelli also says it is possible that the play was written in 1504.

14. See Bertelli, "When Did Machiavelli Write *Mandragola*," 321.

15. Ibid., 322–23.

16. Mansfield writes: "Machiavelli's *Art of War* does not appear to be as Machiavellian as his other major prose works" (Mansfield, *Machiavelli's Virtue*, 191).

17. See Machiavelli's "Dedicatory Letter" to Lorenzo de' Medici at the start of *The Prince* and his "Greeting" letter to Zanobi Buondelmonti and Cosimo Rucellai at the start of *Discourses on Livy*. Also see Mansfield's commentary in *Machiavelli's Virtue*, 58.

18. Mansfield, *Machiavelli's Virtue*, 194.

19. Niccolò Machiavelli, "A Dialogue on Language," in *The Literary Works of Machiavelli*, ed. and trans. J. R. Hale (London: Oxford University Press, 1961), 188.

20. Machiavelli had worked as a secretary and assistant for Piero Soderini, the Gonfaloniere of the Florentine republic. However, in September 1512 the Medici ousted Soderini from power. In November, Machiavelli was purged from office. He was subsequently arrested and tortured because his name was found on a list of anti-Medici conspirators. See Sebastian de Grazia, *Machiavelli in Hell* (Princeton: Princeton University Press, 1989), 32–40.

21. Machiavelli, *Clizia*, Pr.

22. Timothy J. Lukes, "Fortune Comes of Age (in Machiavelli's Literary Works)," *Sixteenth Century Journal* 11, no. 4 (1980): 37 n. 15.

23. Machiavelli, "A Dialogue on Language," 188.

24. See Flaumenhaft, *The Civic Spectacle*, 108.

25. See Theodore A. Sumberg, "*La Mandragola*: An Interpretation," *Journal of Politics* 23 (1961): 320–40. Sumberg writes that the play "contains some dangerous elements of Machiavelli's political teaching meant only for the few who will understand and apply them" (321).

26. See Flaumenhaft, *The Civic Spectacle*, 86–88.

27. See Matt. 5–7.

28. See Mansfield, *Machiavelli's Virtue*, 9.

29. See *D* 1.15, 2.2, 8, 19. Also see *D* 2.1 and *P* 3.

30. See Mansfield, *Machiavelli's Virtue*, 8–11.

31. See *D* 1.12.2.

32. Hanna Fenichel Pitkin writes, "No epithet is more frequent or more powerful in Machiavelli's vocabulary of abuse than 'effeminate'" (Pitkin, *Fortune Is a Woman: Gender and Politics in the Thought of Machiavelli* [Chicago: University of Chicago Press, 1984], 109–10).

33. The following discussion is based on Mansfield's analysis in *Machiavelli's Virtue*, 6–7.

34. Machiavelli also writes in this passage: "one cannot attribute to fortune or to virtue what [Agathocles] achieved without either" (*P* 8).

35. Machiavelli also tells us initially that Agathocles was "without religion" and friendship. Machiavelli later claims that Agathocles remedied his "state with God and with men" through the effective use of cruelty (*P* 8).

36. See Mansfield, *Machiavelli's Virtue*, 6–7. A similar point is made by Victoria Kahn in "*Virtù* and the Example of Agathocles in Machiavelli's *Prince*," in *Machiavelli and the Discourse of Literature,* ed. Albert Russel Ascoli and Victoria Kahn (Ithaca: Cornell University Press, 1993), 195–217.

37. Strauss, *Thoughts on Machiavelli,* 134. Strauss gives numerous instances in which Machiavelli's account of Livy is markedly different from Livy himself (134–36).

38. Mansfield and Tarcov, Introduction to their translation of *Discourses on Livy,* xix–xx.

39. Livy's account of Lucretia occurs in *History of Rome,* 1.57–59. I use B. O. Foster's translation of Livy in the Loeb edition (Cambridge, Mass.: Harvard University Press, 1919).

40. Livy, 1.58.10–11.

41. Livy, 1.60.2–3.

42. Ronald L. Martinez, "The Pharmacy of Machiavelli: Roman Lucretia in *Mandragola,*" *Renaissance Drama,* 14 (1983): 43.

43. See *D* 2.1, 2.2.2.

44. For an essay exploring the links between Lady Fortune and Madonna Lucrezia, see Susan Behuniak-Long, "The Significance of Lucrezia in Machiavelli's *La Mandragola,*" *Review of Politics* 51, no. 2 (1989): 264–80.

45. See Flaumenhaft's "Note on the Names of Characters" in her translation of *Mandragola,* 57.

46. Charles VIII invaded France in 1494–95. The action of the play is set ten years later, in 1504.

47. See Flaumenhaft, *The Civic Spectacle,* 90–91.

48. See especially book 3 of Boethius's *The Consolation of Philosophy.*

49. Flaumenhaft claims that the misspelling suggests "the sort of bovine mildness that is easily led by the nose" (Flaumenhaft, *The Civic Spectacle,* 89).

50. See Flaumenhaft's "Note on the Names of Characters" in her translation of *Mandragola,* 57.

51. This argument is made by Harvey Mansfield in "The Cuckold in Machiavelli's *Mandragola*," in *The Comedy and Tragedy of Machiavelli: Essays on the Literary Works*, ed. Vickie B. Sullivan (New Haven: Yale University Press, 2000), 25–29.

52. See Mansfield, "The Cuckhold in *Mandragola*," 29. Also see Pitkin, *Fortune is a Woman*, 30.

53. See Mansfield, "The Cuckold in *Mandragola*," 28.

54. Ibid.

55. See Mansfield, *Machiavelli's Virtue*, 49–50.

56. This translation is found in James B. Atkinson and David Sices, trans. and eds., *Machiavelli and His Friends: Their Personal Correspondence* (Dekalb: Northern Illinois University Press, 1996), 336. Flaumenhaft, *The Civic Spectacle*, 99, associates Machiavelli's reflections in this letter with the character Timoteo.

57. See *D* 2.2.2.

58. See Flaumenhaft, *The Civic Spectacle*, 106.

59. See Flaumenhaft, "Note on Names of Characters," *Mandragola*, 57.

60. Flaumenhaft, *The Civic Spectacle*, 104–5, links Timoteo to the Pauline "Timothy."

61. Ligurio later identifies yet another donna in the church (3.4).

62. See Behuniak-Long, "The Significance of Lucrezia," 269.

63. Livy, 1.58.9–10.

64. See Ian Donaldson, *The Rapes of Lucretia: A Myth and its Transformations* (Oxford: Clarendon Press, 1982), 91–92.

65. See Gen. 19:37–38. Also see Flaumenhaft, *The Civic Spectacle*, 104.

66. See *CG* 14.2–4, 11–26.

67. See 1.16.50 of the *Commentary*. I use Denis J. Kavanagh's translation of the *Commentary* in Augustine, *Commentary on the Lord's Sermon on the Mount with Seventeen Related Sermons*, vol. 11 of *The Fathers of the Church* (New York: Fathers of the Church, 1951).

68. 1 Cor. 7:4. Paul says in the same verse, "likewise the husband does not have authority over his own body, but the wife does." However, in Paul's subsequent discussion about head veiling, he argues that a husband has greater authority in a marriage: "Christ is the head of every man, and the husband is the head of his wife. . . . [A] man ought not to have his head veiled, since he is the image and reflection of God; but woman is the reflection of man. Indeed, man was not made from woman, but woman from man. Neither was man created for the sake of woman, but woman for the sake of man. For this reason, a woman ought to have a symbol of authority on her head" (1 Cor. 11:3, 7–10).

69. Augustine, *Commentary on the Lord's Sermon on the Mount*, 1.16.50.

70. Ibid.

71. Timoteo tells Lucrezia, "I have been at my books more than two hours studying this case" (3.11).

72. Augustine deals with the issue of rape, chastity and suicide in relation to Lucretia in *CG* 1.16–28.

73. Ian Donaldson first identified the link between Timoteo's statement and Augustine's reflections in *City of God*, 1.25. See Donaldson, *The Rapes of Lucretia*, 92. Also see Behuniak-Long, "The Significance of Lucrezia," 275.

74. See Friedrich Meinecke, *Machiavellism*, trans. D. Scott (New Haven: Yale University Press, 1957), 33; Berlin, "Originality of Machiavelli," 197–98; de Grazia, *Machiavelli in Hell*, 221–232; Shadia B. Drury, "Augustinian Radical Transcendence: Source of Political Excess," *Humanitas* 12, no. 2 (1999): 29–30.

75. de Grazia, *Machiavelli in Hell*, 222.

76. Ibid., 232.

77. Berlin, "Originality of Machiavelli," 197–98.

78. See Carnes Lord, "Allegory in Machiavelli's *Mandragola*," in *Political Philosophy and the Human Soul: Essays in Memory of Allan Bloom*, ed. Michael Palmer and Thomas L. Pangle (Lanham, Md.: Rowman and Littlefield, 1995), 153–54; Mansfield, "The Cuckold in *Mandragola*," 1–2.

79. Behuniak-Long argues that the name "Lucrezia" also alludes to Machiavelli's contemporary Lucrezia Borgia, daughter of Pope Alexander VI and sister of Cesare Borgia. Behuniak-Long writes that Lucrezia Borgia had a reputation for "promiscuity, manipulation, and murder. She was said to have access to the Borgia venom, used to poison enemies of the family" (Behuniak-Long, "The Significance of Lucrezia," 267).

80. Ovid, *Fasti*, 2.847; Valerius Maximus, *Facta et dicta memorabilia*, 6.1. For a commentary on this perception of Lucretia as "manly," see Donaldson, *The Rapes of Lucretia*, 10–11.

81. Behuniak-Long writes: "Perhaps Lucrezia was never of the virtuous nature that the other characters assume. . . . If this is correct, there is no dramatic change in her, and therefore, no fall" (Behuniak-Long, "The Significance of Lucrezia," 265).

82. Callimaco attributes these words to Lucrezia when he relates the account of the previous night to Ligurio.

83. For an account of the difficulty of always changing with the times, see *P* 25. For a commentary on the relation between Lucrezia's ability to change and Machiavelli's reflections in *The Prince*, see Giulio Ferroni, "'Transformation' and 'Adaptation' in Machiavelli's *Mandragola*," trans. Ronald L. Martinez, in *Machiavelli and the Discourse of Literature*, 114–15.

84. This is not to say that Aristotle would have celebrated Lucretia's decision to commit suicide.

85. Orwin, "Machiavelli's Unchristian Charity," 1218.

86. Mansfield, Introduction to his translation of *The Prince*, xix.

87. The deed Machiavelli refers to in this passage is Romulus's murder of his brother—an act that led to the founding of Rome. Machiavelli claims this killing was good because Romulus did it for the "common good and not for his own ambition" (*D* 1.9.2).

88. Mansfield writes: "It is sometimes claimed in extenuation of Machiavelli that he never said, 'the end justifies the means.' No, but he said worse: that the end

makes the means honorable, and that moral men believe this" (Mansfield, *Machiavelli's Virtue*, 27).

89. Orwin, "Machiavelli's Unchristian Charity," 1226.

90. See Mansfield, *Machiavelli's Virtue*, 8, 43–52.

91. Lucrezia uses divine providence to justify her actions (5.4); Callimaco promises to "pray to God" (4.2); Sostrata possesses a nominally Christian faith; Nicia rushes Lucrezia off to church in "fear of God" (5.5); and Timoteo thinks his ministry serves the Lord.

92. For example, he encourages Callimaco to use his Latin to trick Nicia (1.3); he tells Nicia to feign deafness in front of Timoteo (3.2); he employs Sostrata's "easy-virtue" and Timoteo's "religion" to dispose Lucrezia (2.6); and he even sets Siro on simple tasks (2.2, 4.9).

93. Mansfield, *Machiavelli's Virtue*, 236–37.

94. Mansfield argues this in "The Cuckold in *Mandragola*," 27.

95. This is Mansfield's phrase in *Machiavelli's Virtue*, 8.

96. Most scholars argue that Ligurio is the character who is most like Machiavelli himself. See Sumberg, "*La Mandragola*: An Interpretation," 338; Flaumenhaft, *The Civic Spectacle*, 91; Pitkin, *Fortune Is a Woman*, 30–32. Mansfield argues that Nicia is most like Machiavelli. See Mansfield, "The Cuckold in *Mandragola*," 27–29.

97. See Mansfield, "The Cuckold in *Mandragola*," 29.

98. Mansfield, *Machiavelli's Virtue*, 44; emphasis in original.

Chapter 6. The "Fantastical Duke of Dark Corners"

In this chapter I use the edition of *Measure for Measure* contained in *The Complete Works of Shakespeare*, ed. David Bevington. I refer to act, scene, and line numbers in parentheses.

1. Matt. 7:2; Mark 4:24; Luke 6:38.

2. *Measure for Measure* was first performed on December 26, 1604, shortly after the ascension of James I in 1603. For accounts of how the Duke in *Measure for Measure* reflects Jacobean notions of kingship, see J. W. Lever's introduction to *Measure for Measure: The Arden Shakespeare Series*, ed. J. W. Lever (London: Metheun, 1965), xlviii–li; Darryl J. Gless, *"Measure for Measure," the Law, and the Convent* (Princeton: Princeton University Press, 1979), 156–67. For a general account of *Measure for Measure* as a "Jacobean play," see N. W. Bawcutt, General Introduction to *The Oxford Shakespeare: "Measure for Measure,"* ed. N. W. Bawcutt (Oxford: Clarendon Press, 1991), 1–12.

3. G. Wilson Knight is the most popular proponent of this reading. See G. Wilson Knight, *Wheel of Fire: Interpretations of Shakespeare's Tragedy* (London:

Methuen, 1949), 73–96. Also see R. W. Chambers, "The Jacobean Shakespeare and *Measure for Measure*," *Proceedings of the British Academy* 23 (1937): 30–58; R. W. Battenhouse, "*Measure for Measure* and the Christian Doctrine of Atonement," *Publications of the Modern Language Association* 61 (1946): 1029–59; Paul N. Siegel, "*Measure for Measure*: The Significance of the Title," *Shakespeare Quarterly* 4 (1952): 317–20, and *Shakespeare in His Time and Ours* (Notre Dame: University of Notre Dame Press, 1968), 190–98; Arthur Kirsch, "*Measure for Measure*," *Shakespeare and the Experience of Love* (Cambridge: Cambridge University Press, 1981). Gless argues that it is impossible to read the play as a simple Christian allegory. Nevertheless, he argues that the moral message of the play is predominantly Christian and that the Duke's actions simulate divine providence. He describes the Duke as the "intermittent immanence of Godhead." See Gless, "*Measure for Measure*," *the Law, and the Convent*, 4–5, 214–55.

4. *All's Well That End's Well, Troilus and Cressida,* and *Measure for Measure* are the works most commonly referred to as Shakespeare's "problem plays," although other plays such as *Hamlet* and *Antony and Cleopatra* are occasionally cited. Frederick Boas is the first critic to use the term "problem play," but he admits that the phrase was already being widely used in theatrical circles long before he put it in writing. Boas writes: "We may therefore borrow a convenient phrase from the theatre of today and class them [*Measure for Measure, All's Well That Ends Well, Troilus and Cressida,* and *Hamlet*] together as Shakespeare's problem plays" (Boas, *Shakespeare and His Predecessors* [London: John Murray, 1896], 345). For further discussion of *Measure for Measure* as a problem play, see William Witherle Lawrence, *Shakespeare's Problem Comedies* (Harmondsworth: Penguin Books, 1969), 80–114; E. M. W. Tillyard, *Shakespeare's Problem Plays* (Toronto: University of Toronto Press, 1950), 118–38; and Ernest Schanzer, *The Problem Plays of Shakespeare: A Study of "Julius Caesar, "Measure for Measure," and "Antony and Cleopatra,"* (New York: Schocken Books, 1963), 71–131.

5. Samuel Taylor Coleridge, *Coleridge's Shakespearean Criticism,* vol. 2, ed. T. M. Raysor (Cambridge, Mass.: Everyman's Library, 1930), 352.

6. This practice was established by Boas, who reserves his use of the term "problem play" for dramas that "cannot be strictly called comedies or tragedies" (Boas, *Shakespeare and His Predecessors,* 345). Similarly, Lawrence writes, "The term 'problem play,' then, is particularly useful to apply to those productions which clearly do not fall into the category of tragedy, and yet are too serious and analytic to fit the commonly accepted conception of comedy" (Lawrence, *Shakespeare's Problem Comedies,* 22).

7. See Tillyard, *Shakespeare's Problem Plays,* 129–43. Also see A. P. Rossiter, *Angel with Horns and Other Shakepearean Lectures,* ed. Graham Storey (London: Longman, 1961), 164; Harriet Hawkins, *Likeness and Truth in Elizabethan and Restoration Drama* (Oxford: Clarendon Press, 1972), 51–52, 76; Rosalind Miles, *The Problem of "Measure for Measure"* (New York: Barnes and Noble, 1976), 261–62.

Northrop Frye also identifies two distinct parts in *Measure for Measure,* but he does not argue that they are incompatible. Frye argues that a "reversal of action" occurs in the play—a dramatic change from bad fortune to good. This reversal of action, according to Frye, is firmly in the mold of classic comedy and makes the play a unified, structured whole. Contrary to most previous scholars, Frye claims that *Measure for Measure* is easily categorized as a comedy and is, thus, not a "problem." See Frye, *The Myth of Deliverance: Reflections on Shakespeare's Problem Comedies* (Toronto: University of Toronto Press, 1983), 4–5, 22–25, 32–33.

   8. Miles, *The Problem of "Measure for Measure,"* 287.

   9. Schanzer, *The Problem Plays of Shakespeare,* 106.

   10. Harold Bloom, *Shakespeare: The Invention of the Human* (New York: Riverhead Books, 1998), 359.

   11. Whetstone also wrote a prose novella of *Promos and Cassandra* in the *Heptameron of Civil Discourses* (1582). The story in each text is essentially the same. Whetstone probably derived his story from the work of the Italian writer G. B. Giraldi Cinthio. Cinthio wrote a novella in his *Hecatommithi* (1565) and a play called *Epitia* (posthumously published in 1583) that bear striking similarities to Whetstone's *Promos and Cassandra.* Shakespeare probably had access to both Whetstone and Cinthio, but it is speculated that he relied chiefly on Whetstone to form the basic plot of *Measure for Measure.* See Mark Eccles, ed., *A New Variorum Edition of Shakespeare: "Measure for Measure"* (New York: Modern Language Association of America, 1980), 301–5. Eccles provides a copy of Whetstone's *Promos and Cassandra* and the novella in *Heptameron,* as well as a translation of relevant excerpts from Cinthio's *Hecatommithi* (305–87). Extracts from Cinthio's *Epitia* have been translated by Geoffrey Bullough in his *Narrative and Dramatic Sources of Shakespeare,* vol. 2: *The Comedies, 1597–1603* (London: Routledge and Kegan Paul, 1963), 430–42.

   12. Cesare Borgia (1475–1507) was the natural son of Pope Alexander VI. Machiavelli claims that Borgia was called "Duke Valentino by the vulgar" (*P*7).

   13. Several commentators have noted the parallels between Vincentio and Borgia. See Norman Holland, "*Measure for Measure,* the Duke and the Prince," *Comparative Literature* 11 (1959): 16–20; Harry V. Jaffa, "Chastity as a Political Principle: An Interpretation of Shakespeare's *Measure for Measure,*" in *Shakespeare as Political Thinker,* ed. John Alvis and Thomas G. West (Durham: Carolina Academic Press, 1981): 188–89; Allan Bloom, "*Measure for Measure,*" *Love and Friendship* (New York: Simon and Schuster, 1993), 329–30.

   14. Shakespeare's Machiavellian touches in *Measure for Measure* cause the play to depart dramatically from its analogues in the works of Whetstone and Cinthio, suggesting that Machiavelli's influence on *Measure for Measure* is decisive. That Shakespeare gives his Duke more involvement and more control than the rulers in Cinthio and Whetstone is noted by Bullough: "In none of the analogues [of *Measure for Measure*] is the overlord given the same prominent part as

in *Measure for Measure,* of being first a lurking watcher and then the manipulator of the actions leading to the dénouement" (Bullough, *Narrative and Dramatic Sources of Shakespeare,* 410).

15. On this basis, Gless rejects any parallels between Vincentio and Borgia. Gless argues that Vincentio's motives are primarily moral. He writes: "[Vincentio's] manifest concern for the moral health of his people (1.3.27–39) has nothing in common with the aims often attributed—especially in Shakespeare's era—to disciples of Machiavelli" (Gless, *"Measure for Measure," the Law, and the Convent,* 154 n.15).

16. Holland, *"Measure for Measure*: The Duke and the Prince," 20.

17. See Matt. 5:7–8, 21–30, 39, 42, 44; 6:1–18; 7:5, 12.

18. See 1.2.130; 1.3.38; 2.2.96; 2.4.36; 3.2.21.

19. See the numerous allusions to venereal disease in 1.2.31–57.

20. Lever argues that this inconsistency in the text is either an oversight by Shakespeare or a mistake by a transcriber. See Lever, *Measure for Measure,* 17. However, Stephen Derry makes a very compelling argument regarding this apparent discrepancy in the text. Derry claims that Claudio and the Duke are referring to different things: Claudio is referring to the last time the laws were enforced, which was nineteen years ago, whereas the Duke is referring to the number of years he has ruled to date, which is fourteen. According to Derry, the laws regarding lechery were not first established by the Duke but by a ruler who preceded him. The Duke's immediate predecessor, however, did not enforce the laws for the last five years of his reign. Derry argues that when Duke Vincentio ascended to power fourteen years ago, he was faced with a difficult choice: he could either start to reinforce the laws or continue the lenient policy adopted by his predecessor. The Duke chose the latter and continued with this nonenforcement policy for fourteen years. See Stephen Derry, "Time and Punishment in *Measure for Measure,*" *Notes and Queries* 41, no. 4 (December 1994): 489–90.

21. The Duke's words echo passages from the Gospels. See Matt. 5:14–6 and Luke 8:16. For commentary, see Gless, *"Measure for Measure," the Law, and the Convent,* 25–27.

22. Allan Bloom writes, "The Duke surely knows what Angelo is prior to appointing him" (Bloom, *Love and Friendship,* 331). Harold C. Goddard writes, "[The Duke] knows at the time he appoints his deputy of a previous act of turpitude on his part" (Goddard, *The Meaning of Shakespeare* [Chicago: University of Chicago Press, 1951], 438).

23. See 4.1.8–9 and 4.1.25. Mariana suggests that she has known the Duke for a long time and has grown to trust him.

24. See Bloom, *Love and Friendship,* 331.

25. The status of Claudio's "true contract" with Juliet and its similarity to Angelo's "contract" with Mariana have been the subject of much speculation. Many scholars have attempted to show how these marriage contracts correspond to Elizabethan betrothal laws. Lever writes:

English common law recognized two forms of "spousals." *Sponsalia per verba de praesenti,* a declaration by both parties that each took the other at the present time as spouse, was legally binding irrespective of any change of circumstances, and, whether the union was later consecrated or not, amounted to a full marriage. *Sponsalia per verba de futuro,* a sworn declaration of intention to marry in the future, was not thus absolutely binding. Failure of certain conditions to materialize, notably failure to furnish the agreed dowry, justified a unilateral breach. (Lever, Introduction to *Measure for Measure,* liii–liv)

Notwithstanding the claim that a *de praesenti* contract amounted to a full marriage, the Church argued that such contracts did not allow partners to live together and enter conjugal relations. In Elizabethan England, such marriage contracts had to be publicly solemnized by the Church before they could be legally consummated. It was also a civil law that *de futuro* contracts became absolute marriages if the partners had sexual relations. See Ernest Schanzer, "The Marriage-Contracts in *Measure for Measure," Shakespeare Survey* 13 (1960): 83, 86. Schanzer argues that the "true contract" between Claudio and Juliet is *de praesenti,* whereas the "contract" between Angelo and Mariana is *de futuro* (81–86). S. Nagarajan argues exactly the opposite—that Claudio and Juliet have a *de futuro* arrangement, whereas Angelo and Mariana have a *de praesent* contract (Nagarajan, "*Measure for Measure* and Elizabethan Betrothals," *Shakespeare Quarterly* 14 [1963]: 115–19).

    26. Some scholars claim that Angelo's application of the law, though merciless, is in full accord with Elizabethan and Jacobean statutes regarding marriage. Schanzer writes, "Angelo's condemnation of Claudio was, and no doubt was intended by Shakespeare to appear, absolutely tyrannical, but it was also unquestionably legal" (Schanzer, "The Marriage-Contracts in *Measure for Measure,*" 82–83). Also see Davis P. Harding, "Elizabethan Betrothals and *Measure for Measure," Journal of English and Germanic Philology* 49 (1950): 139–58; Nagarajan, "*Measure for Measure* and Elizabethan Betrothals," 115–19. However, other scholars argue exactly the opposite—that Angelo's application of the law is illegal from the standpoint of contemporary English betrothal laws. See Karl P. Wentersdorf, "The Marriage Contracts in "*Measure for Measure*": A Reconsideration," *Shakespeare Survey* 32 (1979): 129–44. Also see Arthur Underhill, "Law" in *Shakespeare's England,* vol. 1 (Oxford: Clarendon Press, 1916), 406–8; Elizabeth M. Pope, "The Renaissance Background of '*Measure for Measure,*'" *Shakespeare Survey* 2 (1949): 76. These contradictory conclusions are based on scholarly interpretations of Elizabethan marriage contracts, specifically the *de praesenti* and *de futuro* contracts that were available to Shakespeare's contemporaries. The wide variety of scholarly speculation on the contracts has led Harriett Hawkins to conclude that any investigation of Elizabethan betrothal laws will not help us understand the legal issues at work in *Measure for Measure.* See Hawkins, "What Kind of Pre-Contract had Angelo? A Note on Some Non-Problems in Elizabethan Drama," *College English* 36, no. 1 (1974–75): 173–79. In accord with Hawkins, I think it is best to turn to *Measure for Measure* itself to

determine if it is legal for Claudio to consummate his marriage on the basis of his "true contract." It is revealing that none of the characters in the play claim that Claudio is innocent before the law. Characters familiar with the law—such as Escalus and the Provost—do not argue that Claudio's execution is illegal. Even Claudio never protests his innocence; he simply complains that he is the unlucky person slated for execution. Whatever the nature of Claudio's "true contract"—regardless of whether it corresponds to an Elizabethan *de praesenti* or *de futuro* compact—all the evidence suggests that it did not permit him to consummate his marriage. Consequently, Angelo can proceed against Claudio legally. Rossiter makes this argument: "Critics who say Angelo's actions were *tyranny* depart utterly from the text. . . . Claudio is simply a 'hard case'—not a case of illegality or wrestling with the law" (Rossiter, *Angel with Horns*, 161 n. 2).

27. See 3.2.179–83; 3.2.254–75; 4.1.59–64; 4.2.108–13; 4.3.93–101. These five short passages exhaust the extent of Vincentio's soliloquizing.

28. See Lever, Introduction to *Measure for Measure*, lxxxvii; Jaffa, *Shakespeare as Political Thinker*, 195; Barbara Tovey, "Wisdom and the Law: Thoughts on the Political Philosophy of *Measure for Measure*," in *Shakespeare's Political Pageant: Essays in Literature and Politics,* ed. Joseph Alulis and Vickie Sullivan (London: Rowman and Littlefield, 1996), 65–67; Bloom, *Love and Friendship,* 335–56; Bloom, *Shakespeare: The Invention of the Human,* 369; Leon Craig, *Of Philosophers and Kings: Political Philosophy in Shakespeare's "Macbeth" and "King Lear"* (Toronto: University of Toronto Press, 2001), 241–42.

29. See Bloom, *Love and Friendship,* 336.

30. See W. M. T. Dodds, "The Character of Angelo in *Measure for Measure*," *Modern Language Review,* 41 (1946): 250–51.

31. Augustine's story of a sexual ransom in *Commentary on the Lord's Sermon on the Mount* (1.16.50) is frequently cited as a source or analogue of *Measure for Measure.* See Mary Lascelles, *Shakespeare's "Measure for Measure"* (London: Athlone Press, 1953), 6–7. Also see Bullough, *Narrative and Dramatic Sources of Shakespeare,* 399–40; and Eccles, *New Variorum Edition,* 387. As we have seen, there are strong indications that Machiavelli used the same passage from Augustine's *Commentary* when formulating Timoteo's arguments in *Mandragola.* If true, then Augustine's *Commentary* is a significant shared source of both *Mandragola* and *Measure for Measure.*

32. In this passage, Isabella claims that Claudio's request is incestuous: "Is 't not a kind of incest, to take life / From thine own sister's shame?" (3.1.141–42). This comment has frequently puzzled scholars. Marc Shell interprets Isabella's claim in light of Augustine's *Commentary on the Lord's Sermon on the Mount* (1.16.50). In Augustine's story of a sexual ransom, a condemned man gives his wife permission to have carnal relations with another man to save his own life. According to Augustine, the woman can do this only if she has the permission of her husband, who has authority over her body and who can determine how it should be used. Augustine argues that when the wife has intercourse with the other man, she actually

yields "her body to her husband only, although [her husband] was now desirous of using it in order to save his life, and not in the usual manner of marital intercourse" (1.16.50). In *Measure for Measure,* however, the situation is somewhat different. Claudio asks his sister, not his wife, to save his life by having intercourse with Angelo. That is to say, he acts as if he has a husband's authority over Isabella's body. In this sense, Claudio's request is a "kind of incest" because he wants to have sexual proprietorship of his sister. See Marc Shell, *The End of Kinship:"Measure for Measure," Incest, and the Ideal of Universal Siblinghood* (Baltimore: Johns Hopkins University Press, 1988), 105.

33. See Marcia Riefer, "'Instruments of Some Mightier Member': The Constriction of Female Power in *Measure for Measure," Shakespeare Quarterly* 35, no. 2 (Summer 1984): 162.

34. There is not a single instance of the word *God* in the play. There are, however, forty-four occurrences of *heaven, heavens,* or *heaven's.* See T. H. Howard-Hill, ed., *Oxford Shakespeare Concordances: "Measure for Measure": A Concordance to the Text of the First Folio* (Oxford: Oxford University Press, 1969), 105. It is possible that all references to "God" were replaced by "heaven" when Ralph Crane transcribed the play from Shakespeare's foul papers for the First Folio in 1623. Crane would have been acting in accordance with the parliamentary act of May 1606 that forbade the use of God's name on stage. See Lever, Introduction to *Measure for Measure,* xxi; Eccles, *A New Variorum Edition,* 295; Bawcutt, Textual Introduction to *The Oxford Shakespeare,* 68–69. However, it is unlikely that Isabella's reference to "Jove" is a later revision. In this passage, she not only speaks of "Jove" but also of his thunderbolts, thereby evoking the classical association of Jupiter with lightning. Isabella's reference to the Roman deity appears to be intended by Shakespeare.

35. See Jaffa, "Chastity as a Political Principle," 204.

36. In an aside, Lucio compliments Isabella for her reinterpretation of the word *bribe,* but suggests that she almost ruined everything ("You had marred all else" [2.2.154]).

37. Isabella enters Angelo's court with Lucio in 2.2. Before they enter, Angelo is told by a servant that Isabella is "the sister of the man condemned" (2.2.21). Perhaps sensing that Isabella will appeal for clemency, Angelo tells the Provost, who is on his way out, to "Stay a little while" (2.2.29). Angelo wants to have a witness present when Isabella is in the room.

38. Commentators of the play have not noticed this point. It is usually assumed that Isabella, in 2.4, returns the next day. This assumption is difficult to defend because the action in the surrounding scenes—2.2, 2.3, and 3.1—is continuous and occurs on the same day. In all these scenes, Claudio's execution is scheduled for "tomorrow," and there is no mention that his execution has been delayed a day while Angelo reconsiders. There is, thus, a time discrepancy if Isabella's second encounter with Angelo in 2.4 occurs on the day after the first in 2.2. However, if we accept that Isabella returns to Angelo on the same day, then this time discrepancy is

no longer a problem. Lest we rule out the possibility that Isabella would flagrantly disobey Angelo's orders by returning earlier than requested, it is helpful to consider what happens later in the play. At the end of 2.4, Angelo asks Isabella to return "tomorrow" to say whether she will pay the sexual ransom for Claudio's life (2.4.168). Isabella, however, will return later that *same* day to tell Angelo—fallaciously—that she will pay the ransom (see 3.1.245–47, 263–70; 4.1.29–47). In one day, Isabella makes three trips to Angelo's court.

The issues surrounding Isabella's visitations to Angelo raise general questions about the time frame of *Measure for Measure*. Many commentators have identified several apparent time discrepancies in the play and have concluded that Shakespeare did not intend the time frame to be realistic. See Lever, Introduction to *Measure for Measure,* xiv–xvii; and Bernard Beckerman, "A Shakespeare Experiment: The Dramaturgy of *Measure for Measure*," in *The Elizabethan Theatre II*, ed. David Galloway (Hamden, Conn: Archon Books, 1970), 87–107. However, most of the apparent time discrepancies in the play are resolved if we accept that the two scenes between Angelo and Isabella occur on the same day. A realistic time frame for the entire play emerges: an indefinite amount of time (days? weeks? months?) passes between 1.1 and 1.2; twenty-four hours pass between 1.2 and 4.3 (morning one day to morning the next day); 4.4 and 4.5 occur at night, at least twelve hours after 4.3; 4.6 and 5.1 occur the following morning. Thus forty-eight hours pass between 1.2 and 5.1.

39. In fact, the official warrant for the execution stipulates that Claudio is to be killed "by eight tomorrow" (4.2.63–65).

40. Harold Bloom remarks that Isabella's words in this passage anticipate the "peculiar accent" of the Marquis de Sade. He writes that Isabella "further excites Angelo's sadism (and ours, if we would admit it). It is one of Shakespeare's most effective outrages that Isabella is his most sexually provocative female character" (Bloom, *Shakespeare: The Invention of the Human,* 365).

41. See Schanzer, "The Marriage-Contracts in *Measure for Measure*," 85; Hawkins, "What Kind of Pre-contract Had Angelo?" 175; Wentersdorf, "The Marriage Contracts in *Measure for Measure*: A Reconsideration," 142–43.

42. Allan Bloom writes: "[The Duke] asks Isabella to participate in arranging an act of carnal knowledge. She does so willingly, partly because she seems concerned primarily with *her* chastity and *her* honor" (Bloom, *Love and Friendship,* 338; emphasis in original).

43. Isabella does not know that the "friar" is the Duke in disguise until he unveils himself at 5.1.363. Mariana is probably cognizant of Vincentio's costume throughout the play. Her awareness of the Duke's identity is suggested by what she says in 4.1.8–9, 25, and 4.6.4. Mariana is in awe of the monk's authority, insinuating that she knows she is not dealing with a simple "friar."

44. This time is earlier than originally scheduled. Angelo had initially told the Provost to execute Claudio "by nine tomorrow" (2.1.34). The official "warrant" for the execution stipulates that Claudio is to be killed "by eight tomorrow" (4.2.63–65). Finally, when Angelo's private note arrives for the Provost, Claudio is to "be executed

by four of the clock" (4.2.120–22). The Duke later suggests that a request for an earlier execution time cannot be granted unless it is certified by a "special warrant" from
the Duke himself (5.1.464–71). It is difficult to determine how seriously this "special
warrant" is to be taken. The Provost makes no mention of such a warrant.

45. The Duke originally thinks it will take him "four days" to realize his new
plan and "return" to the city (4.2.198). Later, when he is forced to reveal the letter
to the Provost announcing the Duke's arrival in "two days," he commits himself to
a forty-eight-hour time frame (4.2.198). By the time he speaks with Isabella, the
Duke realizes he can fulfill his scheme in a little over twenty-four hours. The Duke's
uncertainty over the amount of time he needs reveals that he is improvising.

46. Shakespeare's use of the pronouns *he* and *him* in this scene requires some
degree of interpretation. I have given my interpretation in brackets. Most of the
pronouns in this passage refer to the Duke—except for line 2, which certainly refers
to Angelo. It is possible that the "he" referred to by Isabella in lines 4 and 5 is Friar
Peter rather than the Duke. Accordingly, it could be argued that Peter has instructed
the two women how to act. However, the "he" referred to by Isabella in line 6 ("He
speak against me") is certainly the Duke. It is also illuminating to compare Mariana's statement in line 5 ("Be ruled by him") to what Mariana and Isabella say to
the Duke in other passages ("I am always bound to you" [4.1.24]; "I am directed by
you" [4.3.136]).

47. Goddard writes, "In spite of the Duke's professed love of retirement and
hatred of crowds and applause, he is the very reverse of a hermit, and intends . . .
to burst forth out of the clouds of disguise in full dramatic glory, as he does in the
fifth act" (Goddard, *Meaning of Shakespeare*, 438).

48. Lucio claims to know "Lodowick" after Isabella speaks the name. This
would suggest that Lucio has heard the name before. However, Lucio had seen Isabella speaking with the mysterious friar in prison two days earlier (see 4.3.149–58).
In Act 5, Lucio simply assumes that Isabella is speaking about the same friar. The
Duke, in disguise, never mentions his pseudonym to Lucio in their two conversations
(see 3.2.41–178; 4.3.149–77).

49. Of course, Isabella's claim contradicts the Lord's Prayer: "Your will be
done, on earth as it is in heaven" (Matt. 6:10).

50. Angelo proves true to his words in Act 2:

> You may not so extenuate [Claudio's] offense
> For I have had such faults; but rather tell me,
> When I that censure him do so offend,
> Let mine own judgment pattern out my death
> And nothing come in partial.
>
> (2.1.27–31)

51. Allan Bloom writes: "The Duke is a refined torturer in such matters. Angelo . . . will probably spend the rest of his life comparing Mariana with Isabella.

And before his eyes he will see the woman he truly lusted after enjoyed by the Duke. Perhaps the lesson is that these things are all the same in the dark, but Angelo will never believe that. This would be the philosophy of Mistress Overdone's house. The Duke is diabolical" (Bloom, *Love and Friendship,* 339).

52. In the Geneva Bible, which Shakespeare used, this verse reads: "all mine are thine, and thine are mine" (*The Geneva Bible: A facsimile of the 1560 edition* [Madison: University of Wisconsin Press, 1969]). The oldest source of this proverb is found in Plautus's play *Trinummus,* where the character Lysiteles says, "what's yours is mine, and of course all mine is yours" (2.2.329). This translation is by Paul Nixon in the Loeb edition of *Trinummus* in *Plautus V* (Cambridge, Mass.: Harvard University Press, 1938).

53. See Gless, *"Measure for Measure," the Law, and the Convent,* 255; Shell, *The End of Kinship,* 166–67.

54. See Jaffa, "Chastity as a Political Principle," 188.

55. Ibid., 189.

56. Ibid., 191–92; emphasis in original.

57. For instance, Frye writes, "*Measure for* Measure is not a play about the philosophy of government, the responsibilities of rulers, the social problem of prostitution, or any of the things that so many commentators insist that it is. It is a play about the relation of all such things to the structure of comedy. . . . *Measure for Measure,* then, is a comedy about comedy" (Frye, *The Myth of Deliverance,* 24–25).

Epilogue II. Machiavellianism and Providence

1. Bauman, *Modernity and the Holocaust,* 116.

2. Machiavelli identifies "virtue" and human "necessity" in *D* 3.12.1. This effectively transforms "necessary evils" into goods.

3. T. S. Eliot, *For Lancelot Andrewes: Essays on Style and Order* (London: Faber and Gwyer, 1928), 63.

4. Augustine writes: "True justice is found only in that commonwealth whose founder and ruler is Christ" (*CG* 2.21). Augustine also writes: "If a soul does not serve God it cannot with any kind of justice command the body, nor can a man's reason control the vicious elements in the soul. And if there is no justice in such a man, there can be no sort of doubt that there is no justice in a gathering which consists of such men" (*CG* 19.21). However, the very need for worldly regimes to administer "justice"—to punish criminals and defend those who have been wronged—is a result of our fallen condition. Even if partial justice is possible in societies of Christian citizens, it cannot bring eschatological peace because justice in this world is at constant war with vice. The same is true of all other virtues, such as temperance, prudence, and courage. For Augustine, virtue—even true moral virtue—is not enough. The need for moral virtue is a consequence of human sin. See *CG* 19.4.

5. Prezzolini, "The Christian Roots of Machiavelli's Moral Pessimism," 35. Also see Henry Paolucci's comments in his introduction to *The Political Writings of St. Augustine*, ed. Henry Paolucci (Washington, D.C.: Regnery Gateway, 1962), xii–xiii.

6. Machiavelli claims that every society is composed of "two diverse humours": the "great," who "desire to command and oppress the people"; and the "people," who "desire neither to be commanded nor oppressed by the great" (P 9; also see *D* 1.4.1). Politics must always contend with the demands of these two humors—one that is adept at acquiring and the other that is not. This requires expedient management. It is sometimes possible to accommodate both humours, but not always. See Mansfield's commentary in *Machiavelli's Virtue*, 75–76.

7. For a commentary on Augustine's distinction between world history (the City of Man) and spiritual history (the City of God), see Theodor E. Mommsen, "St. Augustine and the Christian Idea of Progress: The Background of *City of God*," in *Medieval and Renaissance Studies*, ed. Eugene F. Rice Jr. (Ithaca: Cornell University Press, 1959), 265–98.

8. See Mansfield's and Tarcov's introduction to their translation of *Discourses on Livy*, xlii. Also see Mansfield's analysis of "Machiavelli's virtue" in his *Machiavelli's Virtue*, 47–52.

9. See *D* 3.1.

10. Eric Voegelin, "Machiavelli's Prince: Background and Formation," *Review of Politics* 13 (1951): 165.

11. This phrase is used by Gless to describe Vincentio in *"Measure for Measure," the Law, and the Convent*, 4–5, 214–55. However, Gless thinks that Shakespeare is presenting Vincentio as a benign ruler.

12. Eric Voegelin, *The World of the Polis*, vol. 2 of *Order and History* (Baton Rouge: Louisiana State University Press, 1957), 257.

13. Baudrillard, *The Perfect Crime*, 67.

14. This passage is found in Augustine's *Enchiridion*. The translation is by Albert C. Outler in *The Library of Christian Classics*, vol. VII: *Augustine: Confessions and Enchiridion*, ed. John Baillie, John T. McNeill, and Henry P. Van Dusen (Philadelphia: Westminster Press, n.d.), 342 (3.11).

15. This statement appears in Luther's *The Bondage of the Will*. The translation is by J. I. Packer and A. R. Johnston in *Martin Luther: Selections from His Writings*, ed. John Dillenberger (New York: Doubleday, 1962), 193. This translation was originally published in *The Bondage of the Will* (London: James Clarke and Co, 1957).

Conclusion

1. Camus makes this statement in the context of a discussion of the surrealist Pierre Naville. Camus quotes Naville saying that the common feature of all modern revolutionary movements is found in "'the intention of accompanying

man to his downfall and of overlooking nothing that could ensure that his perdition might be useful'" (*R* 95). This statement, for Camus, is a mixture of "Machiavellianism and Augustinism."

2. Jean Baudrillard, *The Illusion of the End,* trans. Chris Turner (Stanford: Stanford University Press, 1994), 82.

3. Ibid.

4. He writes in the *Discourses*: "I judge the world always to have been in the same mode and there to have been as much good as wicked in it" (*D* 2. Pr.2).

5. Baudrillard, *The Perfect Crime,* 122.

6. G. W. F. Hegel, Preface to *Philosophy of Right,* trans. T. M. Knox (London: Oxford University Press, 1967), 10.

7. G. W. F. Hegel, *Introduction to "The Philosophy of History,"* trans. Leo Rauch (Indianapolis: Hackett, 1988), 35.

8. Emmanuel Levinas, "Transcendence and Evil," in *Of God Who Comes to Mind,* trans. Bettina Bergo (Stanford: Stanford University Press, 1998), 127–28; emphasis in original. The essay was first published as "Transcendance et Mal" in *Le Nouveau Commerce* 41 (Autumn 1978): 55–78.

9. Baudrillard, *Transparency of Evil,* 139.

10. The superfluity of evil also means that human consciousness is incapable of comprehending evil entirely as a phenomenon. Evil cannot be absorbed into limited systems of human thought since evil is sheer excess and constantly shifting forms. In other words, there can be no complete "theory of evil." On this point, see Richard Bernstein, *Radical Evil: A Philosophical Interrogation* (Cambridge: Polity, 2002).

11. Ibid., 128.

12. Jean Baudrillard, *The Spirit of Terrorism,* trans. Chris Turner (London: Verso, 2002), 13.

13. Friedrich Nietzsche, *Human, All Too Human,* trans. R. J. Hollingdale (Cambridge: Cambridge University Press, 1996), 265–66 (2.220); emphasis in original.

14. For a commentary on the celebratory and somber aspects of the City Dionysia, see Flaumenhaft, *The Civic Spectacle,* 67–81.

15. Flaumenhaft writes: "The Athenian *theatron* is somewhere between the *thiasos* [the Bacchic revelers] and *theôria* (contemplation) and it aims at making [the Athenian spectators] fuller human beings than they would be without it" (*The Civic Spectacle,* 79).

16. Voegelin, *The World of the Polis,* 243.

17. Ibid., 253.

18. Ibid., 255.

19. Martha Nussbaum observes: "Greek tragedy shows good people being ruined because of things that just happen to them, things that they do not control. . . . Tragedy also, however, shows something more deeply disturbing: it shows good people doing bad things, things otherwise repugnant to their ethical character and

commitments, because of circumstances whose origin does not lie with them" (Nussbaum, *The Fragility of Goodness: Luck and Ethics in Greek Tragedy and Philosophy* [Cambridge: Cambridge University Press, 1986], 25).

20. Camus, *Carnets 1942–1951*, 77. Euben makes a similar comment. He writes: "Tragedy does not so much provide us with a solution as insist on the depth of the problems and the dangers of a 'problem-solving' mentality" (Euben, *Tragedy of Political Theory*, 58).

21. Camus, *Lyrical and Critical Essays*, 301–2. Nussbaum makes a similar argument. She argues, on the basis of plays by Aeschylus and Sophocles, that a tragic hero is forced into a situation where he must decide between the conflicting demands of particular gods, all of whom have both good and bad on their respective sides. Any choice the hero makes entails committing evil, even though he might delude himself into thinking it is good. Regardless of which course he chooses, it will inevitably offend some divinity. For this he will be made to suffer. See Nussbaum, *The Fragility of Goodness*, 25–84.

22. Camus, *Lyrical and Critical Essays*, 296–97, 303.

23. Ibid., 303.

24. Lines 451–52. The translation is by David Grene in *The Complete Greek Tragedies*, vol. 2: *Sophocles*, 418.

25. According to Nietzsche, this is typical of Greek mythology. He writes: "In this way the gods served in those days to justify man to a certain extent even in his wickedness, they served as the originators of evil" (Nietzsche, *Genealogy of Morals*, 2.23, in *Basic Writings of Nietzsche*, 530).

26. Bertolt Brecht, "A Short Organum for the Theatre," in *Brecht on Theatre*, ed. and trans. John Willett (New York: Hill and Wang, 1964), 193.

27. See Brecht's comparison between "Dramatic Theatre" and "Epic Theatre" in his essay "The Modern Theatre is the Epic Theatre," in *Brecht on Theatre*, 37.

28. In "A Short Organum for the Theatre," Brecht goes so far as to declare Sophoclean and Shakespearean tragedy "barbaric." He writes that Sophocles and Shakespeare provided "Barbaric delights" for the audience. A new theatre—one that stresses human power rather than oppressive fate—must replace such primitive entertainment. As Brecht puts it: "We know that the barbarians have their art. Let us create another" (189).

29. Bertolt Brecht, *The Good Person of Szechwan*, vol. 6, pt. 1, of *Bertolt Brecht: Collected Plays*, trans. John Willett, ed. John Willett and Ralph Mannheim (London: Metheun, 1985), 109.

30. Brecht, *Brecht on Theatre*, 37.

31. Antonin Artaud, *The Theatre and Its Double*, trans. Mary Caroline Richards (New York: Grove Press, 1958), 51–52. See also Artaud's "Letter to *Comœdia*," in *Twentieth Century Theatre: A Sourcebook*, ed. Richard Drain, trans. Richard Drain and Micheline Mabille (London: Routledge, 1995), 266–67.

32. Artaud, *The Theatre and Its Double*, 102.

33. Ibid., 103.

34. Ibid., 30.

35. See Artaud's chapter "No More Masterpieces," in *The Theatre and Its Double*, 74–83.

36. Ibid., 86.

37. See Artaud's chapters "On the Balinese Theatre" and "Oriental and Occidental Theatre" in *The Theatre and Its Double*, 53–73.

38. Ibid., 31.

39. Ibid.

40. In "On the Future of Tragedy," Camus refers to Artaud's *Theatre and Its Double* as a "fine book," and he places Artaud in a group of theorists who have "once more brought the tragic dimension to center stage in our thoughts" (*Lyrical and Critical Essays*, 300). The similarities between Artaud and Camus's Caligula are striking. Both understand themselves as perpetrators of a purifying plague that will pulverize the universe. It is likely that Camus was thinking of Artaud when he wrote *Caligula*, for *Theatre and Its Double* was published in 1938, the same year that Camus started writing *Caligula*. It is obvious that Camus tried to use some of Artaud's techniques in the play—shocking the audience with vivid portrayals of violence, sexuality, and murder. However, contrary to Artaud, *Caligula* is "literary" to a fault: the play contains more philosophical argumentation than sensory stimulation. Furthermore, Camus, for the most part, employed "cruelty" in the play to criticize the desire for purity and transfiguration. Notwithstanding Camus's favourable assessment of *Theatre and Its Double*, it is clear that Camus's own understanding of tragedy did not correspond to Artaud's "theatre of cruelty." Nevertheless, as we have seen, Camus's thought occasionally resonates with Artaud's, insofar as Camus suggests that the desire for cataclysm and purity is praiseworthy.

41. Artaud, *The Theatre and Its Double*, 102–3.

42. Ibid., 104.

43. In *Impossible Theatre*, Kantor writes: "The notion of freedom in art, defined and affirmed for the first time in surrealism, its program for a total and indivisible reality, is the very principle of new art." For Kantor, this principle applies to the theatre, which can use methods from other aesthetic realms to realize a new reality: "In the shows realised at the Cricot 2 Theatre in the years 1955–1957, the collage method was carried through into all the material used. . . . Everything was based on the break-up of logical links; the process was to superimpose, to 'tot up,' in order to create a new reality." These passages from *Impossible Theatre* are translated by Richard Drain and Micheline Mabille in *Twentieth Century Theatre*, 64–65.

44. Strauss, *Thoughts on Machiavelli*, 292. Strauss's claim that there is no tragedy in Machiavelli has not gone uncontested. See Vickie B. Sullivan, "Introduction," and Ronald L. Martinez, "Tragic Machiavelli," in *The Comedy and Tragedy of Machiavelli*, ix–xxi, 102–3.

45. Stockhausen made these comments on September 17, 2001, on a German radio program. They were later published in the *New York Times* (September 30, 2001). I have used the translation of Stockhausen's words provided by Christopher Balme in "Forum on Theatre and Tragedy in the Wake of September 11, 2001," *Theatre Journal* 54 (2002): 115. Stockhausen makes reference to 5,000 people being killed in the 9/11 attacks, a number based on the inflated casualty figures of that time. The official number of deaths turned out to be just under 3,000.

46. Ibid., 116.

47. Baudrillard, *Spirit of Terrorism*, 30.

48. See Francis Fukuyama, "The End of History?" *National Interest* 16 (Summer 1989): 3–18.

49. The president's statement was later quoted in the Bush administration's National Security Strategy statement released in September 2002. Also see David Frum and Richard Perle, *An End to Evil: How to Win the War on Terror* (New York: Random House, 2003). Frum is a former speechwriter for President Bush, and Perle is a former assistant secretary of defense.

50. Lifton, *Superpower Syndrome*, 39.

51. Ibid., 4.

52. Richard Bernstein refers to this political orientation as "pragmatic fallibilism," by which he means a democratic ethos that is unflinchingly realistic about the evils that threaten Western democracies but which is also acutely conscious of our fallibility when confronting these evils. See Bernstein, *The Abuse of Evil*, 18–67. Bernstein's book came to my attention while my own was in press, but he provides a similar critique of religious and political orientations that speak in moral absolutes and divide the world into simplistic categories of good and evil. He contrasts this position with a more nuanced approach advocated by American pragmatic philosophers such as William James, Charles S. Pierce, and John Dewey. Bernstein's "pragmatic fallibilism" is based on his analysis of this philosophical tradition. Interestingly, Bernstein refers us to Sidney Hook's 1974 book, *Pragmatism and the Tragic Sense of Life*, in which Hook argues that pragmatism is rooted in tragic experience. See Bernstein, *The Abuse of Evil*, 55–57.

BIBLIOGRAPHY

Abraham, Claude K. "*Caligula*: Drama of Revolt or Drama of Deception?" *Modern Drama* 5, no. 4 (February 1963): 451–53.

Alford, C. Fred. *The Psychoanalytic Theory of Greek Tragedy.* New Haven: Yale University Press, 1994.

———. *What Evil Means to Us.* Ithaca: Cornell University Press, 1997.

———. *Think No Evil: Korean Values in the Age of Globalization.* Ithaca: Cornell University Press, 1999.

Anglo, Sydney. *Machiavelli: A Dissection.* London: Victor Gollancz, 1969.

Aquinas, Thomas. *Summa Theologica.* 3 vols. Trans. Fathers of the English Dominican Province. New York: Benzinger Bros., 1948.

Archambault, Paul. *Camus' Hellenic Sources.* Chapel Hill: University of North Carolina Press, 1972.

Arendt, Hannah. *Eichmann in Jerusalem: A Report on the Banality of Evil.* New York: Viking Press, 1965.

———. *The Life of the Mind.* San Diego: Harcourt Brace Jovanovich, 1978.

Aristotle. *Nicomachean Ethics.* Trans. Martin Ostwald. New York: Macmillan, 1962.

Artaud, Antonin. *The Theatre and Its Double.* Trans. Mary Caroline Richards. New York: Grove Press, 1958.

Ascoli, Albert Russel, and Victoria Kahn, eds. *Machiavelli and the Discourse of Literature.* Ithaca: Cornell University Press, 1993.

Asmus, Walter. "Beckett Directs Godot." *Theatre Quarterly* 5, no. 19 (1975): 19–26.

Atkinson, James B. "An Essay on Machiavelli and Comedy." In *The Comedies of Machiavelli,* ed. and trans. David Sices and James B. Atkinson. Hanover: University Press of New England, 1985.

Atkinson, James B., and David Sices, eds. and trans. *Machiavelli and His Friends: Their Personal Correspondence.* Dekalb: Northern Illinois University Press, 1996.

Augustine, Aurelius. *Enchiridion.* In *Augustine: Confessions and Enchiridion,* ed. and trans. Albert C. Outler. Vol. 7 of *The Library of Christian Classics,* ed. John Baillie, John T. McNeill, and Henry P. Van Dusen. Philadelphia: Westminster Press, n.d.

———. "De Symbolo ad Catechumenos." Vol. 40 of *Patrologiae Latina,* ed. J. P. Migne. Paris: n.p., 1945.

———. *Commentary on the Lord's Sermon on the Mount with Seventeen Related Sermons.* Trans. Denis J. Kavanaugh. Vol. 11 of *The Fathers of the Church.* New York: Fathers of the Church, 1951.

———. *The Writings against the Manichaeans and against the Donatists.* Vol. 4 of *Nicene and Post-Nicene Fathers of the Christian Church,* ed. Philip Schaff. Grand Rapids: Eerdmans, 1956.

———. *City of God.* Trans. Henry Bettenson. London: Penguin Books, 1972.

———. *Confessions.* Trans. Henry Chadwick. Oxford: Oxford University Press, 1991.

———. *Two Books on Genesis against the Manichees.* In *On Genesis,* vol. 84 of *The Fathers of the Church,* ed. Thomas P. Halton, trans. Roland J. Teske. Washington, D.C.: Catholic University of America, 1991.

———. *De Genesis Contra Manichaeos.* In vol. 91 of *Sancti Augustini Opera,* ed. Dorothea Weber. Wien: Österreichischen Akademie der Wissenschaften, 1998.

Banham, Martin, ed. *The Cambridge Guide to the Theatre.* Rev. ed. Cambridge: Cambridge University Press, 1992.

Barrett, Anthony A. *Caligula: The Corruption of Power.* New Haven: Yale University Press, 1989.

Battenhouse, R. W. "*Measure for Measure* and the Christian Doctrine of Atonement." *Publications of the Modern Language Association* 61 (1946): 1029–59.

Baudrillard, Jean. *The Transparency of Evil: Essays on Extreme Phenomena.* Trans. James Benedict. London: Verso, 1993.

———. *The Illusion of the End.* Trans. Chris Turner. Stanford: Stanford University Press, 1994.

———. *The Perfect Crime.* Trans. Chris Turner. London: Verso, 1996.

———. *Paroxysm.* Trans. Chris Turner. London: Verso, 1998.

———. *Impossible Exchange.* Trans. Chris Turner. London: Verso, 2001.

———. *The Spirit of Terrorism.* Trans. Chris Turner. London: Verso, 2002.

Bauman, Zygmunt. *Modernity and the Holocaust.* Ithaca: Cornell University Press, 1989.

———. "A Century of Camps?" In *The Bauman Reader,* ed. Peter Beilharz. Malden: Blackwell, 2001. Originally published in Zygmunt Bauman, *Life in Fragments: Essays in Postmodern Morality* (Oxford: Blackwell, 1995).

Bawcutt, N. W. "Some Elizabethan Allusions to Machiavelli." *English Miscellany* 20 (1969): 53–74.

———, ed. *The Oxford Shakespeare: "Measure for Measure."* Oxford: Clarendon Press, 1991.

Beckerman, Bernard. "A Shakespeare Experiment: The Dramaturgy of *Measure for Measure.*" In *The Elizabethan Theatre II,* ed. David Galloway. Hamden, Conn: Archon Books, 1970.

Beckett, Samuel. "Dante . . . Bruno. Vico . . . Joyce." In *Our Exagmination Round His Factification for Incamination of Work in Progress*. Paris: Shakespeare and Co., 1929. Reprint, London: Faber and Faber, 1961.

———. *En attendant Godot*. Paris: Editions de Minuit, 1952.

———. *Waiting for Godot*. New York: Grove Press, 1954.

———. *Disjecta: Miscellaneous Writings and a Dramatic Fragment*. Ed. Ruby Cohn. New York: Grove Press, 1983.

Behuniak-Long, Susan. "The Significance of Lucrezia in Machiavelli's *La Mandragola*." *Review of Politics* 51, no. 2 (1989): 264–80.

Berkeley, George. *Three Dialogues between Hylas and Philonous*. Ed. Jonathan Dancy. Oxford: Oxford University Press, 1998.

Berlin, Isaiah. "The Originality of Machiavelli." In *Studies on Machiavelli*, ed. Myron P. Gilmore. Florence: G. C. Sansoni, 1972.

Bernardino, Angelo Di, ed. *Encyclopedia of the Early Church*. Trans. Adrian Walford. New York: Oxford University Press, 1992.

Bernstein, Richard J. *Radical Evil: A Philosophical Interrogation*. Cambridge: Polity, 2002.

———. *The Abuse of Evil: The Corruption of Politics and Religion since 9/11*. Cambridge: Polity, 2005.

Bertelli, Sergio. "When Did Machiavelli Write *Mandragola?*" *Renaissance Quarterly* 24 (1971): 317–26.

Bloom, Allan. *Love and Friendship*. New York: Simon and Schuster, 1993.

Bloom, Harold. *Shakespeare: The Invention of the Human*. New York: Riverhead Books, 1998.

Boas, Frederick. *Shakespeare and His Predecessors*. London: John Murray, 1896.

Bouchard, Larry. *Tragic Method and Tragic Theology: Evil in Contemporary Drama and Religious Thought*. University Park: Pennsylvania State University Press, 1989.

Boughner, Daniel C. *The Devil's Disciple: Ben Jonson's Debt to Machiavelli*. New York: Philosophical Library, 1978.

Boyle, A. J. *Tragic Seneca: An Essay in the Theatrical Tradition*. London: Routledge, 1997.

Boyle, Kay. "All Mankind Is Us." In *Samuel Beckett: A Collection of Criticism*, ed. Ruby Cohn. New York: McGraw-Hill, 1975.

Brecht, Bertolt. *Brecht on Theatre*. Ed. and trans. John Willett. New York: Hill and Wang, 1964.

———. *The Good Person of Szechwan*. Trans. John Willett. Vol. 6, pt. 1 of *Bertolt Brecht: Collected Plays*, ed. John Willett and Ralph Mannheim. London: Metheun, 1985.

Bree, Germaine. "Camus' *Caligula*: Evolution of a Play." *Symposium* 12 (1958): 43–51.

Bullough, Geoffrey. *Narrative and Dramatic Sources of Shakespeare*. Vol. 2: *The Comedies, 1597–1603*. London: Routledge and Kegan Paul, 1963.

Bynum, Caroline Walker, and Paul Freedman, eds. *Last Things: Death and the Apocalypse in the Middle Ages*. Philadelphia: University of Pennsylvania Press, 2000.

Camus, Albert. *Le Malentendu suivi de Caligula*. Paris: Librairie Gallimard, 1944.

———. *Myth of Sisyphus and Other Essays*. Trans. Justin O' Brien. New York: Vintage Books, 1955.

———. *The Rebel*. Trans. Anthony Bower. New York: Vintage International, 1956.

———. *Caligula and Three Other Plays*. Trans. Justin O'Brien. New York: Vintage Books, 1958.

———. *Théâtre, Récits, Nouvelles*. Ed. Roger Quilliot. Paris: Éditions Gallimard, 1962.

———. *Carnets 1935–1942*. Trans. Philip Thody. London: Hamish Hamilton, 1963.

———. *Carnets II: Janvier 1942–Mars 1951*. N.p.: Éditions Gallimard, 1964.

———. *Essais*. Ed. Roger Quilliot and Louis Faucon. Paris: Gallimard, Bibliothèque de la Pléiade, 1965.

———. *Carnets: 1942–1951*. Trans. Philip Thody. London: Hamish Hamilton, 1966.

———. *Lyrical and Critical Essays*. Ed. Philip Thody. Trans. Ellen Conroy Kennedy. New York: Vintage Books, 1970.

———. "Neither Victims nor Executioners." In *Between Hell and Reason: Essays from the Resistance Newspaper "Combat," 1944–1947*, trans. Alexandre de Gramont. Hanover: Wesleyan University Press, 1991.

Caputo, John D. *Deconstruction in a Nutshell: A Conversation with Jacques Derrida*. New York: Fordham University Press, 1997.

Chambers, R. W. "The Jacobean Shakespeare and *Measure for Measure*." *Proceedings of the British Academy* 23 (1937): 30–58.

Cohn, Norman. *The Pursuit of the Millennium*. New York: Oxford University Press, 1957.

———. *Cosmos, Chaos, and the World to Come: The Ancient Roots of Apocalyptic Faith*. New Haven: Yale University Press, 1993.

Cohn, Ruby. *Back to Beckett*. Princeton: Princeton University Press, 1973.

———, ed. *Casebook on Waiting for Godot*. New York: Grove Press, 1967.

Coleridge, Samuel Taylor. *Coleridge's Shakespearean Criticism*. Vol. 2. Ed. T. M. Raysor. Cambridge, Mass.: Everyman's Library, 1930.

Collins, John J., ed. *The Encyclopedia of Apocalypticism, Volume I: The Origins of Apocalypticism in Judaism and Christianity*. New York: Continuum, 1999.

Cook, David. "Albert Camus' *Caligula*: The Metaphysics of an Emperor." In *Domination*, ed. Alkis Kontos. Toronto: University of Toronto Press, 1975.

Copjec, Joan, ed. *Radical Evil*. London: Verso, 1996.

Corey, Paul. "Canadian Theatre and the Tragic Experience of Evil." *Theatre Research in Canada* 27, no. 2 (2006): 282–305.

Craig, Hardin, ed. *Machiavelli's Prince: An Elizabethan Translation*. Chapel Hill: University of North Carolina Press, 1944.

Craig, Leon. *Of Philosophers and Kings: Political Philosophy in Shakespeare's "Macbeth" and "King Lear."* Toronto: University of Toronto Press, 2001.

Cronin, Anthony. *Samuel Beckett: The Last Modernist*. London: Flamingo, 1996.

Cruickshank, John. *Albert Camus and the Literature of Revolt*. New York: Oxford University Press, 1960.

D'Andrea, Antonio. "Studies on Machiavelli and His Reputation in the Sixteenth Century: I, Marlowe's Prologue to *The Jew of Malta*." *Medieval and Renaissance Studies* 5 (1960): 214–48.

de Grazia, Sebastian. *Machiavelli in Hell*. Princeton: Princeton University Press, 1989.

Derrida, Jacques. *Specters of Marx: The State of Debt, the Work of Mourning, and the New International*. Trans. Peggy Kamuf. New York: Routledge, 1994.

Derry, Stephen. "Time and Punishment in *Measure for Measure*." *Notes and Queries* 41, no. 4 (December 1994): 489–90.

Dodds, W. M. T. "The Character of Angelo in *Measure for Measure*." *Modern Language Review* 41 (1946): 246–55.

Donaldson, Ian. *The Rapes of Lucretia: A Myth and Its Transformations*. Oxford: Clarendon Press, 1982.

Drain, Richard, ed. *Twentieth Century Theatre: A Sourcebook*. London: Routledge, 1995.

Driver, Tom. "Beckett by the Madeleine." *Columbia University Forum* 4, no. 3 (Summer 1961): 21–25.

Drury, Shadia B. "Augustinian Radical Transcendence: Source of Political Excess." *Humanitas* 12, no. 2 (1999): 27–45.

Duckworth, Colin. *Samuel Beckett: En attendant Godot*. London: George G. Harrap, 1966.

Eccles, Mark, ed. *A New Variorum Edition of Shakespeare: "Measure for Measure."* New York: Modern Language Association of America, 1980.

Eliade, Mircea. *Myth and Reality.* Trans. Willard R. Trask. New York: Harper Torchbooks, 1963.

Eliot, T. S. *For Lancelot Andrewes: Essays on Style and Order*. London: Faber and Gwyer, 1928.

Esslin, Martin. *The Theatre of the Absurd*. London: Penguin Books, 1961.

Euben, J. Peter. *Tragedy of Political Theory: The Road Not Taken*. Princeton: Princeton University Press, 1990.

Filorama, G. "Eschatology." In *Encyclopedia of the Early Church*, 2 vols., ed. Angelo Di Bernardino, trans. Andrian Walford. New York: Oxford University Press, 1992.

Flaumenhaft, Mera. "The Comic Remedy: Machiavelli's *Mandragola*." *Interpretation: A Journal of Political Philosophy* 7, no. 2 (1978): 33–74.

———. *The Civic Spectacle: Essays on Drama and Community.* Lanham: Rowman and Littlefield, 1994.

Fletcher, Beryl S., and John Fletcher. *A Student's Guide to the Plays of Samuel Beckett*. London: Faber and Faber, 1985.

Fletcher, John. "Roger Blin at Work." *Modern Drama* 8, no. 4 (February 1966): 403–8.

"Forum on Theatre and Tragedy in the Wake of September 11, 2001." *Theatre Journal* 54 (2002): 95–138.

Freeman, E. "Camus, Suetonius, and the Caligula Myth." *Symposium* 24, no. 3 (Fall 1970): 230–42.

Frum, David, and Richard Perle. *An End to Evil: How to Win the War on Terror.* New York: Random House, 2003.

Frye, Northrop. *The Myth of Deliverance: Reflections on Shakespeare's Problem Comedies.* Toronto: University of Toronto Press, 1983.

Fukuyama, Francis. "The End of History?" *National Interest* 16 (Summer 1989): 3–18.

Gane, Mike, ed. *Baudrillard Live: Selected Interviews.* London: Routledge, 1993.

Geneva Bible: A facsimile of the 1560 edition. Madison: University of Wisconsin Press, 1969.

Gentillet, Innocent. *A Discourse upon the Meanes of Wel Governing and Maintaining in Good Peace a Kingdom.* Trans. Simon Patericke. London, 1602.

Gerber, A. "All of the Five Fictitious Italian Editions of the Writings of Machiavelli and Three of Those of Pietro Aretino, Printed by John Wolfe of London (1584–88)." *Modern Language Notes* 22 (1907): 129–35.

Gilbert, Allan. *Machiavelli's Prince and Its Forerunners.* Durham: Duke University Press, 1968.

Gless, Darryl J. *"Measure for Measure," the Law, and the Convent.* Princeton: Princeton University Press, 1979.

Goddard, Harold C. *The Meaning of Shakespeare.* Chicago: University of Chicago Press, 1951.

Goldberg, L. "A Note on John Wolfe, Eliabethan Printer." *Historical Studies: Australia and New Zealand* 7, no. 25 (1955): 55–61.

Gourevitch, Philip. *We Wish to Inform You That Tomorrow We Will Be Killed with Our Families: Stories from Rwanda.* New York: Picador, 1999.

Grene, David, and Richmond Lattimore, eds. *The Complete Greek Tragedies.* 2d ed. Chicago: University of Chicago Press, 1991.

Harding, Davis P. "Elizabethan Betrothals and *Measure for Measure.*" *Journal of English and Germanic Philology* 49 (1950): 139–58.

Hawkins, Harriet. *Likeness and Truth in Elizabethan and Restoration Drama.* Oxford: Clarendon Press, 1972.

———. "What Kind of Pre-Contract Had Angelo? A Note on Some Non-Problems in Elizabethan Drama." *College English* 36, no. 1 (1974–75): 173–79.

Hegel, Georg W. F. *Philosophy of Right.* Trans. T. M. Knox. London: Oxford University Press, 1967.

———. *Introduction to "The Philosophy of History."* Trans. Leo Rauch. Indianapolis: Hackett, 1988.

Herrick, Marvin T. *Italian Comedy in the Renaissance.* Urbana: University of Illinois Press, 1960.

———. *Italian Tragedy in the Renaissance.* Urbana: University of Illinois Press, 1965.

Hobson, Harold. "Samuel Beckett, Dramatist of the Year." In *International Theatre Annual*, no. 1. London: John Calder, 1956.

Holland, Norman. "*Measure for Measure*, the Duke and the Prince." *Comparative Literature* 11 (1959): 16–20.

Homer. *The Odyssey of Homer*. Trans. Richmond Lattimore. New York: Harper Perennial, 1965.

Hook, Sidney. *Pragmatism and the Tragic Sense of Life*. New York: Basic Books, 1974.

Howard-Hill, T. H., ed. *Oxford Shakespeare Concordances: "Measure for Measure": A Concordance to the Text of the First Folio*. Oxford: Oxford University Press, 1969.

Ionesco, Eugène. *Notes and Counternotes: Writings on the Theatre by Eugène Ionesco*. Trans. Donald Watson. New York: Grove Press, 1964.

Jaffa, Harry V. "Chastity as a Political Principle: An Interpretation of Shakespeare's *Measure for Measure*." In *Shakespeare as Political Thinker*, ed. John Alvis and Thomas G. West. Durham: Carolina Academic Press, 1981.

Jonas, Hans. *The Gnostic Religion: The Message of the Alien God and the Beginnings of Christianity*. 2d ed., rev. Boston: Beacon Press, 1963.

Jowitt, Ken. *New World Disorder: The Leninist Extinction*. Berkeley: University of California Press, 1992.

Kahn, Victoria. "*Virtù* and the Example of Agathocles in Machiavelli's *Prince*." In *Machiavelli and the Discourse of Literature*, ed. Albert Russel Ascoli and Victoria Kahn. Ithaca: Cornell University Press, 1993.

Kant, Immanuel. *Religion within the Limits of Reason Alone*. Trans. Theodore M. Greene and Hoyt H. Hudson. New York: Harper Torchbooks, 1960.

———. *Foundations of the Metaphysics of Morals*. Trans. Lewis White Beck. New York: Macmillan, 1990.

Kantorowicz, Ernst H. *The King's Two Bodies: A Study in Mediaeval Political Theology*. Princeton: Princeton University Press, 1957.

Kenner, Hugh. *A Reader's Guide to Samuel Beckett*. Syracuse: Syracuse University Press, 1996.

Kirsch, Arthur. *"Measure for Measure," Shakespeare and the Experience of Love*. Cambridge: Cambridge University Press, 1981.

Klaić, Dragan. *Plot of the Future: Utopia and Dystopia in Modern Drama*. Ann Arbor: University of Michigan Press, 1991.

Knight, G. Wilson. *Wheel of Fire: Interpretations of Shakespeare's Tragedy*. London: Methuen, 1949.

Knowlson, James. *Damned to Fame: The Life of Samuel Beckett*. New York: Touchstone, 1996.

Lascelles, Mary. *Shakespeare's "Measure for Measure."* London: Athlone Press, 1953.

Lawrence, William Witherle. *Shakespeare's Problem Comedies*. Harmondsworth: Penguin Books, 1969.

Lever, J. W., ed. *Measure for Measure: The Arden Shakespeare Series*. London: Metheun, 1965.

Levinas, Emmanuel. "Transcendence and Evil." In *Of God Who Comes to Mind,* trans. Bettina Bergo. Stanford: Stanford University Press, 1998.

Lifton, Robert Jay. *Superpower Syndrome: America's Apocalyptic Confrontation with the World.* New York: Thunder's Mouth Press/Nation Books, 2003.

Livy. *Livy.* Trans. B. O. Foster. Loeb Classical Library. Cambridge, Mass.: Harvard University Press, 1919.

Lord, Carnes. "Allegory in Machiavelli's *Mandragola.*" In *Political Philosophy and the Human Soul: Essays in Memory of Allan Bloom,* ed. Michael Palmer and Thomas L. Pangle. Lanham, Md.: Rowman and Littlefield, 1995.

Lukes, Timothy J. "Fortune Comes of Age (in Machiavelli's Literary Works)." *Sixteenth Century Journal* 11, no. 4 (1980): 33–50.

Luther, Martin. *The Bondage of the Will.* Trans. J. I. Packer and A. R. Johnston. In *Martin Luther: Selections from His Writings,* ed. John Dillenberger. New York: Doubleday, 1962. Originally published in Martin Luther, *The Bondage of the Will,* trans. J. I. Packer and A. R. Johnston. London: James Clarke, 1957.

Machiavelli, Niccolò. "A Dialogue on Language." In *The Literary Works of Machiavelli,* ed. and trans. J. R. Hale. London: Oxford University Press, 1961.

———. *Il teatro e gli scritti letterari.* Ed. Franco Gaeta. Milan: Feltrinelli, 1965.

———. *Mandragola.* Trans. Mera J. Flaumenhaft. Prospect Heights: Waveland Press, 1981.

———. *The Prince.* Trans. Harvey C. Mansfield Jr. Chicago: University of Chicago Press, 1985.

———. *Clizia.* Trans. Daniel T. Gallagher. Prospect Heights: Waveland Press, 1996.

———. *Discourses on Livy.* Trans. Harvey C. Mansfield Jr. and Nathan Tarcov. Chicago: University of Chicago Press, 1996.

Mansfield, Harvey. "The Cuckold in Machiavelli's *Mandragola.*" In *The Comedy and Tragedy of Machiavelli: Essays on the Literary Works,* ed. Vickie B. Sullivan. New Haven: Yale University Press, 2000.

———. *Machiavelli's Virtue.* Chicago: University of Chicago Press, 1996.

Marlowe, Christopher. *The Jew of Malta.* In *The Complete Plays.* ed. J. B. Steane. London: Penguin Books, 1969.

Martinez, Ronald L. "The Pharmacy of Machiavelli: Roman Lucretia in *Mandragola.*" *Renaissance Drama* 14 (1983): 1–43.

Masters, Roger D. *Machiavelli, Leonardo, and the Science of Power.* Notre Dame: University of Notre Dame Press, 1996.

McGinn, Bernard. "Introduction: John's Apocalypse and the Apocalyptic Mentality." In *The Apocalypse in the Middle Ages,* ed. Richard K. Emmerson and Bernard McGinn. Ithaca: Cornell University Press, 1992.

McMillan, Dougald, and James Knowlson, eds. *The Theatrical Notebooks of Samuel Beckett.* Vol. 1, *Waiting for Godot.* New York: Grove Press, 1993.

Meier, Christian. *The Political Art of Greek Tragedy.* Trans. Andrew Webber. Baltimore: Johns Hopkins University Press, 1993.

Meinecke, Friedrich. *Machiavellism*. Trans. D. Scott. New Haven: Yale University Press, 1957.

Meyer, Edward. *Machiavelli and the Elizabethan Drama*. Weimar: Litterarhistorische Forschungen, 1897.

Miles, Rosalind. *The Problem of "Measure for Measure."* New York: Barnes and Noble, 1976.

Milgram, Stanley. "Some Conditions of Obedience and Disobedience to Authority." In *The Individual in a Social World*. Reading: Addison-Wesley, 1977.

Mommsen, Theodor E. "St. Augustine and the Christian Idea of Progress: The Background of *City of God.*" In *Medieval and Renaissance Studies*, ed. Eugene F. Rice Jr. Ithaca: Cornell University Press, 1959.

Morris, Christopher. "Machiavelli's Reputation in Tudor England." *Il pensiero politico* 2 (1969): 416–33.

Morrison, Kristin. *Canters and Chronicles: The Use of Narrative in the Plays of Samuel Beckett and Harold Pinter*. Chicago: University of Chicago Press, 1983.

Nagarajan, S. *"Measure for Measure* and Elizabethan Betrothals." *Shakespeare Quarterly,* 14 (1963): 115–19.

Neiman, Susan. *Evil in Modern Thought: An Alternative History of Philosophy.* Princeton: Princeton University Press, 2002.

Nietzsche, Friedrich. *On the Genealogy of Morals.* Trans. Walter Kaufmann. In *Basic Writings of Nietzsche*, ed. Walter Kaufmann. New York: Modern Library, 1992.

———. *Human, All Too Human.* Trans. R. J. Hollingdale. Cambridge: Cambridge University Press, 1996.

Nussbaum, Martha. *The Fragility of Goodness: Luck and Ethics in Greek Tragedy and Philosophy.* Cambridge: Cambridge University Press, 1986.

Orr, John. *Tragic Drama and Modern Society: Studies in the Social and Literary Theory of Drama from 1870 to the Present.* London: Macmillan, 1981.

Orsini, Napoleone. "Machiavelli's *Discourses*: A MSS Translation of 1599." *Times Literary Supplement* 10 (October 1936): 820.

———. "Elizabethan Manuscript Translations of Machiavelli's *Prince.*" *Journal of the Warburg and Courtauld Institutes* 1 (1937–38): 166–69.

Orwin, Clifford. "Machiavelli's Unchristian Charity." *American Political Science Review* 72 (1978): 1217–28.

Paolucci, Henry. Introduction to *The Political Writings of St. Augustine.* Ed. Henry Paolucci. Washington, D.C.: Regnery Gateway, 1962.

Parkin, David, ed. *The Anthropology of Evil.* Cambridge, Mass.: Blackwell, 1985.

Pavis, Patrice. *Dictionary of the Theatre: Terms, Concepts, and Analysis.* Trans. Christine Shantz. Toronto: University of Toronto Press, 1998.

Penman, Bruce, ed. *Five Italian Renaissance Comedies.* Harmondsworth: Penguin Books, 1978.

Pitkin, Hanna Fenichel. *Fortune Is a Woman: Gender and Politics in the Thought of Machiavelli.* Chicago: University of Chicago Press, 1984.

Plautus. *Trinummus*. In *Plautus V,* trans. Paul Nixon. Loeb Classical Library. Cambridge, Mass.: Harvard University Press, 1938.

Pope, Elizabeth M. "The Renaissance Background of '*Measure for Measure.*'" *Shakespeare Survey* 2 (1949): 66–82.

Praz, Mario. "Machiavelli and the Elizabethans." *Proceedings of the British Academy* 13 (1928): 49–97.

Prezzolini, Giuseppe. "The Christian Roots of Machiavelli's Moral Pessimism." *Review of National Literatures* 1, no. 1 (Spring 1970): 26–37.

Raab, Felix. *The English Face of Machiavelli.* London: Routledge and Kegan Paul, 1964.

Radcliff-Ulmstead, Douglas. *The Birth of Modern Comedy in Renaissance Italy.* Chicago: University of Chicago Press, 1969.

Reid, Alec. *All I Can Manage, More than I Could: An Approach to the Plays of Samuel Beckett.* Dublin: Dolmen Press, 1968.

Ribner, Irving. "The Significance of Gentillet's *Contre-Machiavel.*" *Modern Language Quarterly* 10 (1949): 177–87.

———. "Marlow and Machiavelli." *Comparative Literature* 6 (1954): 348–56.

Richards, Kenneth, and Laura Richards. *The Commedia dell'Arte: A Documentary History.* Oxford: Blackwell, 1990.

Richards, Laura. "Machiavelli, Niccolo." In *The Cambridge Guide to the Theatre,* ed. Martin Banham. Rev. ed. Cambridge University Press, 1992.

Ricoeur, Paul. *The Symbolism of Evil.* Trans. Emerson Buchanan. Boston: Beacon Press, 1969.

Riefer, Marcia. "'Instruments of Some Mightier Member': The Constriction of Female Power in *Measure for Measure.*" *Shakespeare Quarterly* 35, no. 2 (Summer 1984): 157–69.

Rossiter, A. P. *Angel with Horns and Other Shakespearean Lectures.* Ed. Graham Storey. London: Longman, 1961.

Rousseau, Jean-Jacques. *Emile or On Education.* Trans. Allan Bloom. New York: Basic Books, 1979.

———. *Letter to M. d'Alembert on the Theatre.* In *Politics and the Arts,* ed. and trans. Allan Bloom. New York: Cornell University Press, 1989.

———. *The Discourses and Other Early Political Writings.* Ed. and trans. Victor Gourevitch. New York: Cambridge University Press, 1997.

Ruffo-Fiore, Silvia. *Niccolò Machiavelli.* Boston: Twayne Publishers, 1982.

Schanzer, Ernest. "The Marriage-Contracts in *Measure for Measure.*" *Shakespeare Survey* 13 (1960): 81–89.

———. *The Problem Plays of Shakespeare: A Study of "Julius Caesar," "Measure for Measure," and "Antony and Cleopatra."* New York: Schocken Books, 1963.

Schmithals, Walter. *The Apocalyptic Movement: Introduction and Interpretation.* Trans. John E. Steely. Nashville: Abingdon Press, 1975.

Schneider, Alan. "Waiting for Beckett: A Personal Chronicle." In *Casebook on Waiting for Godot,* ed. Ruby Cohn. New York: Grove Press, 1967.

Scott, Margaret. "Machiavelli and the Machiavel." *Renaissance Drama* 15 (1984): 147–74.

Segal, Erich. *Roman Laughter: The Comedy of Plautus.* Cambridge, Mass.: Harvard University Press, 1968.

Shakespeare, William. *The Complete Works of Shakespeare.* Ed. David Bevington. 4th ed. New York: Longman, 1997.

Shell, Marc. *The End of Kinship: "Measure for Measure," Incest, and the Ideal of Universal Siblinghood.* Baltimore: Johns Hopkins University Press, 1988.

Shenker, Israel. "Moody Man of Letters." *New York Times,* 6 May 1956, sec. 2.

Siegel, Paul N. "*Measure for Measure*: The Significance of the Title." *Shakespeare Quarterly* 4 (1952): 317–20.

———. *Shakespeare in His Time and Ours.* Notre Dame: University of Notre Dame Press, 1968.

Sjursen, Nina. "La puissance et l'impuissance: Dialogue entre *Caligula* et *En attendant Godot*." In *Camus et le Theatre,* ed. Jacqueline Lévi-Valensi. Paris: Imec Éditions, 1992.

Sonnenfeld, Albert. "Albert Camus as Dramatist: The Sources of His Failure." *Tulane Drama Review* 5, no. 4 (June 1961): 106–23.

Southwold, Martin. "Buddhism and Evil." In *The Anthropology of Evil,* ed. David Parkin. Cambridge, Mass.: Blackwell, 1985.

Spiekerman, Tim. *Shakespeare's Political Realism: The English History Plays.* Albany: State University of New York Press, 2001.

Spivack, Bernard. *Shakespeare and the Allegory of Evil.* New York: Columbia University Press, 1958.

Sprintzen, David. *Camus: A Critical Examination.* Philadelphia: Temple University Press, 1988.

Srigley, Ronald D. "Albert Camus's Political Philosophy." Unpublished manuscript, 2007.

States, Bert O. *Shape of Paradox: An Essay on "Waiting for Godot."* Berkeley: University of California Press, 1978.

Strauss, Leo. *Thoughts on Machiavelli.* Chicago: University of Chicago Press, 1958.

———. "Niccolo Machiavelli." In *History of Political Philosophy,* 3d ed., ed. Leo Strauss and Joseph Cropsey. Chicago: University of Chicago Press, 1987.

———. "The Three Waves of Modernity." In *An Introduction to Political Philosophy: Ten Essays by Leo Strauss,* ed. Hilail Gildin. Detroit: Wayne State University Press, 1989.

Strauss, Walter A. "*Caligula*: Ancient Sources and Modern Parallels." *Comparative Literature* 3, no. 2 (Spring 1951): 160–73.

Suetonius. *Suetonius.* Trans. J. C. Rolfe. Loeb Classical Library. Cambridge, Mass.: Harvard University Press, 1914.

———. *Suétone: Vies des Douze Césars II.* 4th ed. Trans. Henri Ailloud. Paris: Société d'Édition "Les Belles Lettres," 1967.

———. *The Twelve Caesars.* Trans. Robert Graves. Rev. trans. Michael Grant. London: Penguin Books, 1979.

Sullivan, Vickie B., ed. *The Comedy and Tragedy of Machiavelli: Essays on the Literary Works.* New Haven: Yale University Press, 2000.

Sumberg, Theodore A. "*La Mandragola*: An Interpretation." *Journal of Politics* 23 (1961): 320–40.

Suvin, Darko. "Preparing for Godot—or the Purgatory of Individualism." *In Casebook on Waiting for Godot,* ed. Ruby Cohn. New York: Grove Press, 1967.

Tillyard, E. M. W. *Shakespeare's Problem Plays.* Toronto: University of Toronto Press, 1950.

Todd, Oliver. *Albert Camus: A Life.* Trans. Benjamin Ivry. New York: Alfred A. Knopf, 1997.

Tovey, Barbara. "Wisdom and the Law: Thoughts on the Political Philosophy of *Measure for Measure*." In *Shakespeare's Political Pageant: Essays in Literature and Politics,* ed. Joseph Alulis and Vickie Sullivan. London: Rowman and Littlefield, 1996.

Underhill, Arthur. *Shakespeare's England.* Vol. 1. Oxford: Clarendon Press, 1916.

Voegelin, Eric. "Machiavelli's Prince: Background and Formation." *Review of Politics* 13 (1951): 142–68.

———. *New Science of Politics: An Introduction.* Chicago: University of Chicago Press, 1952.

———. *The World of the Polis.* Vol. 2 of *Order and History.* Baton Rouge: Louisiana State University Press, 1957.

———. *The Ecumenic Age.* Vol. 4 of *Order and History.* Baton Rouge: Louisiana State University Press, 1974.

———. "On Debate and Existence." In *Published Essays: 1966–1985,* ed. Ellis Sandoz. Vol. 12 of *The Collected Works of Eric Voegelin.* Baton Rouge: Louisiana State University Press, 1990.

———. *History of Political Ideas, vol. 1: Hellenism, Rome, and Early Christianity.* Ed. Athanasios Moulakis. Vol. 19 of *The Collected Works of Eric Voegelin.* Columbia: University of Missouri Press, 1997.

Walker, I. H. "The Composition of *Caligula*." *Symposium* 20, no. 3 (Fall 1966): 263–77.

Webb, Eugene. *The Plays of Samuel Beckett.* Seattle: University of Washington Press, 1972.

Wentersdorf, Karl P. "The Marriage Contracts in "*Measure for Measure*": A Reconsideration." *Shakespeare Survey* 32 (1979): 129–44.

Willhoite, Fred. *Beyond Nihilism.* Baton Rouge: Louisiana State University Press, 1968.

Wyschogrod, Edith. *Spirit in Ashes: Hegel, Heidegger, and Man-Made Mass Death.* New Haven: Yale University Press, 1985.

Zegel, Sylvain. "At the Théâtre de Babylon: *Waiting for Godot* by Samuel Beckett," trans. Ruby Cohn. In *Casebook on Waiting for Godot,* ed. Ruby Cohn. New York: Grove Press, 1967.

INDEX

Abraham, 89

    Abrahamic traditions, 91, 93, 260

Abraham, Claude K., 288n1

absurd, the, 13, 17–18, 25–26, 31–38,
        48, 49–51, 56, 59, 69–74,
        84, 129, 133, 136–39, 285n15,
        288nn1–2, 291n41, 293n68,
        297n44

    the absurd condition, 69, 71,
        136–37, 139

    the absurd man, 36, 49, 72, 73,
        136–37, 288n2

    ancient religious roots of, 37

    Beckett and, 13, 25, 32–33, 35,
        36–37, 38, 129, 133, 136, 139

    Camus and, 25, 31–35, 37, 38,
        49–51, 59, 69–74, 84, 133,
        136–38, 285n15, 288nn1–2,
        291n41, 293n68

    suicide and, 32, 49, 69–70, 72, 136

    theatre of the absurd, 17–18,
        25–26, 33–37, 133, 136, 138,
        288n1, 297n44

    See also *Caligula* (Camus); *Waiting
        for Godot* (Beckett)

Adam, 88, 257

Adamov, Arthur, 35

Aeschylus, 12, 15, 35, 265–67

    Oresteia, 267

Agathocles the Sicilian, 167, 168,
    309n34

Albee, Edward, 35

Alexander VI, Pope, 3, 311n79, 314n12

Alexander the Great, 15, 55

Alford, C. Fred, 6–7, 15–16, 280n32,
    280n35, 281n53

Al-Qaeda, xiii–xiv

Anouilh, Jean, 34

    Antigone, 34

apocalypticism, 37–38, 42, 44–48, 70,
        75, 90, 120–21, 129, 132, 133,
        135, 256, 257, 259, 273–75

    apocalyptic movements, 37

    Christian, 38, 42, 45, 70, 75,
        89–91, 120, 132, 256, 259

    and de-divinization, 42

    and Gnosticism, 37–38, 42,
        44–48, 90, 133

    and history, 135

    Islamic, 42

    Jewish, 38, 41, 42

    terrorism and, 273–74

Apophis, 41

Aquinas, Thomas, Saint, 146, 257, 258

    natural law, 146

    natural reason, 146

    Summa Theologica, 146, 258

Archambault, Paul, 51, 71

Arendt, Hannah, xiv, 19, 282n70

    "banality of evil," 19

Aristophanes, 13, 161, 267

    Clouds, 161

PAUL COREY

teaches in the religious studies department
at McMaster University.